I0491679

ART BOOKS

FROM CRESCENT MOON PUBLISHING

Leonardo da Vinci
by James Pearson

Early Netherlandish Painting
by Rosalind Mutter

Piero della Francesca
by Naomi Haskell

Giovanni Bellini
by Julia Davis

Eric Gill: Nuptials of God
by Anthony Hoyland

Minimal Art and Artists In the 1960s and After
by Laura Garrard

Postwar Art
by George Knighton

Vincent van Gogh: Visionary Landscapes
by Stuart Morris

Max Beckmann
by Stuart Morris

Egon Schiele: Sex and Death in Purple Stockings
by D. Simon Eade

Mark Rothko: The Art of Transcendence
by Julia Davis

Jasper Johns
by L.M. Poole

Brice Marden
by Laura Garrard

Frank Stella: American Abstract Artist
by James Pearson

The Light Eternal: J.M.W. Turner
by Jeremy Mark Robinson

Maurice Sendak and the Art of Children's Book Illustration
by L.M. Poole

Sex in Art: Pornography and Pleasure in Painting and Sculpture
by Cassidy Hughes

Glorification: Religious Abstraction
In Renaissance and 20th Century Painting
by Jeremy Mark Robinson

The Art of Andy Goldsworthy
by William Malpas

Andy Goldsworthy: Touching Nature
by William Malpas

Andy Goldsworthy In Close-Up
by William Malpas

The Art of Richard Long
by William Malpas

Constantin Brancusi: Sculpting the Essence of Things
by James Pearson

Alison Wilding: The Embrace of Sculpture
by Susan Quinnell

The Erotic Object: Sexuality in Sculpture
From Prehistory to the Present Day
by Susan Quinnell

Land Art: A Complete Guide to Landscape, Environmental,
Earthworks, Nature, Sculpture and Installation Art
by William Malpas

Land Art In Close-Up
by William Malpas

Colourfield Painting: Minimal, Cool, Hard Edge, Serial
and Post-Painterly Abstract Art From the Sixties to the Present
by Laura Garrard

WOMEN IN THE FINE ARTS

WOMEN IN THE FINE ARTS

FROM THE SEVENTH CENTURY B.C. TO THE TWENTIETH CENTURY A.D.

CLARA ERSKINE CLEMENT

CRESCENT MOON

First published in 1904. This edition © 2020.

Set in Book Antiqua 10 on 14pt.
Designed by Radiance Graphics.

Thanks to the authors and publishers quoted.

British Library Cataloguing in Publication data

ISBN-13 978186171717252

CRESCENT MOON PUBLISHING
P.O. Box 1312, Maidstone, Kent, ME14 5XU
Great Britain, www.crmoon.com

CONTENTS

NOTE ON THE TEXT

The text is from *Women In the Fine Arts From the Seventh Century B.C. To the Twentieth Centiry A.D.* by Clara Erskine Clement, published by Houghton, Mifflin, New York, 1904.

The illustrations discussed in the book are included in the illustrations section, along with many other works.

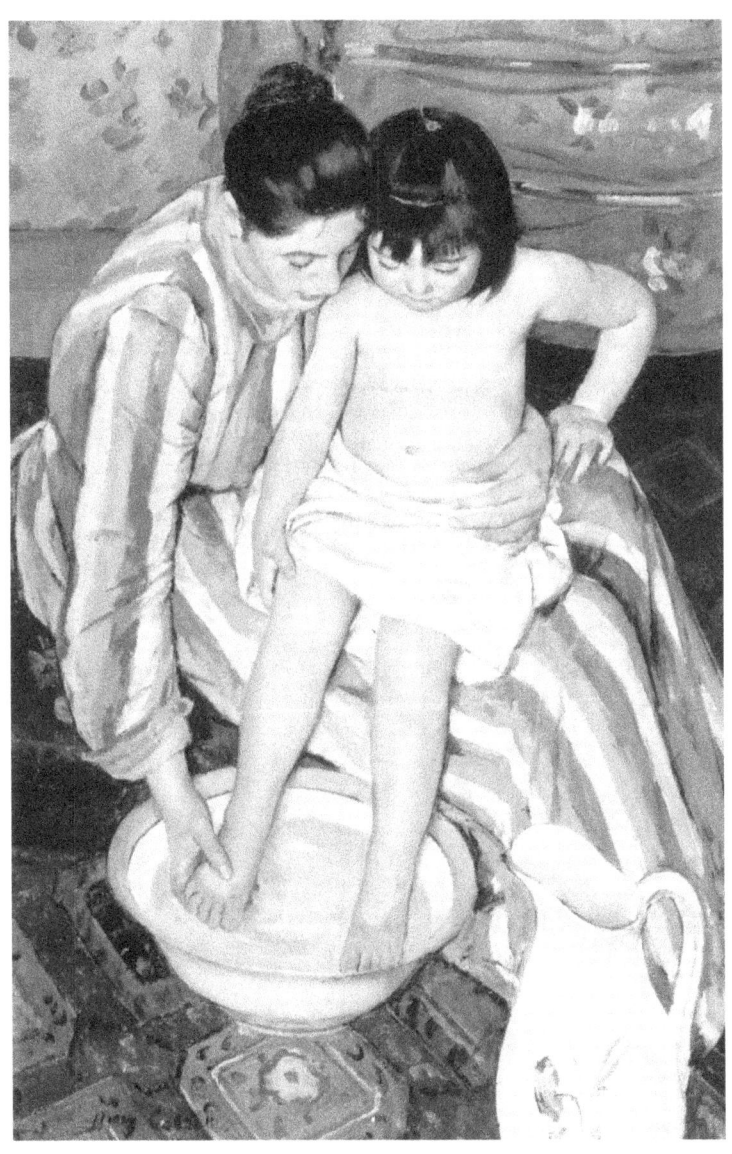

Mary Cassatt, The Bath, 1891

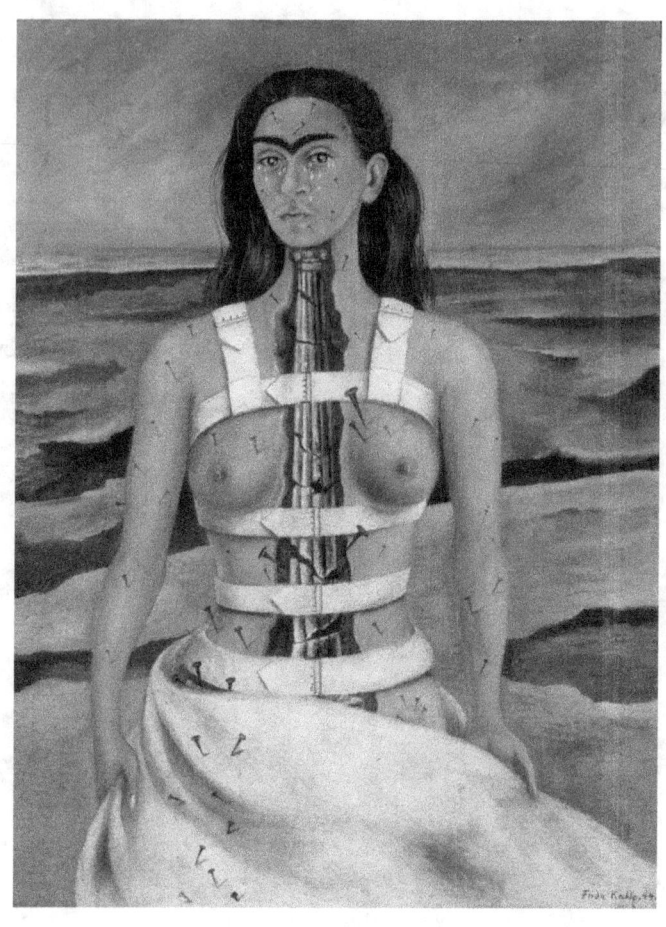

Frida Kahlo, The Broken Column, 1944,
Museo Dolores Olmedo Patino, Mexico City

PREFATORY NOTE

As a means of collecting material for this book I have sent to many artists in Great Britain and in various countries of Europe, as well as in the United States, a circular, asking where their studies were made, what honors they have received, the titles of their principal works, etc.

I take this opportunity to thank those who have cordially replied to my questions, many of whom have given me fuller information than I should have presumed to ask; thus assuring correctness in my statements, which newspaper and magazine notices of artists and their works sometimes fail to do.

I wish especially to acknowledge the courtesy of those who have given me photographs of their pictures and sculpture, to be used as illustrations.

CLARA ERSKINE CLEMENT.

INTRODUCTION

In studying the subject of this book I have found the names of more than a thousand women whose attainments in the Fine Arts – in various countries and at different periods of time before the middle of the nineteenth century – entitle them to honorable mention as artists, and I doubt not that an exhaustive search would largely increase this number. The stories of many of these women have been written with more or less detail, while of others we know little more than their names and the titles of a few of their works; but even our scanty knowledge of them is of value.

Of the army of women artists of the last century it is not yet possible to speak with judgment and justice, although many have executed works of which all women may be proud.

We have some knowledge of women artists in ancient days. Few stories of that time are so authentic as that of Kora, who made the design for the first bas-relief, in the city of Sicyonia, in the seventh century B. C. We have the names of other Greek women artists of the centuries immediately preceding and following the Christian era, but we know little of their lives and works.

Calypso was famous for the excellence of her character pictures, a remarkable one being a portrait of Theodorus, the Juggler. A picture found at Pompeii, now at Naples, is attributed to this artist; but its authorship is so uncertain that little importance can be attached to it. Pliny praised Eirene, among whose pictures was one of "An Aged Man" and a portrait of "Alcisthenes, the Dancer."

In the annals of Roman Art we find few names of women. For this reason Laya, who lived about a century before the Christian era, is important. She is honored as the original painter of miniatures, and her works on ivory were greatly esteemed. Pliny says she did not marry, but pursued her art with absolute devotion; and he considered her pictures worthy of great praise.

A large picture in Naples is said to be the work of Laya, but, as in the case of Calypso, we have no assurance that it is genuine. It is also said that Laya's portraits commanded larger prices than those of Sopolis and Dyonisius, the most celebrated portrait painters of their time.

Our scanty knowledge of individual women artists of antiquity – mingled with fable as it doubtless is – serves the important purpose of proving that women, from very ancient times, were educated as artists and creditably followed their profession beside men of the same periods.

This knowledge also awakens imagination, and we wonder in what other ancient countries there were women artists. We know that in Egypt inheritances descended in the female line, as in the case of the Princess Karamat; and since we know of the great architectural works of Queen Hashop and her journey to the land of Punt, we may reasonably assume that the women of ancient Egypt had their share in all the interests of life. Were there not artists among them who decorated temples and tombs with their imperishable colors? Did not women paint those pictures of Isis – goddess of Sothis – that are like precursors of the pictures of the Immaculate Conception? Surely we may hope that a papyrus will be brought to light that will reveal to us the part that women had in the decoration of the monuments of ancient Egypt.

At present we have no reliable records of the lives and works of women artists before the time of the Renaissance in Italy.

•

M. Taine's philosophy which regards the art of any people or period as the necessary result of the conditions of race, religion, civilization, and manners in the midst of which the art was produced – and esteems a knowledge of these conditions as sufficient to account for the character of the art, seems to me to exclude many complex and mysterious influences, especially in individual cases, which must affect the work of the artists. At the same time an intelligent study of the art of any nation or period demands a study of the conditions in which it was produced, and I shall endeavor in this *résumé* of the history of women in Art – mere outline as it is – to give an idea of the atmosphere in which they lived and worked, and the influences which affected the results of their labor.

It has been claimed that everything of importance that originated in Italy from the thirteenth to the seventeenth century bore the distinctive mark of Fine Art. So high an authority as John Addington Symonds is in accord with this view, and the study of these four centuries is of absorbing interest.

Although the thirteenth century long preceded the practice of art by women, its influence was a factor in the artistic life into which they later came. In this century Andrea Tan, Guido da Siena, and other devoted souls were involved in the final struggles of Mediæval Art, and at its close Cimabue and Duccio da Siena – the two masters whose Madonnas were borne in solemn procession through the streets of Florence and Siena, mid music and the pealing of bells – had given the new impulse to painting which brought them immortal fame. They were the heralds of the time when poetry of sentiment, beauty of color, animation and individuality of form should replace Mediæval formality and ugliness; a time when the spirit of art should be revived with an impulse prophetic of its coming glory.

But neither this portentous period nor the fourteenth century is memorable in the annals of women artists. Not until the fifteenth, the century of the full Renaissance, have we a record of their share in the great rebirth.

It is important to remember that the art of the Renaissance

had, in the beginning, a distinct office to fill in the service of the Church. Later, in historical and decorative painting, it served the State, and at length, in portrait and landscape painting, in pictures of genre subjects and still-life, abundant opportunity was afforded for all orders of talent, and the generous patronage of art by church, state, and men of rank and wealth, made Italy a veritable paradise for artists.

Gradually, with the revival of learning, artists were free to give greater importance to secular subjects, and an element of worldliness, and even of immorality, invaded the realm of art as it invaded the realms of life and literature.

This was an era of change in all departments of life. Chivalry, the great "poetic lie," died with feudalism, and the relations between men and women became more natural and reasonable than in the preceding centuries. Women were liberated from the narrow sphere to which they had been relegated in the minstrel's song and poet's rhapsody, but as yet neither time nor opportunity had been given them for the study and development which must precede noteworthy achievement.

Remarkable as was the fifteenth century for intellectual and artistic activity, it was not productive in its early decades of great genius in art or letters. Its marvellous importance was apparent only at its close and in the beginning of the sixteenth century, when the works of Leonardo, Michael Angelo, Raphael, Titian, and their followers emphasized the value of the progressive attainments of their predecessors.

The assertion and contradiction of ideas and theories, the rivalries of differing schools, the sweet devotion of Fra Angelico, the innovations of Masolino and Masaccio, the theory of perspective of Paolo Uccello, the varied works of Fabriano, Antonello da Messina, the Lippi, Botticelli, Ghirlandajo, the Bellini, and their contemporaries, culminated in the inimitable painting of the Cinquecento – in works still unsurpassed, ever challenging artists of later centuries to the task of equalling or excelling them.

The demands of the art of the Renaissance were so great, and so unlike those of earlier days, that it is not surprising that few women, in its beginning, attained to such excellence as to be remembered during five centuries. Especially would it seem that an insurmountable obstacle had been placed in the way of women, since the study of anatomy had become a necessity to an artist. This, and kindred hindrances, too patent to require enumeration, account for the fact that but two Italian women of this period became so famous as to merit notice – Caterina Vigri and Onorata Rodiana, whose stories are given in the biographical part of this book.

•

In Flanders, late in the fourteenth and early in the fifteenth centuries, women were engaged in the study and practice of art. In Bruges, when the Van Eycks were inventing new methods in the preparation of colors, and painting their wonderful pictures, beside them, and scarcely inferior to them, was their sister, Margaretha, who sacrificed much of her artistic fame by painting portions of her brothers' pictures, unless the fact that they thought her worthy of thus assisting them establishes her reputation beyond question.

In the fifteenth century we have reason to believe that many women practised art in various departments, but so scanty and imperfect are the records of individual artists that little more than their names are known, and we have no absolute knowledge of the value of their works, or where, if still existing, they are to be seen.

The art of the Renaissance reached its greatest excellence during the last three decades of the fifteenth and the first half of the sixteenth century. This was a glorious period in the History of Art. The barbarism of the Middle Ages was essentially a thing of the past, but much barbaric splendor in the celebration of ceremonies and festivals still remained to satisfy the artistic sense, while every-day costumes and customs lent a picturesqueness to ordinary life. So much of the pagan spirit as endured was modified by the spirit of the Renaissance. The result was a new order of things especially favorable to painting.

An artist now felt himself as free to illustrate the pagan myths as to represent the events in the lives of the Saviour, the Virgin and the saints, and the actors in the sacred subjects were represented with the same beauty and grace of form as were given the heroes and heroines of Hellenic legend. St. Sebastian was as beautiful as Apollo, and the imagination and senses were moved alike by pictures of Danae and the Magdalene – the two subjects being often the work of the same artist.

The human form was now esteemed as something more than the mere habitation of a soul; it was beautiful in itself and capable of awakening unnumbered emotions in the human heart. Nature, too, presented herself in a new aspect and inspired the artist with an ardor in her representation such as few of the older painters had experienced in their devotion to religious subjects.

This expansion of thought and purpose was inaugurating an art attractive to women, to which the increasing liberty of artistic theory and practice must logically make them welcome; a result which is a distinguishing feature of sixteenth-century painting.

•

The sixteenth century was noteworthy for the generous patronage of art, especially in Florence, where the policy of its ruling house could not fail to produce marvellous results, and the history of the Medici discloses many reasons why the bud of the Renaissance perfected its bloom in Florence more rapidly and more gloriously than elsewhere.

For centuries Italy had been a treasure-house of Greek, Etruscan, and Byzantine Art. In no other country had a civilization like that of ancient Rome existed, and no other land had been so richly prepared to be the birthplace and to promote the development of the art of the Renaissance.

The intellectually progressive life of this period did much for the advancement of women. The fame of Vittoria Colonna, Tullia d'Aragona, Olympia Morata, and many others who merit association in this goodly company, proves the generous spirit of the age, when in the scholastic centres of Italy women were free to study all branches of learning.

The pursuit of art was equally open to them and women were pupils in all the schools and in the studios of many masters; even Titian instructed a woman, and all the advantages for study enjoyed by men were equally available for women. Many names of Italian women artists could be added to those of whom I have written in the biographical portion of this book, but too little is known of their lives and works to be of present interest. There is, however, little doubt that many pictures attributed to "the School of" various masters were painted by women.

•

Art did not reach its perfection in Venice until later than in Florence, and its special contribution, its glorious color, imparted to it an attraction unequalled on the sensuous plane. This color surrounded the artists of that sumptuous city of luxurious life and wondrous pageants, and was so emphasized by the marvellous mingling of the semi-mist and the brilliancy of its atmosphere that no man who merited the name of artist could be insensible to its inspiration.

The old Venetian realism was followed, in the time of the Renaissance, by startling developments. In the works of Tintoretto and Veronese there is a combination of gorgeous draperies, splendid and often licentious costumes, brilliant metal accessories, and every possible device for enhancing and contrasting colors, until one is bewildered and must adjust himself to these dazzling spectacles – religious subjects though they may be – before any serious thought or judgment can be brought to bear upon their artistic merit; these two great contemporaries lived and worked in the final decades of the sixteenth century.

We know that many women painted pictures in Venice before the seventeenth century, although we have accurate knowledge of but few, and of these an account is given later in this book.

We who go from Paris to London in a few hours, and cross the

St. Gothard in a day, can scarcely realize the distance that separated these capitals from the centres of Italian art in the time of the Renaissance. We have, however, abundant proof that the sacred fire of the love of Art and Letters was smouldering in France, Germany, and England – and when the inspiring breath of the Renaissance was wafted beyond the Alps a flame burst forth which has burned clearer and brighter with succeeding centuries.

From the time of Vincent de Beauvais, who died in 1264, France had not been wanting in illustrious scholars, but it could not be said that a French school of art existed. François Clouet or Cloet, called Jehannet, was born in Tours about 1500. His portraits are seen in the Gallery of the Louvre, and have been likened to those of Holbein; but they lack the strength and spirit of that artist; in fact, the distinguishing feature of Clouet's work is the remarkable finish of draperies and accessories, while the profusion of jewels distracts attention from the heads of his subjects.

The first great French artists were of the seventeenth century, and although Clouet was painter to Francis I. and Henry II., the former, like his predecessors, imported artists from Italy, among whom were Leonardo da Vinci and Benvenuto Cellini.

In letters, however, there were French women of the sixteenth century who are still famous. Marguerite de Valois was as cultivated in mind as she was generous and noble in character. Her love of learning was not easily satisfied. She was proficient in Hebrew, the classics, and the usual branches of "profane letters," as well as an accomplished scholar in philosophy and theology. As an author – though her writings are somewhat voluminous and not without merit – she was comparatively unimportant; her great service to letters was the result of the sympathy and encouragement she gave to others.

Wherever she might be, she was the centre of a literary and religious circle, as well as of the society in which she moved. She was in full sympathy with her brother in making his "*Collège*" an institution in which greater liberty was accorded to the expression of individual opinion than had before been known in France, and by reason of her protection of liberty in thought and speech she suffered much in the esteem of the bigots of her day.

The beautiful Mlle. de Heilly – the Duchesse d'Etampes – whose influence over Francis I. was pre-eminent, while her character was totally unlike that of his sister, was described as "the fairest among the learned, and the most learned among the fair." When learning was thus in favor at Court, it naturally followed that all capacity for it was cultivated and ordinary intelligence made the most of; and the claim that the intellectual brilliancy of the women of the Court of Francis I. has rarely been equalled is generally admitted. There were, however, no artists among them – they wielded the pen rather than the brush.

•

In England, as in France, there was no native school of art in the sixteenth century, and Flemish, Dutch, and German artists crossed the channel when summoned to the English Court, as the Italians crossed the Alps to serve the kings of France.

English women of this century were far less scholarly than those of Italy and France. At the same time they might well be proud of a queen who "could quote Pindar and Homer in the original and read every morning a portion of Demosthenes, being also the royal mistress of eight languages." With our knowledge of the queen's scholarship in mind we might look to her for such patronage of art and literature as would rival that of Lorenzo the Magnificent; but Elizabeth lacked the generosity of the Medici and that of Marguerite de Valois. Hume tells us that "the queen's vanity lay more in shining by her own learning than in encouraging men of genius by her liberality."

Lady Jane Grey and the daughters of Sir Anthony Cooke are familiar examples of learned women, and many English titled and gentlewomen were well versed in Greek and Latin, as well as in Spanish, Italian, and French. Macaulay reminded his readers that if an Englishwoman of that day did not read the classics she could read little, since the then existing books – outside the Italian – would fill a shelf but scantily. Thus English girls read Plato, and doubtless English women excelled Englishmen in their proficiency in foreign languages, as they do at present.

•

In Germany the relative position of Art and Letters was the opposite to that in France and England. The School of Cologne was a genuinely native school of art in the fourteenth century. Although the Niebelungen Lied and Gudrun, the Songs of Love and Volkslieder, as well as Mysteries and Passion Plays, existed from an early date, we can scarcely speak of a German Literature before the sixteenth century, when Albert Dürer and the younger Holbein painted their great pictures, while Luther, Melanchthon and their sympathizers disseminated the doctrines of advancing Protestantism.

At this period, in the countries we may speak of collectively as German, women artists were numerous. Many were miniaturists, some of whom were invited to the English Court and received with honor.

In 1521 Albert Dürer was astonished at the number of women artists in different parts of what, for conciseness, we may call Germany. This was also noticeable in Holland, and Dürer wrote in his diary, in the above-named year: "Master Gerard, of Antwerp, illuminist, has a daughter, eighteen years of age, named Susannah, who illuminated a little book which I purchased for a few guilders. It is wonderful that a woman could do so much!"

Antwerp became famous for its women artists, some of whom visited France, Italy, and Spain, and were honorably recognized for their talent and attainments, wherever they went.

•

In the later years of the sixteenth century a difference of opinion and purpose arose among the artists of Italy, the effects of which were shown in the art of the seventeenth century. Two distinct schools were formed, one of which included the conservatives who desired to preserve and follow the manner of the masters of the Cinquecento, at the same time making a deeper study of Nature – thus the devotional feeling and many of the older traditions would be retained while each master could indulge his individuality more freely than heretofore. They aimed to unite such a style as Correggio's – who belonged to no school – with that of the severely mannered artists of the preceding centuries. These artists were called Eclectics, and the Bolognese school of the Carracci was the most important centre of the movement, while Domenichino, a native of Bologna – 1581-1631 – was the most distinguished painter of the school.

The original aims of the Eclectics are well summed up in a sonnet by Agostino Carracci, which has been translated as follows: "Let him who wishes to be a good painter acquire the design of Rome, Venetian action and Venetian management of shade, the dignified color of Lombardy – that is of Leonardo da Vinci – the terrible manner of Michael Angelo, Titian's truth and nature, the sovereign purity of Correggio's style and the just symmetry of a Raphael, the decorum and well-grounded study of Tibaldi, the invention of the learned Primaticcio, and a *little* of Parmigianino's grace; but without so much study and weary labor let him apply himself to imitate the works which our Niccolò – dell Abbate – left us here." Kugler calls this "a patchwork ideal," which puts the matter in a nut-shell.

At one period the Eclectics produced harmonious pictures in a manner attractive to women, many of whom studied under Domenichino, Giovanni Lanfranco, Guido Reni, the Campi, and others. Sofonisba Anguisciola, Elisabetta Sirani, and the numerous women artists of Bologna were of this school.

The greatest excellence of this art was of short duration; it declined as did the literature, and indeed, the sacred and political institutions of Italy in the seventeenth century. It should not, however, be forgotten, that the best works of Guercino, the later pictures of Annibale Carracci, and the important works of Domenichino and Salvator Rosa belong to this period.

The second school was that of the Naturalists, who professed to study Nature alone, representing with brutal realism her repulsive aspects. Naples was the centre of these painters, and the poisoning of Domenichino and many other dark and terrible deeds have been attributed to them. Few women were attracted to this school, and the only one whose association with the Naturalisti is recorded – Aniella di Rosa – paid for her temerity with her life.

•

In Rome, Florence, Bologna, Venice, and other Italian cities, there were, in the seventeenth century, many women who made enviable reputations as artists, some of whom were also known for their literary and musical attainments. Anna Maria Ardoina, of Messina, made her studies in Rome. She was gifted as a poet and artist, and so excelled in music that she had the distinguished honor of being elected to the Academy of Arcadia.

Not a few gifted women of this time are remembered for their noble charities. Chiara Varotari, under the instruction of her father and her brother, called Padovanino, became a good painter. She was also honored as a skilful nurse, and the Grand Duke of Tuscany placed her portrait in his gallery on account of his admiration and respect for her as a comforter of the suffering.

Giovanna Garzoni, a miniaturist, conferred such benefits upon the Academy of St. Luke that a monument was there erected to her memory. Other artists founded convents, became nuns, and imprinted themselves upon their age in connection with various honorable institutions and occupations.

•

French Art in the seventeenth century was academic and prosaic, lacking the spontaneity, joyousness, and intensely artistic feeling of Italian Art – a heritage from previous centuries which had not been lost, and in which France had no part. The works of Poussin, which have been likened to painted reliefs, afford an excellent example of French Art in his time – 1594-1665 – and this in spite of the fact that he worked and studied much in Rome.

The Académie des Beaux-Arts was established by Louis XIV., and there was a rapidly growing interest in art. As yet, however, the women of France affected literature rather than painting, and in the seventeenth century they were remarkable for their scholarly attainments and their influence in the world of letters.

Madame de Maintenon patronized learning; at the Hôtel Rambouillet men and women of genius met the world of rank and fashion on common ground. Madame Dacier, of whom Voltaire said, "No woman has ever rendered greater services to literature," made her translations from the classics; Madame de Sevigné wrote her marvellous letters; Mademoiselle de Scudéry and Madame Lafayette their novels; Catherine Bernard emulated the manner of Racine in her dramas; while Madame de Guyon interpreted the mystic Song of Solomon.

Of French women artists of this period we can mention several names, but they were so overshadowed by authors as to be unimportant, unless, like Elizabeth Chéron, they won both artistic and literary fame.

•

The seventeenth century was an age of excellence in the art of Flanders, Belgium, and Holland, and is known as the second great epoch of painting in the Netherlands, this name including the three countries just mentioned.

After the calamities suffered under Charles V. and Philip II., with returning peace and prosperity an art was developed, both original and rich in artistic power. The States-General met in 1600, and the greatest artists of the Netherlands did their work in the succeeding fifty years; and before the century closed the appreciation of art and the patronage which had assured its elevation were things of the past.

Rubens was twenty-three years old in 1600, just ready to begin his work which raised the school of Belgium to its highest attainments. When we remember how essentially his art dominated his own country and was admired elsewhere, we might think – I had almost said fear – that his brilliant, vigorous, and voluptuous manner would attract all artists of his day to essay his imitation. But among women artists Madame O'Connell was the first who could justly be called his imitator, and her work was done in the middle of the nineteenth century.

When we turn to the genre painting of the Flemish and Dutch artists we find that they represented scenes in the lives of coarse, drunken boors and vulgar women – works which brought these artists enduring fame by reason of their wonderful technique; but we can mention one woman only, Anna Breughel, who seriously attempted the practice of this art. She is thought to have been of the family of Velvet Breughel, who lived in the early part of the seventeenth century.

Like Rubens, Rembrandt numbered few women among his imitators. The women of his day and country affected pleasing delineations of superficial motives, and Rembrandt's earnestness and intensity were seemingly above their appreciation – certainly far above their artistic powers.

A little later so many women painted delicate and insipid subjects that I have not space even for their names. A critic has said that the Dutch school "became a nursery for female talent." It may have reached the Kindergarten stage, but went no farther.

Flower painting attained great excellence in the seventeenth century. The most elaborate masters in this art were the brothers De Heem, Willem Kalf, Abraham Mignon, and Jan van Huysum. Exquisite as the pictures by these masters are, Maria van Oosterwyck and Rachel Ruysch disputed honors with them, and many other women excelled in this delightful art.

An interesting feature in art at this time was the intimate association of men and women artists and the distinction of women thus associated.

Gerard Terburg, whose pictures now have an enormous value, had two sisters, Maria and Gezina, whose genre pictures were not unworthy of comparison with the works of their famous brother. Gottfried Schalken, remarkable for his skill in the representation of scenes by candle light, was scarcely more famous than his sister Maria. Eglon van der Neer is famous for his pictures of elegant women in marvellous satin gowns. He married Adriana Spilberg, a favorite portrait painter. The daughters of the eminent engraver Cornelius Visscher, Anna and Maria, were celebrated for their fine etching on glass, and by reason of their poems and their scholarly acquirements they were called the "Dutch Muses," and were associated with the learned men of their day. This list, though incomplete, suggests that the co-education of artists bore good fruit in their co-operation in their profession.

•

In England, while there was a growing interest in painting, the standard was that of foreign schools, especially the Dutch. Foreign artists found a welcome and generous patronage at the English Court. Mary Beale and Anne Carlisle are spoken of as English artists, and a few English women were miniaturists. Among these was Susannah Penelope Gibson, daughter of Richard Gibson, the Dwarf. While these women were not wanting in artistic taste, they were little more than copyists of the Dutch artists with whom they had associated.

•

In the early years of the seventeenth century there were a number of Danish women who were painters, engravers, and modellers in wax. The daughter of King Christian IV., Elenora Christina, and her daughter, Helena Christina, were reputable artists. The daughter of Christian V., Sophie Hedwig, made a reputation as a portrait, landscape, and flower painter, which extended beyond her own country; and Anna Crabbe painted a series of portraits of Danish princes, and added to them descriptive verses of her own composition.

•

The Art of Spain attained its greatest glory in the seventeenth century – the century of Velasquez, Murillo, Ribera, and other less distinguished but excellent artists.

In the last half of this century women artists were prominent in the annals of many Spanish cities. In the South mention is made of these artists, who were of excellent position and aristocratic connection. In Valencia, the daughter of the great portrait painter Alonzo Coello was distinguished in both painting and music. She married Don Francesco de Herrara, Knight of Santiago.

In Cordova the sister of Palomino y Vasco – the artist who has been called the Vasari of Spain on account of his Museo Pictorio – was recognized as a talented artist. In Madrid, Velasquez numbered several noble ladies among his pupils; but no detailed accounts of the works of these artists is available – if any such exist – and their pictures are in private collections.

•

The above outline of the general conditions of Art in the seventeenth century will suggest the reasons for there being a larger number of women artists in Italy than elsewhere – especially as they were pupils in the studios of the best masters as well as in the schools of the Carracci and other centres of art study.

•

Italian artists of the eighteenth century have been called scene painters, and, in truth, many of their works impress one as hurried attempts to cover large spaces. Originality was wanting and a wearisome mediocrity prevailed. At the same time certain national artistic qualities were apparent; good arrangement of figures and admirable effects of color still characterized Italian painting, but the result was, on the whole, academic and uninteresting.

The ideals cherished by older artists were lost, and nothing worthy to replace them inspired their followers. The sincerity, earnestness, and devotion of the men who served church and state in the decoration of splendid monuments would have been out of place in the service of amateurs and in the decoration of the salons and boudoirs of the rich, and the painting of this period had little permanent value, in comparison with that of preceding centuries.

Italian women, especially in the second half of the century, were professors in universities, lectured to large audiences, and were respectfully consulted by men of science and learning in the various branches of scholarship to which they were devoted. Unusual honors were paid them, as in the case of Maria Portia Vignoli, to whom a statue was erected in the public square of Viterbo to commemorate her great learning in natural science.

An artist, Matilda Festa, held a professorship in the Academy of St. Luke in Rome, and Maria Maratti, daughter of the Roman painter Carlo Maratti, made a good reputation both as an artist and a poetess.

In Northern Italy many women were famous in sculpture, painting, and engraving. At least forty could be named, artists of good repute, whose lives were lacking in any unusual interest, and whose works are in private collections. One of these was a princess of Parma, who married the Archduke Joseph of Austria, and was elected to the Academy of Vienna in 1789.

•

In France, in the beginning of this century Watteau, 1684-1721, painted his interesting pictures of *La Belle Société*, reproducing the court life, costumes, and manners of the reign of Louis XIV. with fidelity, grace, and vivacity. Later in the century, Greuze, 1725-1805, with his attractive, refined, and somewhat mannered style, had a certain influence. Claude Vernet, 1714-1789, and David, 1748-1825, each great in his way, influenced the nineteenth as well as the eighteenth century. Though Vien, 1716-1809, made a great effort to revive classic art, he found little sympathy with his aim until the works of his pupil David won recognition from the world of the First Empire.

French Art of this period may be described by a single word – eclectic – and this choice by each important artist of the style he would adopt culminated in the Rococo School, which may be defined as the unusual and fantastic in art. It was characterized by good technique and pleasing color, but lacked purpose, depth, and warmth of feeling. As usual in a *pot-pourri*, it was far enough above worthlessness not to be ignored, but so far short of excellence as not to be admired.

In France during this century there was an army of women artists, painters, sculptors, and engravers. Of a great number we know the names only; in fact, of but two of these, Adelaide Vincent and Elizabeth Vigée Le Brun, have we reliable knowledge of their lives and works.

The eighteenth century is important in the annals of women artists, since their numbers then exceeded the collective number of those who had preceded them – so far as is known – from the earliest period in the history of art. In a critical review of the time, however, we find a general and active interest in culture and art among women rather than any considerable number of noteworthy artists.

Germany was the scene of the greatest activity of women artists. France held the second place and Italy the third, thus reversing the conditions of preceding centuries.

•

Many German women emulated the examples of the earlier flower painters, but no one was so important as to merit special attention, though a goodly number were elected to academies and several appointed painters to the minor courts.

Among the genre and historical painters we find the names of Anna Amalia of Brunswick and Anna Maria, daughter of the Empress Maria Theresa, both of whom were successful artists.

In Berlin and Dresden the interest in art was much greater in the eighteenth than in previous centuries, and with this new impulse many women devoted themselves to various specialties in art. Miniature and enamel painting were much in vogue, and collections of these works, now seen in museums and private galleries, are exquisitely beautiful and challenge our admiration, not only for their beauty, but for the delicacy of their handling and the infinite patience demanded for their execution.

The making of medals was carried to great excellence by German women, as may be seen in a medal of Queen Sophie Charlotte, which is preserved in the royal collection of medals. It is the work of Rosa Elizabeth Schwindel, of Leipsic, who was well known in Berlin in the beginning of the century.

The cutting of gems was also extensively done by women. Susannah Dorsch was famous for her accomplishment in this art. Her father and grandfather had been gem-cutters, and Susannah could not remember at what age she began this work. So highly was she esteemed as an artist that medals were made in her honor.

As frequently happens in a study of this kind, I find long lists of the names of women artists of this period of whose lives and works I find no record, while the events related in other cases are too trivial for repetition. This is especially true in Holland, where we find many names of Dutch women who must have been reputable artists, since they are mentioned in Art Chronicles of their time; but we know little of their lives and can mention no pictures executed by them.

•

A national art now existed in England. Hogarth, who has been called the Father of English Painting, was a man of too much originality to be a mere imitator of foreign artists. He devoted his art to the representation of the follies of his time. As a satirist he was eminent, but his mirth-provoking pictures had a deeper purpose than that of amusing. Lord Orford wrote: "Mirth colored his pictures, but benevolence designed them. He smiled like Socrates, that men might not be offended at his lectures, and might learn to laugh at their own folly."

Sir Joshua Reynolds and Thomas Gainsborough were born and died in the eighteenth century; their famous works were contemporary with the founding of the Royal Academy in 1768, when these artists, together with Angelica Kauffman and Mary Moser, were among its original members.

It was a fashion in England at this time for women to paint; they principally affected miniature and water-color pictures, but of the many who called themselves artists few merit our attention; they practised but a feeble sort of imitative painting; their works of slight importance cannot now be named, while their lives were

★ 34

usually commonplace and void of incident. Of the few exceptions to this rule I have written in the later pages of this book.

•

The suggestion that the nineteenth century cannot yet be judged as to its final effect in many directions has already been made, and of nothing is this more true than of its Art. Of one phase of this period, however, we may speak with confidence. No other century of which we know the history has seen so many changes – such progress, or such energy of purpose so largely rewarded as in the century we are considering.

To one who has lived through more than three score years of this period, no fairy tale is more marvellous than the changes in the department of daily life alone.

When I recall the time when the only mode of travel was by stage-coach, boat, or private carriage – when the journey from Boston to St. Louis demanded a week longer in time than we now spend in going from Boston to Egypt – when no telegraph existed – when letter postage was twenty-five cents and the postal service extremely primitive – when no house was comfortably warmed and women carried foot-stoves to unheated churches – when candles and oil lamps were the only means of "lighting up," and we went about the streets at night with dim lanterns – when women spun and wove and sewed with their hands only, and all they accomplished was done at the hardest – when in our country a young girl might almost as reasonably attempt to reach the moon as to become an artist – remembering all this it seems as if an army of magicians must incessantly have waved their wands above us, and that human brains and hands could not have invented and put in operation the innumerable changes in our daily life during the last half-century.

When, in the same way, we review the changes that have taken place in the domains of science, in scholarly research in all directions, in printing, bookmaking, and the methods of illustrating everything that is printed – from the most serious and learned writing to advertisements scattered over all-out-of-doors –

when we add to these the revolutions in many other departments of life and industry, we must regard the nineteenth as the century *par excellence* of expansion, and in various directions an epoch-making era.

•

When we turn to our special subject we find an activity and expansion in nineteenth-century art quite in accordance with the spirit of the time. This expansion is especially noticeable in the increased number of subjects represented in works of art, and in the invention of new methods of artistic expression.

Prior to this period there had been a certain selection of such subjects for artistic representation as could be called "picturesque," and though more ordinary and commonplace subjects might be rendered with such skill – such drawing, color, and technique – as to demand approbation, it was given with a certain condescension and the feeling was manifested that these subjects, though treated with consummate art, were not artistic. The nineteenth century has signally changed these theories.

Nothing that makes a part in human experience is now too commonplace or too unusual and mysterious to afford inspiration to painter and sculptor; while the normal characteristics of human beings and the circumstances common to their lives are not omitted, the artist frequently endeavors to express in his work the most subtle experiences of the heart and soul, and to embody in his picture or statue an absolutely psychologic phenomenon.

The present easy communication with all nations has awakened interest in the life of countries almost unknown to us a half-century ago. So customary is it for artists to wander far and wide, seeking new motives for their works, that I felt no surprise when I recently received a letter from a young American woman who is living and painting in Biskra. How short a time has passed since this would have been thought impossible!

It is also true that subjects not new in art are treated in a nineteenth-century manner. This is noticeable in the picturing of historical subjects. The more intimate knowledge of the world enables the historical painter of the present to impart to his representations of the important events of the past a more human and emotional element than exists in the historical art of earlier centuries. In a word, nineteenth-century art is sympathetic, and has found inspiration in all countries and classes and has so treated its subjects as to be intelligible to all, from the favored children for whom Kate Greenaway, Walter Crane, and many others have spent their delightful talents, to men and women of all varieties of individual tastes and of all degrees of ability to comprehend and appreciate artistic representations.

A fuller acquaintance with the art and art-methods of countries of which but little had before been known has been an element in art expansion. Technical methods which have not been absolutely adopted by European and English-speaking artists have yet had an influence upon their art. The interest in Japanese Art is the most important example of such influence, and it is also true that Japanese artists have been attracted to the study of the art of America and Europe, while some foreign artists resident in Japan – notably Miss Helen Hyde, a young American – have studied and practised Japanese painting to such purpose that Japanese juries have accorded the greatest excellence and its honors to their works, exhibited in competition with native artists.

Other factors in the expansion of art have been found in photography and the various new methods of illustration that have filled books, magazines, and newspapers with pictures of more or less (?) merit. Even the painting of "posters" has not been scorned by good artists, some of whom have treated them in such a manner as to make them worthy a place in museums where only works of true merit are exhibited.

Other elements in the nineteenth-century expansion in art are seen in the improved productions of the so-called Arts and Crafts which are of inestimable value in cultivating the artistic sense in all classes. Another influence in the same direction is the improved decoration of porcelain, majolica, and pottery, which, while not equal to that of earlier date in the esteem of connoisseurs, brings artistic objects to the sight and knowledge of all, at prices suited to moderate means.

•

In America the unparalleled increase of Free Libraries has brought, not books alone, but collections of photographs and other reproductions of the best Painting, Sculpture, and Architecture in the world, as well as medals, book-plates, artistic bindings, etc., within reach of students of art.

Art Academies and Museums have also been greatly multiplied. It is often a surprise to find, in a comparatively small town, a fine Art Gallery, rich in a variety of precious objects. Such an one is the Art Museum of Bowdoin College, in Brunswick, Me. The edifice itself is the most beautiful of the works by McKim that I have seen. The frescoes by La Farge and Vedder are most satisfactory, and one exhibit, among many of interest – that of original drawings by famous Old Masters – would make this Museum a worthy place of pilgrimage. Can one doubt that such a Museum must be an element of artistic development in those who are in contact with it?

I cannot omit saying that this splendid monument to the appreciation of art and to great generosity was the gift of women, while the artists who perfected its architecture and decorations are Americans; it is an impressive expression of the expansion of American Art in the nineteenth century.

•

The advantages for the study of Art have been largely improved and increased in this period. In numberless studios small classes of pupils are received; in schools of Design, schools of National Academies, and in those of individual enterprise, all possible advantages for study under the direction of the best artists are provided, and these are supplemented by scholarships which relieve the student of limited means from providing for daily needs.

All these opportunities are shared by men and women alike. Every advantage is as freely at the command of one as of the other, and we equal, in this regard, the centuries of the Renaissance, when women were Artists, Students, and Professors of Letters and of Law, filling these positions with honor, as women do in these days.

In 1859 T. Adolphus Trollope, in his "Decade of Italian Women," in which he wrote of the scholarly women of the Renaissance, says: "The degree in which any social system has succeeded in ascertaining woman's proper position, and in putting her into it, will be a very accurate test of the progress it has made in civilization. And the very general and growing conviction that our own social arrangements, as they exist at present, have not attained any satisfactory measure of success in this respect, would seem, therefore, to indicate that England in her nineteenth century has not yet reached years of discretion after all."

Speaking of Elisabetta Sirani he says: "The humbly born artist, admirable for her successful combination in perfect compatibility of all the duties of home and studio." Of how many woman artists we can now say this.

Trollope's estimate of the position of women in England, which was not unlike that in America, forty-five years ago, when contrasted with that of the present day, affords another striking example of the expansion of the nineteenth century.

•

Although no important changes occur without some preparation, this may be so gradual and unobtrusive in its work that the result appears to have a Minerva-like birth. Doubtless there were influences leading up to the remarkable landscape painting of this century. The "Norwich School," which took shape in 1805, was founded by Crome, among whose associates were Cotman, Stark, and Vincent. Crome exhibited his works at the Royal Academy in 1806, and the twelve following years, and died in 1821 when the pictures of Constable were attracting unusual attention; indeed, it may be said that by his exhibitions at the Royal Academy, Constable inaugurated modern landscape painting, which is a most important feature of art in this century.

Not forgetting the splendid landscapes of the Dutch masters, of the early Italians, of Claude and Wilson, the claim that landscape painting was perfected only in the nineteenth century, and then largely as the result of the works of English artists, seems to me to be well founded. To this excellence Turner, contemporary with Constable, David Cox, De Wint, Bonington, and numerous others gloriously contributed.

The English landscapes exhibited at the French Salon in the third decade of the century produced a remarkable effect, and emphasized the interest in landscape painting already growing in France, and later so splendidly developed by Rousseau, Corot, Millet, and their celebrated contemporaries. In Germany the Achenbachs, Lessing, and many other artists were active in this movement, while in America, Innes, A. H. Wyant, and Homer Martin, with numerous followers, were raising landscape art to an eminence before unknown.

Formerly landscapes had been used as backgrounds, oftentimes attractive and beautiful, while the real purpose of the pictures centred in the human figures. The distinctive feature of nineteenth-century landscape is the representation of Nature alone, and the variety of method used and the differing aims of the artists cover the entire gamut between absolute Realism and the most pronounced Impressionism.

•

About the middle of the century there emerged from the older schools two others which may be called the Realist and Idealist, and indeed there were those to whom both these terms could be applied, both methods being united in their remarkable works. Of the Realists Corot and Courbet are distinguished, as were Puvis de Chavannes and Gustave Moreau among the Idealists.

Millet, with his marvellous power of observation, painted his landscapes with the fidelity of his school in that art, and so keenly realized the religious element in the peasant life about him – the poetry of these people – that he portrayed his figures in a manner quite his own – at the same time realistic and full of idealism. MacColl in his "Nineteenth-Century Art" called Millet "the most religious figure in modern art after Rembrandt," and adds that "he discovered a patience of beauty, a reconciling, in the concert of landscape mystery with labor."

Shall we call Bastien Lepage a follower of Millet, or say that in these men there was a unity of spirit; that while they realized the poetry of their subjects intensely, they fully estimated the reality as well?

The "Joan of Arc" is a phenomenal example of this art. The landscape is carefully realistic, and like that in which a French peasant girl of any period would live. But here realism ceases and the peasant girl becomes a supremely exalted being, entranced by a vision of herself in full armor.

This art, at once realistic and idealistic, is an achievement of the nineteenth century – so clear and straightforward in its methods as to explain itself far better than words can explain it.

•

Contemporary with these last-named artists were the Pre-raphaelites. The centre of this school was called the Brotherhood, which was founded by J. E. Millais, W. Holman Hunt, Dante Gabriel Rossetti, and William Michael Rossetti. To these were added Thomas Woolner the sculptor, James Collins, and F. G. Stephens. Other important artists known as Pre-raphaelites, not belonging to the Brotherhood, are Ford Madox Brown and Burne Jones, as well as the water-color painters, Mason, Walker, Boyce, and Goodwin.

The aim of these artists was to represent with sincerity what they saw, and the simple sincerity of painters who preceded Raphael led them to choose a name which Ruskin called unfortunate, "because the principles on which its members are working are neither pre- nor post-Raphaelite, but everlasting. They are endeavoring to paint with the highest possible degree of completion what they see in nature, without reference to conventional established rules; but by no means to imitate the style of any past epoch. To paint Nature – Nature as it was around them, by the help of modern science, was the aim of the Brotherhood."

At the time when the Pre-raphaelite School came into being the art of other lands as well as that of England was in need of an awakening impulse, and the Pre-raphaelite revolt against conventionality and the machine-like art of the period roused such interest, criticism, and opposition as to stimulate English art to new effort, and much of its progress in the last half-century is doubtless due to the discussions of the theories of this movement as well as of the works it produced.

Pre-raphaelitism, scorned and ridiculed in its beginning, came to be appreciated in a degree that at first seemed impossible, and though its apostles were few, its influence was important. The words of Burne Jones, in which he gave his own ideal, appeal to many artists and lovers of art: "I mean by a picture a beautiful, romantic dream of something that never was, never will be – in a light better than any light that ever shone – in a land no one can define or remember, only desire – and the forms divinely beautiful."

Rossetti's "Girlhood of Virgin Mary," Holman Hunt's "Light of the World," and Millais' "Christ in the House of His Parents" have been called the Trilogy of Pre-raphaelite Art.

Millais did not long remain a strict disciple of this school, but soon adopted the fuller freedom of his later work, which may be called that of modern naturalism. Rossetti remained a Pre-raphaelite through his short life, but his works could not be other than individual, and their distinct personality almost forbade his being considered a disciple of any school.

Holman Hunt may be called the one persistent follower of this cult. He has consistently embodied his convictions in his pictures, the value of which to English art cannot yet be determined. This is also true of the marvellous work of Burne Jones; but although they have but few faithful followers, Pre-raphaelite art no longer needs defence nor apology.

Its secondary effect is far-reaching. To it may be largely attributed the more earnest study of Nature as well as the simplicity of treatment and lack of conventionality which now characterizes English art to an extent before unknown.

•

Impressionism is the most distinctive feature of nineteenth-century art, and is too large a subject to be treated in an introduction – any proper consideration of it demands a volume.

The entire execution of a picture out-of-doors was sometimes practised by Constable, more frequently by Turner, and some of the peculiarities of the French impressionist artists were shared by the English landscape painters of the early part of the century. While no one could dream of calling Constable an impressionist, it is interesting to recall the reception of his "Opening of Waterloo Bridge." Ridiculed in London, it was accepted in Paris, and is now honored at the Royal Academy.

This picture was covered with pure white, in impasto, a method dear to impressionists. Was Constable in advance of his critics? is a question that comes involuntarily to mind as we read the life of this artist, and recall the excitement which the exhibition of his works caused at the Salon of 1824, and the interest they aroused in Delacroix and other French painters.

The word Impressionism calls to mind the names of Manet, Monet, Pissaro, Mme. Berthe Morisot, Paul Cézanne, Whistler, Sargent, Hassam, and many others. Impressionists exhibited their pictures in Paris as early as 1874; not until 1878 were they seen to advantage in London, when Whistler exhibited in the Grosvenor Gallery; and the New English Art Club, founded in 1885, was the outcome of the need of this school to be better represented in its special exhibitions than was possible in other galleries.

In a comprehensive sense Impressionism includes all artists who represent their subjects with breadth and collectiveness rather than in detail – in the way in which we see a view at the first glance, before we have time to apprehend its minor parts.

The advocates of impressionism now claim that it is the most reformatory movement in modern painting; it is undeniably in full accord with the spirit of the time in putting aside older methods and conventions and introducing a new manner of seeing and representing Nature.

The differing phases of Painting in the nineteenth century have had their effect upon that art as a whole. Each one has been important, not only in the country of its special development, but in other lands, each distinctive quality being modified by individual and national characteristics.

•

In the early decades of the past century Sculpture was "classic" and conventional rather than natural and sincere. A revolt against these conditions produced such artists as Rodin, St. Gaudens, MacMonnies, and many less famous men who have put life, spirit, and nature into their art.

In Sculpture as in Painting many more subjects are treated than were formerly thought suited to representation in marble and bronze, and a large proportion of these recent *motifs* demand a broad method of treatment – a manner often called "unfinished" by those who approve only the smooth polish of an antique Venus, and would limit sculpture to the narrow class of subjects with which this smoothness harmonizes.

The best sculptors of the present treat the minor details of their subjects in a sketchy, or, as some critics contend, in a rough imperfect manner, while others find that this treatment of detail, combined with a careful, comprehensive treatment of the important parts, emphasizes the meaning and imparts strength to the whole, as no smoothness can do.

Although the highest possibilities in sculpture may not yet be reached, it is animated with new spirit of life and nature. Nineteenth-century aims and modes of expression have greatly enlarged its province. Like Painting, Sculpture has become democratic. It glorifies Labor and all that is comprised in the term "common, every-day life," while it also commemorates noble and useful deeds with genuine sympathy and an intelligent appreciation of the best to which humanity attains; at the same time poetical fancies, myths, and legends are not neglected, but are rendered with all possible delicacy and tenderness.

At present a great number of women are sculptors. The important commissions which are given them in connection with the great expositions of the time – the execution of memorial statues and monuments, fountains, and various other works which is confided to them, testifies to their excellence in their art with an emphasis beyond that of words.

•

Want of space forbids any special mention of etching, metal work, enamelling, designing, and decorative work in many directions in which women in great numbers are engaged; indeed, in what direction can we look in which women are not employed – I believe I may say by thousands – in all the minor arts? Between the multitude that pursue the Fine Arts and kindred branches for a maintenance – and are rarely heard of – and those fortunate ones who are commissioned to execute important works, there is an enormous middle class. Paris is their Mecca, but they are known in all art centres, and it is by no means unusual for an artist to study under Dutch, German, and Italian masters, as well as French.

The present method of study in Paris – in such academies as that of Julian and the Colarossi – secures to the student the criticism and advice of the best artists of the day, while in summer – in the country and by the sea – there are artistic colonies in which students lead a delightful life, still profiting by the instruction of eminent masters.

Year by year the opportunities for art-study by women have been increased until they are welcome in the schools of the world, with rare exceptions. The highest goal seems to have been reached by their admission to the competition for the *Grand prix de Rome* conferred by *l'École des Beaux Arts*.

I regret that the advantages of the American Art Academy in

Rome are not open to women. The fact that for centuries women have been members and professors in the Academy of St. Luke, and in view of the recent action of *l'École des Beaux Arts*, this narrowness of the American Academy in the Eternal City is especially pronounced.

One can but approve the encouragement afforded women artists in France, by the generosity with which their excellence is recognized.

To be an officer in the French Academy is an honor surpassed in France by that of the Legion of Honor only. Within a twelvemonth two hundred and seventy-five women have been thus distinguished, twenty-eight of them being painters and designers. From this famous Academy down, through the International Expositions, the Salons, and the numberless exhibitions in various countries, a large proportion of medals and other honors are conferred on women, who, having now been accorded all privileges necessary for the pursuit of art and for its recompense, will surely prove that they richly merit every good that can be shared with them.

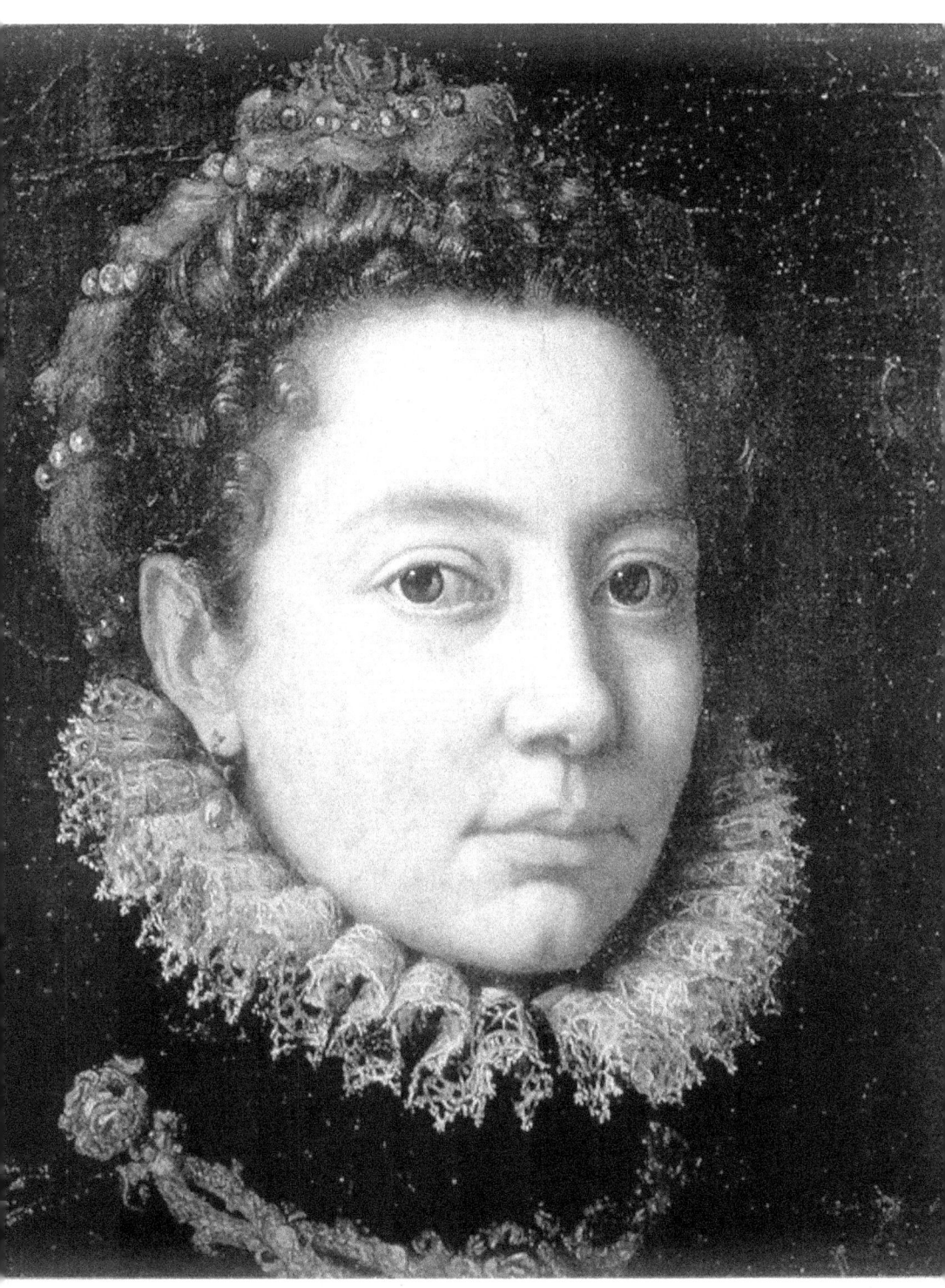

Sofonisba Anguissola, Self-Portrait, 1560

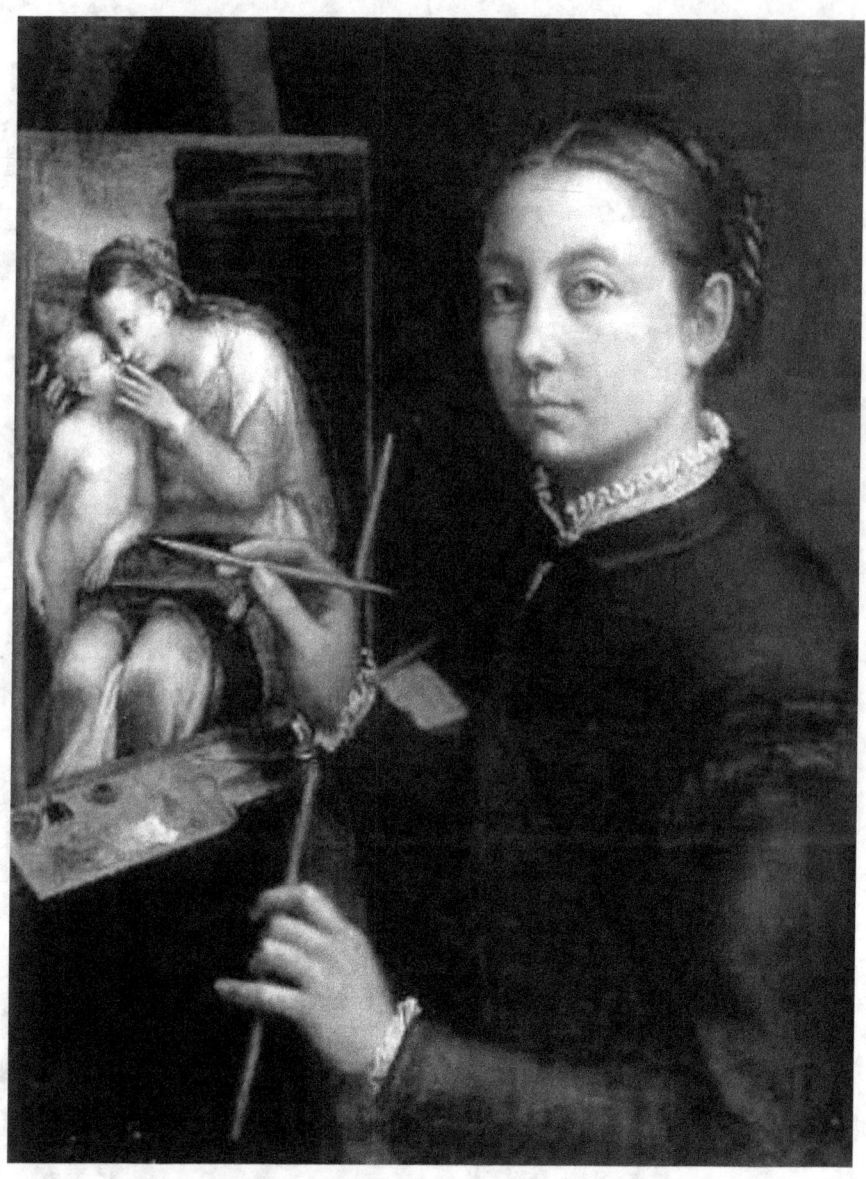

Sofonisba Anguissola, Self-Portrait, 1556, Lancut Museum, Poland

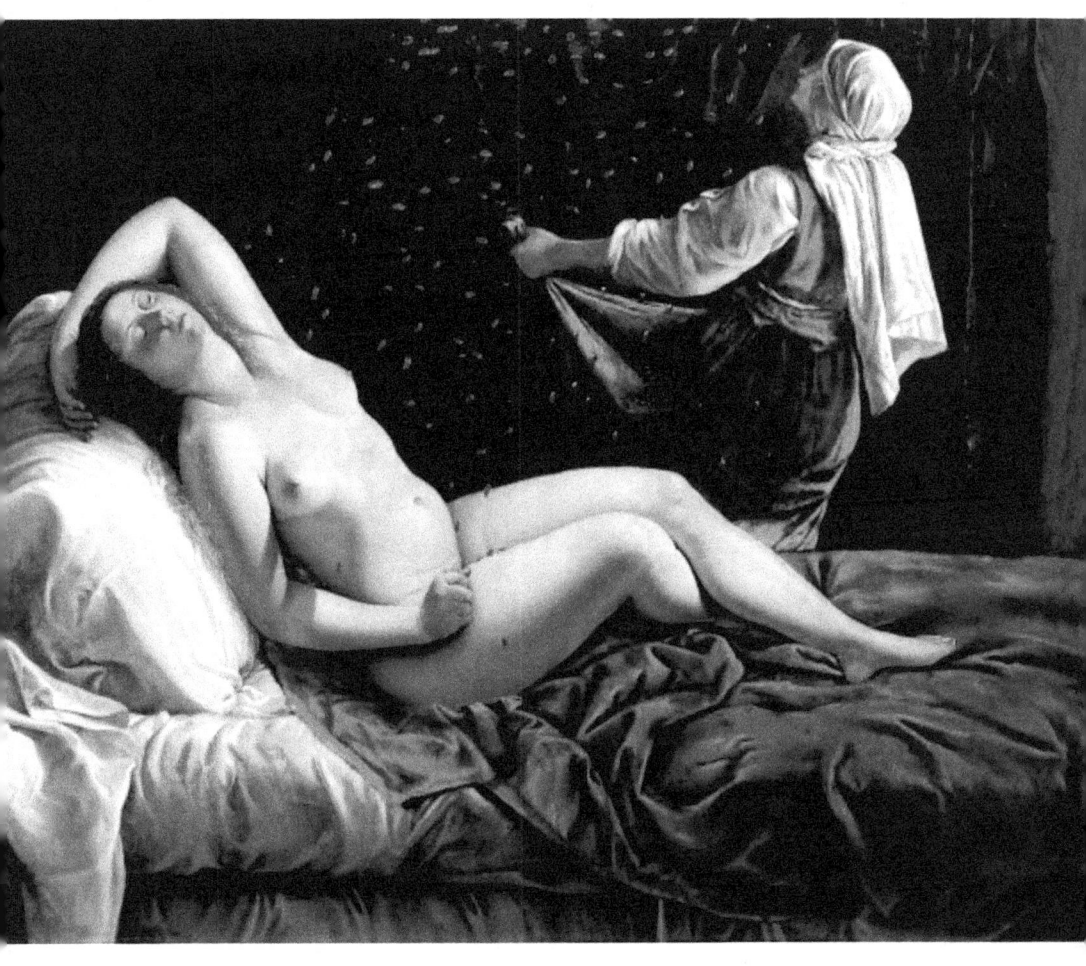

Artemisia Gentileschi, Danaë, c.1612, St Louis Art Museum.

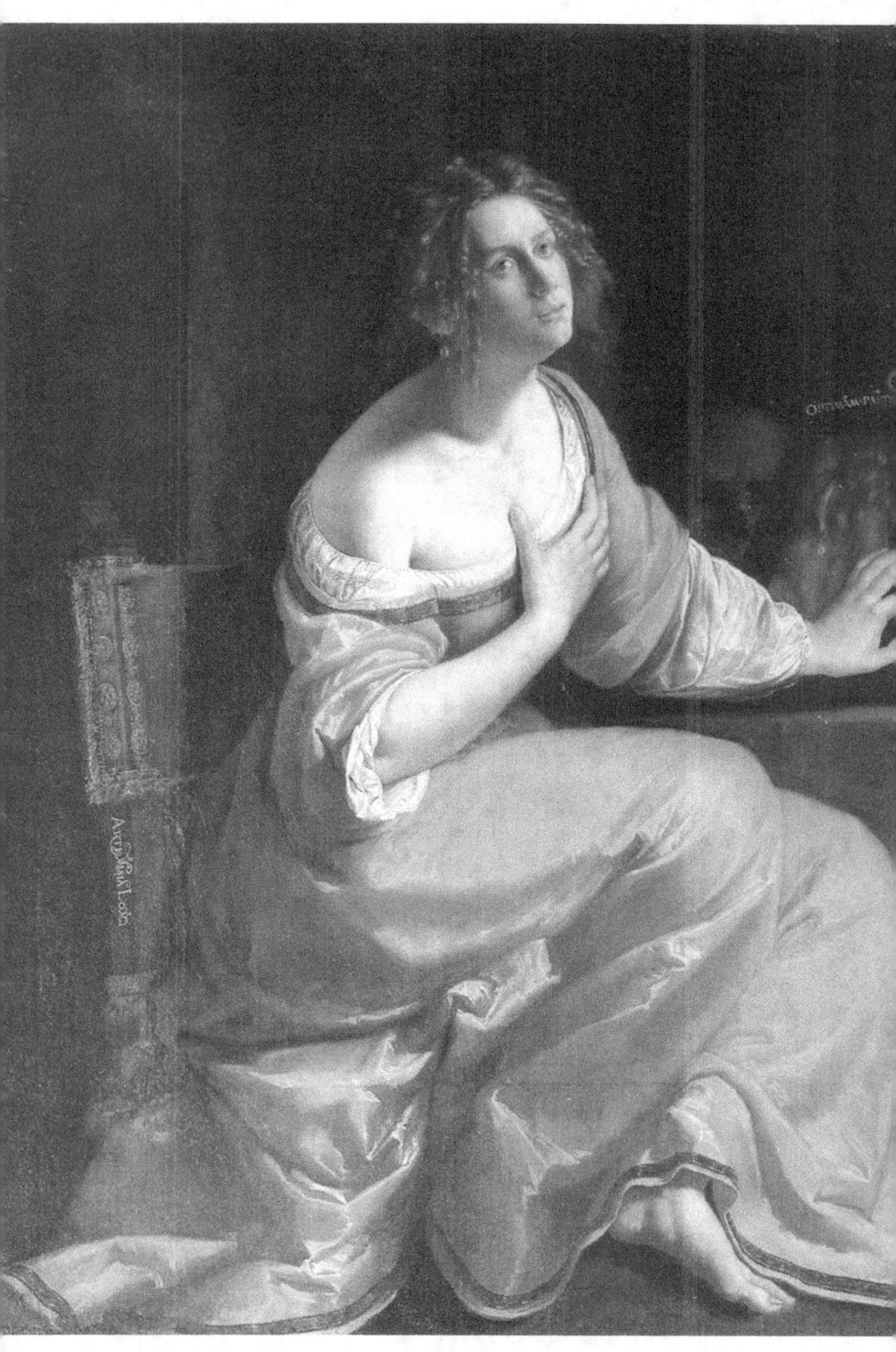

Artemsia Gentileschi, Mary Magdalene

Artemisia Gentileshi, Self-Portrait as a Martyr, 1615

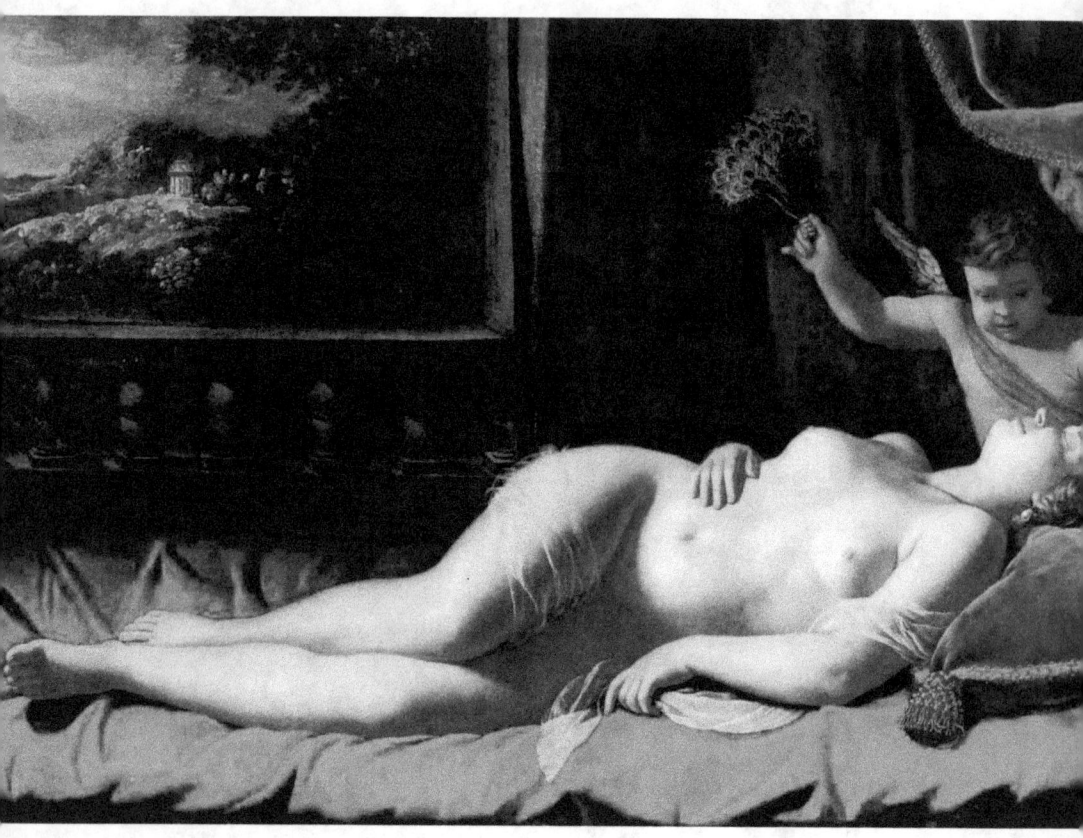

Artemisia Gentileschi, Sleeping Venus, 1625-30,
Barbara Piasecka Johnson Foundation, Princeton, New Jersey

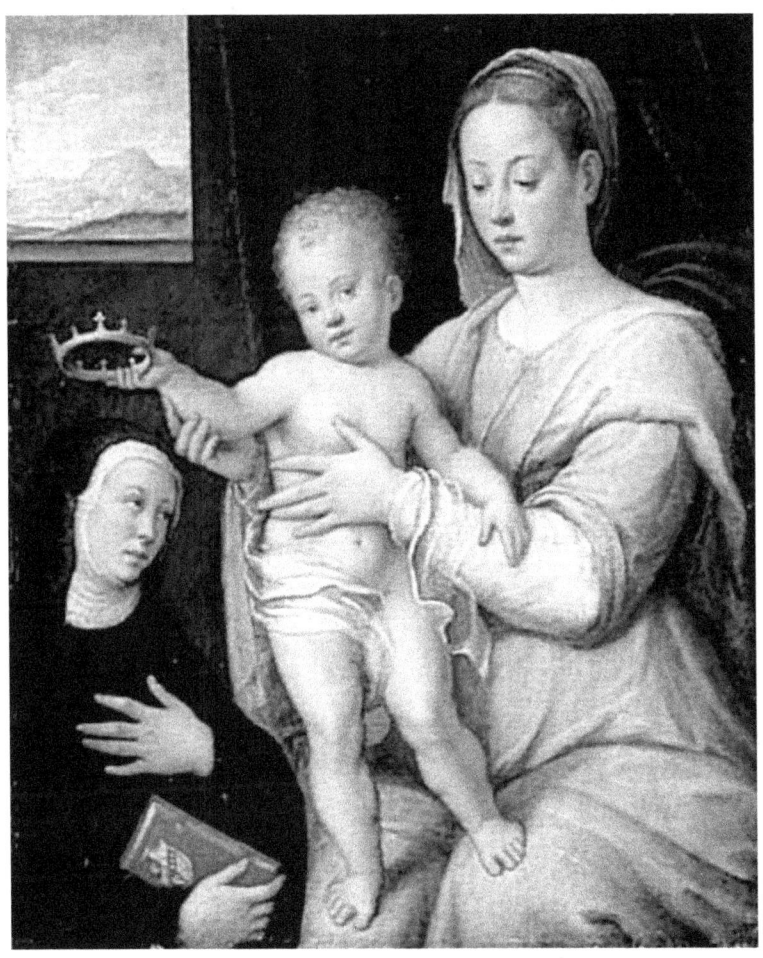

Barbara Longhi, Madonna and Child

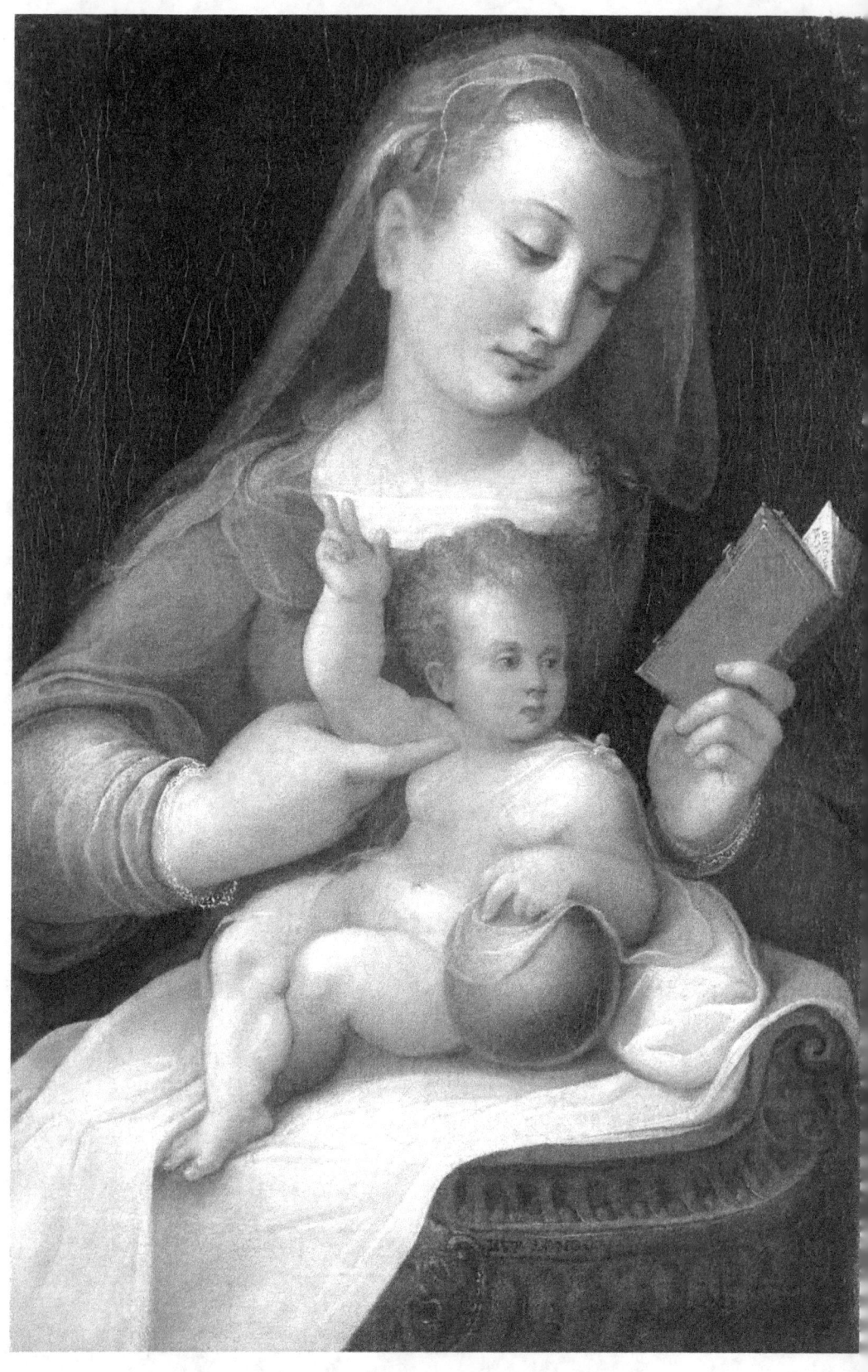

Barbara Longhi, Madonna and Child, 1580-85, Indianapolis

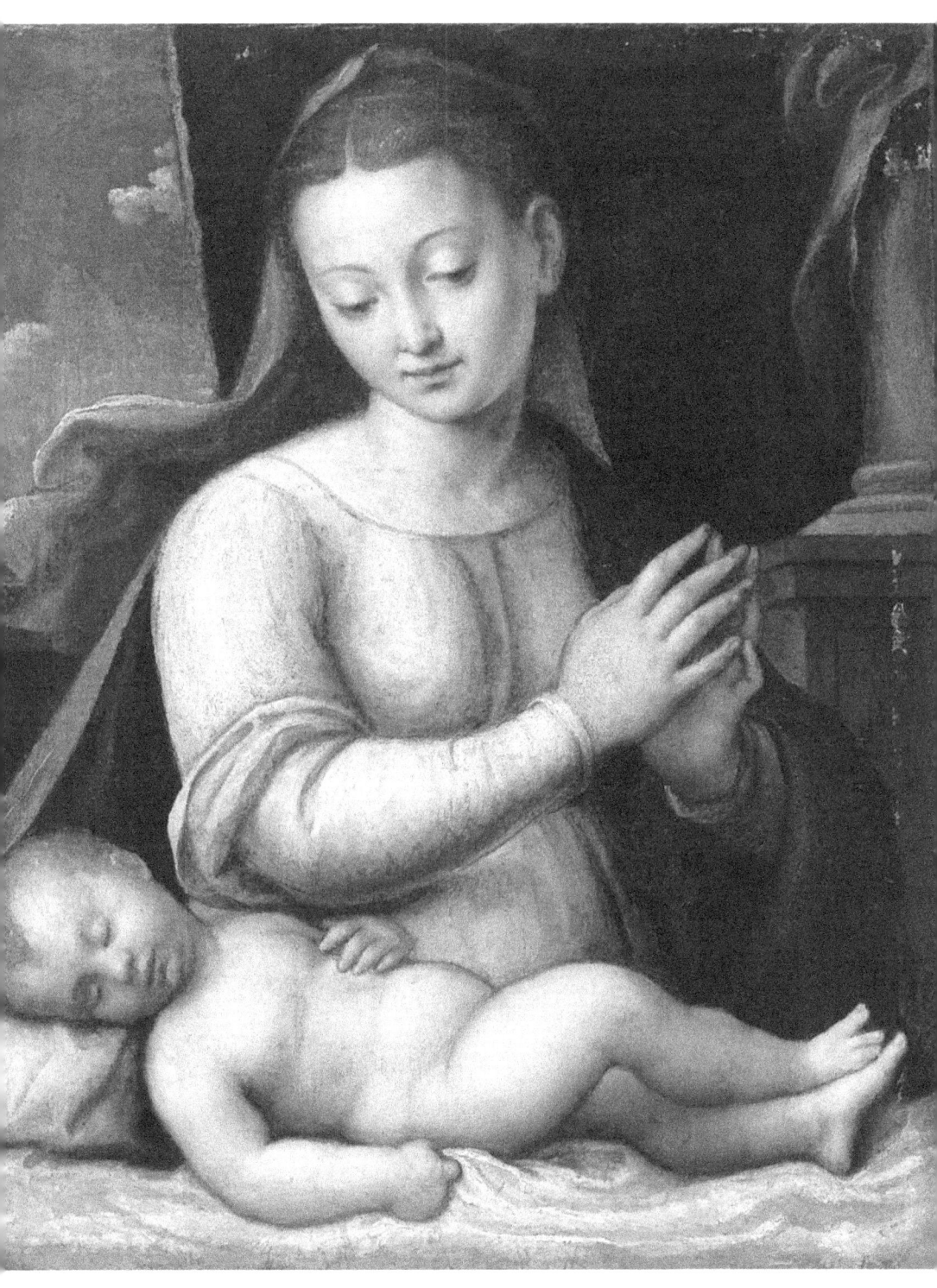

Barbara Longhi, Madonna Adoring the Child

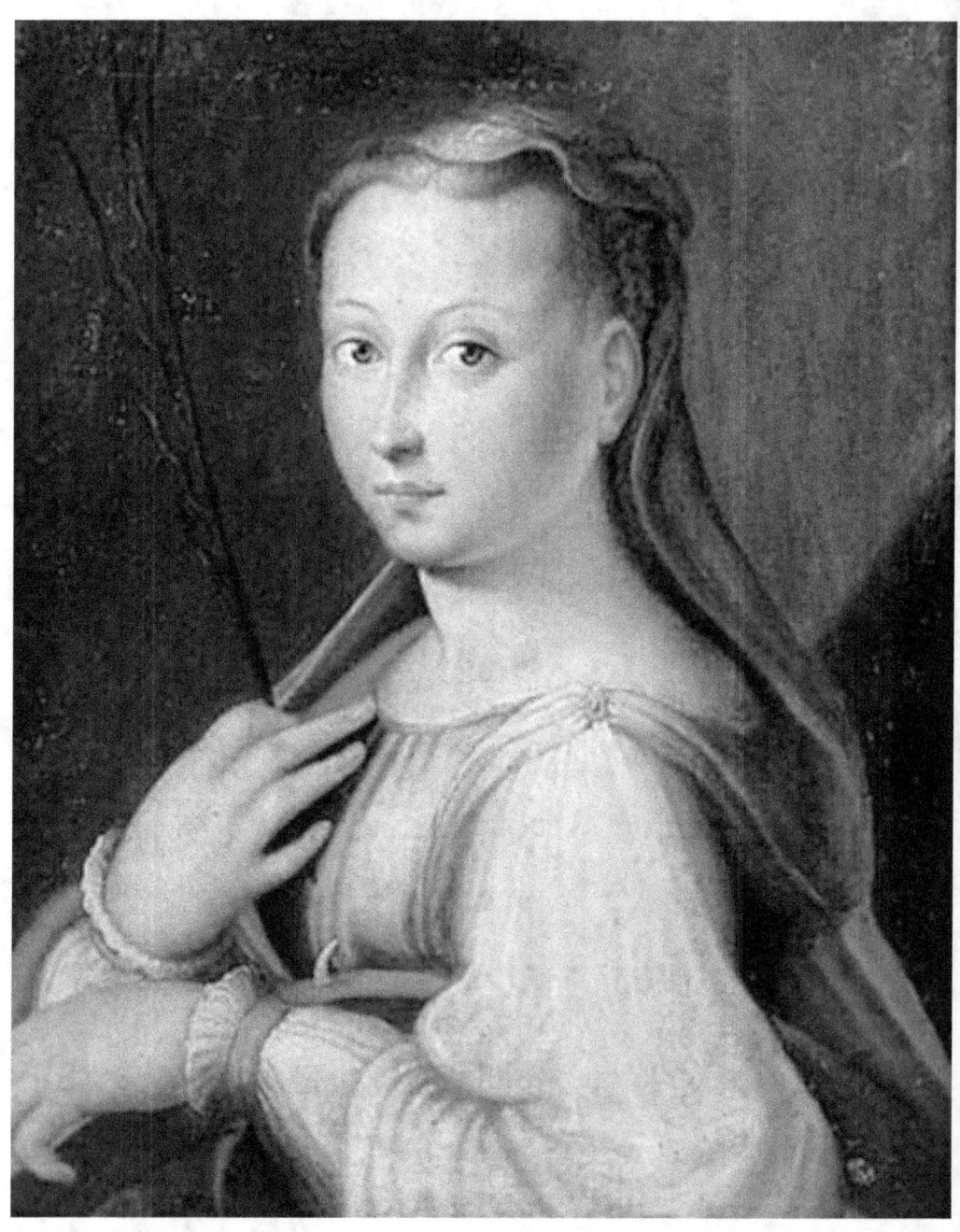

Barbara Longhi, Self-Portrait as St. Catherine of Alexandria, 1589

WOMEN IN THE FINE ARTS

Aarestrup, Marie Helene. Born at Flekkefjord, Norway, 1829. She made her studies in Bergen, under Reusch; under Tessier in Paris; and Vautier in Düsseldorf. She excelled in genre and portrait painting. Her "Playing Child" and "Shepherd Boy" are in the Art Union in Christiania; the "Interior of Hotel Cluny" and a "Flower Girl" are in the Museum at Gottenburg.

Abbatt, Agnes Dean. Bronze medal, Cooper Union; silver medal, Massachusetts Charitable Mechanics' Association. Member of American Water Color Society.

[*No reply to circular.*]

Abbema, Mme. Louise. Officer of the Mérite des Arts; honorable mention, Salon of 1881; bronze medal, Paris Exposition, 1900; Hors Concours, 1903, at Exposition of Limoges. Born at Étampes, 1858. Pupil of Chaplin, Henner, and Carolus-Duran. She exhibited a "Portrait of Sarah Bernhardt," 1876; "The Seasons," 1883; "Portrait of M. Abbema," 1887; "Among the Flowers," 1893; "An April Morning," 1894; "Winter," 1895, etc.

This artist has also executed numerous decorations for ceilings and decorative panels for private houses. Her picture of "Breakfast in the Conservatory" is in the Museum of Pau.

Mme. Abbema illustrated "La Mer," by Maizeroy, and has contributed to the *Gazette des Beaux-Arts* and several other Parisian publications.

At the Salon of the Artistes Français, 1902, she exhibited the "Portrait of Pierre," and in 1903 a portrait of the Countess P. S.

Mme. Abbema wears her hair short, and affects such absolute simplicity in her costume that at first sight she reminds one of a charming young man. In no other direction, however, is there a masculine touch about this delightful artist. She has feminine grace, a love for poetry, a passion for flowers, which she often introduces in her pictures; she has, in short, a truly womanly character, which appears in the refinement and attractiveness of her work.

Abbott, Katherine G. Bronze medal, Paris Exposition, 1900; honorable mention, Buffalo Exposition, 1901.

Achille-Fould, Mlle. Georges. Medal, third class, Versailles, 1888; honorable mention, Paris Salon, 1894; medal, third class, 1895; medal, second class, 1897; Hors Concours; bronze medal at Paris Exposition, 1900. Officer of Public Instruction; member of the Société des Artistes Français. Born at Asnières (Seine). Pupil of Cabanel, Antoine Vollon, and Léon Comerre.

A painter of figure subjects and portraits. Several of her works are in private collections in the United States. Among these are the "Flower-Seller," the "Knife-Grinder," "M. de Richelieu's Love Knots," exhibited in the Salon of 1902, and "Going to School."

"The Dull Season" is in London; "Cinderella" and many others in Paris.

This artist, when still in short skirts, sent her first picture, "In the Market Place," to the Salon of 1884. She is most industrious, and her history, as she herself insists, is in her pictures. She has been surrounded by a sympathetic and artistic atmosphere. Her mother was an art critic, who, before her second marriage to Prince Stirberg, signed her articles Gustave Haller. Her home, the Château de Bécon, is an ideal home for an artist, and one can well understand her distaste for realism and the professional model.

"M. de Richelieu's Love Knots" is very attractive and was one of the successes of 1902. He is a fine gentleman to whom a bevy of young girls is devoted, tying his ribbons, and evidently admiring him and his exquisite costume. The girls are smiling and much amused, while the young man has an air of immense satisfaction.

At the Salon of 1903 Mlle. Fould exhibited "La Chatouilleuse" – Tickling – and "Nasturtiums." The first shows a young woman seated, wearing a décolleté gown, while a mischievous companion steals up behind and tickles her neck with a twig. It is less attractive than many of this artist's pictures.

In 1890 Mlle. Fould painted a portrait of her stepfather, and for a time devoted herself to portraits rather than to the subjects she had before studied with such success. In 1893 she painted a portrait of Rosa Bonheur, in her studio, while the latter paused from her work on a large picture of lions. This portrait presents the great animal painter in a calm, thoughtful mood, in the midst of her studio, surrounded by sketches and all the accessories of her work. In the opinion of many who knew the great artist most intimately this is the best portrait of her in existence.

Mlle. Fould, at different periods, has painted legendary subjects, at other times religious pictures, but in my judgment the last were the least successful of her works.

Her "Cinderella" is delightful; the two "Merry Wives of Windsor," sitting on the basket in which Falstaff is hidden, and from which he is pushing out a hand, is an excellent illustration of this ever-amusing story, and, indeed, all her pictures of this class may well be praised.

To the Exposition of 1900 she sent an allegorical picture, called "The Gold Mine." A young woman in gold drapery drops gold coins from her hands. In the background is the entrance to a mine, lighted dimly by a miner's lamp, while a pickaxe lies at the feet of the woman; this picture was accorded a bronze medal.

Adam, Mme. Nanny. First prize from the Union of Women Painters and Sculptors, Paris. Medal from the Salon des Artistes Français, and "honors in many other cities." Member of the Société des Artistes Français. Born at Crest (Drôme). Her studies were made under Jean Paul Laurens. Her pictures called "Calme du Soir" and "Le Soir aux Martignes" are in private collections. "Les Remparts de la Ville Close, Concarneau," exhibited at the Salon Artistes Français in 1902, was purchased by the French Government. In 1903 she exhibited "June Twilight, Venice," and "Morning Fog, Holland."

Adelsparre, Sophie Albertine. Born in Oland 1808-62. In Stockholm she received instruction from the sculptor Ovarnström and the painter Ekman; after her father's death she went to Paris and entered the atelier of Cogniet, and later did some work under the direction of her countrymen Wickenberg and Wahlbom. She had, at this time, already made herself known through her copies of some of the Italian masters and Murillo. Her copy of the Sistine Madonna was placed by Queen Josephine in the Catholic church at Christiania. After her return from Dresden where she went from Paris, she painted portraits of King Oscar and Queen Josephine. In 1851, having received a government scholarship, she went to Munich, Bologna, and Florence, and lived three years and a half in Rome, where she was associated with Fogelberg, Overbeck, and Schnetz, and became a Catholic. During this time she copied Raphael's "Transfiguration," now in the Catholic church at Stockholm, and painted from life a portrait of Pius IX. for the castle at Drottningholm. She also painted a "Roman Dancing Girl" and a "Beggar Girl of Terracina."

Ahrens, Ellen Wetherald. Second Toppan prize, Pennsylvania Academy of Fine Arts. Second prize and silver medal, Carnegie Institute, Pittsburg, 1902. Member of the Pennsylvania Academy, the Plastic Club, and the Pennsylvania Society of Miniature Painters. Born in Baltimore. Studied at Boston Museum of Fine Arts under Grundmann, Champney, and Stone; Pennsylvania Academy under Thomas Eakins; Drexel Institute under Howard Pyle.

Many of her portraits are in private hands. That called "Sewing," a prize picture, will be in the St. Louis Exhibition. Her portrait of Mr. Ellwood Johnson is in the Pennsylvania Academy. That of Mary Ballard – a miniature – was solicited for exhibition by the Copley Society, Boston.

Miss Ahrens is also favorably known as a designer for stained-glass windows.

Alcott, May – Mme. Nieriker. Born in Concord, Massachusetts, 1840-79. A sister of the well-known author, Louisa M. Alcott. This artist studied in the Boston School of Design, in Krug's Studio, Paris, and under Müller. She made wonderful copies of Turner's pictures, both in oil and water colors, which were greatly praised by Ruskin and were used in the South Kensington Art Schools for the pupils to copy. Her still-life and flower pictures are in private collections and much valued.

She exhibited at the Paris Salon and in the Dudley Gallery, London, and, student as she still was, her works were approved by art critics on both sides of the Atlantic, and a brilliant future as an artist was foretold for her. Her married life was short, and her death sincerely mourned by a large circle of friends, as well as by the members of her profession who appreciated her artistic genius and her enthusiasm for her work.

Alexander, Francesca. Born in Florence, Italy. Daughter of the portrait painter, Francis Alexander. Her pen-and-ink drawing is her best work. The exquisite conceits in her illustrations were charmingly rendered by the delicacy of her work. She thus illustrated an unpublished Italian legend, writing the text also.

Mr. Ruskin edited her "Story of Ida" and brought out "Roadside Songs of Tuscany," collected, translated, and illustrated by this artist. A larger collection of these songs, with illustrations, was published by Houghton, Mifflin & Co., entitled "Tuscan Songs."

Alippi-Fabretti, Quirina. Silver medal at Perugia in 1879; honorary member of the Royal Academy in Urbino and of the Academy of Fine Arts in Perugia. Born in Urbino, 1849. She was the daughter of the jurisconsult Luigi Alippi. She studied drawing and painting in Rome with Ortis and De Sanctis. Following her father to Perugia in 1874, whither he had been called to the Court of Appeals, she continued her study under Moretti. She married

Ferdinando Fabretti in 1877. She made admirable copies of some of the best pictures in Perugia, notably Perugino's "Presepio" for a church in Mount Lebanon, Syria. She was also commissioned to paint an altar-piece, representing St. Stephen, for the same church. Her interiors are admirable. She exhibited an "Interior of the Great Hall of the Exchange of Perugia" in 1884, at Turin. She painted two interior views of the church of San Giovanni del Cambio in Perugia, and an interior of the vestibule of the Confraternity of St. Francis. Her other works, besides portraits, include an "Odalisk," an "Old Woman Fortune-teller," and a "St. Catherine."

Allingham, Helen. Honorable mention at Paris Exhibition, 1900; silver medal from Brussels Exhibition, 1901; bronze medal from the Columbian Exhibition, Chicago. Member of the Royal Society of Painters in Water Colors, London. Born near Burton-on-Trent, 1848. Began the study of art at fourteen, in Birmingham School of Art, where she remained about five years, when she entered the schools of the Royal Academy, where instruction is given by the Royal Academicians in turn. In 1868 she went to Italy.

Her first exhibition at the Royal Academy occurred in 1874, under the name Helen Patterson; her pictures were "Wait for Me" and "The Milkmaid." Since that time Mrs. Allingham has constantly exhibited at the Academy and many other exhibitions.

Her pictures are of genre subjects, chiefly from English rural life and landscapes. She has also been successful as an illustrator for the *Graphic*, the *Cornhill Magazine*, and other publications. Her water-color portraits of Carlyle in his later years are well known. She introduced his cat "Tib" into a portrait taken in his Chelsea garden.

Among her most ambitious works are the "Young Customers," the "Old Men's Garden, Chelsea Hospital," the "Lady of the Manor," "Confidences," "London Flowers," and others of kindred motives.

The "Young Customers," water-color, was exhibited at Paris in 1878. When seen at the Academy in 1875, Ruskin wrote of it: "It happens curiously that the only drawing of which the memory remains with me as a possession out of the Old Water-Color Exhibition of this year – Mrs. Allingham's 'Young Customers' – should be not only by an accomplished designer of woodcuts, but itself the illustration of a popular story. The drawing with whatever temporary purpose executed, is forever lovely; a thing which I believe Gainsborough would have given one of his own paintings for – old-fashioned as red-tipped dresses are, and more precious than rubies." – *Notes of the Academy*, 1875.

Alma-Tadema, Lady Laura Therese. Gold medal at International Art Exhibition, Berlin, 1876; medal at Chicago, 1893; second-class medal at Paris Exhibition, 1900. Born in London. From early childhood this artist was fond of drawing and had the usual drawing-class lessons at school and also drew from the antique in the British Museum. Her serious study, however, began at the age of eighteen, under the direction of Laurenz Alma-Tadema.

Her pictures are principally of domestic scenes, child-life, and other genre subjects. "Battledore and Shuttlecock" is an interior, with a graceful girl playing the game, to the amusement of a young child sitting on a nurse's lap. The room is attractive, the accessories well painted, and a second girl just coming through the door and turning her eyes up to the shuttlecock is an interesting figure.

Of quite a different character is the picture called "In Winter." The landscape is very attractive. In a sled, well wrapped up, is a little girl, with a doll on her lap; the older boy – brother? – who pushes the sled from behind, leaning over the child, does his part with a will, and the dignified and serious expression on the face of the little girl in the sled indicates her sense of responsibility in the care of the doll as well as a feeling of deep satisfaction in her enjoyable outing.

Among the more important pictures by Lady Alma-Tadema are "Hush-a-Bye," "Parting," in the Art Gallery at Adelaide, New South Wales, "Silent Persuasion," "The Carol," and "Satisfaction." Her picture in the Academy Exhibition, 1903, a Dutch interior with a young mother nursing "The Firstborn," was much admired and was in harmony with the verse,

> Lie on mother's knee, my own,
>> Dance your heels about me!
> Apples leave the tree, my own.
>> Soon you'll live without me."

Amen, Madame J. Honorable mention, Paris, 1901.
[*No reply to circular.*]

Anguisciola, Lucia. A pupil of her sister Sofonisba, painted a life-size portrait of Piermaria, a physician of Cremona. It is in the gallery of the Prado, Madrid, and is signed, "Lucia Angvisola Amilcares. F. Adolescens."

Lucia's portrait of her sister Europa is at Brescia. Some authorities believe that the small portrait in the Borghese Gallery is by Lucia, although it has been attributed to Sofonisba.

Vasari relates that Europa and a younger sister, Anna Maria, were artists. A picture of the Holy Family, inscribed with Europa's name, was formerly in the possession of a vicar of the church of San Pietro; it was of far less merit than the works of her sisters.

Anguisciola, Sofonisba. Born in Cremona, about 1539. Daughter of the patrician, Amilcare Anguisciola, whose only fame rests on the fact that he was the father of six daughters, all of whom were distinguished by unusual talents in music and painting. Dear old Vasari was so charmed by his visit to their palace that he pronounced it "the very home of painting and of all other accomplishments."

Sofonisba was the second daughter. The actual date of her

birth is unknown, but from various other dates that we have concerning her, that given above is generally adopted. She was educated with great care and began her study of drawing and painting when but seven years old, under the care of Bernardino Campi, the best artist of the five Campi of Cremona. Later she was a pupil of Bernardino Gatti, "il Sojaro," and in turn she superintended the artistic studies of her sisters.

Sofonisba excelled in portraits, and when twenty-four years old was known all over Italy as a good artist. Her extraordinary proficiency at an early age is proved by a picture in the Yarborough collection, London – a portrait of a man, signed, and dated 1551, when she was not more than twelve years old.

When presented at the court of Milan, then under Spanish rule, Sofonisba was brought to the notice of Philip II., who, through his ambassador, invited her to fill the office of court painter at Madrid. Flattering as this invitation must have been to the artist and her family, it is not surprising that she hesitated and required time for consideration of this honorable proposal.

The reputation of the ceremonious Spanish court, under its gloomy and exacting sovereign, was not attractive to a young woman already surrounded by devoted admirers, to one of whom she had given her heart. The separation from her family, too, and the long, fatiguing journey to Spain, were objections not easily overcome, and her final acceptance of the proposal was a proof of her energy and strength of purpose.

Her journey was made in 1560 and was conducted with all possible care for her comfort. She was attended by two noble ladies as maids of honor, two chamberlains, and six servants in livery – in truth, her mode of travelling differed but little from that of the young ladies of the royal family. As she entered Madrid she was received by the king and queen, and by them conducted to the royal palace.

We can imagine Sofonisba's pleasure in painting the portrait of the lovely Isabella, and her pictures of Philip and his family soon raised her to the very summit of popularity. All the grandees of Madrid desired to have their portraits from her hand, and rich jewels and large sums of money were showered upon her.

Gratifying as was her artistic success, the affection of the queen, which she speedily won, was more precious to her. She was soon made a lady-in-waiting to her Majesty, and a little later was promoted to the distinguished position of governess to the Infanta Clara Eugenia.

That Sofonisba fully appreciated her gentle mistress is shown in her letter to Pope Pius IV., who had requested her to send him a portrait of the queen. She wrote that no picture could worthily figure the royal lady, and added: "If it were possible to represent to your Holiness the beauty of the Queen's soul, you could behold nothing more wonderful."

The Pope bestowed rich gifts on Sofonisba, among which were sacred relics, set with gems. He also wrote an autograph letter, still in existence, in which he assured her that much as he admired her skill in painting, he had been led to believe this the least of her many gifts.

Sofonisba soon gained the approval of the serious and solemn King, for while Philip was jealous of the French ladies of the court and desired Isabella to be wholly under Spanish influence, he proposed to the artist a marriage with one of his nobles, by which means she would remain permanently in the Queen's household. When Philip learned that Sofonisba was already betrothed to Don Fabrizio de Monçada – a Sicilian nobleman – in spite of his disappointment he joined Isabella in giving her a dowry of twelve thousand crowns and a pension of one thousand.

It would seem that one who could so soften the heart and manners of Philip II. as did Queen Isabella, must have had a charm of person and character that no ordinary mortal could resist. One is compelled to a kindly feeling for this much-hated man, who daily visited the Queen when she was suffering from smallpox. In her many illnesses he was tenderly devoted to her, and when we remember the miseries of royal ladies whose children are girls, we almost love Philip for comforting Isabella when her first baby was not a son. Philip declared himself better pleased that she had given him a daughter, and made the declaration good by devotion to this child so long as he lived.

Isabella, in a letter to her mother, wrote: "But for the happiness I have of seeing the King every day I should find this court the dullest in the world. I assure you, however, madame, that I have so kind a husband that even did I deem this place a hundredfold more wearisome I should not complain."

While Sofonisba was overwhelmed with commissions in Spain, her sisters were far from idle in Cremona. Europa sent pictures to Madrid which were purchased for private collections, and a picture by Lucia is now in the Gallery of the Queen at Madrid.

When the time for Sofonisba's marriage came she was sorry to leave her "second home," as she called Madrid, and as Don Fabrizio lived but a short time, the King urged her return to Spain; but her desire to be once more with her family impelled her to return to Italy.

The ship on which she sailed from Sicily was commanded by one of the Lomellini, a noble family of Genoa, with whom Sofonisba fell so desperately in love that she offered him her hand – which, says her biographer, "he accepted like a generous man." Does this mean that she had been ungenerous in depriving him of the privilege of asking for what she so freely bestowed?

In Genoa she devotedly pursued her art and won new honors, while she was not forgotten in Madrid. Presents were sent her on her second marriage, and later the Infanta Clara Eugenia and other Spaniards of exalted rank visited her in Genoa. Her palace became a centre of attraction to Genoese artists and men of letters, while many strangers of note sought her acquaintance. She contributed largely to the restoration of art and literature to the importance that had been accorded them in the most brilliant days of Genoese power.

We have not space to recount all the honors conferred on

Sofonisba, both as a woman and an artist. She lived to an extreme old age, and, although she lost her sight, her intellect was undimmed by time or blindness. Vandyck, who was frequently her guest, more than once declared that he "was more benefited by the counsels of the blind Sofonisba than by all his studies of the masters of his art!" From a pupil of Rubens this was praise indeed!

The chief characteristics of Sofonisba's painting were grace and spirit. Her portrait of herself when at her best is in possession of the Lomellini. A second is the splendid picture at Althorpe, in which she is represented as playing the harpsichord. One can scarcely imagine a place in which a portrait would be more severely tested than in the gallery of the Earl of Spencer, beside portraits of lovely women and famous men, painted by master artists. Yet this work of Sofonisba's is praised by discerning critics and connoisseurs. Of the other portraits of herself, that in the Uffizi is signed by her as "of Cremona," which suggests that it was painted before she went to Spain. That in the Vienna Gallery is dated 1551, and inscribed Sophonisba Anguissola. Virgo. Sc. Ipsam Fecit. Still another, in which a man stands beside her, is in the Sienna Gallery. He holds a brush in his hand, and is probably one of her masters.

Her portrait of her sisters playing chess, while an old duenna looks on, was in the collection of Lucien Bonaparte and is said to be now in a private gallery in England. Her religious pictures are rare; a "Marriage of St. Catherine" is in the gallery at Wilton House.

She painted several pictures of three of her sisters on one canvas; one is in the National Museum of Berlin, and a second, formerly in the Leuchtenberg Gallery, is in the Hermitage at Petersburg. A small Holy Family, signed and dated 1559, belonged to the art critic and author, Morelli.

One regrets that so remarkable a woman left no record of her unusual experiences. How valuable would be the story of Don Carlos from so disinterested a person. How interesting had she told us of the *bal masqué*, given by Isabella in the fashion of her own country, when Philip condescended to open the ball with the Queen; or of the sylvan fêtes at Aranjuez, and of the gardens made under the direction of Isabella. Of all this she has told us nothing. We glean the story of her life from the works of various authors, while her fame rests securely on her superiority in the art to which she was devoted.

Ancher, Anna Kristine. Genre painter, won high praise at Berlin in 1900 for two pictures: "Tischgebet," which was masterly in its smoothness and depth of expression, and "Eine blinde Frau in ihrer Stube," in which the full sunlight streaming through the open window produced an affecting contrast. She was born at Skagen, 1859, the daughter of Erik Brondum, and early showed her artistic tendencies. Michael Ancher (whom she married in 1880) noticed and encouraged her talent, which was first displayed in small crayons treating pathetic or humorous subjects. From 1875-78 she studied with Khyn, and later more or less under the direction of her husband. She has painted exclusively small pictures, dealing with simple and natural things, and each picture, as a rule, contains but a single figure. She believes that a dilapidated Skagen hovel may meet every demand of beauty. "Maageplukkerne" – "Gull plucking" – exhibited in 1883, has been called one of the most sympathetic and unaffected pieces of genre painting ever produced by a Danish artist.

An "Old Woman of Skagen," "A Mother and Child," and "Coffee is Ready" were among the most attractive of her pictures of homely, familiar Danish life. The last represents an old fisher, who has fallen asleep on the bench by the stove, and a young woman is waking him with the above announcement.

"A Funeral Scene" is in the Copenhagen Gallery. The coffin is hung with green wreaths; the walls of the room are red; the people stand around with a serious air. The whole story is told in a simple, homely way.

In the "History of Modern Painters" we read: "All her pictures are softly tender and full of fresh light. But the execution is downright and virile. It is only in little touches, in fine and delicate traits of observation which would probably have escaped a man, that these paintings are recognized as the work of a feminine artist."

Antigna, Mme. Hélène Marie. Born at Melun. Pupil of her husband, Jean Pierre Antigna, and of Delacroix. Her best works are small genre subjects, which are excellent and much admired by other artists.

In 1877 she exhibited at the Paris Salon "On n'entre pas!" and the "New Cider"; in 1876, an "Interior at Saint Brieuc" and "A Stable"; in 1875, "Tant va la cruche à l'eau," etc.

Appia, Mme. Thérèse. Member of the Society of the Permanente Exposition of the Athénée, Geneva. Born at Lausanne. Pupil of Mercié and Rodin at Paris.

Mme. Appia, before her marriage, exhibited at the Paris Salon several years continuously. Since then she has exhibited at Turin and Geneva.

She has executed many portrait busts; among them are those of M. Guillaume Monod, Paris, Commander Paul Meiller, and a medallion portrait of Père Hyacinthe, etc.

Argyll, Her Royal Highness, the Princess Louise, Duchess of. This artist has exhibited her work since, 1868. Although her sketches in water-color are clever and attractive, it is as a sculptor that her best work has been done. Pupil of Sir J. E. Boehne, R.A., her unusual natural talent was carefully developed under his advice, and her unflagging industry and devotion to her work have enabled her to rival sculptors who live by their art.

Her busts and lesser subjects are refined and delicate, while possessing a certain individuality which this lady is known to exercise in her direction of the assistant she is forced to employ. Her chief attainment, the large seated figure of Queen Victoria in

Kensington Gardens, is a work of which she may well be proud.

Of this statue Mr. M. H. Spielmann writes: "The setting up of the figure, the arrangement of the drapery, the modelling, the design of the pedestal – all the parts, in fact – are such that the statue must be added to the short list of those which are genuine embellishments to the city of London."

The Duchess of Argyll has been commissioned to design a statue of heroic size, to be executed in bronze and placed in Westminster Abbey, to commemorate the colonial troops who gave up their lives in South Africa in the Boer war.

Arnold, Annie R. Merrylees. Born at Birkenhead. A Scotch miniature painter. Studied in Edinburgh, first in the School of Art, under Mr. Hodder, and later in the life class of Robert Macgregor; afterward in Paris under Benjamin-Constant.

Mrs. Arnold writes me that she thinks it important for miniature painters to do work in a more realistic medium occasionally, and something of a bolder character than can be done in their specialty. She never studied miniature painting, but took it up at the request of a patroness who, before the present fashion for this art had come about, complained that she could find no one who painted miniatures. This lady gave the artist a number of the *Girls' Own Journal*, containing directions for miniature painting, after which Mrs. Arnold began to work in this specialty. She has painted a miniature of Lady Evelyn Cavendish, owned by the Marquis of Lansdowne; others of the Earl and Countess of Mar and Kellie, the first of which belongs to the Royal Scottish Academy; one of Lady Helen Vincent, one of the daughter of Lionel Phillips, Esquire, and several for prominent families in Baltimore and Washington. Her work is seen in the exhibitions of the Royal Academy, London.

In 1903 she exhibited miniatures of Miss M. L. Fenton, the late Mrs. Cameron Corbett, and the Hon. Thomas Erskine, younger son of the Earl of Mar and Kellie.

Ashe, Margaret L.
[*No reply to circular.*]

Assche, Amélie van. Portrait painter and court painter to Queen Louise Marie of Belgium. She was born in 1804, and was the daughter of Henri Jean van Assche. Her first teachers were Mlle. F. Lagarenine and D' Antissier; she later went to Paris, where she spent some time as a pupil of Millet. She made her début at Ghent in 1820, and in Brussels in 1821, with water-colors and pastels, and some of her miniatures figured in the various exhibitions at Brussels between 1830 and 1848, and in Ghent between 1835 and 1838. Her portraits, which are thought to be very good likenesses, are also admirable in color, drawing, and modelling; and her portrait of Leopold I., which she painted in 1839, won for her the appointment at court.

Assche, Isabel Catherine van. She was born at Brussels, 1794. Landscape painter. She took a first prize at Ghent in 1829, and became a pupil of her uncle, Henri van Assche, who was often called the painter of waterfalls. As early as 1812 and 1813 two of her water-colors were displayed in Ghent and Brussels respectively, and she was represented in the exhibitions at Ghent in 1826, 1829, and 1835; at Brussels in 1827 and 1842; at Antwerp in 1834, 1837, and 1840; and at Lüttich in 1836. Her subjects were all taken from the neighborhood of Brussels, and one of them belongs to the royal collection in the Pavilion at Haarlem. In 1828 she married Charles Léon Kindt.

Athes-Perrelet, Louise. First prize and honorable mention, class Gillet and Hébert, 1888; class Bovy, first prize, 1889; Academy class, special mention, 1890; School of Arts, special mention, hors concours, 1891; also, same year, first prize for sculpture, offered by the Society of Arts; first prize offered by the Secretary of the Theatre, 1902. Member of the Union des Femmes and Cercle Artistique. Born at Neuchâtel. Studies made at Geneva under Mme. Carteret and Mme. Gillet and Professors Hébert and B. Penn, in drawing and painting; M. Bovy, in sculpture; and of various masters in decorative work and engraving. Has executed statues, busts, medallion portraits; has painted costumes, according to an invention of her own, for the Theatre of Geneva, and has also made tapestries in New York. All her works have been commended in the journals of Geneva and New York.

Austen, Winifred. Member of Society of Women Artists, London. Born at Ramsgate. Pupil of Mrs. Jopling-Rowe and Mr. C. E. Swan. Miss Austen exhibits in the Royal Academy exhibitions; her works are well hung – one on the line.

Her favorite subjects are wild animals, and she is successful in the illustration of books. Her pictures are in private collections. At the Royal Academy in 1903 she exhibited "The Day of Reckoning," a wolf pursued by hunters through a forest in snow. A second shows a snow scene, with a wolf baying, while two others are apparently listening to him. "While the wolf, in nightly prowl, bays the moon with hideous howl," is the legend with the picture.

Auzon, Pauline. Born in Paris, where she died. 1775-1835. She was a pupil of Regnault and excelled in portraits of women. She exhibited in the Paris Salon from 1793, when but eighteen years old. Her pictures of the "Arrival of Marie Louise in Compiègne" and "Marie Louise Taking Leave of her Family" are in the Versailles Gallery.

Babiano y Mendez Nuñez, Carmen. At the Santiago Exposition, 1875, this artist exhibited two oil paintings and two landscapes in crayon; at Coruña, 1878, a portrait in oil of the Marquis de Mendez Nuñez; at Pontevedra, 1880, several pen and water-color studies, three life-size portraits in crayon, and a work in oil, "A Girl Feeding Chickens."

Baily, Caroline A. B. Gold medal, Paris Exposition, 1900; third-class medal, Salon, 1901.

[*No reply to circular.*]

Baker, Elizabeth Gowdy. Medal at Cooper Union. Member of Boston Art Students' Association and Art Workers' Club for Women, New York. Born at Xenia, Ohio. Pupil of the Cooper Union, Art Students' League, New York School of Art, Philadelphia Academy of Fine Arts, Cowles Art School, Boston; under Frederick Freer, William Chase, and Siddons Mowbray.

This artist has painted numerous portraits and has been especially successful with pictures of children. She has a method of her own of which she has recently written me.

She claims that it is excellent for life-size portraits in water-colors. The paper she uses is heavier than any made in this country, and must be imported; the water-colors are very strong. Mrs. Baker claims that in this method she gets "the strength of oils with the daintiness of water-colors, and that it is *beautiful* for women and children, and sufficiently strong for portraits of men."

She rarely exhibits, and her portraits are in private houses.

Bakhuyzen, Juffrouw Gerardina Jacoba van de Sande. Silver medal at The Hague, 1857; honorary medal at Amsterdam, 1861; another at The Hague, 1863; and a medal of distinction at Amsterdam Colonial Exhibition, 1885. Daughter of the well-known animal painter. From childhood she painted flowers, and for a time this made no especial impression on her family or friends, as it was not an uncommon occupation for girls. At length her father saw that this daughter, Gerardina – for he had numerous daughters, and they all desired to be artists – had talent, and when, in 1850, the Minerva Academy at Groningen gave out "Roses and Dahlias" as a subject, and offered a prize of a little more than ten dollars for the best example, he encouraged Gerardina to enter the contest. She received the contemptible reward, and found, to her astonishment, that the Minerva

Academy considered the picture as belonging to them.

However, this affair brought the name of the artist to the knowledge of the public, and she determined to devote herself to the painting of flowers and fruit, in which she has won unusual fame. There is no sameness in her pictures, and her subjects do not appear to be "arranged" – everything seems to have fallen into its place by chance and to be entirely natural.

Gerardina Jacoba and her brother Julius van de Sande Bakhuyzen, the landscape painter, share one studio. She paints with rapidity, as one must in order to picture the freshness of fast-fading flowers.

Johan Gram writes of her: "If she paints a basket of peaches or plums, they look as if just picked by the gardener and placed upon the table, without any thought of studied effect; some leaves covering the fruit, others falling out of the basket in the most natural way. If she paints the branch of a rose-tree, it seems to spring from the ground with its flowers in all their luxurious wantonness, and one can almost imagine one's self inhaling their delightful perfume. This talented artist knows so well how to depict with her brush the transparency and softness of the tender, ethereal rose, that one may seek in vain among a crowd of artists for her equal... The paintings are all bright and sunny, and we are filled with enthusiasm when gazing at her powerful works."

This artist was born in 1826 and died in 1895. She lived and died in her family residence. In 1850, at Groningen, she took for her motto, "Be true to nature and you will produce that which is good." To this she remained faithful all her days.

Baldwin, Edith Ella. Born at Worcester, Massachusetts. Studied in Paris at Julian Academy, under Bouguereau and Robert-Fleury; at the Colarossi studios under Courtois, also under Julius Rolshoven and Mosler.

Paints portraits and miniatures. At the Salon of the Champ de Mars she exhibited a portrait in pastel, in 1901; at exhibitions of the Society of American Artists in 1898 and 1899 she exhibited miniatures; also pictures in oils at Worcester, 1903.

Ball, Caroline Peddle. Honorable mention at Paris Exhibition, 1900. Member of the Guild of Arts and Crafts and of Art Students' League. Born at Terre Haute, Indiana. Pupil at the Art Students' League, under Augustus St. Gaudens and Kenyon Cox.

This sculptor exhibited at Paris a Bronze Clock. She designed for the Tiffany Glass Company the figure of the Young Virgin and that of the Christ of the Sacred Heart.

A memorial fountain at Flushing, Long Island, a medallion portrait of Miss Cox of Terre Haute, a monument to a child in the same city, a Victory in a quadriga, seen on the United States Building, Paris, 1900, and also at the Buffalo Exhibition, 1901, are among her important works.

Bañuelos, Antonia. At the Paris Exposition of 1878 several portraits by this artist attracted attention, one of them being a portrait of herself. At the Exposition of 1880 she exhibited "A Guitar Player."

Barrantes Manuel de Aragon, Maria del Cármen. Member of the Academy of San Fernando, Madrid, 1816. This institution possesses a drawing by her of the "Virgin with the Christ-Child" and a portrait in oil of a person of the epoch of Charles III.

Bashkirtseff, Marie. Born in Russia of a noble family. 1860-84. This remarkable young woman is interesting in various phases of her life, but here it is as an artist that she is to be considered. Her journal, she tells us, is absolutely truthful, and it is but courteous to take the story of her artistic career from that. She had lessons in drawing, as many children do, but she gives no indication of a special love for art until she visits Florence when fourteen years old, and her love of pictures and statues is awakened. She spent hours in galleries, never sitting down, without fatigue, in spite of her delicacy. She says: "That is because the things one loves do not tire one. So long as there are pictures and, better still, statues to be seen, I am made of iron." After questioning whether she dare say it, she confides to her readers: "I don't like the Madonna della Sedia of Raphael. The countenance of the Virgin is pale, the color is not natural, the expression is that of a waiting-maid rather than of a Madonna. Ah, but there is a Magdalen of Titian that enchanted me. Only – there must always be an only – her wrists are too thick and her hands are too plump – beautiful hands they would be on a woman of fifty. There are things of Rubens and Vandyck that are ravishing. The 'Mensonge' of Salvator Rosa is very natural. I do not speak as a connoisseur; what most resembles nature pleases me most. Is it not the aim of painting to copy nature? I like very much the full, fresh countenance of the wife of Paul Veronese, painted by him. I like the style of his faces. I adore Titian and Vandyck; but that poor Raphael! Provided only no one knows what I write; people would take me for a fool; I do not criticise Raphael; I do not understand him; in time I shall no doubt learn to appreciate his beauties. The portrait of Pope Leo X. – I think it is – is admirable, however." A surprising critique for a girl of her age!

When seventeen she made her first picture of any importance. "While they were playing cards last night I made a rough sketch of the players – and this morning I transferred the sketch to canvas. I am delighted to have made a picture of persons sitting down in different attitudes; I copied the position of the hands and arms, the expressions of the countenance, etc. I had never before done anything but heads, which I was satisfied to scatter over the canvas like flowers."

Her enthusiasm for her art constantly increased. She was not willing to acknowledge her semi-invalidism and was filled with the desire to do something in art that would live after her. She was opposed by her family, who wished her to be in fashionable society. At length she had her way, and when not quite eighteen began to study regularly at the Julian Academy. She worked eight and nine hours a day. Julian encouraged her, she rejoiced in being with "real artists who have exhibited in the Salon and whose pictures are bought," and declared herself "happy, happy!" Before long M. Julian told her that she might become a great artist, and the first time that Robert-Fleury saw her work and learned how little she had studied, and that she had never before drawn from a living model, he said: "Well, then, you have extraordinary talent for painting; you are specially gifted, and I advise you to work hard."

Her masters always assured her of her talent, but she was much of the time depressed. She admired the work of Mlle. Breslau and acknowledged herself jealous of the Swiss artist. But after a year of study she took the second prize in the Academy, and admitted that she ought to be content.

Robert-Fleury took much interest in her work, and she began to hope to equal Breslau; but she was as often despondent as she was happy, which no doubt was due to her health, for she was already stricken with the malady from which she died. Julian wondered why, with her talent, it was so difficult for her to paint; to herself she seemed paralyzed.

In the autumn of 1879 she took a studio, and, besides her painting, she essayed modelling. In 1880 her portrait of her sister was exhibited at the Salon, and her mother and other friends were gratified by its acceptance.

At one time Mlle. Bashkirtseff had suffered with her eyes, and, getting better of that, she had an attack of deafness. For these reasons she went, in the summer of 1880, to Mont-Dore for treatment, and was much benefited in regard to her deafness, though not cured, and now the condition of her lungs was recognized, and what she had realized for some time was told to her family. She suffered greatly from the restrictions of her condition. She could not read very much, as her eyes were not strong enough to read and paint; she avoided people because of her deafness; her cough was very tiresome and her breathing difficult.

At the Salon of 1881 her picture was well hung and was

praised by artists. In the autumn of that year she was very ill, but happily, about the beginning of 1882, she was much better and again enthusiastic about her painting. She had been in Spain and excited admiration in Madrid by the excellence of her copy of "Vulcan," by Velasquez. January 15th she wrote: "I am wrapped up in my art. I think I caught the sacred fire in Spain at the same time that I caught the pleurisy. From being a student I now begin to be an artist. This sudden influx of power puts me beside myself with joy. I sketch future pictures; I dream of painting an Ophelia. Potain has promised to take me to Saint-Anne to study faces of the mad women there, and then I am full of the idea of painting an old man, an Arab, sitting down singing to the accompaniment of a kind of guitar; and I am thinking also of a large affair for the coming Salon – a view of the Carnival; but for this it would be necessary that I should go to Nice – to Naples first for the Carnival, and then to Nice, where I have my villa, to paint it in open air."

She now met Bastien-Lepage, who, while he was somewhat severe in his criticism of her work, told her seriously that she was "marvellously gifted." This gave her great pleasure, and, indeed, just at this time the whole tone of the journal and her art enthusiasm are most comforting after the preceding despairing months. From this time until her death her journal is largely occupied with her health, which constantly failed, but her interest in art and her intense desire to do something worthy of a great artist – something that Julian, Robert-Fleury, and, above all, Bastien-Lepage, could praise, seemed to give her strength, and, in spite of the steady advance of the fell tuberculosis from which she was dying, she worked devotedly.

She had a fine studio in a new home of the family, and was seized with an ardent desire to try sculpture – she did a little in this art – but that which proved to be her last and best work was her contribution to the Salon of 1884. This brought her to the notice of the public, and she had great pleasure, although mingled with the conviction of her coming death and the doubts of her ability to do more. Of this time she writes: "Am I satisfied? It is easy to answer that question; I am neither satisfied nor dissatisfied. My success is just enough to keep me from being unhappy. That is all."

Again: "I have just returned from the Salon. We remained a long time seated on a bench before the picture. It attracted a good deal of attention, and I smiled to myself at the thought that no one would ever imagine the elegantly dressed young girl seated before it, showing the tips of her little boots, to be the artist. Ah, all this is a great deal better than last year! Have I achieved a success, in the true, serious meaning of the word? I almost think so."

The picture was called the "Meeting," and shows seven gamins talking together before a wooden fence at the corner of a street. François Coppée wrote of it: "It is a *chef d'oeuvre*, I maintain. The faces and the attitudes of the children are strikingly real. The glimpse of meagre landscape expresses the sadness of the poorer neighborhoods."

Previous to this time, her picture of two boys, called "Jean and Jacques," had been reproduced in the Russian *Illustration*, and she now received many requests for permission to photograph and reproduce her "Meeting," and connoisseurs made requests to be admitted to her studio. All this gratified her while it also surprised. She was at work on a picture called "Spring," for which she went to Sèvres, to paint in the open.

Naturally she hoped for a Salon medal, and her friends encouraged her wish – but alas! she was cruelly disappointed. Many thought her unfairly treated, but it was remembered that the year before she had publicly spoken of the committee as "idiots"!

People now wished to buy her pictures and in many ways she realized that she was successful. How pathetic her written words: "I have spent six years, working ten hours a day, to gain what? The knowledge of all I have yet to learn in my art, and a fatal disease!"

It is probable that the "Meeting" received no medal because it was suspected that Mlle. Bashkirtseff had been aided in her work. No one could tell who had originated this idea, but as some medals had been given to women who did not paint their pictures alone, the committee were timid, although there seems to have been no question as to superiority.

A friendship had grown up between the families Bashkirtseff and Bastien-Lepage. Both the great artist and the dying girl were very ill, but for some time she and her mother visited him every two or three days. He seemed almost to live on these visits and complained if they were omitted. At last, ill as Bastien-Lepage was, he was the better able of the two to make a visit. On October 16th she writes of his being brought to her and made comfortable in one easy-chair while she was in another. "Ah, if I could only paint!" he said. "And I?" she replied. "There is the end to this year's picture!"

These visits were continued. October 20th she writes of his increasing feebleness. She wrote no more, and in eleven days was dead.

In 1885 the works of Marie Bashkirtseff were exhibited. In the catalogue was printed François Coppée's account of a visit he had made her mother a few months before Marie's death. He saw her studio and her works, and wrote, after speaking of the "Meeting," as follows:

"At the Exhibition – Salon – before this charming picture, the public had with a unanimous voice bestowed the medal on Mlle. B., who had been already 'mentioned' the year before. Why was this verdict not confirmed by the jury? Because the artist was a foreigner? Who knows? Perhaps because of her wealth. This injustice made her suffer, and she endeavored – the noble child – to avenge herself by redoubling her efforts.

"In one hour I saw there twenty canvases commenced; a hundred designs – drawings, painted studies, the cast of a statue, portraits which suggested to me the name of Frans Hals, scenes made from life in the open streets; notably one large sketch of a landscape – the October mist on the shore, the trees half stripped, big yellow leaves strewing the ground. In a word, works in which is incessantly sought, or more often asserts itself, the sentiment of the sincerest and most original art, and of the most personal talent."

Mathilde Blind, in her "Study of Marie Bashkirtseff," says: "Marie loved to recall Balzac's questionable definition that the genius of observation is almost the whole of human genius. It was natural it should please her, since it was the most conspicuous of her many gifts. As we might expect, therefore, she was especially successful as a portrait painter, for she had a knack of catching her sitter's likeness with the bloom of nature yet fresh upon it. All her likenesses are singularly individual, and we realize their character at a glance. Look, for example, at her portrait of a Parisian swell, in irreproachable evening dress and white kid gloves, sucking his silver-headed cane, with a simper that shows all his white teeth; and then at the head and bust of a Spanish convict, painted from life at the prison in Granada. Compare that embodiment of fashionable vacuity with this face, whose brute-like eyes haunt you with their sadly stunted look. What observation is shown in the painting of those heavily bulging lips, which express weakness rather than wickedness of disposition – in those coarse hands engaged in the feminine occupation of knitting a blue and white stocking!"

Bauck, Jeanna. Born in Stockholm in 1840. Portrait and landscape painter. In 1863 she went to Dresden, and studied figure work with Professor Ehrhardt; later she moved to Düsseldorf, where she devoted herself to landscape under Flamm, and in 1866 she settled in Munich, where she has since remained, making long visits to Paris, Venice, and parts of Switzerland. Her later work is marked by the romantic influence of C. Ludwig, who was for a time her instructor, but she shows unusual breadth and sureness in dealing with difficult subjects, such as dusky forests with dark waters or bare ruins bordered with stiff, ghost-like trees. Though not without talent and boldness, she lacks a feeling for style.

Bauerlé, Miss A.
[No reply to circular.]

Baxter, Martha Wheeler.
[No reply to circular.]

Beale, Mary. 1632-97. This artist was the daughter of the Rev. Mr. Cradock. She married Mr. Beale, an artist and a color-maker. She studied under Sir Peter Lely, who obtained for her the privilege of copying some of Vandyck's most famous works.

Mrs. Beale's portraits of Charles II., Cowley, and the Duke of Norfolk are in the National Portrait Gallery, London, and that of Archbishop Tillotson is in Lambeth Palace. This portrait was the first example of an ecclesiastic represented as wearing a wig instead of the usual silk coif.

Her drawing was excellent and spirited, her color strong and pure, and her portraits were sought by many distinguished persons.

Several poems were written in praise of this artist, in one of which, by Dr. Woodfall, she is called "Belasia." Her husband, Charles Beale, an inferior artist, was proud of his wife, and spent much time in recording the visits she received, the praises lavished on her, and similar matters concerning her art and life. He left more than thirty pocket-notebooks filled with these records, and showed himself far more content that his wife should be appreciated than any praise of himself could have made him.

Beaury-Saurel, Mme. Amélie. Prize of honor at Exposition of Black and White, 1891; third-class medal, Salon, 1883; bronze medal, Exposition, 1889. Born at Barcelona, of French parents. Pupil of Julian Academy. Among her principal portraits are those of Léon Say, Félix Voisin, Barthélemy Saint-Hilaire, Mme. Sadi-

Carnot, Coralie Cohen, Princess Ghika, etc. She has also painted the "Two Vanquished Ones," "A Woman Physician," and a "Souvenir of a Bull-Fight," pastel, etc.

This artist has also contributed to several magazines. At the Salon of the Artistes Français, 1902, she exhibited a portrait and a picture of "Hamlet"; in 1903 a picture, "In the Train." Mme. Beaury-Saurel is also Mme. Julian, wife of the head of the Academy in which she was educated.

Beaux, Cecilia. Mary Smith prize at the Pennsylvania Academy of Fine Arts, 1885, 1887, 1891, 1892; gold medal, Philadelphia Art Club, 1893; Dodge prize, National Academy of Design, 1893; bronze medal, Carnegie Institute, 1896; first-class gold medal, $1,500, Carnegie Institute, 1899; Temple gold medal, Pennsylvania Academy, 1900; gold medal, Paris Exposition, 1900; gold medal, (?) 1901. Associate of National Academy of Design, member of Society of American Artists, associate of Société des Beaux-Arts, Paris. Born in Philadelphia. Studied under Mrs. T. A. Janvier, Adolf van der Weilen, and William Sartain in Philadelphia; under Robert-Fleury, Bouguereau, and Benjamin-Constant, in Paris.

Her portraits are numerous. In 1894 she exhibited a portrait of a child at the Exhibition of the Society of American Artists, which was much admired and noticed in the *Century Magazine*, September, 1894, as follows: "Few artists have the fresh touch which the child needs and the firm and rapid execution which allows the painter to catch the fleeting expression and the half-forms which make child portraits at once the longing and the despair of portrait painters. Miss Beaux's technique is altogether French, sometimes reminding me a little of Carolus Duran and of Sargent; but her individuality has triumphed over all suggestions of her foreign masters, and the combination of refinement and strength is altogether her own."

Seven years later, in the *International Studio*, September, 1901, we read: "The mention of style suggests a reference to the portraits by Miss Cecilia Beaux, while the allusion to characterization suggests at the same time their limitation. The oftener one sees her 'Mother and Daughter,' which gained the gold medal at Pittsburg in 1899 and the gold medal also at last year's Paris Exposition, the less one feels inclined to accept it as a satisfactory example of portraiture. Magnificent assurance of method it certainly has, controlled also by a fine sobriety of feeling, so that no part of the ensemble impinges upon the due importance of the other parts; it is a balanced, dignified picture. But in its lack of intimacy it is positively callous. One has met these ladies on many occasions, but with no increase of acquaintanceship or interest on either side – our meetings are sterile of any human interest. So one turns with relief to Miss Beaux's other picture of 'Dorothea and Francesca' – an older girl leading a younger one in the steps of a dance. They are not concerned with us, but at least interested in one another; and we can attach ourselves, if only as outsiders, to the human interest involved.

"These pictures suggest a moment's consideration of the true meaning of the term 'style' as applied to painting. Is it not more than the mere ableness of method, still more than the audacity of brush work, that often passes for style? Is it possible to dissociate the manner of a picture from its embodiment of some fact or idea? For it to have style in the full sense of the word, surely it must embody an expression of life as serious and thorough as the method of record." – *Charles H. Caffin.*

In the *International Studio* of March, 1903, we read: "The portrait of Mrs. Roosevelt, by Miss Cecilia Beaux, seemed to me to be one of the happiest of her creations. Nothing could exceed the skill and daintiness with which the costume is painted, and the characterization of the head is more sympathetic than usual, offering a most winsome type of beautiful, good womanhood. A little child has been added to the picture – an afterthought, I understand, and scarcely a fortunate one; at least in the manner of its presentment. The figure is cleverly merged in half shadow, but the treatment of the face is brusque, and a most unpleasant smirk distorts the child's mouth. It is the portrait of the mother that carries the picture, and its superiority to many of Miss Beaux's portraits consists in the sympathy with her subject which the painter has displayed." – *Charles H. Caffin.*

A writer in the *Mail and Express* says: "Miss Beaux has approached the task of painting the society woman of to-day, not as one to whom this type is known only by the exterior, but with a sympathy as complete as a similar tradition and an artistic temperament will allow. Thus she starts with an advantage denied to all but a very few American portrait painters, and this explains the instinctive way in which she gives to her pictured subjects an air of natural ease and good breeding."

Miss Beaux's picture of "Brighton Cats" is so excellent that one almost regrets that she has not emulated Mme. Ronner's example and left portraits of humans to the many artists who cannot paint cats!

[*No reply to circular.*]

Beck, Carol H. Mary Smith prize at Pennsylvania Academy of Fine Arts, 1899. Fellow of above Academy and member of the Plastic Club, Philadelphia. Born in Philadelphia. Studied in schools of Pennsylvania Academy, and later in Dresden and Paris.

Miss Beck paints portraits and her works have been frequently exhibited. Her portraits are also seen in the University of Pennsylvania, in the Woman's Medical College, Philadelphia, in Wesleyan College, at the capitols of Pennsylvania and New Jersey, and other public places, as well as in many private homes.

Miss Beck edited the Catalogue of the Wilstach Collection of Paintings in Memorial Hall, Fairmount Park, Philadelphia.

Beckington, Alice.
[*No reply to circular.*]

Beernaerts, Euphrosine. Landscape painter. In 1873 she won a medal at Vienna, in 1875 a gold medal at the Brussels Salon, and still other medals at Philadelphia (1876), Sydney (1879), and Teplitz (1879). She was made Chévalier de l'Ordre de Léopold in 1881. Mlle. Beernaerts was born at Ostend, 1831, and studied under Kuhner in Brussels. She travelled in Germany, France, and Italy, and exhibited admirable landscapes at Brussels, Antwerp, and Paris, her favorite subjects being Dutch. In 1878 the following pictures by her were shown in Paris: "Lisière de bois dans les Dunes (Zélande)," "Le Village de Domburg (Zélande)," and "Intérieur de bois à Oost-Kapel (Holland)." Other well-known works are "Die Campine" and "Aus der Umgebung von Oosterbeck."

Begas, Luise Parmentier. Born in Vienna. Pupil of Schindler and Unger. She travelled extensively in Europe and the Orient, and spent some time in Sicily. She married Adalbert Begas in 1877 and then established her studio in Berlin. Her subjects are landscape, architectural monuments, and interiors. Some of the latter are especially fine. Her picture of the "Burial Ground at Scutari" was an unusual subject at the time it was exhibited and attracted much attention.

Her rich gift in the use of color is best seen in her pictures of still life and flowers. In Berlin, in 1890, she exhibited "Before the Walls of Constantinople" and "From Constantinople," which were essentially different from her earlier works and attracted much attention. "Taormina in Winter" more nearly resembled her earlier pictures.

Fräulein Parmentier also studied etching, in which art Unger was her instructor. In her exquisite architectural pictures and landscapes she has represented Italian motives almost exclusively. Among these are her views of Venice and other South Italian sketches, which are also the subjects of some of her etchings.

Belle, Mlle. Andrée. Member of the Société Nationale des

Beaux Arts. Born in Paris. Pupil of Cazin. Paints in oils and pastels, landscapes especially, of which she exhibited seventeen in June, 1902. The larger part of these were landscape portraits, so to speak, as they were done on the spots represented with faithfulness to detail. The subjects were pleasing, and the various hours of day, with characteristic lighting, unusually well rendered.

At the Salon des Beaux Arts, 1902, this artist exhibited a large pastel, "A Halt at St. Mammès" and a "Souvenir of Bormes," showing the tomb of Cazin. In 1903 she exhibited a pastel called "Calvary," now in the Museum at Amiens, which has been praised for its harmony of color and the manner in which the rainbow is represented. Her pictures of "Twilight" and "Sunset" are unusually successful.

Benato-Beltrami, Elisabetta. Painter and sculptor of the nineteenth century, living in Padua since 1858. Her talent, which showed itself early, was first developed by an unknown painter named Soldan, and later at the Royal Academy in Venice. She made copies of Guido, Sassoferrato and Veronese, the Laokoon group, and the Hercules of Canova, and executed a much-admired bas-relief called "Love and Innocence." Among her original paintings are an "Atala and Chactas," "Petrarch's First Meeting with Laura," a "Descent from the Cross" for the church at Tribano, a "St. Sebastian," "Melancholy," a "St. Ciro," and many Madonnas. Her pictures are noble in conception and firm in execution.

Benito y Tejada, Benita. Born in Bilboa, where she first studied drawing; later she went to Madrid, where she entered the Escuela superior. In the Exposition of 1876 at Madrid "The Guardian" was shown, and in 1881 a large canvas representing "The First Step."

Bernhardt, Sarah. In 1869 this famous actress watched

Mathieu-Meusnier making a bust. She made her criticisms and they were always just. The sculptor told her that she had the eye of an artist and should use her talent in sculpture. Not long after she brought to him a medallion portrait of her aunt. So good was it that Mathieu-Meusnier seriously encouraged her to persevere in her art. She was fascinated by the thought of what might be possible for her, took a studio, and sent to the Salon in 1875 a bust, which attracted much attention. In 1876 she exhibited "After the Tempest," the subject taken from the story of a poor woman who, having buried two sons, saw the body of her last boy washed ashore after a storm. This work was marvellously effective, and a great future as a sculptress was foretold for the "divine Sara." At the Salon of 1878 she exhibited two portrait busts in bronze.

This remarkable woman is a painter also, and exhibited a picture called "La jeune Fille et la Mort." One critic wrote of it: "Sarah's picture shows very considerable feeling for color and more thought than the vast majority of modern paintings. The envious and evil speakers, who always want to say nasty things, pretend to trace in the picture very frequent touches of Alfred Stevens, who has been Sarah's master in painting, as Mathieu-Meusnier was in sculpture. However that may be, Sarah has posed her figures admirably and her coloring is excellent. It is worthy of notice that, being as yet a comparative beginner, she has not attempted to give any expression to the features of the young girl over whose shoulder Death is peeping."

One of the numerous ephemeral journals which the young and old jeunesse of the Latin Quarter is constantly creating has made a very clever caricature of the picture in a sort of Pompeian style. Death is represented by the grinning figure of Coquelin aîné. The legend is "'La Jeune Fille et la Mort,' or Coquelin aîné, presenting Sarah Bernhardt the bill of costs of her fugue." In other words, Coquelin is Death, handing to Sarah the undertaker's bill – 300,000 francs – for her civil burial at the Comédie Française.

Bethune, Louise. This architect, whose maiden name was Blanchard, was born in Waterloo, New York, 1856. She studied drawing and architecture, and in 1881 opened an office, being the first woman architect in the United States. Since her marriage to Robert A. Bethune they have practised their art together. Mrs. Bethune is the only woman holding a fellowship in the American Institute of Architects.

[*No reply to circular.*]

Beveridge, Kühne. Honorable mention in Paris twice. Born in Springfield, Illinois. Studied under William R. O'Donovan in New York, and under Rodin in Paris.

Among her works are a statue called "Rhodesia," "Rough Rider Monument," a statue called "Lascire," which belongs to Dr. Jameson, busts of Cecil Rhodes, King Edward VII., Grover Cleveland, Vice-President Stevenson, Joseph Jefferson, Buffalo Bill, General Mahon, hero of Mafeking, Thomas L. Johnson, and many others.

Miss Beveridge was first noticed as an artist in this country in 1892, when her busts of ex-President Cleveland and Mr. Jefferson called favorable attention to her.

In 1899 she married Charles Coghlan, and soon discovered that he had a living wife at the time of her marriage and obtained a divorce. Before she went to South Africa Miss Beveridge had executed several commissions for Cecil Rhodes and others living in that country.

Her mother is now the Countess von Wrede, her home being in Europe, where her daughter has spent much time. She has married the second time, an American, Mr. Branson, who resides at Johannesburg, in the Transvaal.

Biffin, Sarah. 1784-1850. It seems a curious fact that several persons born without arms and hands have become reputable artists. This miniature painter was one of these. Her first teacher, a man named Dukes, persuaded her to bind herself to live in his house and give her time to his service for some years. Later, when the Earl of Morton made her acquaintance, he proved to her that her engagement was not legally binding and wished her to give it up; but Miss Biffin was well treated by the Dukes and preferred to remain with them.

The Earl of Morton, however, caused her to study under Mr. Craig, and she attained wonderful excellence in her miniatures. In 1821 the Duke of Sussex, on behalf of the Society of Arts, presented her with a prize medal for one of her pictures.

She remained sixteen years with the Dukes, and during this time never received more than five pounds a year! After leaving them she earned a comfortable income. She was patronized by George III. and his successors, and Queen Victoria and the Prince Consort were her generous patrons, as well as many other distinguished persons.

After the death of the Earl of Morton she had no other friend to aid her in getting commissions or selling her finished pictures, and she moved to Liverpool. A small annuity was purchased for her, which, in addition to the few orders she received, supported her until her death at the age of sixty-six. Her miniatures have been seen in loan collections in recent years. Her portrait of herself, on ivory, was exhibited in such a collection at South Kensington.

Bilders, Marie. Family name Van Bosse. Born in Amsterdam, 1837; died in Wiesbaden, 1900. Pupil of Van de Sande-Bakhuyzen, Bosboom, and Johannes W. Bilders. Settled in Oosterbeck, and painted landscapes from views in the neighborhood. This artist was important, and her works are admired especially by certain Dutch artists who are famous in all countries. These facts are well known to me from good authority, but I fail to find a list of her works or a record of their present position.[1]

---

1 See Supplement.

Bilinska, Anna. Received the small gold medal at Berlin in 1891, and won distinguished recognition at other international exhibitions in Berlin and Munich by her portraits and figure studies. She was born in Warsaw in 1858, and died there in 1893. She studied in Paris, where she quickly became a favorite painter of aristocratic Russians and Poles. Her pictures are strong and of brilliant technique.

Biondi, Nicola. Born at Capua, 1866. This promising young Italian painter was a pupil of the Institute of Fine Arts in Naples. One of her pictures, called "Una partita," was exhibited at Naples and attracted much attention. It was purchased by Duke Martini. Another, "Ultima Prova," was exhibited in Rome and favorably noticed.

Blau, Tina. Honorable mention in Paris, 1883, for her "Spring in the Prater." Her "Land Party" is in the possession of the Emperor of Austria, and "In Spring-time" belongs to the Prince Regent of Bavaria. This talented landscape painter was born in Vienna, 1847. She was a pupil of Schäffer in Vienna, and of W. Lindenschmitt in Munich. After travelling in Austria, Holland, and Italy, she followed her predilection for landscape, and chose her themes in great part from those countries. In 1884 she married Heinrich Lang, painter of battle scenes (who died in 1891), and she now works alternately in Munich and Vienna. In 1890 she gave an exhibition of her pictures in Munich; they were thought to show great vigor of composition and color and much delicacy of artistic perception. Her foreign scenes, especially, are characterized by unusual local truth and color. Among her best works are "Studies from the Prater in Vienna," "Canal at Amsterdam," "Harvest Day in Holland," "The Arch of Titus in Rome," "Street in Venice," and "Late Summer."

Bloch, Mme. Elisa. Honorable mention, 1894. Officer of public instruction, Commander of the Order of the Liberator; Chevalier of the Order of the Dragon of Annam. Born at Breslau, Silesia, 1848. Pupil of Chapu. She first exhibited at the Salon of 1878, a medallion portrait of M. Bloch; this was followed by "Hope," the "Golden Age," "Virginius Sacrificing his Daughter," "Moses Receiving the Tables of the Law," etc. Mme. Bloch has made numerous portrait busts, among them being the kings of Spain and Portugal, Buffalo Bill, C. Flammarion, etc.

At the Salon of the Artistes Français, 1903, Mme. Bloch exhibited a "Portrait of M. Frédéric Passy, Member of the Institute."

Boccardo, Lina Zerbinah. Rome.
[*No reply to circular.*]

Boemm, Ritta. A Hungarian artist. Has been much talked of in Dresden. She certainly possesses distinguished talents, and is easily in the front rank of Dresden women artists. Her gouache pictures dealing with Hungarian subjects, a "Village Street," a "Peasant Farm," a "Churchyard," exhibited at Dresden in 1892, were well drawn and full of sentiment, but lacking in color sense and power. She works unevenly and seems pleased when she succeeds in setting a scene cleverly. She paints portraits also, mostly in pastel, which are spirited, but not especially good likenesses. What she can do in the way of color may be seen in her "Village Street in Winter," a picture of moderate size, in which the light is exquisite; unfortunately most of her painting is less admirable than this.

Boissonnas, Mme. Caroline Sordet. Honorable mention at the Salon of Lyons, 1897. Member of the Exposition Permanente Amis des Beaux-Arts, Geneva. Born in Geneva. Pupil of the School of Fine Arts, Geneva, under Prof. F. Gillet and M. E. Ravel.

This artist paints portraits principally. She has been successful, and her pictures are in Geneva, Lausanne, Vevey, Paris, Lyons, Marseilles, Dresden, Naples, etc.

Bompiani-Battaglia, Clelia. Born in Rome, 1847. Pupil of her father, Roberto Bompiani, and of the professors in the Academy of St. Luke. The following pictures in water-colors have established her reputation as an artist: "Confidential Communication," 1885; the "Fortune-Teller," 1887; "A Public Copyist," 1888; and "The Wooing," 1888.

Bonheur, Juliette – Mme. Peyrol. Born at Paris. Sister of Rosa Bonheur, and a pupil of her father. Among her pictures are "A Flock of Geese," "A Flock of Sheep Lying Down," and kindred subjects. The last-named work was much remarked at the Salon of 1875. In 1878 she exhibited "The Pool" and "The Mother's Kiss."

Mme. Peyrol was associated with her famous sister in the conduct of the Free School of Design, founded by Rosa Bonheur in 1849.

Bonheur, Marie Rosalie. 1822-99. Member of Antwerp Institute, 1868. Salon medals, 1845, 1848, 1855, 1867; Legion of Honor, 1865; Leopold Cross, 1880; Commander's Cross, Royal Order of Isabella the Catholic, 1880. Born in Bordeaux. She was taught drawing by her father, who, perceiving that she had unusual talent, permitted her to give up dressmaking, to which, much against her will, she had been apprenticed. From 1855 her fame was established; she was greatly appreciated, and her works competed for in England and the United States, as well as in European countries.

Her chief merit is the actual truthfulness with which she represented animals. Her skies might be bettered in some cases – the atmosphere of her pictures was sometimes open to question – but her animals were anatomically perfect and handled with such virility as few men have excelled or even equalled. Her position as an artist is so established that no quoted opinions are needed when speaking of her – she was one of the most famous women of her century.

Her home at By was near Fontainebleau, where she lived quietly, and for some years held gratuitous classes for drawing. She left, at her death, a collection of pictures, studies, etchings, etc., which were sold by auction in Paris soon after.

Her "Ploughing in the Nivernais," 1848, is in the Luxembourg Gallery; "The Horse Fair," 1853, is seen in the National Gallery, London, in a replica, the original being in the United States, purchased by the late A. T. Stewart. Her "Hay Harvest in the Auvergne," 1855, is one of her most important works. After 1867 Mlle. Bonheur did not exhibit at the Salon until 1899, a few weeks before her death.

One must pay a tribute to this artist as a good and generous woman. She founded the Free School of Design for Girls, and in 1849 took the direction of it and devoted much of her valuable time to its interests. How valuable an hour was to her we may understand when we remember that Hamerton says: "I have seen work of hers which, according to the price given, must have paid her a hundred pounds for each day's labor."

The story of her life is of great interest, and can be but slightly sketched here.

She was afoot betimes in the morning, and often walked ten or twelve miles and worked hard all day. The difficulty of reaching her models proved such a hindrance to her that she conceived the idea of visiting the abattoirs, where she could see animals living and dead and study their anatomy.

It is not easy to imagine all the difficulties she encountered in doing this – the many repulsive features of such places – while the company of drovers and butchers made one of the disagreeables of her pursuits. Her love for the animals, too, made it doubly hard for her to see them in the death agony and listen to their pitiful cries for freedom.

In all this experience, however, she met no rude or unkind treatment. Her drawings won the admiration of the men who watched her make them and they treated her with respect. She pursued her studies in the same manner in the stables of the

Veterinary School at Alfort and in the Jardin des Plantes.

At other times she studied in the country the quiet grazing herds, and, though often mistaken for a boy on account of the dress she wore, she inspired only admiration for her simplicity and frankness of manner, while the graziers and horse-dealers respectfully regarded her and wondered at her skill in picturing their favorite animals. Some very amusing stories might be told of her comical embarrassments in her country rambles, when she was determined to preserve her disguise and the pretty girls were equally determined to make love to her!

Aside from all this laborious study of living animals, she obtained portions of dead creatures for dissection; also moulds, casts, and illustrated anatomical books; and, in short, she left no means untried by which she could perfect herself in the specialty she had chosen. Her devotion to study and to the practice of her art was untiring, and only the most engrossing interest in it and an indomitable perseverance, supplemented and supported by a physically and morally healthful organization, could have sustained the nervous strain of her life from the day when she was first allowed to follow her vocation to the time when she placed herself in the front rank of animal painters.

A most charming picture is drawn of the life of the Bonheur family in the years when Rosa was making her progressive steps. They lived in an humble house in the Rue Rumfort, the father, Auguste, Isidore, and Rosa all working in the same studio. She had many birds and a pet sheep. As the apartment of the Bonheurs was on the sixth floor, this sheep lived on the leads, and from time to time Isidore bore him on his shoulders down all the stairs to the neighboring square, where the animal could browse on the real grass, and afterward be carried back by one of the devoted brothers of his mistress. They were very poor, but they were equally happy. At evening Rosa made small models or illustrations for books or albums, which the dealers readily bought, and by this means she added to the family store for needs or pleasures.

In 1841, when Rosa was nineteen years old, she first experienced the pleasures, doubts, and fears attendant upon a public exhibition of one's work. Two small pictures, called "Goats and Sheep" and "Two Rabbits," were hung at the Salon and were praised by critics and connoisseurs. The next year she sent three others, "Animals in a Pasture," "A Cow Lying in a Meadow," and "A Horse for Sale." She continued to send pictures to the Salon and to some exhibitions in other cities, and received several bronze and silver medals.

In 1845 she sent twelve works to the Salon, accompanied by those of her father and her brother Auguste, who was admitted that year for the first time. In 1848 Isidore was added to the list, exhibiting a picture and a group in marble, both representing "A Combat between a Lioness and an African Horseman." And, finally, the family contributions were completed when Juliette, now Madame Peyrol, added her pictures, and the works of the five artists were seen in the same Exhibition.

In 1849 Rosa Bonheur's "Cantal Oxen" was awarded the gold medal, and was followed by "Ploughing in the Nivernais," so well known the world over by engravings and photographs. When the medal was assigned her, Horace Vernet proclaimed her triumph to a brilliant assemblage, and also presented to her a magnificent vase of Sèvres porcelain, in the name of the French Government. This placed her in the first rank of living artists, and the triumph was of double value to her on account of the happiness it afforded her father, to see this, his oldest child, of whose future he had often despaired, taking so eminent a place in the artistic world.

This year of success was also a year of sorrow, for before its end the old Raymond had died. He had been for some time the director of the Government School of Design for Girls, and, being freed from pecuniary anxiety, he had worked with new courage and hope. After her father's death Rosa Bonheur exhibited nothing for two years, but in 1853 she brought out her "Horse Fair," which added to her fame.

She was perfectly at home in the mountains, and spent much time in the huts of charcoal burners, huntsmen, or woodcutters, contented with the food they could give her and happy in her study. Thus she made her sketches for "Morning in the Highlands," "The Denizens of the Mountains," etc. She once lived six weeks with her party on the Spanish side of the Pyrenees, where they saw no one save muleteers going and coming, with their long lines of loaded mules. Their only food was frogs' legs, which they prepared themselves, and the black bread and curdled milk which the country afforded. At evening the muleteers would amuse the strangers by dancing the national dances, and then repose in picturesque groups just suited to artistic sketching. In Scotland and in Switzerland, as well as in various portions of her own country, she had similar experiences, and her "Hay-Making in Auvergne" proves that she was familiar with the more usual phases of country life. At the Knowles sale in London, in 1865, her picture of "Spanish Muleteers Crossing the Pyrenees," one of the results of the above sojourn in these mountains, sold for two thousand guineas, about ten thousand dollars. I believe that, in spite of the large sums of money that she received, her habitual generosity and indifference to wealth prevented her amassing a large fortune, but her fame as an artist and her womanly virtues brought the rewards which she valued above anything that wealth could bestow – such rewards as will endure through centuries and surround the name of Rosa Bonheur with glory, rewards which she untiringly labored to attain.

Bonsall, Elizabeth F. First Toppan prize, and Mary Smith prize twice, at Pennsylvania Academy of Fine Arts. Member of Plastic Club, Philadelphia. Born at Philadelphia. Studied at the above-named Academy and in Paris; also at the Drexel Institute, Philadelphia, under Eakins, Courtois, Collin, and Howard Pyle.

Miss Bonsall is well known for her pictures of cats. She illustrated the "Fireside Sphinx," by Agnes Repplier. Her picture of "Hot Milk" is in the Pennsylvania Academy; her "Suspense," in a private gallery in New York.

An interesting chapter in Miss Winslow's book, "Concerning Cats," is called "Concerning Cat Artists," in which she writes: "Elizabeth Bonsall is a young American artist who has exhibited some good cat pictures, and whose work promises to make her famous some day if she does not 'weary in well-doing.'"

Miss Bonsall has prepared a "Cat Calendar" and a "Child's Book about Cats," which were promised to appear in the autumn of 1903.

Bonsall, Mary M. First Toppan prize at Pennsylvania Academy of Fine Arts. Member of the Plastic Club, Philadelphia. Studied at above academy under Vonnoh, De Camp, William Chase, and Cecilia Beaux.

This artist paints portraits, which are in private hands.

Bonte, Paula. Born in Magdeburg, 1840, and from 1862 to 1864 was a pupil of Pape in Berlin. She travelled and studied in Northern Italy and Switzerland, and from these regions, as well as from Northern Germany, took her subjects. She has exhibited pictures at various exhibitions, and among her best works should be mentioned: "The Beach at Clovelly in Devonshire," "From the Bernese Oberland," "The Riemenstalden Valley," etc.

Boott, Elizabeth. Born in Cambridge. Miss Boott was one of those pupils of William M. Hunt to whom he imparted a wonderful artistic enthusiasm, energy, and devotion. After studying in Boston she studied in Paris under Duveneck – whom she afterward married – and under Couture. Her subjects were genre, still-life, and flowers, and were well considered. Among her genre pictures are "An Old Man Reading," an "Old Roman Peasant," and a "Girl with a Cat." When in Italy she painted a number of portraits, which were successful. Miss Brewster, who lived in Rome, was an excellent critic, and she wrote: "I must say a few words about a studio I have lately visited – Miss Boott's. I saw there three very fine portraits, remarkable for strength and character, as well as rich coloring: one of Mr. Boott, one of Bishop Say, and the third of T. Adolphus Trollope, the well-known writer and brother of the novelist, Anthony Trollope. All are good likenesses and are painted with vigor and skill, but the one of Mr. Trollope is especially clever. Trollope's head and face, though a good study, are not easy to paint, but Miss Boott has succeeded to perfection. His head and beard are very fine. The face in nature, but for the melancholy, kindly look about the eyes and mouth, would be stern; Miss Boott has caught this expression and yet retained all the firm character of the countenance. It is remarkable that an artist who paints male heads with such a vigorous character should also give to flowers softness, transparency, and grace. Nothing can be more lovely than Miss Boott's flower studies. She has some delicious poppies among wheat, lilies, thistles. She gets a transparency into these works that is not facile in oil. A bunch of roses in a vase was as tender and round and soft-colored as in nature. Among all the many studios of Rome I do not know a more attractive one than Miss Boott's."

Bortolan, Rosa. Born at Treviso. She was placed in the Academy at Venice by her family, where she had the benefit of such masters as Grigoletti, Lipparini, Schiavoni, and Zandomeneghi. She early showed much originality, and after making thorough preliminary studies she began to follow her own ideas. She was of a mystical and contemplative turn of mind, and a great proportion of her work has been of a religious nature. Her pictures began to attract attention about 1847, and she had many commissions for altar-pieces and similar work. The church of Valdobbiadene, at Venice, contains "San Venanziano Fortunatus, Bishop." "Saint Louis" was painted as a commission of Brandolin da Pieve; "Comte Justinian Replying to Bonaparte in Treviso" was a subscription picture presented to Signor Zoccoletto. Portraits of the Countess Canossa-Portalupi and her son, of Luigia

Codemo, and of Luigi Giacomelli are thought to possess great merit; while those of Dr. Pasquali (in the Picture Gallery at Treviso) and Michelangelo Codemo have been judged superior to those of Rosalba Carriera and Angelica Kauffmann. Her sacred pictures, strong and good in color, are full of a mystical and spiritual beauty. Her drawing is admirable and her treatment of detail highly finished.

Borzino, Leopoldina. Milanese water-color painter. Has shown excellent genre pictures at various exhibitions. "The Holiday" and the "Return from Mass" were both exhibited and sold at Rome in 1883; "The Way to Calvary" was seen at Venice in 1887. "The Rosary," "Anguish," and "Going to the Fountain" are all distinguished by good color as well as by grace and originality of composition.

Bouguereau, Mme. Elizabeth Jane. See Gardner.

Boulanger, Mme. Marie Elizabeth. Medals at the Paris Salon in 1836 and 1839. Born in Paris, 1810. Her family name was Blavot, and after the death of M. Boulanger she married M. Cavé, director of the Academy of the Beaux-Arts. Her picture of "The Virgin in Tears" is in the Museum of Rouen; and "The Children's Tournament," a triptych, was purchased by the Government.

Bourrillon-Tournay, Mme. Jeanne. Medal of the second class at Exposition Universelle at Lyons; silver medal at Versailles; honorable mention at Paris Salon, 1896; the two prizes of the Union des Femmes Peintres et Sculpteurs – les Palmes Académique, 1895; the Rosette of an Officer of the Public Instruction in 1902. Member of the Société des Artistes Français, of the Union des Femmes Peintres et Sculpteurs, and of the Association de Baron Taylor. Born at Paris, 1870. Pupil of Ferdinand Humbert and G. C. Saintpierre.

This artist paints portraits, and among them are those of a

"Young Girl," which belongs to the general Council of the Seine; one of the Senator Théophile Roussel, of the Institute, and a portrait of an "Aged Lady," both purchased by the Government; one of M. Auguste Boyer, councillor of the Court of Cassation, and many others.

At the Salon des Artistes Français, 1902, Mme. Bourrillon-Tournay exhibited two portraits, one being that of her mother; in 1903, that of M. Boyer and one of Mme. B.

Bowen, Lota. Member of Society of Women Artists, London, the Tempera Society, and the "91" Art Club. Born at Armley, Yorkshire. Studied in Ludovici's studio, London; later in Rome under Santoro, and in the night classes of the Circolo Artistico.

Her pictures are principally landscapes, and are chiefly in private collections in England. Among the most important are "On the Venetian Lagoons," "Old Stone Pines, Lido, Venice," "Evening on Lake Lugano," "Evening Glow on the Dolomites," "The Old Bird Fancier," "Moonrise on Crowborough, Sussex." All these have been exhibited at the Academy.

"Miss Lota Bowen constantly receives most favorable notices of her works in magazines and journals. She is devotedly fond of her art, and has sought subjects for her brush in many European byways, as well as in North Africa, Turkey, and Montenegro. She paints portraits and figure subjects; has a broad, swinging brush and great love of 'tone.' Miss Bowen has recently built a studio, in Kensington, after her own design. She is in London from Christmas time to August, when she makes an annual journey for sketching."

Bozzino, Candida Luigia. Silver medal at Piacenza. Born at Piacenza, 1853. Pupil of her father. Her portrait of Alessandro Manzoni was her prize picture. The "Madonna of the Sacred Heart of Jesus" was painted on a commission from the Bishop of Piacenza, who presented it to Pope Pius IX.; after being exhibited at the Vatican, it was sent to the Bishop of Jesi, for the church of

Castelplanio. Other celebrated works of hers are a "Holy Family," the "Madonna of Lourdes," and several copies of the "Viâ Crucis," by Viganoni.

In 1881 this artist entered the Ursuline Convent at Piacenza, where she continues to paint religious pictures.

Bracken, Julia M. First prize for sculpture, Chicago, 1898; appointed on staff of sculptors for the St. Louis Exposition. Member of Arts Club, Western Society of Artists, Municipal Art League, and Krayle Workshop, Chicago. Born at Apple River, Ill., 1871. Pupil of Chicago Art Institute. Acted as assistant to Lorado Taft, 1887-92. Was much occupied with the decorations for the Columbian Exposition, and executed on an independent commission the statue of "Illinois Welcoming the Nations." There are to be five portrait statues placed in front of the Educational Building at St. Louis, each to be executed by a well-known artist. One of these is to be the work of Miss Bracken, who is the only woman among them. Miss Bracken has modelled an heroic portrait statue of President Monroe; beside the figure is a globe, on which he points out the junction of the Mississippi and Missouri rivers.

[*No reply to circular.*]

Bracquemond, Mme. Marie. Pupil of Ingres. A portrait painter, also painter of genre subjects. At the Salon of 1875 she exhibited "The Reading"; in 1874 "Marguerite." She has been much occupied in the decoration of the Haviland faience, a branch of these works, at Auteuil, being at one time in charge of her husband, Félix Bracquemond. In 1872 M. Bracquemond was esteemed the first ceramic artist in France. An eminent French critic said of M. and Mme. Bracquemond: "You cannot praise too highly these two artists, who are as agreeable and as clever as they are talented and esteemed."

Mme. Bracquemond had the faculty of employing the faience colors so well that she produced a clearness and richness not attained by other artists. The progress made in the Haviland faience in the seventies was very largely due to Mme. Bracquemond, whose pieces were almost always sold from the atelier before being fired, so great was her success.

Brandeis, Antoinetta. Many prizes at the Academy of Venice. Born of Bohemian parents in Miscova, Galitza, 1849. Pupil of Iavurek, of Prague, in the beginning of her studies, but her father dying and her mother marrying again, she was taken to Venice, where she studied in the Academy several years under Grigoletti, Moja, Bresolin, Nani, and Molmenti. Although all her artistic training was received in Italy and she made her first successes there, most of her works have been exhibited in London, under the impression that she was better understood in England.

Annoyed by the commendation of her pictures "as the work of a woman," she signed a number of her canvases Antonio Brandeis. Although she painted religious subjects for churches, her special predilection is for views of Venice, preferably those in which the gondola appears. She has studied these in their every detail. "Il canale Traghetto de' San Geremia" is in the Museum Rivoltella at Trieste. This and "Il canale dell' Abbazia della Misericordia" have been much commended by foreign critics, especially the English and Austrians. Other Venetian pictures are "La Chiese della Salute," "Il canale de' Canalregio," and "La Pescaria."

Breslau, Louisa Catherine. Gold medal at Paris Exposition, 1889; gold medal at Paris Exposition, 1900. Chevalier of the Legion of Honor, 1901. Member of the Société Nationale des Beaux-Arts. A Swiss artist, who made her studies at the Julian Academy under Robert-Fleury.

She has painted many portraits. Her picture "Under the Apple-Tree" is in the Museum at Lausanne; the "Little Girls" or "The Sisters" and the "Child Dreamer" – exhibited at Salon, 1902 – are in the Gallery of the Luxembourg; the "Gamins," in the

Museum at Carpentras; the "Tea Party," at the Ministry of the Interior, Paris.

At the Salon of 1902 Mlle. Breslau exhibited six pictures, among which were landscapes, two representing September and October at Saint-Cloud; two of fruit and flowers; all of which were admired, while the "Dreamer" was honored with a place in the Luxembourg. In the same Salon she exhibited six pictures in pastel: four portraits, and heads of a gamin and of a little girl. The portrait of Margot is an ideal picture of a happy child, seated at a table, resting her head on her left hand while with the right she turns the leaves of a book. A toy chicken and a doll are on the table beside her. In the Salon of 1903 she exhibited five pictures of flowers and another called the "Child with Long Hair."

I was first interested in this artist by the frequent references to her and her work in the journal of Marie Bashkirtseff. They were fellow-pupils in the Julian Academy. Soon after she began her studies there Marie Bashkirtseff writes: "Breslau has been working at the studio two years, and she is twenty; I am seventeen, but Breslau had taken lessons for a long time before coming here... How well that Breslau draws!"

"That miserable Breslau has composed a picture, 'Monday Morning, or the Choice of a Model.' Every one belonging to the studio is in it – Julian standing between Amalie and me. It is correctly done, the perspective is good, the likenesses – everything. When one can do a thing like that, one cannot fail to become a great artist. You have guessed it, have you not? I am jealous. That is well, for it will serve as a stimulus to me."

"I am jealous of Breslau. She does not draw at all like a woman."

"I am terrified when I think of the future that awaits Breslau; it fills me with wonder and sadness. In her compositions there is nothing womanish, commonplace, or disproportioned. She will attract attention at the Salon, for, in addition to her treatment of it, the subject itself will not be a common one."

The above prophecy has been generously fulfilled. Mlle.

Breslau is indeed a poet in her ability to picture youth and its sweet intimacies, and she does this so easily. With a touch she reveals the grace of one and the affectations of another subject of her brush, and skilfully renders the varying emotions in the faces of her pictures. Pleasure and suffering, the fleeting thought of the child, the agitation of the young girl are all depicted with rare truthfulness.

Brewster, Ada Augusta.
[*No reply to circular.*]

Brickdale, Miss Eleanor Fortescue.
[*No reply to circular.*]

Bricci or Brizio, Plautilla. Very little is known of this Roman artist of the seventeenth century, but that little marks her as an unusually gifted woman, since she was a practical architect and a painter of pictures. She was associated with her brother in some architectural works in and near Rome, and was the only woman of her time in this profession.

She is believed to have erected a small palace near the Porta San Pancrazio, unaided by her brother, and is credited with having designed in the Church of San Luigi de' Francesi the third chapel on the left aisle, dedicated to St. Louis, and with having also painted the altar-piece in this chapel.

Bridges, Fidelia. Associate of the National Academy of Design in 1878, when but three other women were thus honored. Born in Salem, Massachusetts. Studied with W. T. Richards in Philadelphia, and later in Europe during one year. She exhibited her pictures from 1869 in Philadelphia, New York, and Boston. Her subjects were landscapes and flowers. In 1871 she first painted in water-colors, which suited many of her pictures better than oils. She was elected a member of the Water-Color Society in 1875. To the Philadelphia Exposition, 1876, she sent a "Kingfisher and

Catkins," a "Flock of Snow Birds," and the "Corner of a Rye-Field." Of the last a writer in the *Art Journal* said: "Miss Bridges' 'Edge of a Rye-Field,' with a foreground of roses and weeds, is a close study, and shows that she is as happy in the handling of oil colors as in those mixed with water."

Another critic wrote: "Her works are like little lyric poems, and she dwells with loving touches on each of her buds, 'like blossoms atilt' among the leaves."

Her pictures are in private collections, and are much valued by their owners.

Brooks, Maria.
[*No reply to circular.*]

Brownscombe, Jennie. Pupil of the National Academy and the Art Students' League, New York, and of Henry Mosler in Paris.

Paints genre subjects, among which are: "Love's Young Dream," "Colonial Minuet," "Sir Roger de Coverly at Carvel Hall," "Battle of Roses," etc.

The works of this artist have been reproduced in engravings and etchings, and are well known in black and white. Her water-colors, too, have been published in photogravure.

Miss Brownscombe exhibits at many American exhibitions and has had her work accepted at the Royal Academy, London.

Browne, Matilda. Honorable mention at Chicago, 1893; Dodge prize at National Academy of Design, 1899; Hallgarten prize, 1901. Born in Newark, New Jersey. Pupil of Miss Kate Greatorex; of Carleton Wiggins, New York; of the Julian Academy, Paris; of H. S. Birbing in Holland, and of Jules Dupré on the coast of France. When a child this artist lived very near Thomas Moran and was allowed to spend much time in his studio, where she learned the use of colors.

She exhibited her first picture at the National Academy of Design when twelve years old, and has been a constant contributor to its exhibitions since that time; also to the exhibitions of the American Water-Color Society.

Her earliest pictures were of flowers, and during several years she had no teacher. At length she decided to study battle painting, and, after a summer under Carleton Wiggins, she went abroad, in 1890, and remained two years, painting in the schools in winter and out of doors in summer. Miss Browne exhibited at the Salon des Beaux-Arts in 1890, and many of her works have been seen in exhibits in this country. The Dodge prize was awarded to a picture called "The Last Load," and the Hallgarten prize to "Repose," a moonlight scene with cattle. Her pictures are in private collections.

Brown, Mrs. Agnes – Mrs. John Appleton Brown. Born in Newburyport. This artist paints in oils. Her subjects are landscapes, flowers, and still life. She has also painted cats successfully.

I have a winter landscape by Mrs. Brown which is unusually attractive and is often admired. She sends her works to the exhibitions of the Boston Art Club and to some exhibitions in New York.

Browne, Mme. Henriette. Born at Paris; 1829-1901. Pupil of Chaplin. The family name of this artist was Bouteiller, and she married M. Jules de Saux, but as an artist used the name of an ancestress. Her pictures of genre subjects very early attracted attention, especially in 1855, when she sent to the Salon "A Brother of the Christian School," "School for the Poor at Aix," "Mutual Instruction," and "Rabbits." Her works were popular and brought good prices. In 1868 "The Sisters of Charity" sold for £1,320.

In 1878 she exhibited "A Grandmother" and "Convalescence." Her Oriental scenes were much admired. Among these were "A Court in Damascus," "Nubian Dancing Girls," and a "Harem in Constantinople." Mme. Browne was also skilful as an engraver.

T. Chasrel wrote in *L'Art*: "Her touch without over-minuteness has the delicacy and security of a fine work of the needle. The accent is just without that seeking for virile energy which too often spoils the most charming qualities. The sentiment is discreet without losing its intensity in order to attract public notice. The painting of Mme. Henriette Browne is at an equal distance from grandeur and insipidity, from power and affectation, and gathers from the just balance of her nature some effects of taste and charm of which a parvenu in art would be incapable."

The late Rev. Charles Kingsley wrote of the picture of the "Sisters of Charity," of the sale of which I have spoken, as follows: "The picture which is the best modern instance of this happy hitting of this golden mean, whereby beauty and homely fact are perfectly combined, is in my eyes Henrietta Browne's picture of the 'Sick Child and the Sisters of Charity.' I know not how better to show that it is easy to be at once beautiful and true, if one only knows how, than by describing that picture. Criticise it, I dare not; for I believe that it will surely be ranked hereafter among the very highest works of modern art. If I find no fault in it, it is because I have none to find; because the first sight of the picture produced in me instantaneous content and confidence. There was nothing left to wish for, nothing to argue about. The thing was what it ought to be, and neither more nor less, and I could look on it, not as a critic, but as a learner only."

This is praise indeed from an Englishman writing of a Frenchwoman's picture – an Englishman with no temptation to say what he did not think; and we may accept his words as the exact expression of the effect the picture made on him.

Brune, Mme. Aimée Pagès. Medal of second class at Salon of 1831; first class in 1841. Born in Paris. 1803-66. Pupil of Charles Meynier. Painted historical and genre subjects. In 1831 she exhibited "Undine," the "Elopement," "Sleep," and

"Awakening." In 1841 a picture of "Moses." She painted several Bible scenes, among which were the "Daughter of Jairus" and "Jephthah's Daughter."

Buechmann, Frau Helene. Her pictures have been seen at some annual exhibitions in Germany, but she is best known by her portraits of celebrated persons. Born in Berlin, 1849. Pupil of Steffeck and Gussow. Among her portraits are those of Princess Carolath-Beuthen, Countess Brühl, Prince and Princess Biron von Kurland, and the youngest son of Prince Radziwill. She resides in Brussels.

Butler, Mildred A. Associate of the Royal Society of Painters in Water-Colors and of the Society of Lady Artists. Pupil of Naftel, Calderon, and Garstin. Has exhibited at the Royal Academy and New Gallery. Her picture called the "Morning Bath," exhibited at the Academy in 1896, was purchased under the Chantry Bequest and is in the Tate Gallery. It is a water-color, valued at £50.

Miss Butler exhibited "A Corner of the Bargello, Florence," at the London Academy in 1903.

[*No reply to circular.*]

Butler, Lady Elizabeth. Born in Lausanne about 1844. Elizabeth Southerden Thompson. As a child this artist was fond of drawing soldiers and horses. She studied at the South Kensington School, at Florence under Bellucci, and in Rome. She worked as an amateur some years, first exhibiting at the Academy in 1873 her picture called "Missing," which was praised; but the "Roll-Call," of the following year, placed her in the front rank of the Academy exhibitors. It was purchased by the Queen and hung in Windsor Castle. She next exhibited the "Twenty-Eighth Regiment at Quatre Bras," the "Return from Inkerman," purchased by the Fine Art Society for £3,000. This was followed by kindred subjects.

In 1890 Lady Butler exhibited "Evicted," in 1891 the "Camel Corps," in 1892 "Halt in a Forced March," in 1895 the "Dawn of

Waterloo," in 1896 "Steady the Drums and Fifes," in 1902 "Tent Pegging in India," in 1903 "Within Sound of the Guns."

In 1869 she painted a religious picture called the "Magnificat." In water-colors she has painted "Sketches in Tuscany" and several pictures of soldiers, among which are "Scot's Grays Advancing" and "Cavalry at a Gallop."

Lady Butler has recently appeared as an author, publishing "Letters from the Holy Land," illustrated by sixteen most attractive drawings in colors. The *Spectator* says: "Lady Butler's letters and diary, the outcome of a few weeks' journeyings in Palestine, express simply and forcibly the impressions made on a devout and cultivated mind by the scenes of the Holy Land."

In 1875 Ruskin wrote in "Notes of the Academy": "I never approached a picture with more iniquitous prejudice against it than I did Miss Thompson's – 'Quatre Bras' – partly because I have always said that no woman could paint, and secondly because I thought what the public made such a fuss about *must* be good for nothing. But it is Amazon's work this, no doubt of it, and the first fine pre-Raphaelite picture of battle we have had; profoundly interesting, and showing all manner of illustrative and realistic faculty... The sky is most tenderly painted, and with the truest outline of cloud of all in the Exhibition; and the terrific piece of gallant wrath and ruin on the extreme left, when the cuirassier is catching round the neck of his horse as he falls, and the convulsed fallen horse, seen through the smoke below, is wrought through all the truth of its frantic passion with gradations of color and shade which I have not seen the like of since Turner's death."

The *Art Journal*, 1877, says: "'Inkerman' is simply a marvellous production when considered as the work of a young woman who was never on the field of battle... No matter how many figures she brings into the scene, or how few, you may notice character in each figure, each is a superb study."

Her recent picture, "Within Sound of the Guns," shows a company of mounted soldiers on the confines of a river in South

Africa.

[*No reply to circular.*]

Cameron, Katherine. Member of the Royal Scottish Society of Painters in Water-Colors; Modern Sketch Club, London; Ladies' Art Club, Glasgow. Born in Glasgow. Studied at Glasgow School of Art under Professor Newbery, and at the Colarossi Academy, Paris, under Raphael Collin and Gustave Courtois.

Her pictures are of genre subjects principally, and are in private collections. "'The Sea Urchin,'" Miss Cameron writes, "is in one of the public collections of Germany. I cannot remember which." She also says: "Except for my diploma R. S. W. and having my drawings sometimes in places of honor, usually on the line, and often reproduced in magazines, I have no other honors. I have no medals."

In the *Magazine of Art*, June, 1903, her picture of a "Bull Fight in Madrid" is reproduced. It is full of action and true to the life of these horrors as I have seen them in Madrid. Doubtless the color is brilliant, as the costumes of the toreadors are always so, and there are two in this picture. This work was displayed at the exhibition of the Royal Scottish Academy, June, 1903 – of which a writer says: "A feeling for color has always been predominant in the Scottish school, and it is here conspicuously displayed, together with a method of handling, be it in the domain of figure or landscape, which is personal to the artist and not a mere academic tradition."

In the *Studio* of May, 1903, J. L. C., who writes of the same exhibition, calls this picture "admirable in both action and color."

Carl, Kate A. Honorable mention, Paris Salon, 1890; Chevalier of the Legion of Honor, 1896; honorable mention, Paris Exposition, 1900. Associé de la Société Nationale des Beaux-Arts. Born in New Orleans. Pupil of Julian Academy and of Courtois in Paris.

This artist's name has been made prominent by the fact of her being selected to paint a portrait of the Empress of China. Miss

Carl has frequently exhibited at the Salon. In 1902 she sent portraits in both oil and water-colors. One of these works, called "Angelina," impresses one as a faithful portrait of a model. She is seated and gracefully posed – the face is in a full front view, the figure turned a little to one side and nude to the waist, the hands are folded on the lap and hold a flower, a gauze-like drapery falls about the left shoulder and the arms, but does not conceal them; the background is a brocade or tapestry curtain.

I have seen a reproduction only, and cannot speak of the color. The whole effect of the picture is attractive. For the purpose of painting the portrait of the Chinese Empress, Miss Carl was assigned an apartment in the palace. It is said that the picture was to be finished in December, 1903, and will probably be seen at the St. Louis Exhibition.

[*No reply to circular.*]

Carlisle, Mistress Anne. Died in 1680. Was a favorite artist of King Charles I. It is said that on one occasion the King bought a quantity of ultramarine, for which he paid £500, and divided it between Vandyck and Mistress Carlisle. Her copies after the Italian masters were of great excellence.

She painted in oils as well as in water-colors. One of her pictures represents her as teaching a lady to use the brush. When we remember that Charles, who was so constantly in contact with Vandyck, could praise Mistress Carlisle, we must believe her to have been a good painter.

Mistress Anne has sometimes been confounded with the Countess of Carlisle, who was distinguished as an engraver of the works of Salvator Rosa, etc.

Carpenter, Margaret Sarah. The largest gold medal and other honors from the Society of Arts, London. Born at Salisbury, England. 1793-1872. Pupil of a local artist in Salisbury when quite young. Lord Radnor's attention was called to her talent, and he permitted her to copy in the gallery of Longford Castle, and advised her sending her pictures to London, and later to go there herself. She made an immediate success as a portrait painter, and from 1814 during fifty-two years her pictures were annually exhibited at the Academy with a few rare exceptions.

Her family name was Geddis; her husband was Keeper of the Prints and Drawings in the British Museum more than twenty years, and after his death his wife received a pension of £100 a year in recognition of his services.

Her portraits were considered excellent as likenesses; her touch was firm, her color brilliant, and her works in oils and water-colors as well as her miniatures were much esteemed. Many of them were engraved. Her portrait of the sculptor Gibson is in the National Portrait Gallery, London. A life-size portrait of Anthony Stewart, miniature painter, called "Devotion," and the "Sisters," portraits of Mrs. Carpenter's daughters, with a picture of "Ockham Church," are at South Kensington.

She painted a great number of portraits of titled ladies which are in the collections of their families. Among the more remarkable were those of Lady Eastnor, 1825; Lady King, daughter of Lord Byron, 1835; Countess Ribblesdale, etc.

Her portraits of Fraser Tytler, John Girkin, and Bonington are in the National Portrait Gallery, London. In the South Kensington Gallery are her pictures of "Devotion – St. Francis," which is a life-size study of Anthony Stewart, the miniature painter; "The Sisters," "Ockham Church," and "An Old Woman Spinning."

Carpentier, Mlle. Madeleine. Honorable mention, 1890; third-class medal, 1896. Born in Paris, 1865. Pupil of Bonnefoy and of Jules Lefebvre at the Julian Academy. Since 1885 this artist has exhibited many portraits as well as flower and fruit pieces, these last in water-colors. In 1896 her pictures were the "Communicants" and the "Candles," a pastel, purchased by the city of Paris; "Among Friends" is in the Museum of Bordeaux.

At the Salon of the Artistes Français, 1902, Mlle. Carpentier exhibited a picture called "Reflection," and in 1903 a portrait of

Mme. L. T. and the "Little Goose-Herders."

Carriera, Rosalba, better known as Rosalba. Born in Venice 1675-1757 – and had an eventful life. Her artistic talent was first manifested in lace-weaving, which as a child she preferred before any games or amusements. She studied painting under several masters, technique under Antonio Balestra, pastel-painting with Antonio Nazari and Diamantini, and miniature painting, in which she was especially distinguished, was taught her by her brother-in-law, Antonio Pellegrini, whom she later accompanied to Paris and London and assisted in the decorative works he executed there.

Rosalba's fame in Venice was such that she was invited to the courts of France and Austria, where she painted many portraits. She was honored by election to the Academies of Rome, Bologna, and Paris.

This artist especially excelled in portraits of pretty women, while her portraits of men were well considered. Among the most important were those of the Emperor Charles, the kings of France and Denmark, and many other distinguished persons, both men and women.

The Grand Duke of Tuscany asked for her own portrait for his gallery. She represented herself with one of her sisters. Her face is noble and most expressive, but, like many of her pictures, while the head is spirited and characteristic, the rest of the figure and the accessories are weak. A second portrait of herself – in crayons – is in the Dresden Gallery, and is very attractive.

While in England Rosalba painted many portraits in crayon and pastel, in which art she was not surpassed by any artist of her day.

Her diary of two years in Paris was published in Venice. It is curious and interesting, as it sets forth the customs of society, and especially those of artists of the period.

Returning to Venice, Rosalba suffered great depression and was haunted by a foreboding of calamity. She lived very quietly.

In his "Storia della Pittura Veneziana," Zanetti writes of her at this time: "Much of interest may be written of this celebrated and highly gifted woman, whose spirit, in the midst of her triumphs and the brightest visions of happiness, was weighed down by the anticipation of a heavy calamity. On one occasion she painted a portrait of herself, the brow wreathed with leaves which symbolized death. She explained this as an image of the sadness in which her life would end."

Alas, this was but too prophetic! Before she was fifty years old she lost her sight, and gradually the light of reason also, and her darkness was complete.

An Italian writer tells the following story: "Nature had endowed Rosalba with lofty aspirations and a passionate soul; her heart yearned for the admiration which her lack of personal attraction forbade her receiving. She fully realized her plainness before the Emperor Charles XI. rudely brought it home to her. When presented to him by the artist Bertoli, the Emperor exclaimed: 'She may be clever, Bertoli mio, this painter of thine, but she is remarkably ugly.' From which it would appear that Charles had not believed his mirror, since his ugliness far exceeded that of Rosalba! Her dark eyes, fine brow, good expression, and graceful pose of the head, as shown in her portrait, impress one more favorably than would be anticipated from this story."

Many of Rosalba's works have been reproduced by engravings; a collection of one hundred and fifty-seven of these are in the Dresden Gallery, together with several of her pictures.

Cassatt, Mary. Born in Pittsburg. Studied in Pennsylvania schools, and under Soyer and Bellay in Paris. She has lived and travelled much in Europe, and her pictures, which are of genre subjects, include scenes in France, Italy, Spain, and Holland.

Among her principal works are "La tasse de thé," "Le lever du bébé," "Reading," "Mère et Enfant," and "Caresse Maternelle."

Miss Cassatt has exhibited at the Paris Salon, the National Academy, New York, and various other exhibitions, but her works are rarely if ever exhibited in recent days. It is some years since William Walton wrote of her: "But in general she seems to have attained that desirable condition, coveted by artists, of being able to dispense with the annual exhibitions."

Miss Cassatt executed a large, decorative picture for the north tympanum of the Woman's Building at the Columbian Exhibition.

A writer in the *Century Magazine*, March, 1899, says: "Of the colony of American artists, who for a decade or two past have made Paris their home, few have been more interesting and none more serious than Miss Cassatt... Miss Cassatt has found her true bent in her recent pictures of children and in the delineation of happy maternity. These she has portrayed with delicacy, refinement, and sentiment. Her technique appeals equally to the layman and the artist, and her color has all the tenderness and charm that accompanies so engaging a motif."

In November, 1903, Miss Cassatt held an exhibition of her works in New York. At the winter exhibition of the Philadelphia Academy, 1904, she exhibited a group, a mother and children, one child quite nude. Arthur Hoeber described it as "securing great charm of manner, of color, and of grace."

Cattaneo, Maria. Bronze medal at the National Exposition, Parma, 1870; silver medal at Florence, 1871; silver medal at the centenary of Ariosto at Ferrara. Made an honorary member of the Brera Academy, Milan, 1874, an honor rarely conferred on a woman; elected to the Academy of Urbino, 1875. Born in Milan. Pupil of her father and of Angelo Rossi.

She excels in producing harmony between all parts of her works. She has an exquisite sense of color and a rare technique. Good examples of her work are "The Flowers of Cleopatra," "The Return from the Country," "An Excursion by Gondola." She married the artist, Pietro Michis. Her picture of the "Fish Market in Venice" attracted much attention when it appeared in 1887; it was a most accurate study from life.

Charpentier, Constance Marie. Pupil of David. Her best known works were "Ulysses Finding Young Astyanax at Hector's Grave" and "Alexander Weeping at the Death of the Wife of Darius." These were extraordinary as the work of a woman. Their size, with the figures as large as life, made them appear to be ambitious, as they were certainly unusual. Her style was praised by the admirers of David, to whose teaching she did credit. The disposition of her figures was good, the details of her costumes and accessories were admirably correct, but her color was hard and she was generally thought to be wanting in originality and too close a follower of her master.

Charretie, Anna Maria. 1819-75. Her first exhibitions at the Royal Academy, London, were miniatures and flower pieces. Later she painted portraits and figure subjects, as well as flowers. In 1872 "Lady Betty Germain" was greatly admired for the grace of the figure and the exquisite finish of the details. In 1873 she exhibited "Lady Betty's Maid" and "Lady Betty Shopping." "Lady Teazle Behind the Screen" was dated 1871, and "Mistress of Herself tho' China Fall" was painted and exhibited in the last year of her life.

Chase, Adelaide Cole. Member of Art Students' Association. Born in Boston. Daughter of J. Foxcroft Cole. Studied at the School of the Museum of Fine Arts, under Tarbell, and also under Jean Paul Laurens and Carolus Duran in Paris; and with Vinton in Boston.

Mrs. Chase has painted portraits entirely, most of which are in or near Boston; her artistic reputation among painters of her own specialty is excellent, and her portraits are interesting aside from the persons represented, when considered purely as works of art.

A portrait called a "Woman with a Muff," exhibited recently at the exhibition of the Society of American Artists, in New York, was much admired. At the 1904 exhibition of the Philadelphia Academy Mrs. Chase exhibited a portrait of children, Constance and Gordon Worcester, of which Arthur Hoeber writes: "She has painted them easily, with deftness and feeling, and apparently caught their character and the delicacy of infancy."

Chauchet, Charlotte. Honorable mention at the Salon, 1901; third-class medal, 1902. Member of the Société des Artistes Français and of l'Union des femmes peintres et sculpteurs. Born at Charleville, Ardennes, in 1878. Pupil of Gabriel Thurner, Benjamin-Constant, Jean Paul Laurens, and Victor Marec. Her principal works are "Marée" – Fish – 1899, purchased for the lottery of the International Exposition at Lille; "Breton Interior," purchased by the Society of the Friends of the Arts, at Nantes; "Mother Closmadenc Dressing Fish," in the Museum of Brest; "Interior of a Kitchen at Mont," purchased by the Government; "Portrait of my Grandmother," which obtained honorable mention; "At the Corner of the Fire," "A Little Girl in the Open Air," medal of third class.

The works of Mlle. Chauchet have been much praised. The *Petit Moniteur*, June, 1899, says: "Mlle. Chauchet, a very young girl, in her picture of a 'Breton Interior' shows a vigor and decision very rare in a woman." Of the "Marée," the *Dépêche de Brest* says: "On a sombre background, in artistic disorder, thrown pell-mell on the ground, are baskets and a shining copper kettle, with a mass of fish of all sorts, of varied forms, and changing colors. All well painted. Such is the picture by Mlle. Chauchet."

In the *Courrier de l'Est* we read: "Mlle. Chauchet, taking her grandmother for her model, has painted one of the best portraits of the Salon. The hands, deformed by disease and age, are especially effective; the delicate tone of the hair in contrast with the lace of the cap makes an attractive variation in white."

In the *Union Républicaine de la Marne*, H. Bernard writes: "'Le retour des champs' is a picture of the plain of Berry at evening. We see the back of a peasant, nude above the blue linen pantaloons, with the feet in wooden sabots. He is holding his tired, heavy cow by the tether. The setting sun lights up his powerful bronzed back, his prominent shoulders, and the hindquarters of the cow. It is all unusually strong; the drawing is firm and very bold in the foreshortening of the animal. The effect of the whole is a little sad; the sobriety of the execution emphasizes this effect, and, above all, there is in it no suggestion of the feminine. I have already noticed this quality of almost brutal sincerity, of picturesque realism, in the works of Mlle. Chauchet who successfully follows her methods."

Chaussée, Mlle. Cécile de.
[*No reply to circular.*]

Chéron, Elizabeth Sophie. Born in Paris in 1648. Her father was an artist, and under his instruction Elizabeth attained such perfection in miniature and enamel painting that her works were praised by the most distinguished artists. In 1674 Charles le Brun proposed her name and she was elected to the Academy.

Her exquisite taste in the arrangement of her subjects, the grace of her draperies, and, above all, the refinement and spirituality of her pictures, were the characteristics on which her fame was based.

Her life outside her art was interesting. Her father was a rigid Calvinist, and endeavored to influence his daughter to adopt his religious belief; but her mother, who was a fervent Roman Catholic, persuaded Elizabeth to pass a year in a convent, during which time she ardently embraced the faith of her mother. She was an affectionate daughter to both her parents and devoted her earnings to her brother Louis, who made his studies in Italy.

In her youth Elizabeth Chéron seemed insensible to the attractions of the brilliant men in her social circle, and was indifferent to the offers of marriage which she received; but when sixty years old, to the surprise of her friends, she married Monsieur Le Hay, a gentleman of her own age. One of her biographers, leaving nothing to the imagination, assures us that "substantial esteem and respect were the foundations of their matrimonial happiness, rather than any pretence of romantic sentiment."

Mlle. Chéron's narrative verse was much admired and her spiritual poetry was thought to resemble that of J. B. Rousseau. In 1699 she was elected to the Accademia dei Ricovrati of Padua, where she was known as Erato. The honors bestowed on her did not lessen the modesty of her bearing. She was simple in dress, courteous in her intercourse with her inferiors, and to the needy a helpful friend.

She died when sixty-three and was buried in the church of St. Sulpice. I translate the lines written by the Abbé Bosquillon and placed beneath her portrait: "The unusual possession of two exquisite talents will render Chéron an ornament to France for all time. Nothing save the grace of her brush could equal the excellencies of her pen."

Pictures by this artist are seen in various collections in France, but the larger number of her works were portraits which are in the families of her subjects.

Cherry, Emma Richardson. Gold medal from Western Art Association in 1891. Member of above association and of the Denver Art Club. Born at Aurora, Illinois, 1859. Pupil of Julian and Delécluse Academies in Paris, also of Merson, and of the Art Students' League in New York.

Mrs. Cherry is a portrait painter, and in 1903 was much occupied in this art in Chicago and vicinity. Among her sitters were Mr. Orrington Lunt, the donor of the Library of the Northwestern University, and Bishop Foster, a former president of the same university; these are to be placed in the library. A portrait by Mrs. Cherry of a former president of the American Society of Civil Engineers, Mr. O. Chanute, is to be placed in the club rooms of the society in New York. It has been done at the request of the society.

An exhibition of ten portraits by this artist was held in Chicago in 1903, and was favorably noticed. Mrs. Cherry resides in Houston, Texas.

Clement, Ethel. This artist has received several awards from California State fair exhibits, and her pastel portrait of her mother was hung on the line at the Salon of 1898. Member of San Francisco Art Association and of the Sketch Club of that city. Born in San Francisco in 1874. Her studies began in her native city with drawing from the antique and from life under Fred Yates. At the Cowles Art School, Boston, and the Art Students' League, New York, she spent three winters, and at the Julian Academy, Paris, three other winters, drawing from life and painting in oils under the teaching of Jules Lefebvre and Robert-Fleury, supplementing these studies by that of landscape in oils under George Laugée in Picardie.

Her portraits, figure subjects, and landscapes are numerous, and are principally in private collections, a large proportion being in San Francisco. Her recent work has been landscape painting in New England. In 1903 she exhibited a number of pictures in Boston which attracted favorable attention.

Cohen, Katherine M. Honorary member of the American Art Association, Paris, and of the New Century Club, Philadelphia. Born in Philadelphia, 1859. Pupil of School of Design, Pennsylvania Academy of Fine Arts, and of St. Gaudens at Art Students' League; also six years in Paris schools.

This artist executed a portrait of General Beaver for the Smith Memorial in Fairmount Park. She has made many portraits in busts and bas-reliefs, as well as imaginary subjects and decorative works. "The Israelite" is a life-size statue and an excellent work.

Collaert, Marie. Born in Brussels, 1842. Is called the Flemish Rosa Bonheur and the Muse of Belgian landscape. Her pictures of country life are most attractive. Her powerful handling of her brush is modified by a tender, feminine sentiment.

I quote from the "History of Modern Painters": "In Marie Collaert's pictures may be found quiet nooks beneath clear sky-green stretches of grass where the cows are at pasture in idyllic peace. Here is to be found the cheery freshness of country life."

Coman, Charlotte B. Bronze medal, California Mid-Winter Exposition, 1894. Member of New York Water-Color Club. Born in Waterville, N. Y. Pupil of J. R. Brevoort in America, of Harry Thompson and Émile Vernier in Paris. This artist has painted landscapes, and sent to the Philadelphia Exposition in 1876 "A French Village"; to the Paris Exposition, 1878, "Near Fontainebleau." In 1877 and 1878 she exhibited in Boston, "On the Borders of the Marne" and "Peasant House in Normandy."

[No reply to circular.]

Comerre-Paton, Mme. Jacqueline. Honorable mention, 1881; medal at Versailles; officer of the Academy. Born at Paris, 1859. Pupil of Cabanel. Her principal works are: "Peau d'Ane, Hollandaise," in the Museum of Lille; "Song of the Wood," Museum of Morlaix; "Mignon," portrait of Mlle. Ugalde; the "Haymaker," etc.

Cookesley, Margaret Murray. Decorated by the Sultan of Turkey with the Order of the Chefakat, and with the Medaille des Beaux Arts, also a Turkish honor. Medal for the "Lion Tamers in the Time of Nero." Member of the Empress Club. Born in Dorsetshire. Studied in Brussels under Leroy and Gallais, and spent a year at South Kensington in the study of anatomy. Mrs. Cookesley has lived in Newfoundland and in San Francisco. A visit to Constantinople brought her a commission to paint a portrait of the son of the Sultan. No sittings were accorded her, the Sultan thinking a photograph sufficient for the artist to work from. Fortunately Mrs. Cookesley was able to make a sketch of her subject while following the royal carriage in which he was riding.

The portrait proved so satisfactory to the Sultan that he not only decorated the artist, but invited her to make portraits of some of his wives, for which Mrs. Cookesley had not time. Her pictures of Oriental subjects have been successful. Among these are: "An Arab Café in the Slums of Cairo," much noticed in the Academy Exhibition of 1895; "Noon at Ramazan," "The Snake-Charmer," "Umbrellas to Mend – Damascus," and a group of the "Soudanese Friends of Gordon." Her "Priestess of Isis" is owned in Cairo.

Among her pictures of Western subjects are "The Puritan's Daughter," "Deliver Us from Evil," "The Gambler's Wife." "Widowed" and "Miss Calhoun as Salome" were purchased by Maclean, of the Haymarket Theatre; "Death of the First-Born" is owned in Russia; and "Portrait of Ellen Terry as Imogen" is in a private collection.

"Lion Tamers in the Time of Nero" is one of her important pictures of animals, of which she has made many sketches.

Cooper, Emma Lampert. Awarded medal at World's Columbian Exposition, 1893; bronze medal, Atlanta Exposition, 1895. Member of Water-Color Club and Woman's Art Club, New York; Water-Color Club and Plastic Club, Philadelphia; Woman's Art Association, Canada; Women's International Art Club, London.

Born in Nunda, N. Y. Studied under Agnes D. Abbatt at Cooper Union and at the Art Students' League, New York; in Paris under Harry Thompson and at Delécluse and Colarossi Academies.

Mrs. Cooper's work is principally in water-colors. After several years abroad, in the spring of 1903 she exhibited twenty-two pictures, principally of Dutch interiors, with some sketches in English towns, which last, being more unusual, were thought her best work. Her picture, "Mother Claudius," is in the collection of Walter J. Peck, New York; "High Noon at Cape Ann" is owned by W. B. Lockwood, New York; and a "Holland Interior" by Dr. Gessler, Philadelphia. Of her recent exhibition a critic writes:

"The pictures are notable for their careful attention to detail of drawing. Architectural features of the rich old Gothic churches are faithfully indicated instead of blurred, and the treatment is almost devotional in tone, so sympathetic is the quality of the work. There is a total absence of the garish coloring which has become so common, the religious subjects being without exception in a minor key, usually soft grays and blues. It is indeed in composition and careful drawing that this artist excels rather than in coloring, although this afterthought is suggested by the canvasses treating of secular subjects." – *Brooklyn Standard Union*.

Corazzi, Giulitta. Born at Fivizzano, 1866. Went to Florence when still a child and early began to study art. She took a diploma at the Academy in 1886, having been a pupil of Cassioli. She is a portrait painter, and among her best works are the portraits of the Counts Francesco and Ottorino Tenderini, Giuseppe Erede, and Raffaello Morvanti. Her pictures of flowers are full of freshness and spirit and delightful in color. Since 1885 she has spent much time in teaching in the public schools and other institutions and in private families.

Correlli, Clementina. Member of the Society for the Promotion of the Fine Arts, in Naples. Born in Lesso, 1840. This artist is both a painter and a sculptor. Pupil of Biagio Molinari, she supplemented his instructions by constant visits to galleries and museums, where she could study masterpieces of art. A statue called "The Undeceived" and a group, "The Task," did much to establish her reputation. They were exhibited in Naples, Milan, and Verona, and aroused widespread interest.

Her pictures are numerous. Among them are "St. Louis," "Sappho," "Petrarch and Laura," "Romeo and Juliet," "Hagar and Ishmael in the Desert," "A Devotee of the Virgin," exhibited at Turin in 1884; a series illustrating the "Seasons," and four others representing the arts.

Cosway, Maria. The artist known by this name was born Maria Hadfield, the daughter of an Englishman who acquired a fortune as a hotel-keeper in Leghorn, which was Maria's birthplace. She was educated in a convent, and early manifesting unusual artistic ability, was sent to Rome to study painting. Her friends there, among whom were Battoni, Raphael Mengs, and Fuseli, found much to admire and praise in her art.

After her father's death Maria ardently desired to become a nun, but her mother persuaded her to go to England. Here she came under the influence of Angelica Kauffman, and devoted herself assiduously to painting.

She married Richard Cosway, an eminent painter of miniatures in water-colors. Cosway was a man of fortune with a good position in the fashionable circles of London. For a time after their marriage Maria lived in seclusion, her husband wishing her to acquire the dignity and grace requisite for success in the society which he frequented. Meantime she continued to paint in miniature, and her pictures attracted much attention in the Academy exhibitions.

When at length Cosway introduced her to the London world, she was greatly admired; her receptions were crowded, and the most eminent people sat to her for their portraits. Her picture of the Duchess of Devonshire in the character of Spenser's Cynthia was very much praised. Cosway did not permit her to be paid for her work, and as a consequence many costly gifts were made her in return for her miniatures, which were regarded as veritable treasures by their possessors.

Maria Cosway had a delicious voice in singing, which, in addition to her other talent, her beauty, and grace, made her unusually popular in society, and her house was a centre for all who had any pretensions to a place in the best circles. Poets, authors, orators, lords, ladies, diplomats, as well as the Prince of Wales, were to be seen in her drawing-rooms. A larger house was soon required for the Cosways, and the description of it in "Nollekens and His Times" is interesting:

"Many of the rooms were more like scenes of enchantment pencilled by a poet's fancy, than anything perhaps before displayed in a domestic habitation. Escritoires of ebony, inlaid with mother-of-pearl, and rich caskets for antique gems, exquisitely enamelled and adorned with onyx, opals, rubies, and emeralds; cabinets of ivory, curiously wrought; mosaic tables, set with jasper, blood-stone, and lapis-lazuli, their feet carved into the claws of lions and eagles; screens of old raised Oriental Japan; massive musical clocks, richly chased with ormulu and tortoise-shell; ottomans superbly damasked; Persian and other carpets, with corresponding hearth-rugs bordered with ancient family crests and armorial ensigns in the centre, and rich hangings of English tapestry. The carved chimney-pieces were adorned with the choicest bronzes and models in wax and terra-cotta. The tables were covered with Sèvres, blue Mandarin, Nankin, and Dresden china, and the cabinets were surmounted with crystal cups, adorned with the York and Lancaster roses, which might have graced the splendid banquets of the proud Wolsey."

In the midst of all this fatiguing luxury, Maria Cosway lost her health and passed several years travelling in Europe. Returning to London, she was again prostrated by the death of her only daughter. She then went to Lodi, near Milan, where she founded a college for the education of girls. She spent much time in Lodi, and after the death of her husband established herself there permanently. A goodly circle of friends gathered about her, and she found occupation and solace for her griefs in the oversight of her college.

She continued her painting and the exhibition of her pictures at the Royal Academy. She made illustrations for the works of Virgil, Homer, Spenser, and other poets, and painted portraits of interesting and distinguished persons, among whom were Mme. Le Brun and Mme. Récamier. The life and work of Maria Cosway afford a striking contradiction of the theory that wealth and luxury induce idleness and dull the powers of their possessors. Hers is but one of the many cases in which a woman's a woman "for a' that."

At an art sale in London in 1901, an engraving by V. Green after Mrs. Cosway's portrait of herself, first state, brought $1,300, and a second one $200 less.

Coudert, Amalia Küssner. Born in Terre Haute, Indiana. This distinguished miniaturist writes me that she "never studied." Like Topsy, she must have "growed." By whatever method they are produced or by whatever means the artist in her has been evolved, her pictures would seem to prove that study of a most intelligent order has done its part in her development.

She has executed miniature portraits of the Czar and Czarina of Russia, the Grand Duchess Vladimir, King Edward VII., the late Cecil Rhodes, many English ladies of rank, and a great number of the beautiful and fashionable women of America.

Coutan-Montorgueil, Mme. Laure Martin. Honorable mention, Salon des Artistes Français, 1894. Born at Dun-sur-Auron, Cher. Pupil of Alfred Boucher.

This sculptor has executed the monument to André Gill, Père Lachaise; that of the Poet Moreau, in the cemetery Montparnasse; bust of Taglioni, in the foyer of the Grand Opera House, Paris; bust of the astronomer Leverrier, at the Institute, Paris; a statue, "The Spring," Museum of Bourges; "Sirius," in the Palais of the Governor of Algiers. Also busts of Prince Napoleon, General Boulanger, the Countess de Choiseul, the Countess de Vogué, and numerous statuettes and other compositions.

At the Salon, Artistes Français, 1903, she exhibited "Fortune" and "A Statuette."

Cowles, Genevieve Almeda. Member of the Woman's Art Club, New York; Club of Women Art Workers, New York; and the Paint and Clay Club of New Haven. Born in Farmington, Connecticut, 1871. Pupil of Robert Brandagee; of the Cowles Art School, Boston; and of Professor Niemeyer at the Yale Art School.

Together with her twin sister, Maud, this artist has illustrated various magazine articles. Also several books, among which are "The House of the Seven Gables," "Old Virginia," etc.

Miss G. A. Cowles designed a memorial window and a decorative border for the chancel of St. Michael's Church, Brooklyn. Together with her sister, she designed a window in the memory of the Deaconess, Miss Stillman, in Grace Church, New York City. These sisters now execute many windows and other decorative work for churches, and also superintend the making and placing of the windows.

Regarding their work in the Chapel of Christ Church, New Haven, Miss Genevieve Cowles writes me: "These express the Prayer of the Prisoner, the Prayer of the Soul in Darkness, and the Prayer of Old Age. These are paintings of states of the soul and of deep emotions. The paintings are records of human lives and not mere imagination. We study our characters directly from life."

These artists are now, November, 1903, engaged upon a landscape frieze for a dining-room in a house at Watch Hill.

Miss Genevieve Cowles writes: "We feel that we are only at the beginning of our life-work, which is to be chiefly in mural decoration and stained glass. I desire especially to work for prisons, hospitals, and asylums – for those whose great need of beauty seems often to be forgotten."

Cowles, Maud Alice. Twin sister of Genevieve Cowles. Bronze medal at Paris Exposition, 1900, and a medal at Buffalo, 1901. Her studies were the same as her sister's, and she is a member of the same societies. Indeed, what has been said above is equally true of the two sisters, as they usually work on the same windows and decorations, dividing the designing and execution between them.

Cox, Louise – Mrs. Kenyon Cox. Third Hallgarten prize, National Academy of Design; bronze medal, Paris Exposition, 1900; silver medal at Buffalo, 1901; medal at Charleston, 1902; Shaw Memorial prize, Society of American Artists, 1903. Member of Society of American Artists, and an associate of the Academy of Design. Born at San Francisco, 1865. Studies made at Academy of Design, Art Students' League, under C. Turner, George de Forest Brush, and Kenyon Cox.

Mrs. Cox paints small decorative pictures and portraits, mostly of children. The Shaw prize was awarded to a child's portrait, called "Olive." Among other subjects she has painted an "Annunciation," the "Fates," and "Angiola," reproduced in this book.

A writer in the *Cosmopolitan* says: "Mrs. Cox is an earnest worker and her method is interesting. Each picture is the result of many sketches and the study of many models, representing in a composite way the perfections of all. For the Virgin in her 'Annunciation' a model was first posed in the nude, and then another draped, the artist sketching the figure in the nude, draping it from the second model. The hands are always separately sketched from a model who has a peculiar grace in folding them naturally."

Mrs. Cox gives her ideas about her picture of the "Fates" as follows: "My interpretation of the Fates is not the one usually accepted. The idea took root in my mind years ago when I was a student at the League. It remained urgently with me until I was forced to work it out. As you see, the faces of the Fates are young and beautiful, but almost expressionless. The heads are drooping, the eyes heavy as though half asleep. My idea is, that they are merely instruments under the control of a higher power. They perform their work, they must do it without will or wish of their own. It would be beyond human or superhuman endurance for any conscious instrument to bear for ages and ages the horrible responsibility placed upon the Fates."

Crespo de Reigon, Asuncion. Honorable mention at the National Exhibition, Madrid, 1860. Member of the Academy of San Fernando, 1839. Pupil of her father. To the exhibition in 1860 she sent a "Magdalen in the Desert," "The Education of the

Virgin," "The Divine Shepherdess," "A Madonna," and a "Venus." Her works have been seen in many public exhibitions. In 1846 she exhibited a miniature of Queen Isabel II. Many of her pictures are in private collections.

Cromenburch, Anna von. In the Museum of Madrid are four portraits by this artist: "A Lady of the Netherlands," which belonged to Philip IV.; "A Lady and Child," "A Lady with her Infant before Her," and another "Portrait of a Lady." The catalogue of the Museum gallery says: "It is not known in what place or in what year this talented lady was born. She is said to have belonged to an old and noble family of Friesland. At any rate, she was an excellent portrait painter, and flourished about the end of the sixteenth century. The Museo del Prado is the only gallery in Europe which possesses works signed by this distinguished artist."

Dahn-Fries, Sophie. Born in Munich. 1835-98. This artist was endowed with unusual musical and artistic talent. After the education of her only son, she devoted herself to painting, principally of landscape and flowers. After 1868, so long as she lived she was much interested in Frau von Weber's Art School for Girls. In 1886, when a financial crisis came, Mme. Dahn-Fries saved the enterprise from ruin. She exhibited, in 1887, two pictures which are well known – "Harvest Time" and "Forest Depths."

Damer, Mrs. Anne Seymour. Family name Conway. 1748-1828. She was a granddaughter of the Duke of Argyle, a relative of the Marquis of Hertford, and a cousin of Horace Walpole. Her education was conducted with great care; the history of ancient nations, especially in relation to art, was her favorite study. She had seen but few sculptures, but was fascinated by them, and almost unconsciously cherished the idea that she could at least model portraits and possibly give form to original conceptions.

Allan Cunningham wrote of her thus: "Her birth entitled her to a life of ease and luxury; her beauty exposed her to the assiduity of suitors and the temptations of courts; but it was her pleasure to forget all such advantages and dedicate the golden hours of her youth to the task of raising a name by working in wet clay, plaster of Paris, stubborn marble, and still more intractable bronze."

Before she had seriously determined to attempt the realization of her dreams, she was brought to a decision by a caustic remark of the historian, Hume. Miss Conway was one day walking with him when they met an Italian boy with plaster vases and figures to sell. Hume examined the wares and talked with the boy. Not long after, in the presence of several other people, Miss Conway ridiculed Hume's taste in art; he answered her sarcastically and intimated that no woman could display as much science and genius as had entered into the making of the plaster casts she so scorned.

This decided her to test herself, and, obtaining wax and the proper tools, she worked industriously until she had made a head that she was willing to show to others. She then presented it to Hume; it has been said that it was his own portrait, but we do not know if this is true. At all events, Hume was forced to commend her work, and added that modelling in wax was very easy, but to chisel in marble was quite another task. Piqued by this scant praise she worked on courageously, and before long showed her critic a copy of the wax head done in marble.

Though Hume genuinely admired certain portions of this work, it is not surprising that he also found defects in it. Doubtless his critical attitude stimulated the young sculptress to industry; but the true art-impulse was awakened, and her friends soon observed that Miss Conway was no longer interested in their usual pursuits. When the whole truth was known, it caused much comment. Of course ladies had painted, but to work with the hands in wet clay and be covered with marble dust – to say the least, Miss Conway was eccentric.

She at once began the study of anatomy under Cruikshanks, modelling with Cerrachi, and the handling of marble in the studio of Bacon.

Unfortunately for her art, she was married at nineteen to John Darner, eldest son of Lord Milton, a fop and spendthrift, who had run through a large fortune. He committed suicide nine years after his marriage. It is said that Harrington, in Miss Burney's novel of "Cecilia," was drawn from John Damer, and that his wardrobe was sold for $75,000 – about half its original cost!

Mrs. Damer was childless, and very soon after her husband's death she travelled in Europe and renewed her study and practice of sculpture with enthusiasm. By some of her friends her work was greatly admired, but Walpole so exaggerated his praise of her that one can but think that he wrote out of his cousinly affection for the artist, rather than from a judicial estimate of her talent. He bequeathed to her, for her life, his villa of Strawberry Hill, with all its valuables, and £2,000 a year for its maintenance.

Mrs. Damer executed many portrait busts, some animal subjects, two colossal heads, symbolic of the Thames and the Isis, intended for the adornment of the bridge at Henley. Her statue of the king, in marble, was placed in the Register Office in Edinburgh. She made a portrait bust of herself for the Uffizi Gallery, in Florence. Her portrait busts of her relatives were numerous and are still seen in private galleries. She executed two groups of "Sleeping Dogs," one for Queen Caroline and a second for her brother-in-law, the Duke of Richmond. Napoleon asked her for a bust of Fox, which she made and presented to the Emperor. A bust of herself which she made for Richard Payne Knight was by him bequeathed to the British Museum. Her "Death of Cleopatra" was modelled in relief, and an engraving from it was used as a vignette on the title-page of the second volume of Boydell's Shakespeare.

Those who have written of Mrs. Darner's art have taken extreme views. They have praised *ad nauseam*, as Walpole did when he wrote: "Mrs. Darner's busts from life are not inferior to the antique. Her shock dog, large as life and only not alive, rivals the marble one of Bernini in the Royal Collection. As the ancients have left us but five animals of equal merit with their human figures – viz., the Barberini Goat, the Tuscan Boar, the Mattei Eagle, the Eagle at Strawberry Hill, and Mr. Jennings' Dog – the talent of Mrs. Damer must appear in the most distinguished light."

Cerrachi made a full length figure of Mrs. Damer, which he called the Muse of Sculpture, and Darwin, the poet, wrote:

"Long with soft touch shall Damers' chisel charm,
With grace delight us, and with beauty warm."

Quite in opposition to this praise, other authors and critics have severely denied the value of her talent, her originality, and her ability to finish her work properly. She has also been accused of employing an undue amount of aid in her art. As a woman she was unusual in her day, and as resolute in her opinions as those now known as strong-minded. Englishwoman as she was, she sent a friendly message to Napoleon at the crisis, just before the battle of Waterloo. She was a power in some political elections, and she stoutly stood by Queen Caroline during her trial.

Mrs. Damer was much esteemed by men of note. She ardently admired Charles Fox, and, with the beautiful Duchess of Devonshire and Mrs. Crewe, she took an active part in his election; "rustling their silks in the lowest sinks of sin and misery, and in return for the electors' 'most sweet voices' submitting, it is said, their own sweet cheeks to the salutes of butchers and bargemen." She did not hesitate to openly express her sympathy with the American colonies, and bravely defended their cause.

At Strawberry Hill Mrs. Damer dispensed a generous hospitality, and many distinguished persons were her guests; Joanna Baillie, Mrs. Siddons, Mrs. Garrick, and Mrs. Berry and her daughters were of her intimate circle.

She was fond of the theatre and frequently acted as an amateur in private houses. She was excellent in high comedy and recited poetry effectively. Mrs. Damer was one of the most interesting of Englishwomen at a period of unusual excitement and importance.

When seventy years old she was persuaded to leave Strawberry Hill, and Lord Waldegrave, on whom it was entailed, took possession. Mrs. Damer then purchased York House, the birthplace of Queen Anne, where she spent ten summers, her winter home being in Park Lane, London.

She bequeathed her artistic works to a relative, directed that her apron and tools should be placed in her coffin, and all her letters destroyed, by which she deprived the world of much that would now be historically valuable, since she had corresponded with Nelson and Fox, as well as with other men and women who were active in the important movements of her time. She was buried at Tunbridge, Kent.

Dassel, Mrs. Herminie, whose family name was Borchard. Daughter of a Prussian gentleman, who, having lost his fortune, came to the United States in 1839. His children had enjoyed the advantages of education and of an excellent position in the world, but here, in a strange land, were forced to consider the means of their support. Herminie determined to be a painter, and in some way earned the money to go to Düsseldorf, where she studied four years under Sohn, all the time supporting herself. Her pictures were genre subjects introducing children, which found a ready sale.

She returned to America, determined to earn money to go to Italy. In a year she earned a thousand dollars, and out of it paid some expenses for a brother whom she wished to take with her. Herminie was still young, and so petite in person that her friends were alarmed by her ambitions and strenuously opposed her plans. However, she persevered and reached Italy, but unfortunately the Revolution of 1848 made it impossible for her to remain, and she had many unhappy experiences in returning to New York.

Her pictures were appreciated, and several of them were purchased by the Art Union, then existing in New York. Soon after her return to America she married Mr. Dassel, and although she had a large family she continued to paint. Her picture of "Othello" is in the Düsseldorf Gallery. Her painting of "Effie Deans" attracted much attention.

Mrs. Dassel interested herself in charities and was admired as an artist and greatly respected as a woman. She died in 1857.

Dealy, Jane Mary – Mrs. W. Llewellyn Lewis. Silver medal at Royal Academy School and prize for best drawing of the year. Member of Royal Institute of Painters in Water-Colors. Born in Liverpool. Studied at Slade School and Royal Academy School. Has exhibited several years at the Royal Academy Exhibition and Institute of Painters in Water-Colors.

In 1901 her picture, "A Dutch Bargain," was etched and engraved. "Hush-a-Bye Baby" and "Good-by, Summer," have been published by Messrs. De la Rue et Cie. She has successfully illustrated the following children's books: "Sixes and Sevens," "The Land of Little People," "Children's Prayers," and "Children's Hymns."

To the Academy Exhibition of 1903 Mrs. Lewis sent "On the Mountain-side, Engelberg."

De Angelis, Clotilde. This Neapolitan artist has made a good impression in at least two Italian exhibitions. To the National Exposition, Naples, 1877, she sent "Studio dal Vero" and "Vallata di Porrano," showing costumes of Amalfi. Both her drawing and color are good.

Debillemont-Chardon, Mme. Gabrielle. Third-class medal, Salon, 1894; honorable mention at Paris Exposition, 1900; second-class medal, Salon, 1901. This miniaturist is well known by her works, in which so much grace, freshness, skill, and delicacy are shown; in which are represented such charming subjects with purity of tone and skilful execution in all regards, as well as with an incomparable spirit of attractiveness.

This artist is one of the three miniaturists whose works have a place in the Museum of the Luxembourg. She has had many pupils, and by her influence and example – for they endeavor to imitate their teacher – she has done much to improve and enlarge the style in miniature painting.

De Haas, Mrs. Alice Preble Tucker. Born in Boston. Studied at the Cooper Union and with M. F. H. de Haas, Swain Gifford, William Chase, and Rhoda Holmes Nicholls. Painter of water-color pictures and miniatures.

Her pictures are in private hands in Washington, New York, and Boston.

The following article written at the time of an exhibition by Mrs. de Haas gives a just estimate of her work:

"Mrs. de Haas is especially devoted to the painting in water-color of landscape and sea views, for which the Atlantic coast affords such a wide and varied range. A constant and keen observer of Nature, she has seized her marvellous witchery of light and color, and reproduced them in the glow of the moonlight on the water when in a stormy mood, and the silvery gleam has become an almost vivid orange tint. She is most happy in the tender opalescent hues of the calm sea and the soft sky above, while the little boats seem to rock quietly on the water, barely stirred by the unruffled tide beneath.

"The sunset light is a never-failing source of variety and beauty, and Mrs. de Haas has found a most attractive subject in the steeple of the old church in York Village – whose graceful curves are said to have been designed by Sir Christopher Wren – as it rises above the soft mellow glow of the sky or is pictured against the dark clouds.

"In another mood the artist paints the low rocks among the reeds, with the breakers playing about them, while the distant sea stretches out to a horizon, with dark, stormy clouds brooding over the solitary waste. A remarkable union of the beauty of land and water is produced by a foreground of brilliant fancy flowers relieved by a scrubby tree in the background, with the faint responsive touch of yellow in the clouds over a calm sea, where gentle motion is only indicated by the little boat floating on its surface.

"The schooners on the Magnolia Shore with Norman's Woe in the distance suggest alike the tragic story of the past and the present beauty, for now the sea is calm and the sails are drying in the sun after the storm is over.

"Many other pictures might be mentioned – a quaint old house at Gloucester, a view of Ten Pound Island, with its picturesque surroundings, and the familiar beach, with Fort Head at York Harbor. As a specimen of landscape I would mention a picturesque group of trees at Gerrish Island, full of sunshine.

"But Mrs. de Haas has added another most attractive style of art to her resources, and her miniatures, besides their charm of simplicity of treatment and delicacy of coloring, are said to have the merit of faithful likeness to their originals. Of course portraits, being painted on commission, are not generally available for exhibition, but Mrs. de Haas has a few specimens of her work which warrant all that has been said in their praise.

"One is a charming picture of a child, which for beauty of delineation and delicacy of tinting recalls the memory of our greatest of miniature painters, Malbone.

"Another is the portrait of the artist's father, and is represented with such truth of nature and so much vitality of expression and character as at once to give rise to the remark, 'I must have known that man, he seems so living to me.'"

De Kay, Helena – Mrs. R. Watson Gilder. This artist has exhibited at the National Academy of Design, New York, since 1874, flower pieces and decorative panels. In 1878 she sent "The Young Mother." She was the first woman elected to the Society of American Artists, and to its first exhibition in 1878 she contributed

"The Last Arrow," a figure subject, also a portrait and a picture of still-life.

[*No reply to circular.*]

Delacroix-Garnier, Mme. P. Honorable mention, Salon des Artistes Français; medal at Exposition, Paris, 1900, for painting in oils; and a second medal for a treatise on water-colors. Member of the Société des Artistes Français, of the Union of women painters and sculptors, and vice-president from 1894 to 1900. Pupil of Henry Delacroix in painting in oils and of Jules Garnier in water-colors.

Mme. Delacroix-Garnier has painted numerous portraits; among them those of the Dowager Duchess d'Uzès, Jules Garnier, and the Marquis Guy de Charnac, the latter exhibited at the Salon des Artistes Français, 1903. At the same Salon in 1902 she exhibited the portrait of J. J. Masset, formerly a professor in the Paris Conservatory.

Among her pictures are the "Happy Mother," "Temptation," "Far from Paris," "Maternal Joys," and in the Salon des Artistes Français, 1903, "Youth which Passes."

Delasalle, Angèle. Honorable mention, Salon des Artistes Français, 1895; third-class medal, 1897; second-class medal, 1898; travelling purse, 1899; Prix Piot, of the Institute, 1899; silver medal, Paris Exposition, 1900. Member of the Société des Artistes Français, the Société Nationale des Beaux-Arts, Société des prix du Salon et boursiers de voyage de la Société Nationale. Born in Paris. Pupil of Jean Paul Laurens and Benjamin-Constant.

Her picture of "Diana in Repose" is in the collection of Alphonse de Rothschild; "Return from the Chase," a prehistoric scene, purchased by the Government; "The Forge," in the Museum of Rouen, where is also a "Souvenir of Amsterdam." Portrait of Benjamin-Constant and several other works of Mlle. Delasalle are in the Luxembourg; other pictures in the collections Demidoff, Coquelin, Georges Petit, etc.

At the Salon des Artistes Français, 1902, this artist exhibited the portrait of M. Constant and the "Roof-Maker." At the Salon des Beaux-Arts, 1903, "The Park at Greenwich," "The Pont Neuf," "On the Thames," and a portrait in oils; and in water-colors, "The Coliseum, Rome," "A Tiger Drinking," "A Lion Eating," "Head of a Lion," "The Forge," etc.

In the *Magazine of Art*, June, 1902, B. Dufernex writes of Mlle. Delasalle essentially as follows: This artist came into notice in 1895 by means of her picture of "Cain and Enoch's Daughters." Since then her annual contributions have demonstrated her gradual acquirement of unquestionable mastery of her art. Her characteristic energy is such that her sex cannot be detected in her work; in fact, she was made the first and only woman member of the International Association of Painters under the impression that her pictures – signed simply A. Delasalle – were the work of a man. Attracted by the dramatic aspects of human nature, she finds congenial subjects in the great efforts of humanity in the struggle for life. Her power of observation enables her to give freshness to hackneyed subjects, as in "La Forge." The attitudes of the workmen, so sure and decided, turning the half-fused metal are perfect in the precision of their combined efforts; the fatigue of the men who are resting, overwhelmed and stupefied by their exhausting labor, indicates the work of a profound thinker; whilst the atmosphere, the play of the diffused glow of the molten metal, are the production of an innate colorist. Her portrait of Benjamin-Constant represents not only the masterful man, but is also the personification of the painter. The attentive attitude, discerning eye, the openness of the absorbing look, the cerebral mask where rests so much tranquil power, the impressive shape of the leonine face, all combine to make the painting one of the finest portraits of the French school.

She has a perfect and rare knowledge of the art of drawing and a faculty for seizing the character of things. Mlle. Delasalle exhibited her pictures at the Grafton Gallery, London, in 1902.

Delorme, Berthe. Medals at Nîmes, Montpellier, Versailles, and London. Member of the Société des Artistes Français. Born at Paris. Pupil of A. Chaplin.

Mlle. Delorme has painted a great number of portraits, which are in the hands of her subjects. Her works are exhibited in the Salon au Grand Palais. In 1902 she exhibited a "Portrait of Mlle. Magdeleine D."

Demont-Breton, Virginie. Paris Salon, honorable mention, 1880; medals of third and second class, 1881, 1883; Hors Concours; gold medal at Universal Exposition, Amsterdam, 1883; Paris Expositions, 1889 and 1900, gold medals; medal of honor at Exposition at Antwerp; Chevalier of the Legion of Honor and of the Belgian Order of Leopold; officer of the Nichan Iftikhar, a Turkish order which may be translated "A Sign of Glory"; member and honorary president of the Union des femmes peintres et sculpteurs de France, of the Alliance Feminine, of the Alliance Septentrionale; fellow of the Royal Academy, Antwerp; member of the Société des Artistes Français; member of the committee of the Central Union of Decorative Arts and of the American National Institute; member of the Verein der Schriftstellerinnen und Künstlerinnen of Vienna; one of the founders of the Société Populaire des Beaux-Arts and of the Société de bienfaisance l'Allaitement Maternel, etc. Born at Courrière, Pas de Calais, 1859. Pupil of her father, Jules Breton.

The works of this artist are in a number of museums and in private collections in several countries. "La Plage" is in the Gallery of the Luxembourg, "Les Loups de Mer" in the Museum of Ghent, "Jeanne d'Arc at Domrémy" in a gallery at Lille; other pictures are in New York, Minneapolis, and other American cities; also in Berlin and Alexandria, Egypt.

At the Salon des Artistes Français, in 1902, Mme. Demont-Breton exhibited a picture of "Les Meduses bleues." The fish were left on the beach by the retreating water, and two nude children, a boy and a girl, are watching them with intense interest. The children are very attractive.

At the Salon of 1903 she exhibited "Seaweed." A strong young fisherwoman, standing in the water, draws out her net filled with shells, seaweed, and other products of the sea, while two nude children – again a boy and a girl – are selecting what pleases them in the mother's net.

At the exhibition of Les Femmes Peintres et Sculpteurs, in February, 1903, Mme. Demont-Breton exhibited the "Head of a Young Girl," which attracted much attention. Gray and sober in color, with a firmly closed mouth and serious eyes denoting great strength of character, it is admirably studied and designed and proves the unusual excellence of the art of this gifted daughter of Jules Breton. At the Exposition of Limoges, May to November, 1903, Mme. Demont-Breton was pronounced hors concours in painting.

Dickson, Mary Estelle. Honorable mention, Paris Salon, 1896; bronze medal, Paris Exposition, 1900; honorable mention, Buffalo Exposition, 1901; third-class medal, Paris Salon, 1902.
[*No reply to circular.*]

Diéterle, Mme. M.
[*No reply to circular.*]

Dietrich, Adelheid. Born in Wittemberg, 1827. Daughter and pupil of Edward Dietrich, whose teaching she supplemented by travel in Italy and Germany. She made her home in Erfurt after her journeys and painted flower and fruit subjects. Her pictures were of forest, field, and garden flowers. They are much valued by their owners and are mostly in private collections.

Dietrichsen, Mathilde – née Bonneire. Born in Christiania, 1847. When but ten years old she began the study of art at Düsseldorf, under the direction of O. Mengelberg and Tideman. When but fifteen she married, at Stockholm, the historian of art,

Dietrichsen. She travelled extensively, visiting Germany, France, Italy, and Greece. She passed three years in Rome. Her pictures show refined, poetic feeling as well as good taste and humor.

Dillaye, Blanche. Silver medal at Atlanta Exposition, 1895; medal at American Art Society, 1902. Member of New York and Philadelphia Water-Color Clubs, American Women's Art Association, Paris; first president of Plastic Club, Philadelphia. Pupil of Philadelphia Academy of Fine Arts; has also studied in Europe.

This artist makes a specialty of etching, and the medal she received at Atlanta was for a group of works in that art. She paints in water-colors, and has exhibited at the principal American exhibitions, in London, and in both Paris Salons. Her etchings have been widely noticed. At an early age she showed talent, and preferring etching as a mode of expression, she soon became noted for the qualities which have since made her famous, and is one of the best known among a group of women etchers. Her work, exhibited at the New York Etching Club, is conspicuous on account of its strength, directness, and firmness, allied to delicacy of touch.

"In Miss Dillaye's work one sees the influence of her wanderings in many lands; the quaintness of Holland landscapes, the quiet village life in provincial France, the sleepy towns in Norway, and the quietude of English woods." – *Success*, September, 1902.

Dina, Elisa. A Venetian figure and portrait painter. Is known through the pictures she has shown at many Italian exhibitions. At Venice, in 1881, she exhibited a graceful, well-executed work called "Caldanino della Nonna." "Di Ritorno dalla Chiesa" appeared at Milan in the same year. The latter, which represented a charming young girl coming out of church, prayer-book in hand, is full of sentiment. She sent to Turin, in 1884, "Popolana," which was much admired. Her portraits are said to be exceedingly life-like.

Dringlinger, Sophie Friedericke. Born in Dresden, 1736; died 1791. Pupil of Oeser in Leipzig. In the Dresden Gallery are seven miniatures by her of different members of the Dringlinger family. The head of this house was John Melchior Dringlinger, court jeweller of Augustus the Strong.

Dubourg, Victoria – Mme. Fantin-Latour. Honorable mention, Paris Salon, 1894; medal third class, 1895; picture in Gallery of Luxembourg, 1903. Member of the Société des Artistes Français. Born in Paris, 1840. Studies made at the Museum of the Louvre.

Mme. Dubourg has exhibited her works at the Salons regularly since 1868, and her pictures are now seen in the Museums of Grenoble and Pau, as well as in many private collections. Her subjects are of still life.

At the Salon of the Artistes Français, in 1902, Mme. Dubourg exhibited a "Basket of Flowers."

Dubray, Charlotte Gabrielle. Born at Paris, and was the pupil of her father, Gabriel Vital-Dubray. In 1874 she exhibited at the Salon a marble bust of a "Fellah Girl of Cairo"; in 1875, a silvered bronze bust called the "Study of a Head," in the manner of Florence, sixteenth century; in 1876, "The Daughter of Jephthah Weeping on the Mountain," a plaster statue, a bust in bronze, and "A Neapolitan"; in 1877, "The Coquette," a bust in terra-cotta, and a portrait bust, in bronze, of M. B.

Ducoudray, Mlle. M. Honorable mention, 1898; honorable mention, Paris Exposition, 1900. At the Salon des Artistes Français, in 1902, this sculptor exhibited "Mon Maître Zacharie Astruc," and in 1903, "En Bretagne."

[No reply to circular.]

Dufau, Clémentine Hélène. Awards from the Salon,

Bashkirtseff prize, 1895; medal third class, 1897; travelling purse, 1898; medal second class, 1902; Hors Concours; silver medal, Paris Exposition, 1900. Picture in the Luxembourg, 1902. Member of the Société des Artistes Français and of the Società Heleno Latina, Rome. Born at Quinsac (Gironde).

Studies made at Julian Academy, under Bouguereau and Robert-Fleury. Mlle. Dufau calls her works illustrations and posters, and gives the following as the principal examples:

"Fils des Mariniers," in Museum of Cognac; "Rhythme," "Dryades," "Automne," a study, Manzi collection; "Espagne," "Été," Behourd collection; "Automne," Gallery of the Luxembourg. The latter is a decorative work of rare interest. At the Salon of 1903 Mlle. Dufau exhibited two works – "La grande Voix" and "Une Partie de Pelotte, au Pays basque." The latter was purchased by the Government, and will be hung in the Luxembourg.

Duhem, Marie. Officer of the Academy, 1895; member of the Société Nationale des Beaux-Arts; medal at the Paris Exposition, 1900; diploma of honor at Exposition of Women Artists, London, 1900. Born at Guemps (Pas-de-Calais). Has had no masters, has studied and worked by herself.

Her pictures are in several museums: "The Communicants," at Cambrai; "Easter Eve," at Calais; "Death of a White Sister," at Arras, etc. The picture of St. Francis of Assisi was exhibited at the Salon of the Beaux-Arts, 1903. The saint, with a large aureole, is standing in the midst of a desolate landscape; his left hand raised, as if speaking – perhaps to some living thing, though nothing is revealed in the reproduction in the illustrated catalogue of the Salon.

The other exhibits by Mme. Duhem are flower pictures – jonquils and oranges, chrysanthemums and roses. In 1902 she exhibited "The House with Laurels" in water-colors, and in oils "The High Road" and "The Orison." The first is a scene at nightfall and is rendered with great delicacy and refinement.

Dupré, Amalia. Corresponding member of the Academy of Fine Arts, Florence, and of the Academy of Perugia. Born in Florence, 1845. Pupil of her father, Giovanni Dupré, who detected her artistic promise in her childish attempts at modelling. She has executed a number of notable sepulchral monuments, one for Adèle Stiacchi; one for the daughter of the Duchess Ravaschieri, in Naples, which represents the "Madonna Receiving an Angel in her Arms"; it is praised for its subject and for the action of the figures. "A Sister of Charity" for the tomb of the Cavaliere Aleotti is her work, and for the tomb of her parents, at Fiesole, she reproduced "La Pietà," one of her father's most famous sculptures.

For the facade of the Florence Cathedral she made a statue of "Saint Reparata," and finished the "San Zenobi" which her father did not live to complete.

She has a wide reputation in Italy for her statues of the "Young Giotto," "St. Peter in Prison," and "San Giuseppe Calasanzio."

Durant, Susan D. This English sculptor was educated in Paris, and died there in 1873. She first exhibited at the Royal Academy in 1847. She was the teacher of the Princess Louise, and executed medallion portraits and busts of many members of the royal family of England. Her works were constantly exhibited at the Royal Academy. The *Art Journal*, March, 1873, spoke of her as "one of our most accomplished female sculptors." Her bust of Queen Victoria is in the Middle Temple, London; the "Faithful Shepherdess," an ideal figure, executed for the Corporation of London, is in the Mansion House. Among her other works are "Ruth," a bust of Harriet Beecher Stowe, and a monument to the King of Belgium, at Windsor.

D'Uzès, Mme. la Duchesse. Honorable mention, Paris Salon, 1889. Born in Paris, 1847. Pupil of Bonnassieux and Falguière. The principal works of this artist are "Diana Surprised," in marble;

"Saint Hubert," in the church of the Sacré-Coeur; the same subject for a church in Canada; "The Virgin," a commission from the Government, in the church at Poissy; "Jeanne d'Arc," at Mousson; the monument to Émile Augier, the commission for which was obtained in a competition with other sculptors; and many busts and statuettes.

In the spring of 1903, at the twenty-second exhibition of the Society of Women Painters and Sculptors, the Duchesse d'Uzès exhibited a large statue of the Virgin which is to be erected in the church of St. Clothilde. It is correct anatomically and moulded with great delicacy.

Earl, Maud. A painter of animals, whose "Early Morning" was exhibited at the Royal Academy in 1885, and has been followed by "In the Drifts," "Old Benchers," "A Cry for Help," etc. In 1900 she exhibited "The Dogs of Death"; in 1901, "On Dian's Day."

Miss Earl has painted portraits of many dogs on the Continent and in Great Britain, notably those belonging to Queen Victoria and to the present King and Queen.

This artist exhibits in the United States as well as in the chief cities of England, and has held private exhibitions in Graves' Galleries. In 1902 her principal work was "British Hounds and Gun-Dogs." Many of her pictures have been engraved and published in both England and the United States. Among them are the last-named picture, "Four by Honors," "The Absent-Minded Beggar," and "What We Have We'll Hold."

[*No reply to circular.*]

Egloffstein, Countess Julia. Born at Hildesheim. 1786-1868. This painter of portraits and genre subjects belonged to a family of distinction in the north of Germany. She was a maid of honor at the court of Weimar. Her pictures were praised by Cornelius and other Munich artists. Her portrait of Goethe, in his seventy-seventh year, is in the Museum at Weimar. She also painted portraits of Queen Theresa Charlotte of Bavaria and of the Grand Duchess of Saxe-Weimar. Her picture of "Hagar and Ishmael in the Desert" is well known in Germany.

Egner, Marie. Pupil of Schindler in Vienna. She has exhibited her pictures at the exhibitions of the Vienna Water-Color Club. In 1890 an exquisite series of landscapes and flowers, in 1894 "A Mill in Upper Austria," in gouache, and in 1895 other work in the same medium, confirming previous impressions of her fine artistic ability.

Eisenstein, Rosa von. Born in Vienna, 1844. This artist is one of the few Austrian women artists who made all her studies in her native city. She was a pupil of Mme. Wisinger-Florian, Schilcher, C. Probst, and Rudolf Huber. Her pictures are of still-life. She is especially fond of painting birds and is successful in this branch of her art.

Ellenrieder, Anna Marie. Born at Constance. 1791-1863. A pupil of Einsle, a miniaturist, and later of Langer, in Munich. In Rome, where this artist spent several years, she became a disciple of Overbeck. Returning to Switzerland, she received the appointment of Court painter at Baden in 1829.

Her works are portraits and pictures of historical subjects, many of the latter being Biblical scenes. Among her best works are the "Martyrdom of Saint Stephen," in the Catholic church at Carlsruhe; a "Saint Cecilia," a "Madonna," and "Mary with the Christ-Child Leaving the Throne of Heaven" are in the Carlsruhe Gallery. "Christ Blessing Little Children" is in the church at Coburg. Among her other works are "John Writing his Revelation at Patmos," "Peter Awaking Tabitha," and "Simeon in the Temple."

Her religious subjects sometimes verge on the sentimental, but are of great sweetness, purity, and tenderness. She was happier in her figures of women than in those of men. She also made etchings of portraits and religious subjects in the manner of G. F. Schmidt.

Emmet, Lydia Field. Medal at Columbian Exhibition, Chicago, 1893; medal at Atlanta Exhibition, 1895; honorable mention at Pan-American Exposition, Buffalo, 1901. Member of the Art Students' League and Art Workers' Club for Women. Born at New Rochelle, New York. Studied at Art Students' League under Chase, Mowbray, Cox, and Reid; at the Julian Academy, Paris, under Robert-Fleury, Giacomotti, and Bouguereau; at the Shinnecock School of Art under W. M. Chase; at Académie Vieté, Paris, under Collin, and in a private studio under Mac Monnies.

Miss Emmet has painted many portraits, which are in private hands in New York, Chicago, Boston, and elsewhere. She executed a decorative painting for the Woman's Building at Chicago which is still in that city.

Emmet, Rosina – Mrs. Arthur Murray Sherwood. Silver medal, Paris Exposition, 1889; the Art Department medal, Chicago, 1893; bronze medal, Buffalo, 1901. Member of the Society of American Artists, American Water-Color Society, New York Water-Color Club. Born in New York City. Studied two years under William M. Chase and six months at Julian Academy, Paris.

Miss Emmet exhibited at the National Academy of Design, in 1881, a "Portrait of a Boy"; in 1882, a "Portrait of Alexander Stevens" and "Waiting for the Doctor"; in 1883, "Red Rose Land" and "La Mesciana"; her picture called "September" belongs to the Boston Art Club. The greater number of her works are in private collections.

Escallier, Mme. Éléonore. Medal at Salon, 1868. A pupil of Ziegler. A painter of still-life whose pictures of flowers and birds were much admired. "Chrysanthemums," exhibited in 1869, was purchased by the Government. "Peaches and Grapes," 1872, is in the Museum at Dijon; and in 1875 she executed decorative panels for the Palais de la Légion d'Honneur.

Esch, Mathilde. Born at Kletten, Bohemia, 1820. Pupil of Waldmüller in Vienna. She also studied a long time in Düsseldorf and several years in Paris, finally settling in Vienna. She painted charming scenes from German and Hungarian life, as well as flowers and still-life. Most of her works are in private galleries.

Esinger, Adèle. Born in Salzburg, 1846. In 1874 she became a student at the Art School in Stuttgart, where she worked under the special direction of Funk, and later entered the Art School at Carlsruhe, where she was a pupil of Gude. She also received instruction from Hansch. Her pictures are remarkable for their poetic feeling; especially is this true of "A Quiet Sea," "The Gollinger Waterfall," and "A Country Party."

Eyck, Margaretha van. In Bruges, in the early decades of the fifteenth century, the Van Eycks were inventing new methods in the preparation of colors. Their discoveries in this regard assured them an undying fame, second only to that of their marvellous pictures.

Here, in the quaint old city – a large part of which we still describe as mediæval – in an atmosphere totally unlike that of Italy, beside her devout brothers, Hubert and Jan, was Margaretha. When we examine the minute detail and delicate finish of the pictures of Jan van Eyck, we see a reason why the sister should have been a miniaturist, and do not wonder that with such an example before her she should have excelled in this art. The fame of her miniatures extended even to Southern Italy, where her name was honorably known.

We cannot now point to any pictures as exclusively hers, as she worked in concert with her brothers. It is, however, positively known that a portion of an exquisite Breviary, in the Imperial Library in Paris, was painted by Margaretha, and that she illustrated other precious and costly manuscripts.

She was held in high esteem in Bruges and was honored in Ghent by burial in the Church of St. Bavo, where Hubert van Eyck had been interred. Karl van Mander, an early writer on Flemish art, was poetically enthusiastic in praise of Margaretha, calling her "a gifted Minerva, who spurned Hymen and Lucina, and lived in single blessedness."

A Madonna in the National Gallery in London is attributed to Margaretha van Eyck.

Facius, Angelika. Born at Weimar. 1806-87. This artist was distinguished as an engraver of medals and gems. Pupil of her father, Friedrich Wilhelm Facius. Goethe recommended her to Rauch, and in 1827 she went to Berlin to study in his studio. Under her father's instruction she engraved the medal for the celebration at Weimar, 1825, of the jubilee of the Grand Duke Charles Augustus. Under Rauch's direction she executed the medal to commemorate the duke's death. In 1841 she made the medal for the convention of naturalists at Jena.

After Neher's designs, she modelled reliefs for the bronze doors at the castle of Weimar.

Farncomb, Caroline. Several first prizes in exhibitions in London, Toronto, Montreal, and Ottawa. Member of Women's Art Club, London, Ontario. Born near Toronto, Canada. Pupil of Mr. Judson and Mlle. van den Broeck in London, Canada, and later of William Chase in New York. Now studying in Paris.

Fassett, Cornelia Adèle. 1831-1898. Member of the Chicago Academy of Design and the Washington Art Club. Born in Owasco, New York. Studied water-color painting in New York under an English artist, J. B. Wandesforde. Pupil in Paris of Castiglione, La Tour, and Mathieu. Her artistic life was spent in Chicago and Washington, D. C.

She painted numerous portraits in miniature and a large

number in oils. Among those painted from life were Presidents Grant, Hayes, and Garfield; Vice-President Henry Wilson; Charles Foster, when Governor of Ohio, now in the State House at Columbus, Ohio; Dr. Rankin, president of Howard University, Washington; and many other prominent people of Chicago and Washington.

Her chief work and that by which she is best remembered hangs in the Senate wing of the United States Capitol. No picture in the Capitol attracts more attention, and large numbers of people view it daily. It is the "Electoral Commission in Open Session." It represents the old Senate Chamber, now the Supreme Court Room, with William M. Evarts making the opening argument. There are two hundred and fifty-eight portraits of notable men and women, prominent in political, literary, scientific, and social circles. Many of these were painted from life.

The *Arcadian*, New York, December 15, 1876, in speaking of this picture, says: "Mr. Evarts is addressing the court, and the large number of people present are naturally and easily grouped. There is no stiffness nor awkwardness in the positions, nothing forced in the whole work. There are, in the crowd, ladies in bright colors to relieve the sombreness of the black-coated men, and the effect of the whole picture is pleasing and artistic, aside from its great value as an historical work."

The *Washington Capital*, March 17, 1878: "Mrs. Fassett's 'Electoral Commission' gives evidence of great merit, and this illustration in oil of an historical event in the presidential annals of the country, by the preservation of the likenesses in groups of some of the principal actors, and a few leading correspondents of the press, will be valuable. This picture we safely predict will be a landmark in the history of the nation that will never be erased. It memorizes a most remarkable crisis in our life, and perpetuates, both by reason of its intrinsic value as a chapter of history and its intrinsic worth as an art production, the incident it represents and the name of the artist."

In the *Washington Star*, October, 1903, an article appeared from which I quote as follows: "On the walls of the beautiful tessellated corridor of the eastern gallery floor of the Senate wing of the Capitol at Washington, just opposite the door of the caucus room of the Senate Democrats, hangs a large oil painting that never fails to attract the keenest curiosity of sightseers and legislators alike. And for good reason: that painting depicts in glowing colors a scene of momentous import, a chapter of American political history of graver consequence and more far-reaching results than any other since the Civil War. The printed legend on the frame of the picture reads:

"'The Florida case before the electoral commission, February 5, 1877. Painted from life sittings in the United States Supreme Court room by Cornelia Adèle Fassett.'"

"The painting belongs to Congress, having been purchased from the artist for $15,000. As you face the picture the portraits of two hundred and fifty-eight men and women, who, twenty-six years ago, were part and parcel of the legislative, executive, judicial, social, and journalistic life of Washington, look straight at you as if they were still living and breathing things, as, indeed, many of them are. As a work of art the picture is unique, for each face is so turned that the features can easily be studied, and the likenesses of nearly all are so faithful as to be a source of constant wonder and delight." – *David S. Barry*, in *Pearson's Magazine*.

Fauveau, Félicie de. Second-class medal at Florence in 1827, when she made her début by exhibiting a statue, "The Abbot," and a group, "Queen Christine and Monaldeschi." Born in Florence, of French parents, about 1802. For political reasons she was forced to leave Florence about 1834, when she went to Belgium, but later returned to her native city.

Among her best works are "St. George and the Dragon," bronze; the "Martyrdom of St. Dorothea," "Judith with the Head of Holofernes," "St. Genoveva," marble, and a monument to Dante.

Her works display a wonderful skill in the use of drapery and a purity of taste in composition. She handled successfully the exceedingly difficult subject, a "Scene between Paolo and Francesca da Rimini."

Faux-Froidure, Mme. Eugénie Juliette. Honorable mention at Salon, 1898; the same at the Paris Exposition, 1900; third-class medal at Salon, 1903; first prize of the Union of Women Painters and Sculptors, 1902; chevalier of the Order Nichan Iftikar; Officer of Public Instruction. Member of the Association of Baron Taylor, of the Société des Artistes Français, of the Union of Women Painters and Sculptors, and of the Association of Professors of Design of the City of Paris. Born at Noyen (Sarthe). Pupil of P. V. Galland, Albert Maignan, and G. Saintpierre.

Mme. Faux-Froidure's pictures are principally of fruit and flowers, and three have been purchased by the Government. One, "Raisins" (Grapes), is in the Museum at Commerey; a second, "Hortensias" (Hydrangeas), is in the Museum of Mans; the third, which was in the Salon of 1903, has not yet been placed. In 1899 she exhibited a large water-color called "La Barque fleurie," which was much admired and was reproduced in "L'Illustration." Her water-color of "Clematis and Virginia Creeper" is in the Museum at Tunis. In the summer exhibition of 1903, at Évreux, this artist's "Peonies" and "Iris" were delightfully painted – full of freshness and brilliancy, such as would be the despair of a less skilful hand.

At the Limoges Exposition, May to November, 1903, Mme. Faux-Froidure was announced as hors concours in water-colors.

La Société Français des Amis des Arts purchased from the Salon, 1903, two water-colors by Mme. Faux-Froidure – "Roses" and "Loose Flowers," or "Jonchée fleurie."

Her pictures at the Exposition at Toulouse, spring of 1903, were much admired. In one she had most skilfully arranged "Peaches and Grapes." The color was truthful and delicate. The result was a most artistic picture, in which the art was concealed and nature alone was manifest. A second picture of "Zinnias" was equally admirable in the painting of the flowers, while that of the table on which they were placed was not quite true in its perspective.

Of a triptych, called the "Life of Roses," exhibited at the Salon des Artistes Français, 1903, Jules de Saint Hilaire writes: "Mme. Faux-Froidure was inspired when she painted her charming triptych of 'Rose Life.' In the compartment on the left the roses are twined in a crown resembling those worn in processions; in the centre, in all its dazzling beauty, the red rose, the rose of love, is enthroned; while the panel on the right is consecrated to the faded rose – the souvenir rose, shrivelled, and lying beside the little casket which it still perfumes with its old-time sweetness."

Fischer, Clara Elizabeth. Born in Berlin, 1856. Studied under Biermann six years, and later under Julius Jacob. Her pictures are portraits and genre subjects. Among the latter are "What Will Become of the Child?" 1886; "Orphaned," "In the Punishment Corner," and "Morning Devotion."

Fischer, Helene von. Born in Bremen, 1843. She first studied under a woman portrait painter in Berlin; later she was a pupil of Frische in Düsseldorf, of Robie in Brussels, and of Hertel and Skarbina in Berlin.

She makes a specialty of flowers, fruit, and still-life; her fruit and flower pieces are beautiful, and her pictures of the victims of the chase are excellent.

Flesch-Brunnengen, Luma von. Born in Brünn in 1856. In Vienna she worked under Schöner, the interpreter of Venetian and Oriental life, and later in Munich she acquired technical facility under Frithjof Smith. Travels in Italy, France, and Northern Africa furnished many of her themes – mostly interiors with figures, in which the entering light is skilfully managed. "The Embroiderers," showing three characteristic figures, who watch the first attempt of their seriously earnest pupil, is full of humor. In sharp contrast to this is a "Madonna under the Cross," exhibited at Berlin in 1895, in which the mother's anguish is most sympathetically rendered. "Devotion," "Shelterless," and the "Kitchen Garden" are among the paintings which have won her an excellent reputation as a genre painter.

Fleury, Mme. Fanny.
[*No reply to circular.*]

Focca, Signora Italia Zanardelli. Silver medal at Munich, 1893; diploma of gold medal at Women's Exhibition, London, 1900. Member of Società Amatorie Pittori di Belle Arti, of the Unione degli Artisti, and of the Società Cooperativa, all in Rome.

Born in Padua, 1872. Pupil of Ottin in Paris, and of the Academy of Fine Arts in Rome.

The principal works of this sculptor are a "Bacchante," now in St. Petersburg; "Najade," sold in London; "The Virgin Mother," purchased by Cavaliere Alinari of Florence; portrait of the Minister Merlo, which was ordered by the Ministry of Public Instruction. Many other less important works are in various Italian and foreign cities.

Signora Focca is a professor of drawing in the Normal Schools of Rome.

Foley, Margaret E. A native of New Hampshire. Died in 1877. Without a master, in the quiet of a country village, Miss Foley modelled busts in chalk and carved small figures in wood. At length she made some reputation in Boston, where she cut portraits and ideal heads in cameo. She went to Rome and remained there. She became an intimate friend of Mr. and Mrs. Howitt, and died at their summer home in the Austrian Tyrol.

Among her works are busts of Theodore Parker, Charles Sumner, and others; medallions of William and Mary Howitt, Longfellow, and Bryant; and several ideal statues and bas-reliefs.

In a critical estimate of Miss Foley we read: "Her head of the somewhat impracticable but always earnest senator from Massachusetts – Sumner – is unsurpassable and beyond praise. It is simple, absolute truth, embodied in marble." – *Tuckerman's Book of the Artists.*

"Miss Foley's exquisite medallions and sculptures ought to be reproduced in photograph. Certainly she was a most devoted artist, and America has not had so many sculptors among women that she can afford to forget any one of them." – *Boston Advertiser,* January, 1878.

Fontaine, Jenny. Silver medal, Julian Academy, 1889; silver medal at Amiens Exposition, 1890 and 1894; honorable mention, Paris Salon, 1892; gold medal at Rouen Exposition, 1893; third-class medal, Salon, 1896; bronze medal, Paris Exposition, 1900. Officer of the Academy, 1896; Officer of Public Instruction, 1902. Member of the Société des Artistes Français, Paris; Société de l'Union Artistique, du Pas-de-Calais, at Arras; corresponding member of the Academy of Arras. Pupil of Jules Lefebvre and Benjamin-Constant.

Mlle. Fontaine paints portraits only – of these she has exhibited regularly at the Salons for sixteen years. Among her sitters have been many persons of distinction, both men and women.

At the Salon of 1902 she exhibited her own portrait; in 1903, portraits of MM. Rene et Georges D. The *Journal des Arts,* giving an account of the exhibition at Rheims, summer, 1903, says: "The portraits here are not so numerous as one might expect, but they are too fine to be overlooked. Mlle. Jenny Fontaine has, for a long time, held a distinguished place as a *portraitiste* in our Salons, and two of her works are here: a portrait of a young girl and one of General Jeanningros."

Fontana, Lavinia. Born in Bologna, 1552. Her father was a distinguished portrait painter in Rome in the time of Pope Julius III., but the work of his daughter was preferred before his own.

She was elected to the Academy of Rome, while her charms were extolled in poetry and prose.

Pope Gregory XIII. made her his painter-in-ordinary. Patrician ladies, cardinals, and Roman nobles contended for the privilege of having their portraits from her hand. Men of rank and scholars paid court to her, but, with a waywardness not altogether uncommon, she married a man who was even thought to be lacking in sense.

One of her two daughters was blind of one eye, and her only son was so simple that the loungers in the antechamber of the Pope were accustomed to amuse themselves with his want of wit. She is said to have died of a broken heart after the death of this son, and her portrait of him is considered her masterpiece.

Her own portrait was one of her most distinguished works, and though it is in possession of her husband's family, the Zappi, of Imola, it may be judged by an engraving after it in Rossini's "History of Italian Painting."

Many portraits by Lavinia Fontana are in the private collections of Italian families for whom they were painted. In the Gallery of Bologna there is a night-scene, the "Nativity of the Virgin," by her, and in the Escorial is a Madonna lifting a veil to regard the sleeping Jesus, while SS. Joseph and John stand near by.

In the churches of San Giacomo Maggiore and of the Madonna del Baracano, both in Bologna, are Fontana's pictures of the "Madonna with Saints." In Pieve di Cento are two of her works – a "Madonna" and an "Ascension." It is said that several pictures by this artist are in England, but I have failed to find to what collections they belong.

Lavinia Fontana was a distinguished woman in a notable age, and if, in translating the tributes that were paid her by the authors of her day, we should faithfully render their superlatives, these writings would seem absurd in their exaggerations, and our comparatively cold adjectives would be taxed beyond their power of expression.

Fontana, Veronica. Born in 1576. A pupil of Elisabetta Sirani, who devoted herself to etching and wood-engraving. She is known from her exceedingly fine, delicate portraits on wood and etchings of scenes from the life of the Madonna.

Foord, Miss J. A painter of plants and flowers, which are much praised. An article in the *Studio*, July, 1901, says: "Miss Foord, by patient and observant study from nature, has given us a very pleasing, new form of useful work, that has traits in common; with the illustrations to be found in the excellent botanical books of the beginning of the nineteenth century." After praising the works of this artist, attention is called to her valuable book, "Decorative Flower Studies," illustrated with forty plates printed in colors.

[*No reply to circular.*]

Foote, Mary Hallock. Born in Milton, New York. At New York School of Design for Women this artist studied anatomy and composition under William Rimmer, and drawing on wood and black and white under William J. Linton. Mrs. Foote is a member of the Alumni of the School of Design.

Her illustrations have been exhibited by the publishers for whom they were made. In the beginning her work was suited to the taste and custom of the time. She illustrated the so-called "Gift Books" and poems in the elaborate fashion of the period. Later she was occupied principally in illustrations for the Century Company and Houghton, Mifflin & Co. Mrs. Foote writes that Miss Regina Armstrong – now Mrs. Niehaus – in a series of articles on "Women Illustrators of America," whom she divided into classes, placed her with the "Story-Tellers."

Forbes, Mrs. Stanhope. Mr. Norman Gastin, in an article upon the work of the Royal Academician, Stanhope Forbes, in the *Studio*, July, 1901, pays the following tribute to the wife of the artist, whose maiden name was Elizabeth Armstrong:

"Mrs. Stanhope Forbes's work does not ask you for any of that chivalrous gentleness which is in itself so derogatory to the powers of women. As an artist she stands shoulder to shoulder with the very best; she has taste and fancy, without which she could not be an artist. But what strikes one about her most is summed up in the word 'ability.' She is essentially able. The work which that wonderful left hand of hers finds to do, it does with a certainty that makes most other work look tentative beside hers. The gestures and poses she chooses in her models show how little she fears drawing, while the gistness of her criticism has a most solvent effect in dissolving the doubts that hover round the making of pictures."

[*No reply to circular.*]

Forti, Enrica. Rome.
[*No reply to circular.*]

Fortin de Cool, Delfina. Third-class medal, Madrid, 1864, for the following works reproduced on porcelain: the "Conception" of Murillo, the "Magdalen" of Antolinez, and the portrait of Alonso Cano by Velazquez; also a portrait on ivory of a young girl.

This artist, who was French by birth, was a pupil of her father. For paintings executed in the imperial works at Sèvres, she was awarded prizes at Blois, Besançon, Rouen, Perigueux, and Paris.

Foulques, Elisa. Born in Pjatigorsk, in the Caucasus. She came under Italian influence when but four years old, and was taken to Naples. At the Institute of the Fine Arts she was a pupil of Antoriello, Mancinelli, Perrisi, and Solari. She received a diploma when leaving the Institute. Her picture, "Mendica," was exhibited in Naples, 1886; "Un ultimo Squardo" and "Sogno," 1888. In London, in 1888, "Tipo Napoletano," "Studio dal vero," and "Ricordi" were exhibited. Since 1884 this artist has taught drawing in the Municipal School for Girls in Naples, and has executed many portraits in oil, as well as numerous pastels and water-colors. Among her later works are "La Figlia del Corsaro," "Chiome nere," "Una Carezza al Nonno," and "Di Soppiatto."

Frackleton, Susan Stuart. Medal at Antwerp Exposition, 1894; at Paris Exposition, 1900. Founder and first president of National League of Mineral Painters; member of Park and Outdoor Association. Born at Milwaukee, 1848. Pupil of private studios in Milwaukee and New York.

Mrs. Frackleton's gas-kilns for firing decorated china and glass are well known; also her book, "Tried by Fire," a treatise on china painting. As a ceramic artist she has exhibited in various countries, and has had numerous prizes for her work. She declined the request of the Mexican Government to be at the head of a National School of Ceramic Decoration, etc. She is also a lecturer on topics connected with the so-called arts and crafts.

Freeman, Florence. Born in Boston. 1836-1883. Pupil of Richard S. Greenough in Boston and of Hiram Powers in Florence, Italy. After a year in Florence she went to Rome, where she made her home. Among her works are a bust of "Sandalphon," which belonged to Mr. Longfellow, bas-reliefs of Dante, and a statue of the "Sleeping Child."

She sent to the Exhibition in Philadelphia, 1876, a chimney-piece on which were sculptured "Children and the Yule-Log and Fireside Spirits." This was purchased by Mrs. Hemenway, of Boston.

"Her works are full of poetic fancy; her bas-reliefs of the seven days of the week and of the hours are most lovely and original in conception. Her sketches of Dante in bas-reliefs are equally fine. Her designs for chimney-pieces are gems, and in less prosaic days than these, when people were not satisfied with the work of mechanics, but demanded artistic designs in the commonest household articles, they would have made her famous." – *The*

Revolution, May, 1871.

French, Jane Kathleen. Member of the Water-Color Society of Ireland. Born in Dublin. Studied in Brussels under M. Bourson, and in Wiesbaden under Herr Kögler. Miss French is a miniaturist and exhibited at the Royal Academy, London, in 1901, a case of her works which she was later specially invited to send to an exhibition in Liverpool, and several other exhibits.

The last two years she has exhibited in Ireland only, as her commissions employ her time so fully that she cannot prepare for foreign expositions.

Freyberg, Baroness Marie Electrine. Elected to the Academy of St. Luke, 1822. Born in Strassburg. 1797-1847. Daughter and pupil of the landscape painter, Stuntz. After travelling in France and Italy, making special studies in Rome, she settled in Munich. She painted historical and religious subjects, and a few portraits. "Zacharias Naming the Little St. John" is in the New Picture Gallery, Munich; in the same gallery is also a portrait called the "Boy Playing a Flute"; in the Leuchtenberg Gallery, Petersburg, is her "Three Women at the Sepulchre." She painted a picture called the "Glorification of Religion through Art" and a "Madonna in Prayer." She also executed a number of lithographs and etchings.

Friedländer, Camilla. Born in Vienna, 1856. She was instructed by her father, Friedrich Friedländer. Among her numerous paintings of house furniture, antiquities, and dead animals should be especially mentioned her picture in the Rudolfinum at Prague, which represents all sorts of drinking-vessels, 1888. Some critics affirm that she has shown more patience and industry than wealth of artistic ideas, but her still-life pictures demanded those qualities and brought her success and artistic recognition.

Friedrich, Caroline Friederike. Born in Dresden. 1749-1815. Honorary member of Dresden Academy. In the Dresden Gallery is a picture by this artist, "Pastry on a Plate with a Glass of Wine," signed 1799.

Friedrichson, Ernestine. Born in Dantzig, 1824. Pupil of Marie Wiegmann in Düsseldorf, and later of Jordan and Wilhelm Sohn. While still a student she visited Holland, Belgium, England, and Italy. Her favorite subjects were scenes from the every-day life of Poles and Jews.

Her best pictures were sold to private collectors. Among these are "Polish Raftsmen Resting in the Forest," 1867; "Polish Raftsmen before a Crucifix," 1869; "A Jew Rag-picker," 1870; "The Jewish Quarter in Amsterdam on Friday Evening," 1881; "A Goose Girl," 1891.

Fries, Anna. Silver medal at Berne, 1857; two silver medals from the Academy of Urbino; silver medal at the National Exposition by Women in Florence. Honorary member of the Academy Michael Angela, Florence, and of the Academy of Urbino. Born in Zürich, 1827. She encountered much opposition to her desire to study art, but her talent was so manifest that at length she was permitted to study drawing in Zürich, and her rapid progress was finally recognized and she was taken to Paris, where the great works of the masters were an inspiration to her. She has great individuality in her pictures, which have been immoderately praised. She visited Italy, and in 1857 went to Holland, where she painted portraits of Queen Sophia and the Prince of Orange. She returned to Zürich and was urged to remain in Switzerland, but she was ambitious of further study, and went again to Florence. She there painted a portrait of the Grand Duchess Marie of Russia. She turned her attention to decorative painting, and her success in this may be seen in the facades of the Schmitz villa, the Schemboche establishment, and her own home. When we consider the usual monotony of this art, the charming effects which Mme. Fries has produced make her distinguished in this specialty.

Frishmuth, Harriet Whitney.
[*No reply to circular.*]

Fritze, Margarethe Auguste. Born in Magdeburg, 1845. This genre painter worked first in Bremen, and went in 1873 to Munich, where she studied with Grützner and Liezen-Meyer. The most significant of her pictures is "The Little Handorgan-Player with His Monkey." She has also executed many strong portraits, and her painting is thought to show the influence of A. von Kotzebue and Alexander Wagner. In 1880 she spent some time in Stuttgart, and later settled in Berlin.

Froriep, Bertha. Born in Berlin, 1833. Pupil of Martersteig and Pauwels in Weimar. This artist's pictures were usually of genre subjects. Her small game pictures with single figures are delightful. She also painted an unusually fine portrait of Friedrich Rückert. At an exhibition by the women artists of Berlin, 1892, a pen study by Fräulein Froriep attracted attention and was admired for its spirit and its clear execution.

Frumerie, Mme. de. Honorable mention at the Salon des Artistes Français in 1893 and 1895. Born in Sweden, she studied in the School of Fine Arts in Stockholm. There she gained a prize which entitled her to study abroad during four years.

She has exhibited her works in Paris, and to the Salon of Les Femmes Peintres et Sculpteurs, in February, 1903, she contributed a bust of Strindberg which was a delightful example of life-like portraiture.

Fuller, Lucia Fairchild. Bronze medal, Paris Exposition, 1900; silver medal, Buffalo Exposition, 1901. Member of the Society of American Artists and of the American Society of Miniature

Painters. Born in Boston. Studied at the Cowles Art School, Boston, under Denis M. Bunker, and at the Art Students' League, New York, under H. Siddons Mowbray and William M. Chase.

Mrs. Fuller is a most successful miniature painter. Among her principal works are "Mother and Child," in the collection of Mrs. David P. Kimball, Boston; "Girl with a Hand-Glass," owned by Hearn; and "Girl Drying Her Feet," for which the medal was given in Paris.

Mrs. Fuller's miniatures are portraits principally, and are in private hands. Some of her sitters in New York are Mrs. J. Pierpont Morgan and her children, Mrs. H. P. Whitney and children, J. J. Higginson, Esq., Dr. Edwin A. Tucker, and many others.

Gaggiotti-Richards, Emma. Historical and portrait painter, of the middle of the nineteenth century, is known by her portrait of Alexander von Humboldt (in possession of the Emperor William II.) and by her portrait of herself before her easel. Her historical paintings include "The Crusader" and a "Madonna."

Galli, Emira. Reproduces with great felicity the customs of the lagoons, the boys and fishermen of which she represents with marvellous fidelity. She depicts not only characteristics of features and dress, but of movement. "Giovane veneziana" and "Ragazzo del Popolo" were exhibited at Turin in 1880, and were much admired. "Il Falconiere" was exhibited at both Turin and Milan. "Un Piccolo Accattone" has also been accorded warm praise.

Gardner, Elizabeth Jane. Honorable mention, Paris Salon, 1879; gold medal, 1889; hors concours. Born in Exeter, New Hampshire, 1851, her professional life has been spent in Paris, where she was a pupil of Hugues Merle, Lefebvre, and M. William A. Bouguereau, whom she married.

[*No reply to circular.*]

Garrido y Agudo, Maria de la Soledad. Born in Salamanca. Pupil of Juan Peyró. She exhibited two works at the National Exposition, 1876 – a portrait and a youth studying a picture. In 1878 she sent to the same exposition "The Sacrifice of the Saguntine Women." At the Philadelphia Exposition, 1876, she exhibited her "Messenger of Love." Her "Santa Lucia" is in the church of San Roque de Gardia.

Gasso y Vidal, Leopolda. Honorable mention, 1876. Prizes, 1876, for two works sent to the Provincial Exposition of Leon. Member of the Association of Authors and Artists, 1876. Born in the Province of Toledo. Pupil of Manuel Martinez Ferrer and Isidoro Lozano. At Madrid, in 1881, she exhibited "A Pensioner," "A Beggar," a portrait of Señorita M. J., and a landscape; in 1878, "A Coxcomb," "Street Venders of Ávila," and a landscape; and in 1881, at an exhibition held by D. Ricardo Hernandez, were seen a landscape and a portrait of D. Lucas Aguirre y Juarez.

Geefs, Mmc. Fanny Isabelle Marie. Born at Brussels. 1814-1883. Wife of the sculptor, Guillaume Geefs. A painter of portraits and genre subjects which excel the historical pictures she also painted. Her "Assumption of the Virgin" is in a church at Waterloo; "Christ Appearing to His Disciples," in a church at Hauthem. "The Virgin Consoling the Afflicted" was awarded a medal in Paris, and is in the Hospital of St. John at Brussels. The "Virgin and Child" was purchased by the Belgian Government. Her portraits are good, and among her genre subjects the "Young Mother," the "Sailor's Daughter," and "Ophelia" are attractive and artistic in design and execution.

Gelder, Lucia van. Born in Wiesbaden. 1864-1899. This artist was the daughter of an art dealer, and her constant association as a child with good pictures stimulated her to study. In Berlin she had lessons in drawing with Liezenmayer, and in color with Max Thedy. She was also a constant student at the galleries. She began to work independently when eighteen, and a number of her pictures achieved great popularity, being reproduced in many art magazines. "The Little Doctor," especially, in which a boy is feeling, with a grave expression of knowledge, the pulse of his sister's pet kitten, has been widely copied in photographs, wood-engravings, and in colors. She repeated the picture in varying forms. She died in Munich, where she was favorably known through such works as "The Village Barber," "Contraband," "The Wonderful Story," "At the Sick Bed," and "The Violin Player," the last painted the year before her death.

Gentileschi, Artemisia. 1590-1642. A daughter of Orazio Gentileschi, whom she accompanied to England when he was invited to the court of Charles I. Artemisia has been called the pupil, and again the friend, of Guido Reni. Whatever the relation may have been, there is no doubt that the manner of her painting was influenced by Guido, and also by her study of the works of Domenichino.

Wagner says that she excelled her father in portraits, and her own likeness, in the gallery at Hampton Court, is a powerful and life-like picture. King Charles had several pictures from her hand, one of which, "David with the Head of Goliath," was much esteemed. Her "Mary Magdalene" and "Judith with the Head of Holofernes" are in the Pitti Palace. The latter work is a proof of her talent. Lanzi says: "It is a picture of strong coloring, of a tone and intensity which inspires awe." Mrs. Jameson praised its execution while she regretted its subject.

Her picture of the "Birth of John the Baptist," in the Gallery of the Prado, is worthy of attention, even in that marvellous collection, where is also her "Woman Caressing Pigeons." The Historical Society of New York has her picture of "Christ among the Doctors."

After her return to Italy from England, this artist was married and resided in Naples. Several of her letters are in existence. They tell of the manner of her life and give an interesting picture of

Neapolitan society in her day.

Gessler de Lacroix, Alejandrena – known in art circles as Madame Anselma. Gold medal at Cadiz, 1880. Honorary member of the Academy of Cadiz. She has spent some years in Paris, where her works are often seen in exhibitions. Her medal picture at Cadiz was an "Adoration of the Cross." One of her most successful works is called "The Choir Boys."

Giles, Miss – Mrs. Bernard Jenkin. This sculptor exhibited a life-size marble group, called "In Memoriam," at the Royal Academy in 1900, which attracted much attention. It was graceful in design and of a sympathetic quality. At an open competition in the London Art Union her "Hero" won the prize. In 1901 she exhibited an ambitious group called "After Nineteen Hundred Years, and still They Crucify." It was excellent in modelling, admirable in sentiment, and displayed strength in conception and execution.

Ginassi, Caterina. Born in Rome, 1590. This artist was of noble family, and one of her uncles, a Cardinal, founded the Church of Santa Lucia, in which Caterina, after completing her studies under Lanfranco, painted several large pictures. After the death of the Cardinal, with money which he had given her for the purpose, Caterina founded a cloister, with a seminary for the education of girls.

As Abbess of this community she proved herself to be of unusual ability. In her youth she had been trained in practical affairs as well as in art, and, although she felt that "the needle and distaff were enemies to the brush and pencil," her varied knowledge served her well in the responsibilities she had assumed, and at the head of the institution she had founded she became as well known for her executive ability as for her piety.

Little as the works of Lanfranco appeal to us, he was a notable artist of the Carracci school; Caterina did him honor as her master, and, in the esteem of her admirers, excelled him as a painter.

Girardet, Berthe. Gold medal at the Paris Exposition, 1900; honorable mention, Salon des Artistes Français, 1900; ten silver medals from foreign exhibitions. Member of the Société des Artistes Français and the Union des femmes peintres et sculpteurs. Born at Marseilles. Her father was Swiss and her mother a Miss Rogers of Boston. She was a pupil for three months of Antonin-Carlès, Paris. With this exception, Mme. Girardet writes: "I studied mostly alone, looking to nature as the best teacher, and with energetic perseverance trying to give out in a concrete form all that filled my heart."

Among her works are: "L'Enfant Malade," bought by the city of Paris and placed in the Petit Palais des Champs Élysées; a group called the "Grandmother's Blessing," purchased by the Government and placed in a public museum; the bust of an "Old Woman," acquired by the Swiss Government and placed in the Museum of Neuchâtel; a group, the "Madonna and Child," for which the artist received the gold medal; and two groups illustrating the prayer, "Give us this day our daily bread." Also portrait statues and busts belonging to private collections.

At the Salon des Artistes Français, 1902, Mme. Girardet exhibited the "Grandmother's Blessing" and "L'Enfant Malade." At the same Salon, 1903, the two groups illustrating the Lord's Prayer.

A writer, G. M., in the *Studio* of December, 1902, writes: "Prominent among the women artists of the day whose talents are attracting attention is Mme. Berthe Girardet. She has a very delicate and very tender vision of things, which stamps her work with genuine originality. She does not seek her subjects far from the life around her; quite the reverse; and therein lies the charm of her sculpture – a great, sincere, and simple charm, which at once arouses one's emotion. What, for instance, could be more poignantly sad than this 'Enfant Malade' group, with the father, racked with anxiety, bending over the pillow of his fragile little son, and the mother, already in an attitude of despair, at the foot of the bed? The whole thing is great in its profound humanity.

"The 'Bénédiction de l'Aïeule' is less tragic. Behind the granddaughter, delightful in her white veil and dress of a *première communicante*, stands the old woman, her wrinkled face full of quiet joy. She is thinking of the past, moved by the melancholy of the bells, and she is happy with a happiness with which is mingled something of sorrow and regret. It is really exquisite. By simple means Mme. Berthe Girardet obtains broad emotional effects. She won a great and legitimate success at the Salon of the Société des Artistes Français."

Gleichen, Countess. Bronze medal at Paris Exposition, 1900. Honorable member of Royal Institute of Painters in Water-Colors, of Royal Society of Painter Etchers. Sculptor. Pupil of her father, Prince Victor of Hohenlohe, and of the Slade School, London; also of Professor Legros. She has exhibited regularly at the Royal Academy since 1893.

In 1895 she completed a life-size statue of Queen Victoria for the Victoria Hospital, Montreal. The Queen is represented in royal robes, with one child asleep on her knee, while another, with its arm in a sling, stands on the steps of the throne. Shortly before the Queen's death she gave sittings to Countess Gleichen, who then executed a bust of her majesty, now at the Cheltenham Ladies' College. The Constitutional Club, London, has her bust of Queen Alexandra, which was seen at the Academy in 1895. Her "Satan" attracted much attention when exhibited in 1894. He is represented as seated on a throne composed of snakes, while he has scales and wings and is armed like a knight. In 1899 her statue of "Peace" was more pleasing, while a hand-mirror of jade and bronze was much admired both in London and Paris, where it was seen in the Exposition of 1900. In 1901 she executed a fountain with a figure of a nymph for a garden in Paris; a year later, a second fountain for W. Palmer, Esq., Ascot. She has made a half-length figure of Kubelik. Her sculptured portraits include those of Sir Henry Ponsonby, Mme. Calvé, Mrs. Walter Palmer, and a bust of the late Queen, in ivory, which she exhibited in 1903.

Gleichen, Countess Helena.
[*No reply to circular.*]

Gloag, Isobel Lilian. Born in London, the daughter of Scotch parents. Her early studies were made at St. John's Wood Art School, preparatory to entering the School of the Royal Academy, but the conservative and academic training of these institutions so displeased her that she went to the Slade School. Ill health compelled her to put aside all plans for regular study, and she entered Ridley's studio for private instruction, following this with work at the South Kensington Museum. After still further study with Raphael Collin in Paris, she returned to London and soon had her work accepted at the Royal Academy. Miss Gloag is reported as saying that women have little sense of composition, a failing which she does not seem to share; in this respect and as a colorist she is especially strong. "Rosamond," in which the charming girl in a purple robe, sitting before an embroidery frame, is startled by the shadow of Queen Eleanor bearing the poisoned cup, displays these qualities to great advantage. The leafy bower, the hanging mantle, show great skill in arrangement and a true instinct for color. "The Magic Mantle," "Rapunzel," and the "Miracle of the Roses" have all – especially, the first named – made an impression; another and strikingly original picture, called the "Quick and the Dead," represents a poorhouse, in the ward of which is a group of old women surrounded by the ghosts of men and children. Miss Gloag has also made some admirable designs for stained-glass windows. She has been seriously hampered by ill health, and her achievements in the face of such a drawback are all the more remarkable.

Godewyck, Margaretta. Born at Dort, 1627. A pupil of the

celebrated painter, Nicholas Maas. She excelled as a painter of flowers, and was proficient in both ancient and modern languages. She was called by authors of her time, "the lovely flower of Art and Literature of the Merwestrom," which is a poetical way of saying Dordrecht!

Golay, Mary – Mme. Speich Golay. Silver medal at Geneva Exposition, 1896; eighteen medals and rewards gained in the Art Schools of Geneva, and the highest recompense for excellence in composition and decoration. Member of the Amis des Beaux-Arts, Geneva; Société vaudoise des Beaux Arts, Lausanne. Born in Geneva and studied there under Mittey for flower painting, composition, and ceramic decoration; under Gillet for figure painting.

Mme. Golay has executed a variety of pictures both in oil and water-colors. In an exhibition at the Athénée in Geneva, in the autumn of 1902, she exhibited two pictures of sleep, which afforded an almost startling contrast. They were called "Sweet Sleep" and the "Eternal Sleep." The first was a picture of a beautiful young woman, nude, and sleeping in the midst of roses, while angels watching her inspire rosy dreams of life and love. The roses are of all possible shades, rendered with wonderful freshness – scarlet roses, golden roses – and in such masses and so scattered about the nude figure as to give it a character of purity and modesty. The flesh tints are warm, the figure is supple in effect, and the whole is a happy picturing of the sleep and dream of a lovely young woman who has thrown herself down in the carelessness of solitude.

It required an effort of will to turn to the second picture. Here lies another young woman, in her white shroud, surrounded with lilies as white as her face, on which pain has left its traces. In the artistic speech of the present day, it is a symphony in white. The figure is as rigid as the other is supple; it is frightfully immovable – and yet the drawing is not exaggerated in its firmness. Certainly these contrasting pictures witness to the skill of the artist. Without doubt the last is by far the most difficult, but Mme. Golay has known how to conquer its obstacles.

A third picture by this artist in the exhibition is called the "Abundance of Spring." Mme. Golay's reputation as a flower painter has been so long established that one need not dwell on the excellence of the work. A writer in the Geneva *Tribune* exclaims: "One has never seen more brilliant peonies, more vigorous or finer branches of lilacs, or iris more delicate and distinguished. How they breathe – how they live – how they smile – these ephemeral blossoms!"

Gonzalez, Inés. Member of the Academy San Carlos of Valencia. In the expositions of 1845 and 1846 in that city she was represented by several miniatures, one of which, "Dido," was much admired. Another – the portrait of the Baron of Santa Barbara – was acquired by the Economic Society of Valencia. In the Provincial Museum is her picture of the "Two Smokers."

Granby, Marchioness of. Replies as follows to circular: "Lady Granby has been written about by Miss Tomlinson, 20 Wigmore Street, London, W. And I advise you if you really want any information to get it from her. V. G."

I was not "*really*" anxious enough to be informed about Lady Granby – who drops so readily from the third person to the first – to act on her advice, which I give to my readers, in order that any one who does wish to know about her will be able to obtain the information!

Grant, Mary R. This sculptor studied in Paris and Florence, as well as in London, where she was a pupil of J. H. Foley, R.A. She has exhibited at the Royal Academy since 1870. She has executed portraits of Queen Victoria, Georgina, Lady Dudley, the Duke of Argyll, Mr. C. Parnell, M.P., and Sir Francis Grant, P.R.A.

Her memorial work includes a relief of Dean Stanley, Royal Chapel, Windsor; and a relief of Mr. Fawcett, M.P., on the

Thames Embankment. The late Queen gave Miss Grant several commissions. In Winchester Cathedral is a screen, on the exterior of Lichfield Cathedral a number of figures, and in the Cathedral of Edinburgh a reredos, all the work of this artist. At the Royal Academy, 1903, she exhibited a medallion portrait in bronze.

Gratz, Marie. Born at Karlsruhe, 1839. This portrait painter was a pupil of Bergmann, and later of Schick and Canon. Among her best-known portraits are those of Prince and Princess Lippe-Detmold, Princess Hohenlohe-Langenburg, Prince Wittgenstein, the hereditary Princess Reuss, and Princess Biron von Kurland.

Gray, Sophie de Butts. First honor, Maryland Institute; second honor, World's Fair, New Orleans; gold medal, Autumn Exhibition, Louisville, 1898; first and second premiums, Nelson County Fair, 1898.

[No reply to circular.]

Greatorex, Eliza. In 1869 Mrs. Greatorex was elected associate member of the National Academy, New York, and was the first woman member of the Artists' Fund Society of New York. Born in Ireland. 1820-1897. Studied under Witherspoon and James and William Hart in New York; under Lambinet in Paris; and at the Pinakothek in Munich. Mrs. Greatorex visited England, Paris, Italy, and Germany, spending a summer in Nuremberg and one in Ober-Ammergau.

Among her most important works are "Bloomingdale," which was purchased by Mr. Robert Hoe; "Château of Madame Cliffe," the property of Dykeman van Doren; "Landscape, Amsterdam"; pictures of "Bloomingdale Church," "St. Paul's Church," and the "North Dutch Church," all painted on panels taken from these churches.

Mrs. Greatorex illustrated the "Homes of Ober-Ammergau" with etchings, published in Munich in 1871; also "Summer Etchings in Colorado," published in 1874; and "Old New York from the Battery to Bloomingdale," published in 1875. Eighteen of the drawings for the "Old New York" were at the Philadelphia Exhibition, 1876.

Greenaway, Kate. Member of the Royal Institute of Painters in Water-Colors, 1890. Born in London. 1846-1901. Her father was a well-known wood-engraver. Miss Greenaway first studied her art at the South Kensington School; then at Heatherley's life class and at the Slade School. She began to exhibit at the Dudley Gallery in 1868.

Her Christmas cards first attracted general attention to her as an artist. Their quaint beauty and truthful drawing in depicting children, young girls, flowers, and landscape soon made them more popular than the similar work of other artists. These cards sold by thousands on both sides of the Atlantic and secured consideration for any other work she might do.

She soon made illustrations for *Little Folks* and the *London News*. In 1879 "Under the Window" appeared, and one hundred and fifty thousand copies were sold; it was also translated into French and German. The "Birthday Book," "Mother Goose," and "Little Ann" followed and were accorded the heartiest welcome. It is said that for the above four toy books she received $40,000. Wherever they went – and they were in all civilized countries – they were applauded by artists and critics and loved by all classes of women and children. One can but hope that Kate Greenaway realized the world-wide pleasure she gave to children.

The exhibition of her works at the Gallery of the Fine Arts Society, since her death, was even more beautiful than was anticipated. The grace, delicacy, and tenderness with which her little people were created impressed one in an entire collection as no single book or picture could do.

It has been said that "Kate Greenaway dressed the children of two continents," and, indeed, her revival of the costumes of a hundred years ago was delightful for the children and for everybody who saw them.

Among her papers after her death many verses were found. Had she lived she would doubtless have acquired the courage to give them to the world. She was shy of strangers and the public; had few intimates, but of those few was very fond; the charm of her character was great – indeed, her friends could discover no faults in her; her personality and presence were as lovely to them as were her exquisite flowers.

Greene, Mary Shepard. Third-class medal, 1900, second-class medal, 1902, at Salon des Artistes Français. Her picture of 1902 is thus spoken of in *Success*, September of that year:

"'Une Petite Histoire' is the title of Miss Mary Shepard Greene's graceful canvas. The lithe and youthful figure of a girl is extended upon a straight-backed settle in somewhat of a Récamier pose. She is intently occupied in the perusal of a book. The turn of the head, the careless attitude, and the flesh tints of throat and face are all admirably rendered. The diaphanous quality of the girlish costume is skilfully worked out, as are also the accessories of the room. Miss Greene's work must commend itself to those who recognize the true in art. Technical dexterity and a fine discrimination of color are attributes of this conscientious artist's work. She has a rare idea of grace and great strength of treatment.

"Miss Greene's canvas has a charm all its own, and is essentially womanly, while at the same time it is not lacking in character. Hailing from New England, her first training was in Brooklyn, under Professor Whittaker, from whom she received much encouragement. Afterward she came under the influence of Herbert Adams, and, after pursuing her studies with that renowned artist, she went to Paris, where she was received as a pupil by Raphael Collin. She has exhibited at Omaha, Pittsburg, and at the Salon. Her first picture, called 'Un Regard Fugitif,' won for her a medal of the third class."

[*No reply to circular.*]

Grey, Mrs. Edith F. Member of the Society of Miniaturists,

Royal Institute of Painters in Water-Colors, Bewick Club, and Northumbrian Art Institute, Newcastle-on-Tyne. Born at the last-named place, where she also made her studies in the Newcastle School of Art, and later under private masters in London.

Mrs. Grey has exhibited miniatures and pictures in both oils and water-colors at the Royal Society of British Artists, the Royal Academy, the Royal Institute of Painters in Water-Colors, and the exhibitions at Liverpool, Manchester, and York. Since 1890 she has continuously exhibited at the Academy of the Royal Institute, London, except in 1895 and 1902.

Mrs. Grey was fortunate in having the first picture she sent to London sold, and has continued to find purchasers for her exhibited works, which are now in many private collections and number about one hundred and fifty. "Empty," a child study in oils, 1897, and a water-color, "A Silver Latch," 1900, are among her important works.

To the Academy Exhibition, 1903, she sent a picture of "Nightfall, Cullercoats," and a portrait of "Lily, daughter of Mrs. J. B. Firth."

Guild, Mrs. Cadwallader. I quote from the Boston *Transcript* a portion of an article relative to this sculptor, some of whose works were exhibited in Boston in 1903:

"In spite of the always suspected journalistic laudations of Americans abroad, in spite of the social vogue and intimacy with royalty which these chronicle, the work of Mrs. Guild shows unmistakable talent and such a fresh, free spirit of originality that one can almost accept the alleged dictum of Berlin that Mrs. Guild 'is the greatest genius in sculpture that America has ever had.'

"The list of Mrs. Guild's works executed abroad include a painting belonging to the very beginning of her career, of still-life in oils, which was accepted and well hung at the Royal Academy in London; but it is in Berlin that she has been especially successful. To her credit there are: A bust of her royal highness the Princess Christian of Schleswig-Holstein; Mr. Gladstone, in marble and bronze; G. F. Watts, in bronze, for the 'Permanent Manchester Art Exhibition'; Mr. Peter Brotherhood, inventor of a torpedo engine, in marble and bronze, which held the place of honor at the Royal Academy the year of its exhibition; Princess Henry of Prussia, in marble; her highness Princess Helena of Saxe-Altenburg; his excellency the Baron von Rheinbaben, minister of finance; his excellency Dr. Studt, minister of education in art; Prof. Dr. Henry Thode, of the Heidelberg University; Hans Thoma and Joachim, the violinist; Felix Weingartner; statuette of her royal highness Princess Henry with her little son Prince Henry."

[*No reply to circular.*]

Gunther-Amberg, Julie. Born in Berlin, 1855. Daughter and pupil of Wilhelm Amberg; later she studied under Gussow. She painted attractive scenes of domestic life, the setting for these works often representing a landscape characteristic of the shore of the Baltic Sea. Among these pictures are "Schurr-Meer," "The Village Coquette," "Sunday Afternoon," "At the Garden Gate," and "Harvest Day in Misdroy." In 1886 this artist married Dr. Gunther, of Berlin.

Guyon, Maximiliènne. Medal of third class, Paris salon, 1888; honorable mention and medal of third class at Exposition Universelle, 1889; travelling purse, 1894 – first woman to whom the purse was given; bronze medal, Paris Exposition, 1900; gold medal at Exposition of Black and White, Paris; medal in silver-gilt at Amiens. Mme. Guyon is hors concours at Lyons, Versailles, Rouen, etc. Member of the Société des Artistes Français, Société des Aquarellistes Français, and of the Société des Prix du Salon et Boursiers de Voyage. Born at Paris. Pupil of the Julian Academy under Robert-Fleury, Jules Lefebvre, and Gustave Boulanger.

Mme. Guyon is a successful portrait painter, and her works are numerous. Among her pictures of another sort are the "Violinist" and "The River." In the Salon des Artistes Français,

1902, she exhibited two portraits. In 1903 she exhibited "Mending of the Fish Nets, a scene in Brittany," and "A Study." The net-menders are three peasant women, seated on the shore, with a large net thrown across their laps, all looking down and working busily. They wear the white Breton caps, and but for these – in the reproduction that I have – it seems a gloomy picture; but one cannot judge of color from the black and white. The net is well done, as are the hands, and the whole work is true to the character of such a scene in the country of these hard-working women.

Mme. Guyon is much esteemed as a teacher. She has been an instructor and adviser to the Princess Mathilde, and has had many young ladies in her classes.

In her portraits she succeeds in revealing the individual characteristics of her subjects and bringing out that which is sometimes a revelation to themselves in a pronounced manner. Is not this the key to the charm of her works?

Haanen, Elizabeth Alida – Mme. Kiers. Member of the Academy of Amsterdam, 1838. Born in Utrecht. 1809-1845. Pupil of her brother, Georg G. van Haanen. The genre pictures by this artist are admirable. "A Dutch Peasant Woman" and "The Midday Prayer of an Aged Couple" are excellent examples of her art and have been made familiar through reproductions.

Hale, Ellen Day. Medal at exhibition of Mechanics' Charitable Association. Born in Worcester, Massachusetts. Pupil of William M. Hart and of Dr. Rimmer, in Boston, and of the Julian Academy, Paris.

Her principal works are decorative. The "Nativity" is in the South Congregational Church, Boston; "Military Music," decorative, is in Philadelphia. She also paints figure subjects.

Hallowell, May. See Loud.

Halse, Emmeline. This artist, when in the Royal Academy Schools, was awarded two silver medals and a prize of £30. Her works have been accepted at the Academy Exhibitions since 1888, and occasionally she has sent them to the Paris Salons. Born in London. Studied under Sir Frederick Leighton, at Academy Schools, and in Paris under M. Bogino.

Miss Halse executed the reredos in St. John's Church, Notting Hill, London; a terra-cotta relief called "Earthward Board" (?) is in St. Bartholomew's Hospital, London; a relief, the "Pleiades," was purchased by the Corporation of Glasgow for the Permanent Exhibition; her restoration of the "Hermes" was placed in the British Museum beside the cast from the original.

This artist has made many life-size studies of children, portraits in marble, plaster, and wax, in all sizes, poetical reliefs, and tiny wax figures.

Hammond, Gertrude Demain. Several prizes at the School of the Royal Academy, 1886, 1887, and in 1889 the prize for decorative design; bronze medal at Paris Exposition in 1900. Member of Institute of Painters in Water-Colors. Born at Brixton. After gaining the prize for decorative design Miss Hammond was commissioned to execute her design, in a public building. This was the third time that such a commission was given to a prize student, and the first time it was accorded to a woman.

More recently Miss Hammond has illustrated books and magazines; in 1902 she illustrated the "Virginians" in a new American edition of Thackeray's novels. At the Academy, 1903, she exhibited "A Reading from Plato."

Harding, Charlotte. George W. Childs gold medal at Philadelphia School of Design for Women; silver medal at Women's Exposition, London, 1900. Born in Newark, New Jersey, 1873. Pupil of Philadelphia Academy of Fine Arts and School of Design for Women. In the latter was awarded the Horstman fellowship. Miss Harding is an illustrator whose works are seen in a number of the principal magazines.

Hart, Letitia B. Dodge prize, National Academy of Design, 1898. Born in New York, 1857. Pupil of her father, James M. Hart, and Edgar M. Ward.

Her principal works are "The Keepsake," "Unwinding the Skein," "In Silk Attire," and "The Bride's Bouquet."

Havens, Belle. Awarded third Hallgarten prize at National Academy of Design, winter of 1903. Born in Franklin County, Ohio. Studied at Art Students' League, New York, and at Colarossi Atelier, Paris. In New York Miss Havens was directed by William Chase, and by Whistler in Paris. In Holland she studied landscape under Hitchcock, and a picture called "Going Home" was accepted at the Salon and later exhibited at the Philadelphia Academy; it is owned by Mr. Caldwell, of Pittsburg.

Mr. Harrison N. Howard, in *Brush and Pencil*, writing of the exhibition of the National Academy of Design, says: "'Belle Havens' the 'Last Load' is part and parcel with her other cart-and-horse compositions, commonplace and prosaic in subject, but rendered naturally and forcefully and with no small measure of atmospheric effect. The picture is not one of the winsome sort, and it doubtless makes less appeal to the spectator than any other of the prize-winners."

Hazleton, Mary Brewster. First Hallgarten prize, 1896; first prize travelling scholarship, School of Museum of Fine Arts, Boston, 1899; honorable mention, Buffalo, 1901.

[*No reply to circular.*]

Hedinger, Elise. Family name Neumann. Born in Berlin, 1854. Pupil of Hoguet, Hertel, and Gussow in Berlin, and of Bracht in Paris. In recent years she has exhibited in Berlin and other cities many exquisite landscapes and admirable pictures of still-life, which have been universally praised.

Heeren, Minna. Born in Hamburg; living in Düsseldorf. In the Gallery at Hamburg is her "Ruth and Naomi," 1854; other important works are "The Veteran of 1813 and His Grandson, Wounded in 1870," "The Little Boaster," "A Troubled Hour of Rest," etc.

Helena. A Greek painter of the fourth century B. C. Daughter of Timon, an Egyptian. She executed a picture of the "Battle of Issus," which was exhibited in the Temple of Peace, in the time of Vespasian, 333 B. C.

Herbelin, Mme. Jeanne Mathilde. Third-class medal, Paris Salon, 1843; second class, 1844; and first class, 1847, 1848, and 1855. Born in Brunoy, 1820. A painter of miniatures. One of these works by Mme. Herbelin was the first miniature admitted to the Luxembourg Gallery.

Hereford, Laura. 1831-1870. This artist is distinguished by the fact that she was the first woman to whom the schools of the Royal Academy were opened. She became a pupil there in 1861 or 1862, and in 1864 sent to the Exhibition "A Quiet Corner"; in 1865, "Thoughtful"; in 1866, "Brother and Sister"; and in 1867, "Margaret."

Herman, Hermine von. Born in Komorn, Hungary, 1857. Studied under Darnaut in Vienna, where she made her home. She is a landscape painter and is known through her "Evening Landscape," "Spring," "Eve," and a picture of roses.

Heustis, Louise Lyons. Member of Art Workers' Club for Women and the Art Students' League. Born in Mobile, Alabama. Pupil of Art Students' League, New York, under Kenyon Cox and W. M. Chase; at Julian Academy, Paris, under Charles Lasar.
A portrait painter. At a recent exhibition of the Society of

American Artists, Miss Heustis's genre portrait called "The Recitation" was most attractive and well painted. She has painted portraits of Mr. Henry F. Dimock; Mr. Edward L. Tinker, in riding clothes, of which a critic says, "It is painted with distinction and charm"; the portrait of a little boy in a Russian blouse is especially attractive; and a portrait of Miss Soley in riding costume is well done. These are but a small number of the portraits by this artist. She is clever in posing her sitters, manages the effect of light with skill and judgement, and renders the various kinds of textures to excellent advantage.

As an illustrator Miss Heustis has been employed by *St. Nicholas, Scribner's,* and *Harper's Magazine.*

Hill, Amelia R. A native of Dunfermline, she lived many years in Edinburgh. A sister of Sir Noel and Walter H. Paton, she married D. O. Hill, of the Royal Scottish Academy. Mrs. Hill made busts of Thomas Carlyle, Sir David Brewster, Sir Noel Paton, Richard Irven, of New York, and others. She also executed many ideal figures. She was the sculptor of the memorial to the Regent Murray at Linlithgow, of the statue of Captain Cook, and that of Dr. Livingstone; the latter was unveiled in Prince's Gardens, Edinburgh, in 1876, and is said to be the first work of this kind executed by a woman and erected in a public square in Great Britain.

"Mrs. Hill has mastered great difficulties in becoming a sculptor in established practice." – *Mrs. Tytler's "Modern Painters."*

"Mrs. Hill's Captain Cook – R. Scottish Academy, 1874 – is an interesting figure and a perfectly faithful likeness, according to extant portraits of the great circumnavigator." – *Art Journal,* April, 1874.

Hills, Laura Coombs. Medal at Art Interchange, 1895; bronze medal, Paris Exposition, 1900; silver medal, Pan-American Exposition, 1901; second prize, Corcoran Art Gallery, Washington, D. C, 1901. Member of Society of American Artists, Women's Art

Club, New York, American Society of Miniature Painters, and Water-Color Club, Boston. Born in Newburyport, Massachusetts. Studied in Helen M. Knowlton's studio and at Cowles Art School, Boston, and at Art Students' League, New York.

Miss Hills is a prominent and successful miniaturist, and her numerous pictures are in the possession of her subjects. They are decidedly individual in character. No matter how simple her arrangements, she gives her pictures a cachet of distinction. It may be "a lady in a black gown with a black aigrette in her hair and a background of delicate turquoise blue, or the delicate profile of a red-haired beauty, outlined against tapestry, the snowy head and shoulders rising out of dusky brown velvet; but the effect is gem-like, a revelation of exquisite coloring that is entirely artistic."

"An attractive work," reproduced here, "may be called a miniature picture. It is a portrait of a little lady, apparently six or seven years old, in an artistic old-fashioned gown, the bodice low in neck and cut in sharp point at the waist line in front; elbow sleeves, slippers with large rosettes, just peeping out from her dress, her feet not touching the floor, so high is she seated. Her hair, curling about her face, is held back by a ribbon bandeau in front; one long, heavy curl rests on the left side of her neck, and is surmounted by a big butterfly bow. The costume and pose are delightful and striking at first sight, but the more the picture is studied the more the face attracts the attention it merits. It is a sweet little girl's face, modest and sensible. She is holding the arm of her seat with a sort of determination to sit that way and be looked at so long as she must, but her expression shows that she is thinking hard of something that she intends to do so soon as she can jump down and run away to her more interesting occupations."

Hinman, Leana McLennan.
[*No reply to circular.*]

Hitz, Dora. Born at Altdorf, near Nuremberg, 1856. During eight years she worked under the direction of Lindenschmit, 1870-1878. She was then invited to Bucharest by the Queen of Roumania, "Carmen Sylva." Here the artist illustrated the Queen's poem, "Ada," with a series of water-color sketches, and painted two landscapes from Roumanian scenery. Between 1883 and 1886 she made sketches for the mural decoration of the music-room at the castle of Sinoia. Later, in Brittany and Normandy, she made illustrations for the fisher-romances of Pierre Loti. At Berlin, in 1891-1892, she painted portraits, and then retired to Charlottenburg. Her exhibition of two beautiful pictures in gouache, at Dresden, in 1892, brought her into notice, and her grasp of her subjects and her method of execution were much commended.

Fräulein Hitz could not stem the "classic" art creed of Berlin, where the "new idealism" is spurned. She ventured to exhibit some portraits and studies there in 1894, and was most unfavorably criticised. At Munich, however, in 1895, her exhibition was much admired at the "Secession." Again, in 1898, she exhibited, in Berlin, at the Union of Eleven, a portrait of a young girl, which was received with no more favor than was shown her previous works. In the same year, at the "Livre Esthetique," in Brussels, her pictures were thought to combine a charming grace with a sure sense of light effects, in which the predominating tone was a deep silver gray. A portrait by this artist was exhibited at a Paris Salon in 1895.

Hoffmann, Felicitas. Born in Venice, she died in Dresden, 1760. Pupil of Rosalba Camera. There are four pictures in the Dresden Gallery attributed to her – "St. George," after Correggio; "Diana with an Italian Greyhound," after Camera; "Winter," a half-length figure by herself; and her own portrait. Her principal works were religious subjects and portraits.

Hoffmann-Tedesco, Giulia. Prize at the Beatrice Exposition,

Naples. Born at Wurzburg, 1850. This artist has lived in Italy and made her artistic success there, her works having been seen in many exhibitions. Her prize picture at Naples was called "A Mother's Joy." In 1877 she exhibited in the same city "Sappho" and "A Mother," which were much admired; at Turin, 1880, "On the Water" and "The Dance" were seen; at Milan, 1881, she exhibited "Timon of Athens" and a "Sunset"; at Rome, 1883, "A Gipsy Girl" and "Flowers." Her flower pictures are excellent; they are represented with truth, spirit, and grace.

Hogarth, Mary. Exhibits regularly at the New English Art Club, and occasionally at the New Gallery. Born at Barton-on-Humber, Lincolnshire. Pupil of the Slade School under Prof. Fred Brown and P. Wilson Steer.

Miss Hogarth's contribution to the exhibition of the New English Art Club, 1902, was called "The Green Shutters," a very peculiar title for what was, in fact, a picture of the Ponte Vecchio and its surroundings, in Florence. It was interesting. It was scarcely a painting; a tinted sketch would be a better name for it. It was an actual portrait of the scene, and skilfully done.

Hormuth-Kollmorgen, Margarethe. Born at Heidelberg, 1858. Pupil of Ferdinand Keller at Carlsruhe. Married the artist Kollmorgen, 1882. This painter of flowers and still-life has also devoted herself to decorative work, mural designs, fire-screens, etc., in which she has been successful. Her coloring is admirable and her execution careful and firm.

Hosmer, Harriet G. Born in Watertown, Massachusetts, 1830. Pupil in Boston of Stevenson, who taught her to model; pupil of her father, a physician, in anatomy, taking a supplementary course at the St. Louis Medical School.

Since 1852 she has resided in Rome, where she was a pupil of Gibson. Two heads, "Daphne" and "Medusa," executed soon after she went to Rome, were praised by critics of authority. "Will-o'-

the-Wisp," "Puck," "Sleeping Faun," "Waking Faun," and "Zenobia in Chains" followed each other rapidly.

Miss Hosmer made a portrait statue of "Maria Sophia, Queen of the Sicilies," and a monument to an English lady to be placed in a church in Rome. Her "Beatrice Cenci" has been much admired; it is in the Public Library at St. Louis, and her statue of Thomas H. Benton is in a square of the same city.

For Lady Ashburton Miss Hosmer made her Triton and Mermaid Fountains, and a Siren Fountain for Lady Marian Alford.

Houston, Caroline A.
[*No reply to circular.*]

Houston, Frances C. Bronze medal at Atlanta Exposition; honorable mention at Paris Exposition, 1900. Member of the Water-Color Club, Boston, and of the Society of Arts and Crafts. Born in Hudson, Michigan, 1851. Studied in Julian Academy under Lefebvre and Boulanger.

A portrait painter whose pictures are in private hands. They have been exhibited in Paris, London, Naples, New York, Philadelphia, and Boston.

Mrs. Houston writes me: "I have not painted many pictures of late years, but always something for exhibition every year." She first exhibited at Paris Salon in 1889, in London Academy in 1890, and annually sends her portraits to the Boston, New York, and Philadelphia Exhibitions.

Hoxie, Vinnie Ream. Born in Madison, Wisconsin, 1847. This sculptor was but fifteen years old when she was commissioned to make a life-size statue of Abraham Lincoln, who sat for his bust; her completed statue of him is in the rotunda of the Capitol at Washington. Congress then gave her the commission for the heroic statue of Admiral Farragut, now in Farragut Square, Washington. These are the only two statues that the United States

Government has ordered of a woman.

This artist has executed ideal statues and several bust portraits of distinguished men. Of these the bust of Ezra Cornell is at Cornell University; that of Mayor Powell in the City Hall of Brooklyn, etc.

Hudson, Grace. Gold medal at Hopkins Institute, San Francisco; silver medal at Preliminary World's Fair Exhibition of Pacific States; and medals and honorable mention at several California State exhibitions. Born in Potter Valley, California. Studied at Hopkins Art Institute, San Francisco, under Virgil Williams and Oscar Kunath.

Paints genre subjects, some of which are "Captain John," in National Museum; "Laughing Child," in C. P. Huntington Collection; "Who Comes?" in private hands in Denver, etc.

Mrs. Hudson's pictures of Indians, the Pomas especially, are very interesting, although when one sees the living article one wonders how a picture of him, conscientiously painted and truthful in detail, can be so little repulsive – or, in fact, not repulsive at all. At all events, Mrs. Hudson has no worthy rival in painting California Indians. If we do not sympathize with her choice of subjects, we are compelled to acknowledge that her pictures are full of interest and emphasize the power of this artist in keeping them above a wearisome commonplace.

Her Indian children are attractive, we must admit, and her "Poma Bride," seated in the midst of the baskets that are her dower, is a picture which curiously attracts and holds the attention. Her compositions are simple, and it can only be a rare skill in their treatment that gives them the value that is generally accorded them by critics, who, while approving them, are all the time conscious of surprise at themselves for doing so, and of an unanswered Why? which persists in presenting itself to their thought when seeing or thinking of these pictures.

Hulbert, Mrs. Katherine Allmond. Born in Sacramento Valley,

California. Pupil of the San Francisco School of Design under Virgil Williams; National Academy of Design, New York, under Charles Noel Flagg; Artist Artisan Institute, New York, under John Ward Stimson.

This artist paints in water-colors and her works are much admired. Among the most important are "The Stream, South Egremont," which is in a private gallery in Denver; "In the Woods" belongs to Mr. Whiting, of Great Barrington; and "Sunlight and Shadow" to Mr. Benedict, Albany, New York.

Mrs. Hulbert is also favorably known as an illustrator and decorative designer.

Hunter, Mary Y. Four silver medals at Royal Academy Schools Exhibitions; diploma for silver medal, Woman's International Exhibition, Earl's Court, London. Member of Society of Painters in Tempera. Born in New Zealand. Studied at Royal Academy Schools.

The following list of the titles of Mrs. Hunter's works will give an idea of the subjects she affects: "Dante and Beatrice," "Joy to the Laborer," "An Italian Garden," "Where shall Wisdom be Found?" and the "Roadmenders," in Academy Exhibition, 1903.

The only work of Mrs. Hunter's that I have seen is the "Dante and Beatrice," Academy, 1900, and the impression I received leads me to think an article in the *Studio*, June, 1903, a just estimate of her work. It is by A. L. Baldry, who writes: "In the band of young artists who are at the present time building up sound reputations which promise to be permanent, places of much prominence must be assigned to Mr. J. Young Hunter and his wife. Though neither of them has been before the public for any considerable period, they have already, by a succession of notable works, earned the right to an amount of attention which, as a rule, can be claimed only by workers who have a large fund of experience to draw upon. But though they have been more than ordinarily successful in establishing themselves among the few contemporary painters whose performances are worth watching, they have not sprung suddenly into notice by some special achievement or by doing work so sensational that it would not fail to set people talking. There has been no spasmodic brilliancy in their progress, none of that strange alternation of masterly accomplishment and hesitating effort which is apt at times to mark the earlier stages of the life of an artist who may or may not attain greatness in his later years. They have gone forward steadily year by year, amplifying their methods and widening the range of their convictions; and there has been no moment since they made their first appeal to the public at which they can be said to have shown any diminution in the earnestness of their artistic intentions.

"The school to which they belong is one which has latterly gathered to itself a very large number of adherents among the younger painters – a school that, for want of a better name, can be called that of the new Pre-Raphaelites. It has grown up, apparently, as an expression of the reaction which has recently set in against the realistic beliefs taught so assiduously a quarter of a century ago. At the end of the seventies there was a prevailing idea that the only mission of the artist was to record with absolute fidelity the facts of nature... To-day the fallacy of that creed is properly recognized, and the artists on whom we have to depend in the immediate future for memorable works have substituted for it something much more reasonable... There runs through this new school a vein of romantic fantasy which all thinking people can appreciate, because it leads to the production of pictures which appeal, not only to the eye by their attractiveness of aspect, but also to the mind by their charm of sentiment... It is because Mr. Young Hunter and his wife have carried out consistently the best principles of this school that they have, in a career of some half-dozen years, established themselves as painters of noteworthy prominence. Their romanticism has always been free from exaggeration and from that morbidity of subject and treatment which is occasionally a defect in the work of young artists. They have kept their art wholesome and sincere, and they have cultivated judiciously those tendencies in it which justify most completely the development of the new Pre-Raphaelitism. They are, indeed, standing examples of the value of this movement, which seems destined to make upon history a mark almost as definite as that left by the original Brotherhood in the middle of the nineteenth century. By their help, and that of the group to which they belong, a new artistic fashion is being established, a fashion of a novel sort, for its hold upon the public is a result not of some irrational popular craze, but of the fascinating arguments which are put into visible shape by the painters themselves."

Hyatt, Harriet Randolph – Mrs. Alfred L. Mayer. Silver medal at Exposition in Atlanta, Georgia, 1895. Member of National Art Club, New York. Born at Salem, Massachusetts. Studied at Cowles Art School and with Ross Turner; later under H. H. Kitson and Ernest L. Major.

Among this artist's pictures are "Shouting above the Tide," "Primitive Fishing," "The Choir Invisible," etc.

The plaster group called the "Boy with Great Dane" was the work of this artist and her sister, Anna Vaughan Hyatt, and is at the Bureau of the Society for the Prevention of Cruelty to Animals, in New York.

Hyatt, Anna Vaughan. Member of the Copley Society, Boston. Born in Cambridge, Massachusetts. Studied nature at Bostock's Animal Arena, Norumbega Park, and at Sportsman's Exhibition. Criticism from H. H. Kitson.

The principal works of this artist are the "Boy with Great Dane," already mentioned, made in conjunction with her sister; a "Bison," in a private collection in Boston; and "Playing with Fire."

In November, 1902, Miss Hyatt held an exhibition of her works, in plaster and bronze, at the Boston Art Club. There were many small studies taken from life.

Hyde, Helen. Member of the Art Association, San Francisco.

Born in Lima, New York, but has lived so much in California that she is identified with that State, and especially with San Francisco. She made her studies in San Francisco, Philadelphia, New York, and Paris, where she was a pupil of Felix Regamy and Albert Sterner. She then went to Holland, where she also studied. On her return to San Francisco she became so enamoured of the Oriental life she saw there that she determined to go to Japan to perfect herself in colored etching. Miss Hyde devoted herself to the study she had chosen during three years. She lived in an old temple at Tokio, made frequent excursions into the country, was a pupil of the best Japanese teachers, adapted herself to the customs of the country, worked on low tables, sitting on the floor, and so gained the confidence of the natives that she easily obtained models, and, in a word, this artist was soon accorded honors in Japanese exhibitions, where her pictures were side by side with those of the best native artists.

Miss Hyde has made a visit to America and received many commissions which decided her to return to Japan. A letter from a friend in Tokio, written in October, 1903, says that she will soon return to California.

Ighino, Mary. A sculptor residing in Genoa. Since 1884 she has exhibited a number of busts, bas-reliefs, and statues. At Turin in the above-named year she exhibited a group in plaster, "Love Dominating Evil." She is especially successful in bas-relief portraits; one of these is of the Genoese sculptor, Santo Varin. She has also made a bust of Emanuele Filiberto; and in terra-cotta a bust of Oicetta Doria, the fifteenth-century heroine of Mitylene. She has executed a number of decorative and monumental works, and receives many commissions from both Italians and foreigners.

Inglis, Hester. This artist lived in the last half of the sixteenth and in the early decades of the seventeenth century. In the Library of Christ Church College, Oxford, there is an example of the Psalms, in French, written and decorated by her, which formerly belonged to Queen Elizabeth. In the Royal Library of the British Museum there is also a "Book of Emblems" from her hand.

Itasse, Jeanne. Honorable mention, Paris Salon, 1888, and the purse of the city of Paris; at Paris Exposition, honorable mention, 1889; travelling purse, 1891; medal at Chicago Exposition, 1893; medal third class, Salon, 1896; medal second class, 1899; silver medal, Paris Exposition, 1900. Member of Société des Artistes Français, Société Libre, Société des prix du Salon et boursiers de voyage. Born in Paris. Pupil of her father.

Several works of this sculptor have been purchased by the Government and are in the Bureaux of Ministers or in provincial museums. A "Bacchante" is in the Museum at Agen; a portrait bust in the Museum of Alger. At the Salon of 1902 Mlle Itasse exhibited a "Madonna"; in 1903, a portrait of M, W.

Mlle Itasse knows her art thoroughly. When still a child, at the age when little girls play with dolls, she was in her father's atelier, working in clay with an irresistible fondness for this occupation, and without relaxation making one little object after another, until she acquired that admirable surety of execution that one admires in her work – a quality sometimes lacking in the work of both men and women sculptors.

Since her début at the Salon of 1886 she has annually exhibited important works. In 1887 her bust of the danseuse, Marie Salles, was purchased by the Government for the Opera; in 1888 she exhibited a plaster statue, the "Young Scholar," and the following year the bust of her father; in 1890 a "St. Sebastian" in high relief; in 1891 an "Egyptian Harpist," which gained her a traveller's purse and an invitation from the Viceroy of Egypt; in 1893 a Renaissance bas-relief; in 1894 the superb funeral monument dedicated to her father; in 1896 she exhibited, in plaster, the "Bacchante," which in marble was a brilliant success and gained for her a second-class medal and the palmes académique, while the statue was acquired by the Government.

Mlle. Itasse has also gained official recompenses in provincial exhibitions and has richly won the right to esteem herself mistress of her art.

Jacquemart, Mlle. Nélie. Medals at Paris Salon, 1868, 1869, and 1870. Born in Paris. A very successful portrait painter. Among the portraits she has exhibited at the Paris Salon are those of Marshal Canrobert, General d'Aurelle de Paladines, General de Palikao, Count de Chambrun, M. Dufaure, and many others, both ladies and gentlemen. Her portrait of Thiers in 1872 was greatly admired.

Paul d'Abrest wrote of Mlle. Jacquemart, in the *Zeitschrift für bildende Kunst:* "One feels that this artist does not take her inspirations alone from the sittings of her subjects, but that she finds the best part of her work in her knowledge of character and from her close study of the personnelle of those whom she portrays."

Janda, Herminie von. Born at Klosterbruch, 1854. Pupil of Ludwig Holanska and Hugo Darnaut. Since 1886 her landscapes have been seen in various Austrian exhibitions. One of these was bought for the "Franzens-Museum" at Brünn, while several others were acquired by the Imperial House of Austria.

Jenks, Phoebe A. Pickering. Born in Portsmouth, New Hampshire, 1849. Mrs. Jenks writes that she has had no teachers.

Her works, being portraits, are mostly in the homes of their owners, but that of the son of T. Jefferson Coolidge, Jr., has been exhibited in the Museum of Fine Arts, Boston, and that of Mrs. William Slater and her son is in the Slater Museum at Norwich.

Mrs. Jenks has been constantly busy in portrait painting for twenty-seven years, and has had no time for clubs and societies. She esteems the fact of her constant commissions the greatest honor that she could have. She has probably painted a greater number of portraits than any other Boston contemporary artist.

Jerichau-Baumann, Elizabeth. 1819-1881. Honorable mention, Paris Salon, 1861. Member of the Academy of Copenhagen. Born in Warsaw. Pupil of Karl Sohne and Stilke, in Düsseldorf. In Rome she married the Danish sculptor Jerichau and afterward lived in Copenhagen. She travelled in England, France, Russia, Greece, Turkey, and Egypt.

Her picture of a "Polish Woman and Children Leaving Their Home, which had been Destroyed," is in the Raczynski Collection, Berlin; "Polish Peasants Returning to the Ruins of a Burnt House," in the Lansdowne Collection, London; "A Wounded Soldier Nursed by His Betrothed," in the Gallery at Copenhagen, where is also her portrait of her husband; "An Icelandic Maiden," in the Kunsthalle, Hamburg. Her picture, "Reading the Bible," was painted for Napoleon III. at his request. Mme. Jerichau painted a portrait of the present Queen of England, in her wedding dress. A large number of her works are in private houses in Copenhagen.

One of her most important pictures was a life-size representation of "Christian Martyrs in the Catacombs." This picture was much talked of in Rome, where it was painted, and the Pope desired to see it. Madame Jerichau took the picture to the Vatican. On seeing it the Pope expressed surprise that one who was not of his Church could paint this picture. Mme. Jerichau, hearing this, replied: "Your Holiness, I am a Christian."

Hans Christian Andersen was an intimate friend in the Jerichau family. He attended the wedding in Rome, and wrote the biographies of Professor and Mme. Jerichau.

Théophile Gautier once said that but three women in Europe merited the name of artists – Rosa Bonheur, Henrietta Brown, and Elizabeth Jerichau; and Cornelius called her "the one woman in the Düsseldorf School," because of her virile manner of painting.

Among her important portraits are those of Frederick VII. of Denmark, the brothers Grimm, and "Hans Christian Andersen Reading His Fairy Tales to a Child."

Mme. Jerichau was also an author. In 1874 she published her "Memories of Youth," and later, with her son, the illustrated "Pictures of Travel."

Jopling-Rowe, Louise. Member of Royal Society of British Artists, Society of Portrait Painters, Pastel Society, Society of Women Artists. Born at Manchester, 1843. Pupil of Chaplin in Paris; also studied with Alfred Stevens.

Since 1871 Mrs. Jopling has been a constant exhibitor at the Royal Academy and other London exhibitions, and frequently also at the Paris Salon.

Her pictures are principally portraits and genre subjects. Her first decided success was gained in 1874, when she exhibited at the Academy the "Japanese Tea Party," and from that time she was recognized as an accomplished artist and received as many commissions as she could execute. The Baroness de Rothschild had been convinced of Mrs. Jopling's talent before she became an artist, and had given her great encouragement in the beginning of her career. The portrait of Lord Rothschild, painted for Lord Beaconsfield, is thought to be her best work of this kind, but its owner would not allow it to be exhibited. Her portrait of Ellen Terry, which hangs in the Lyceum Theatre, was at the Academy in 1883. It is in the costume of Portia. Mrs. Jopling's pastels are of an unusual quality, delicate, strong, and brilliant. Her portraits are numerous, and from time to time she has also executed figure subjects.

Of late years Mrs. Jopling has been much occupied with a School of Painting. The large number of pupils who wished to study with her made a school the best means of teaching them, and has been successful. From the beginning they draw from life, and at the same time they also study from the antique.

Many of her pupils receive good prices for their works, and also earn large sums for their portraits in black and white.

Mrs. Jopling writes: "What I know I chiefly learned alone. Hard work and the genius that comes from infinite pains, the eye to see nature, the heart to feel nature, and the courage to follow nature – these are the best qualifications for the artist who would succeed."

In the *Art Journal*, July, 1874, I read: "'The Five-o'Clock Tea' is the largest and most important design we have seen from Mrs. Jopling's hand, and in the disposition of the various figures and the management of color it certainly exhibits very remarkable technical gifts. Especially do we notice in this lady's work a correct understanding of the laws of tone, very rare to find in the works of English painters, giving the artist power to bring different tints, even if they are not harmonious, into right relations with one another."

The above-named picture was sold to the Messrs. Agnew, and was followed by "The Modern Cinderella," which was seen at the Paris Exposition in 1878; at the Philadelphia Exposition in 1876 she exhibited "Five Sisters of York."

Mrs. Jopling is also known as the founder and president of the Society of the Immortals. She has written several short tales, some poems, and a book called "Hints to Amateurs."

At the Royal Academy, 1903, she exhibited "Hark! Hark! the Lark at Heaven's Gate Sings," which is a picture of a poor girl beside a table, on which she has thrown her work, and leaning back in her chair, with hands clasped behind her head, is lost in thought.

Joris, Signorina Agnese – pseudonym, Altissimi. Was accorded the title of professor at the Institute of the Fine Arts, Rome, 1881. She was successful in a competition for a position in the Scuole Tecniche, Rome, 1888. Honorable mention, Florence, 1890; same at Palermo, 1891 and 1892; silver medal of first class and diploma of silver medal, Rome, 1899 and 1900. Member of the Società Cooperativa, Rome. Born in the same city, and pupil of the Institute of Fine Arts and of her brother, Cavaliere Professore Pio Joris.

This artist writes that a list of her works would be too long and require too much time to write it. They are in oils, pastel, and water-colors, with various applications of these to tapestries, etc. She also gives lessons in these different methods of painting. In a private collection in New York is her "Spanish Scene in the Eighteenth Century."

She painted a "portrait of the late King Humbert, arranged in the form of a triptych surrounded by a wreath of flowers, painted from some which had lain on the King's bier." She sent this picture to Queen Margharita, "who not only graciously accepted it, but sent the artist a beautiful letter and a magnificent jewel on which was the Royal Cipher."

Kaerling, Henriette. Born about 1832. Daughter of the artist, J. T. Kaerling, who was her principal teacher. She practised her art as a painter of portraits, genre subjects, and still-life in Budapest during some years before her marriage to the pianist Pacher, with whom she went to Vienna. She there copied some of the works of the great painters in the Gallery, besides doing original work of acknowledged excellence. In addition to her excellent portraits, she painted in 1851 "The Grandmother"; in 1852, "A Garland with Religious Emblems"; in 1855, "A Crucifix Wound with Flowers."

Kalckreuth, Countess Maria. Medal at Chicago Exposition, 1893. Member of the Society of Women Artists in Berlin. Born at Düsseldorf. 1857-1897. Much of her artistic life was passed in Munich. Her picture at Chicago was later exhibited at Berlin and was purchased for the Protestant Chapel at Dachau. It represented "Christ Raising a Repentant Sinner" – a strong work, broadly painted. Among her important pictures are "In the Sunshine," "Fainthearted," "Discontented," and several portraits, all of which show the various aspects of her artistic talent.

Kauffman, Angelica. An original member of the London Academy. She was essentially an Italian artist, since from the age of eleven she lived in Italy and there studied her art. Such different estimates have been made of her works that one may quote a good authority in either praise or blame of her artistic genius and attainment.

Kugler, a learned, unimpassioned critic, says: "An easy talent for composition, though of no depth; a feeling for pretty forms, though they were often monotonous and empty, and for graceful movement; a coloring blooming and often warm, though occasionally crude; a superficial but agreeable execution, and especially a vapid sentimentality in harmony with the fashion of the time – all these causes sufficiently account for her popularity."

Raphael Mengs, himself an artist, thus esteems her: "As an artist she is the pride of the female sex in all times and all nations. Nothing is wanting – composition, coloring, fancy – all are here."

Miss Kate Thompson writes: "Her works showed no originality nor any great power of execution, and, while sometimes graceful, were generally weak and insipid."

For myself I do not find her worthy of superlative praise or condemnation; one cannot deny her grace in design, which was also creditably correct; her poetical subjects were pleasing in arrangement; her historical subjects lacked strength and variety in expression; her color was as harmonious and mellow as that of the best Italian colorists, always excepting a small number of the greatest masters, and in all her pictures there is a something – it must have been the individuality of the artist – that leads one to entertain a certain fondness for her, even while her shortcomings are fully recognized.

The story of Angelica Kauffman's life is of unusual interest. She was born at Coire, in the Grisons. 1742-1807. Her father, an artist, had gone from Schwarzenburg to Coire to execute some frescoes in a church, and had married there. When Angelica was a year old the family settled in Morbegno, in Lombardy. Ten years later, when the child had already shown her predilection for painting and music, a new home was made for her in Como, where there were better advantages for her instruction.

Her progress in music was phenomenal, and for a time she loved her two arts – one as well as the other – and could make no choice between them. In one of her pictures she represented herself as a child, standing between allegorical figures of Music and Painting.

The exquisite scenery about Como, the stately palaces, charming villas, the lake with its fairy-like pleasure boats, and the romantic life which there surrounded this girl of so impressionable a nature, rapidly developed the poetic element born with her, which later found expression through her varied talents. During her long life the recollections of the two years she passed at Como were among the most precious memories associated with her wandering girlhood.

From Como she was taken to Milan, where she had still better advantages for study, and a world of art was opened to her which far exceeded her most ardent imaginings. Leonardo had lived and taught in Milan, and his influence with that of other Lombard masters stirred Angelica to her very soul.

Her pictures soon attracted the attention of Robert d'Este, who became her patron and placed her in the care of the Duchess of Carrara. This early association with a circle of cultured and elegant men and women was doubtless the origin of the self-possession and modest dignity which characterized Angelica Kauffman through life and enabled her becomingly to accept the honors that were showered upon her.

Her happy life at Milan ended all too soon. Her mother died, and her father decided to return to his native Schwarzenburg to execute some extensive decorative works in that vicinity. In the interior decoration of a church Angelica painted in fresco the figures of the twelve apostles after engravings from the works of Piazetta.

The coarse, homely life of Schwarzenburg was in extreme contrast to that of Milan and was most uncongenial to a sensitive nature; but Angelica was saved from melancholy by the companionship she felt in the grand pine forests, which soothed her discontent, while her work left her little time to pine for the happiness she had left or even to mourn the terrible loss of her mother.

Her father's restlessness returned, and they were again in Milan for a short time, and then in Florence. Here she studied assiduously awhile, but again her father's discontent drove him on, and they went to Rome.

Angelica was now eighteen years old, and in a measure was prepared to profit by the aid and advice of Winckelmann. He conceived an ardent friendship for the young artist, and, though no longer young, and engaged in most important and absorbing research, he found time to interest himself in Angelica's welfare, and allowed her to paint his portrait, to which she gave an expression which proved that she had comprehended the spirit of this remarkable man of threescore years.

While at Rome Angelica received a commission to copy some pictures in Naples. After completing these she returned to Rome, in 1764, and continued her studies for a time, but her interests were again sacrificed to her father's unreasonable capriciousness, and she was taken to Bologna and then to Venice. This constant change was disheartening to Angelica and of the greatest disadvantage to her study, and it was most fortunate that she now met Lady Wentworth, who became her friend and afterward took her to England.

Angelica had already executed commissions for English families of rank whom she had met in various cities of Italy, and her friends hoped that she would be able to earn more money in England than in Italy, where there were numberless artists and copyists. After visiting Paris she went to London, where a brilliant career awaited her, not only as an artist, but in the social world as well.

De Rossi thus describes her at this time: "She was not very tall, but slight, and her figure was well proportioned. She had a dark, clear complexion, a gracious mouth, white and equal teeth, and well-marked features;... above all, her azure eyes, so placid and so bright, charmed you with an expression it is impossible to write; unless you had known her you could not understand how eloquent were her looks."

Her English friends belonged to the most cultivated circles, many of them being also of high rank. Artists united to do her honor – showing no professional envy and making no opposition to her election to the Academy. Many interesting incidents in her association with London artists are related, and it is said that both Fuseli and Sir Joshua Reynolds were unsuccessful suitors for her hand. Miss Thackeray, in her novel, "Miss Angel," makes Angelica an attractive heroine.

The royal family were much interested in her, and the mother of the King visited her – an honor never before accorded to an artist – and the Princess of Brunswick gave her commissions for several pictures.

De Rossi says that her letters at this time were those of a person at the summit of joy and tranquillity. She was able to save money and looked hopefully forward to a time when she could make a home for her unthrifty father. But this happy prosperity was suddenly cut short by her own imprudence.

After refusing many eligible offers of marriage, she was secretly married to an adventurer who personated the Count de Horn, and succeeded by plausible falsehoods in convincing her that it was necessary, for good reasons, to conceal their marriage. One day when painting a portrait of Queen Charlotte, who was very friendly to the artist, Angelica was moved to confide the secret of her marriage to the Queen. Until this time no one save her father had known of it.

Her Majesty, who loved Angelica, expressed her surprise and interest and desired that Count de Horn should appear at Court. By this means the deceit which had been practised was discovered, and the Queen, as gently as possible, told Angelica the truth. At first she felt that though her husband was not the Count de Horn and had grossly deceived her, he was the man she had married and the vows she had made were binding. But it was soon discovered that the villain had a living wife when he made his pretended marriage with Angelica, who was thus released from any consideration for him. This was a time to prove the sincerity of friends, and Angelica was comforted by the steadfastness of those who had devoted themselves to her in her happier days. Sir Joshua Reynolds was untiring in his friendly offices for her and for her helpless old father.

There were as many differing opinions in regard to Angelica Kauffman, the woman, as in regard to the quality of her art. Some of her biographers believed her to be perfectly sincere and uninfluenced by flattery. Nollekens takes another view; he calls her a coquette, and, among other stories, relates that when in Rome, "one evening she took her station in one of the most conspicuous boxes in the theatre, accompanied by two artists, both of whom, as well as many others, were desperately enamoured of her. She had her place between her two adorers, and while her arms were folded before her in front of the box, over which she leaned, she managed to clasp a hand of both, so that each imagined himself the cavalier of her choice."

When Angelica could rise above the unhappiness and mortification of her infatuation for the so-called De Horn, she devoted herself to her art, and during twelve years supported her father and herself and strengthened the friendships she had gained in her adopted land. At length, in 1781, her father's failing health demanded their return to Italy; and now, when forty years old, she married Antonio Zucchi, an artist who had long loved her and devoted himself to her and to her father with untiring affection.

The old Kauffman lived to visit his home in Schwarzenburg and to reach Southern Italy, but died soon after.

Signor Zucchi made his home in Rome. He was a member of the Royal Academy, London, and was in full sympathy with his wife in intellectual and artistic pursuits and pleasures. De Rossi says: "It was interesting to see Angelica and her husband before a picture. While Zucchi spoke with enthusiasm Angelica remained silent, fixing her eloquent glance on the finest portions of the work. In her countenance one could read her emotions, while her observations were limited to a few brief words. These, however, seldom expressed any blame – only the praises of that which was worthy of praise. It belonged to her nature to recognize the beauty alone – as the bee draws honey only out of every flower."

Her home in Rome was a centre of attraction to the artistic and literary society of the city, and few persons of note passed any time there without being presented to her. Goethe and Herder were her friends, and the former wrote: "The good Angelica has a most remarkable, and for a woman really unheard-of, talent; one must see and value what she does and not what she leaves undone. There is much to learn from her, particularly as to work, for what she effects is really marvellous." In his work called "Winckelmann and His Century," Goethe again said of her: "The light and pleasing in form and color, in design and execution, distinguish the numerous works of our artist. *No living painter* excels her in dignity or in the delicate taste with which she handles the pencil."

In the midst of the social demands on her time in Rome, she continued to devote herself to her art, and Signor Zucchi, hoping to beguile her into idleness, purchased a charming villa at Castel Gondolfo; but in spite of its attractions she was never content to be long away from Rome and her studio.

Thus in her maturer years her life flowed on in a full stream of prosperity until, in 1795, Signor Zucchi died. Angelica survived him twelve years – years of deep sadness. Not only was her personal sorrow heavy to bear, but the French invasion of her beloved Italy disquieted her. Hoping to regain her usual spirits, she revisited the scenes of her youth and remained some time in Venice with the family of Signor Zucchi. Returning to Rome she resumed her accustomed work, so far as her health permitted.

She held fast to the German spirit through all the changes in her life, with the same determination which made it possible, in her strenuous labors, to retain her gentle womanliness. Just before she died she desired to hear one of Gellert's spiritual odes.

She was buried in Sant' Andrea dei Frati, beside her husband. All the members of the Academy of St. Luke attended her obsequies, and her latest pictures were borne in the funeral procession. Her bust was placed in the Pantheon, and every proper tribute and honor were paid to her memory in Rome, where she was sincerely mourned.

Although Angelica lived and worked so long in London and was one of the thirty-six original members of the Royal Academy, I do not think her best pictures are in the public galleries there. Of course many of the portraits painted in London are in private collections. Her pictures are seen in all the important galleries of Europe. Her etchings, executed with grace and spirit, are much esteemed and sell for large prices. Engravings after her works by Bartolozzi are most attractive; numerous as they were, good prints of them are now rare and costly.

She painted several portraits of herself; one is in the National Portrait Gallery, London, one at Munich, and a third in the Uffizi, Florence. The last is near that of Madame Le Brun, and the contrast between the two is striking. Angelica is still young, but the expression of her face is so grave as to be almost melancholy; she is sitting on a stone in the midst of a lonely landscape; she has a portfolio in one hand and a pencil in the other, and so unstudied is her pose, and so lacking in any attempt to look her best, that one feels that she is entirely absorbed in her work. The Frenchwoman could not forget to be interesting; Angelica was interesting with no thought of being so.

I regard three works by this artist, which are in the Dresden Gallery, as excellent examples of her work; they are "A Young Vestal," "A Young Sibyl," and "Ariadne Abandoned by Theseus."

On the margin of one of her pictures she wrote: "I will not attempt to express supernatural things by human inspiration, but wait for that till I reach heaven, if there is painting done there."

In 1784 Angelica Kauffman painted "Servius Tullius as a

Child" for the Czar of Russia; in 1786 "Hermann and Thusnelda" and "The Funeral of Pallas" for Joseph II. These are now in the Vienna Gallery. Three pictures, "Virgil Reading the Æneid to the Empress Octavia," "Augustus Reading Verses on the Death of Marcellus," and "Achilles Discovered by Ulysses, in Female Attire," were painted for Catherine II. of Russia. "Religion Surrounded by Virtues," 1798, is in the National Gallery, London. A "Madonna" and a "Scene from the Songs of Ossian" are in the Aschaffenburg Gallery. A "Madonna in Glory" and the "Women of Samaria," 1799, are in the New Pinakothek, Munich, where is also the portrait of Louis I. of Bavaria, as Crown Prince, 1805. The "Farewell of Abelard and Heloise," together with other works of this artist, are in the Hermitage, St. Petersburg. A "Holy Family," and others, in the Museo Civico, Venice. "Prudence Warning Virtue against Folly," in the Pennsylvania Academy, Philadelphia. Portraits of Winckelmann in the Städel Institute, Frankfort, and in the Zürich Gallery. Portrait of a Lady, Stuttgart Museum; the Duchess of Brunswick, Hampton Court Palace; the architect Novosielski, National Gallery, Edinburgh. In addition to the portraits of herself mentioned above, there are others in Berlin Museum, the Old Pinakothek, Munich, the Ferdinandeum, Innsbruck, and in the Philadelphia Academy.

Kaula, Mrs. Lee Lufkin. Member of the Woman's Art Club, New York. Born in Erie, Pennsylvania. Pupil in New York of Charles Melville Dewey and the Metropolitan Art Schools; in Paris, during three years, pupil of Girardot, Courtois, the Colarossi Academy, and of Aman-Jean.

Mrs. Kaula is essentially a portrait painter, although she occasionally paints figure subjects. Her portraits are in private hands in various cities, and her works have been exhibited in Paris, New York, Philadelphia, Chicago, Boston, etc. She paints in both oil and water-colors.

Kayser, Ebba. Medals in Vienna, Dresden, and Cologne for

landscapes and flower pieces. Born in Stockholm, 1846. When twenty years old she went to Vienna, where she studied under Rieser, Geyling, and Karl Hannold. She did not exhibit her works until 1881, since when she has been favorably known, especially in Austria. A water-color of a "Mill near Ischl" and several other pictures by this artist have been purchased for the Imperial Collections.

Keith, Dora Wheeler.
[*No reply to circular.*]

Kemp-Welch, Lucy Elizabeth. Fellow and Associate of Herkomer School, and member of the Royal Society of British Artists. Born at Bournemouth, 1869. Has exhibited annually at the Royal Academy since 1894. In 1897 her picture of "Colt Hunting in the New Forest" was purchased by the trustees of the Chantrey Bequest; in 1900 that of "Horses Bathing in the Sea" was bought for the National Gallery at Victoria. In 1901 she exhibited "Lord Dundonald's Dash on Lady-smith."

In July, 1903, in his article on the Royal Academy Exhibition, the editor of the *Magazine of Art*, in enumerating good pictures, mentions: "Miss Lucy Kemp-Welch's well-studied 'Village Street' at dusk, and her clever 'Incoming Tide,' with its waves and rocks and its dipping, wheeling sea gulls."

Mr. Frederick Wetmore, in writing of the Spring Exhibition of the Royal Painter Etchers, says: "Miss Kemp-Welch, whose best work, so delicate that it could only lose by the reduction of a process block, shows the ordinary English country, the sign-post of the crossways, and the sheep along the lane."

[*No reply to circular.*]

Kendell, Marie von. Born in Lannicken, 1838. Pupil of Pape, Otto von Kameke, and Dressier. She travelled in England, Italy, and Switzerland, and many of her works represent scenes in these countries. In 1882 she painted the Cadinen Peaks near

Schluderbach, in the Ampezzo Valley. At the exhibition of the Women Artists in Berlin, 1892, she exhibited two mountain landscapes and a view of "Clovelly in Devonshire." The last was purchased by the Emperor. To the same exhibition in 1894 she contributed two Swiss landscapes, which were well considered.

Kielland, Kitty. Sister of the famous Norwegian novelist, Alexander Kielland. Her pictures of the forests and fjords of Norway are the best of her works and painted *con amore*. Recently she exhibited a portrait which was much praised and said to be so fresh and life-like in treatment, so flexible and vivacious in color, that one is involuntarily attracted by it, without any knowledge of the original.

Killegrew, Anne. Was a daughter of Dr. Henry Killegrew, a prebendary of Westminster Cathedral. Anne was born in 1660, and when still quite young was maid of honor to the Duchess of York, whose portrait she painted as well as that of the future King James II. She also painted historical subjects and still-life.

One of her admirers wrote of her as "A grace for beauty and a muse for wit." A biographer records her death from smallpox when twenty-five years old, "to the unspeakable reluctancy of her relatives." She was buried in the Savoy Chapel, now a "Royal Peculiar," and a mural tablet set forth her beauty, accomplishments, graces, and piety in a Latin inscription.

Anne Killigrew was notable for her poetry as well as for her painting. Dryden wrote an ode in her memory which Dr. Johnson called "the noblest our language has produced." It begins: "Thou youngest virgin daughter of the skies." After praising her poetry Dryden wrote:

"Her pencil drew whate'er her soul designed,
And oft the happy draught surpassed the image of her mind."

Of her portrait of James II. he says:

"For, not content to express his outward part,
Her hand called out the image of his heart;
His warlike mind – his soul devoid of fear –
His high designing thoughts were figured there."

Having repeated these panegyrics, it is but just to add that two opinions existed concerning the merit of Mistress Killigrew's art and of Dryden's ode, which another critic called "a harmonious hyperbole, composed of the Fall of Adam – Arethusa – Vestal Virgins – Dian – Cupid – Noah's Ark – the Pleiades – the fall of Jehoshaphat – and the last Assizes."

Anthony Wood, however, says: "There is nothing spoken of her which she was not equal to, if not superior, and if there had not been more true history in her praises than compliment, her father never would have suffered them to pass the press."

Kindt, Adele. This painter of history and of genre subjects won her first prize at Ghent when less than twenty-two, and received medals at Douai, Cambrai, Ghent, and Brussels before she was thirty-two. Was made a member of the Brussels, Ghent, and Lisbon Academies. Born in Brussels, 1805. Pupil of Sophie Frémiet and of Navez. Her picture of the "Last Moments of Egmont" is in the Ghent Museum; among her other historical pictures are "Melancthon Predicting Prince Willem's Future" and "Elizabeth Sentencing Mary Stuart," which is in the Hague Museum. The "Obstinate Scholar" and "Happier than a King" are two of her best genre pictures.

King, Jessie M. A most successful illustrator and designer of book-covers, who was educated as an artist in the Glasgow School of Decorative Art. In this school and at that of South Kensington she was considered a failure, by reason of her utterly unacademic manner. She did not see things by rule and she persistently represented them as she saw them. Her love of nature is intense, and when she illustrated the "Jungle Book" she could more easily imagine that the animals could speak a language that Mowgli could understand, than an academic artist could bring himself to fancy for a moment. Her work is full of poetic imagination, of symbolism, and of the spirit of her subject.

Walter P. Watson, in a comprehensive critique of her work, says: "Her imaginations are more perfect and more minutely organized than what is seen by the bodily eye, and she does not permit the outward creation to be a hindrance to the expression of her artistic creed. The force of representation plants her imagined figures before her; she treats them as real, and talks to them as if they were bodily there; puts words in their mouths such as they should have spoken, and is affected by them as by persons. Such creation is poetry in the literal sense of the term, and Miss King's dreamy and poetical nature enables her to create the persons of the drama, to invest them with appropriate figures, faces, costumes, and surroundings; to make them speak after their own characters."

Her important works are in part the illustrations of "The Little Princess," "The Magic Grammar," "La Belle Dame sans Merci," "L'Evangile de l'Enfance," "The Romance of the Swan's Nest," etc.

She also makes exquisite designs for book-covers, which have the spirit of the book for which they are made so clearly indicated that they add to the meaning as well as to the beauty of the book.

[*No reply to circular.*]

Kirchsberg, Ernestine von. Medal at Chicago Exposition, 1893. Born in Verona, 1857. Pupil of Schäffer and Darnaut. This artist has exhibited in Vienna since 1881, and some of her works have been purchased for the royal collection. Her landscapes, both in oil and water-colors, have established her reputation as an excellent artist, and she gains the same happy effects in both mediums. Her picture shown at Chicago was "A Peasant Home in Southern Austria."

Kirschner, Marie. Born at Prague, 1852. Pupil of Adolf Lier in

Munich, and Jules Dupré and Alfred Stevens in Paris. In 1883 she travelled in Italy, and has had her studio in Berlin and in Prague. The Rudolfinum at Prague contains her "Village Tulleschitz in Bohemia." She is also, known by many flower pieces and by the "Storm on the Downs of Heyst," "Spring Morning," and a "Scene on the Moldau."

Kitson, Mrs. H. H. Honorable mention, Paris Exposition, 1889; and the same at Paris Salon, 1890; two medals from Massachusetts Charitable Association; and has exhibited in all the principal exhibitions of the United States. Born in Brookline. Pupil of her husband, Henry H. Kitson, and of Dagnan-Bouveret in Paris.

The women of Michigan commissioned Mrs. Kitson to make two bronze statues representing the woods of their State for the Columbian Exhibition at Chicago. Her principal works are the statue of a volunteer for the Soldiers' Monument at Newburyport; Soldiers' Monument at Ashburnham; Massachusetts State Monument to 29th, 35th, and 36th Massachusetts Volunteer Infantry at National Military Park at Vicksburg; also medallion portraits of Generals Dodge, Ransom, Logan, Blair, Howard, A. J. Smith, Grierson, and McPherson, for the Sherman Monument at Washington.

[*No reply to circular.*]

Klumpke, Anna Elizabeth. Honorable mention, Paris Salon, 1885; silver medal, Versailles, 1886; grand prize, Julian Academy, 1889; Temple gold medal, Pennsylvania Academy of Fine Arts, 1889; bronze medal, Paris Exposition, 1889. Member of the Copley Society, Boston; of the Society of Baron Taylor, Paris; and of the Paris Astronomical Society. Born in San Francisco. Pupil of the Julian Academy, under Robert-Fleury, and Jules Lefebvre, where she received, in 1888, the prize of the silver medal and one hundred francs – the highest award given at the annual Portrait Concours, between the men and women students of the above Academy.

Among Miss Klumpke's principal works are: "In the Wash-house," owned by the Pennsylvania Academy of Fine Arts; portrait of Mrs. Nancy Foster, at the Chicago University; "Maternal Instruction," in the collection of Mr. Randolph Jefferson Coolidge, Boston; many portraits, among which are those of Madame Klumpke, Rosa Bonheur, Mrs. Thorp, Mrs. Sargent, Count Kergaradec, etc.

In writing me of her own life-work and that of her family, she says, what we may well believe: "Longfellow's thought, 'Your purpose in life must be to accomplish well your task,' has been our motto from childhood."

Anna Klumpke, being the eldest of the four daughters of her mother, had a double duty: her own studies and profession and the loving aid and care of her sisters. In the beginning of her art studies it was only when her home duties were discharged that she could hasten to the Luxembourg, where, curiously enough, her time was devoted to copying "Le Labourage Nivernais," by Rosa Bonheur, whose beloved and devoted friend she later became.

Meantime Anna Klumpke had visited Boston and other cities of her native land, and made a success, not only as an artist, but as a woman, whose intelligence, cheerfulness, and broad interests in life made her a delightful companion. Sailing from Antwerp one autumn, I was told by a friend that a lady on board had a letter of introduction to me from Madame Bouguereau. It proved to be Miss Klumpke, and the acquaintance thus begun, as time went on, disclosed to me a remarkable character, founded on a remarkable experience, and it was no surprise to me that the great and good Rosa Bonheur found in Anna Klumpke a sympathetic and reliable friend and companion for her last days.

The history of this friendship and its results are too well known to require more than a passing mention. Miss Klumpke is now established in Paris, and writes me that, in addition to her painting, she is writing of Rosa Bonheur. She says: "This biography consists of reminiscences of Rosa Bonheur's life, her impressions of Nature, God, and Art, with perhaps a short sketch of how I became acquainted with the illustrious woman whose precious maternal tenderness will remain forever the most glorious event of my life."

At the Salon des Artistes Français, 1903, Miss Klumpke exhibited a picture called "Maternal Affection."

Knobloch, Gertrude. Born at Breslau, 1867. Pupil of Skirbina in Berlin. Her studio is in Brussels. She paints in oil and water-colors. Among her best pictures are "In the Children's Shoes," "The Forester's Leisure Hours," and a "Madonna with the Christ Child."

Two of her works in gouache are worthy of mention: "An Effeminate" and "Children Returning from School."

Kollock, Mary. Born at Norfolk, Virginia, 1840. Studied at the Pennsylvania Academy under Robert Wylie, and in New York under J. B. Bristol and A. H. Wynant. Her landscapes have been exhibited at the National Academy, New York. Several of these were scenes about Lake George and the Adirondack regions. "Morning in the Mountains" and "On the Road to Mt. Marcy" were exhibited in 1877; "A November Day" and an "Evening Walk," in 1878; "A House in East Hampton, Two Hundred and Twenty Years Old," in 1880; "On Rondout Creek," in 1881; and "The Brook," in 1882.

Koker, Anna Maria de. A Dutch etcher and engraver of the seventeenth century, who pursued her art from pure love of it, never trying to make her works popular or to sell them. A few of her landscapes fell into the hands of collectors and are much valued for their rarity and excellence. Three examples are the "Landscape with a View of a Village," "The Square Tower," and "Huts by the Water."

Komlosi, Irma. Born in Prague, 1850. Pupil of Friederich

Sturm. This flower painter resides in Vienna, where her pictures are much appreciated and are seen in good collections. They have been purchased for the Art Associations of Brünn, Prague, and Budapest.

Kondelka, Baroness Pauline von – Frau von Schmerling. Born at Vienna. 1806-1840. She inherited from her father a strong inclination for art, and was placed by him under the instruction of Franz Potter. In the Royal Gallery, Vienna, is her picture called "Silence," 1834. It represents the Virgin with her finger on her lip to warn against disturbing the sleep of the Infant Jesus. The picture is surrounded by a beautiful arrangement of flowers. In 1836 she painted a charming picture called "A Bunch of Flowers." Her favorite subjects were floral, and her works of this sort are much admired.

Konek, Ida. Born at Budapest, 1856. Her early art studies were under G. Vastagh, C. von Telepy, W. Lindenschmit, and Munkácsy; later she was a pupil at the Julian Academy in Paris and the Scuola libera in Florence. In the Parish Church at Köbölkut are three of her pictures of sacred subjects, and in the Hungarian National Museum a picture of still-life. Her "Old Woman," 1885, is mentioned as attracting favorable notice.

Kora or Callirhoë. It is a well-authenticated fact that in the Greek city of Sicyonia, about the middle of the seventh century before Christ, there lived the first woman artist of whom we have a reliable account.

Her story has been often told, and runs in this wise: Kora, or Callirhoë, was much admired by the young men of Sicyonia for her grace and beauty, of which they caught but fleeting glimpses through her veil when they met her in the flower-market. By reason of Kora's attraction the studio of her father, Dibutades, was frequented by many young Greeks, who watched for a sight of his daughter, while they praised his models in clay.

At length one of these youths begged the modeller to receive him as an apprentice, and, his request being granted, he became the daily companion of both Kora and her father. As the apprentice was skilled in letters, it soon came about that he was the teacher and ere long the lover of the charming maiden, who was duly betrothed to him.

The time for the apprentice to leave his master came all too soon. As he sat with Kora the evening before his departure, she was seized by an ardent wish for a portrait of her lover, and, with a coal from the brazier, she traced upon the wall the outline of the face so dear to her. This likeness her father instantly recognized, and, hastening to bring his clay, he filled in the sketch and thus produced the first portrait in bas-relief! It is a charming thought that from the inspiration of a pure affection so beautiful an art originated, and doubtless Kora's influence contributed much to the artistic fame which her husband later achieved in Corinth.

In the latter city the portrait was preserved two hundred years, and Dibutades became so famous for the excellence of his work that at his death several cities claimed the honor of having been his birthplace.

Krafft, Anna Barbara. Member of the Vienna Academy. She was born at Igto in 1764, and died at Bamberg in 1825. She received instruction from her father, J. N. Steiner, of which she later made good use. Having married an apothecary, she went for a time to Salsburg, and again, after nine years in Prague, spent eighteen years in Salsburg, retiring finally to Bamberg. In the Gallery at Bamberg may be seen her portrait of the founder, J. Hemmerlein; in the Nostitz Gallery, Prague, a portrait of the Archduke Charles; in Strahow Abbey, Prague, a "Madonna"; and in the church at Owencez, near Prague, an altar-piece.

Kuntze, Martha. Born in Heinrichsdorf, Prussia, 1849. Pupil of Steffeck and Gussow in Berlin. In 1881 she went to Paris and studied under Carolus Duran and Henner, and later travelled in

Italy, pursuing her art in Florence, Rome, and Southern Italy. She has an excellent reputation as a portrait painter, and occasionally paints subjects of still-life.

Küssner, Amalia. See Coudert, Amalia Küssner.

Labille, Adelaide Vertus. Was born in Paris in 1749. She early developed a taste for art and a desire to study it. J. E. Vincent was her master in miniature painting, while Latour instructed her in the use of pastels. She was successful as a portrait painter and as a teacher, having some members of the royal family as pupils, who so esteemed her that they became her friends. She is known as Madame Vincent, having married the son of her first master in painting.

Her portrait of the sculptor Gois gained a prize at the Academy, and in 1781 she was made a member of that institution. We know the subjects of some large, ambitious works by Madame Vincent, on which she relied for her future fame, but unhappily they were destroyed in the time of the French Revolution, and she never again had the courage to attempt to replace them. One of these represented the "Reception of a Member to the Order of St. Lazare," the Grand Master being the brother of the King, who had appointed Madame Vincent Painter to the Court. Another of these works was a portrait of the artist before her easel, surrounded by her pupils, among whom was the Duchesse d'Angoulême and other noble ladies.

As Madame Vincent and her husband were staunch royalists, they suffered serious losses during the Revolution; the loss of her pictures was irreparable. She was so disheartened by the destruction of the result of the labors of years that she never again took up her brush with her old-time ambition and devotion.

She died in 1803, at the age of fifty-four, having received many honors as an artist, while she was beloved by her friends and esteemed by all as a woman of noble character.

Laing, Mrs. J. G. Principal studies made in Glasgow under Mr. F. H. Newbery; also in Paris under Jean-Paul Laurens and Aman-Jean.

This artist is especially occupied with portraits of children and their mothers. She has, however, exhibited works of another sort. Her "Sweet Repose" and "Masquerading" were sold from the exhibitions in London and Glasgow, where they were shown. "Bruges Lace-Makers" was exhibited in Munich in 1903.

The Ladies' Club of Glasgow is enterprising and its exhibitions are interesting, but Mrs. Laing is not a member of any club, and sends her pictures by invitation to exhibitions on the Continent as well as in Great Britain, and sometimes has a private exhibition in Glasgow.

Her study at Aman-Jean's and Colarossi's gave a certain daintiness and grace to her work, which is more Parisian than British in style. There is great freedom in her brush and a delicacy well suited to the painting of children's portraits; her children and their mothers really smile, not grin, and are altogether attractive. I cannot say whether the portraits I have seen are good likenesses, but they have an air of individuality which favors that idea.

Lamb, Ella Condie – Mrs. Charles R. Lamb. Dodge prize, National Academy, New York; medal at Columbian Exposition, Chicago, 1893; gold medal, Atlanta Exposition; medal at Pan-American Exposition, 1901. Member of Art Students' League, Woman's Art Club, National Art Club. Born in New York City. Pupil of National Academy of Design and of Art Students' League, New York, under C. Y. Turner, William M. Chase, and Walter Shirlaw; in Paris, pupil of R. Collin and R. Courtois; in England, of Hubert Herkomer, R.A.

Among Mrs. Lamb's works are "The Advent Angel"; "The Christ Child," a life-size painting, copied in mosaic for the Conrad memorial, St. Mary's Church, Wayne, Pennsylvania; "The Arts" and "The Sciences," executed in association with Charles R. Lamb, for the Sage Memorial Apse designed by him for Cornell University.

Of recent years Mrs. Lamb is much occupied in collaborating with her husband in decorative designs for public edifices. One of the works thus executed is a memorial window to Mrs. Stella Goodrich Russell in Wells College at Aurora. It represents three female figures against a landscape background. Literature is seated in the centre, while Science and Art stand in the side panels. It has the effect of a triptych.

Lamb, Rose. Two bronze medals in Boston exhibitions, 1878 and 1879. Member of the Copley Society. Born in Boston, where her studies have been made, chiefly under William M. Hunt.

Miss Lamb has painted portraits principally, a large number of which are in Boston in the homes of the families to which they belong. Among them are Mrs. Robert C. Winthrop, Jr., and her children; Mr. J. Ingersoll Bowditch, Mr. Horace Lamb, the three sons of the late Governor Roger Wolcott, the daughters of Mrs. Shepherd Brooks, the children of Mrs. Walter C. Baylies, etc.

In 1887 Miss Lamb painted an admirable portrait of Mohini Mohun Chatterji, a Brahmin, who spent some months in Boston.

Lanciani, Marcella. Born in Rome, where her studies were made under Professor Giuseppe Ferrari in figure drawing, and under Signor Onorato Carlandi – the great water-color artist of the Roman Campagna – in landscape and coloring.

At the annual spring exhibition in the Palazzo delle Belle Arti, Rome, 1903, this artist exhibited four works: a life-size "Study of the Head of an old Roman Peasant"; a "Sketch near the Mouth of the Tiber at Finniscino"; "An Old Stairway in the Villa d'Este, at Tivoli"; "A View from the Villa Colonna, Rome."

Two of her sketches, one of the "Tiber" and one of the "Villa Medici," are in the collection of Mrs. Pierpont Morgan; two similar sketches are in the collection of Mrs. James Leavitt, New York; a copy of a "Madonna" in an old Umbrian church is in a private gallery in Rome; a "Winter Scene in the Villa Borghese" and two other sketches are owned in Edinburgh; the "Lake in the Villa Borghese" is in the collection of Mr. Richard Corbin, Paris; and several other pictures are in private collections in New York.

Lander, Louisa. Born in Salem, 1826. Manifested a taste for sculpture when quite young, and modelled likenesses of the members of her family. In 1855 she became the pupil of Thomas Crawford in Rome. Among her earlier works are figures in marble of "To-day" and "Galatea," the first being emblematic of America.

She executed many portrait busts, one of them being of Nathaniel Hawthorne. "The Captive Pioneer" is a large group. Among her ideal works are a statue of Virginia Dare – the first child born in America of English parents; "Undine," "Evangeline," "Virginia," etc.

Laukota, Herminie. Born in Prague, 1853. After having studied in Prague, Amsterdam, and Munich, she was a pupil of Doris Raab in etching. She paints portraits, genre and still-life subjects with artistic taste and delicacy. Her studio is in Prague. Among her best pictures are "Battle for Truth," "Sentinels of Peace," "A Contented Old Woman"; and among her etchings may be named "The Veiled Picture of Saïs," "Prometheus," "The Microscopist," "Before the Bar of Reason," etc. The latter was reproduced in *Zeitschrift für bildende Kunst* in 1893, and was said to show a powerful fancy.

In 1875 and 1876 she exhibited her etchings in Vienna. The "Going to Baptism" in the second exhibition was much admired and aroused unusual interest.

La Villette, Mme. Elodie. Third-class medal, Paris Salon, 1875; bronze medal, Paris Exposition, 1889; second-class medal, Melbourne Exposition; numerous diplomas and medals from provincial exhibitions in France; also from Vienna, Brussels,

Antwerp, Amsterdam, London, Copenhagen, Barcelona, Munich, and Chicago. Officer of the Academy. Born at Strasbourg. Educated at Lorient. She began to study drawing and painting under Coroller, a professor in the school she attended. She then studied six months in the Atelier School at Strasbourg, and finally became a pupil of Dubois at Arras. She has exhibited since 1870.

Her picture of the "Strand at Lohic," 1876, is in the Luxembourg Gallery; the "Cliffs of Yport" is in the Museum of Lille; "A Calm at Villers," in the Museum at Lorient; "Coming Tide at Kervillaine," in the museum of Morlaix, etc. Her marine views are numerous and are much admired.

At the Salon of the Artistes Français, 1902, Mme. La Villette exhibited "Twilight, Quiberon, Morbihan"; in 1903, "Fort Penthièvre, Quiberon," and "A Foaming Wave."

Le Brun, Mme. See Vigée.

Lehmann, Charlotte. Born in Vienna, 1860. Daughter of an artist, Katharine Lehmann. Pupil of Schilcher and Pitner. Her works are principally portraits and studies of heads, in which she is successful. Her "Styrian Maiden" belongs to the Austrian Emperor, and is in Gödöllö castle.

Her portraits are seen at many exhibitions, and art critics mention her with respect.

[*No reply to circular.*]

Lemaire, Mme. Jeanne-Madeleine. Honorable mention, 1877; silver medal, Paris Exposition, 1900. Born at Sainte Rosseline. Pupil of an aunt, who was a miniaturist, and later of Chaplin. She first exhibited at the Salon of 1864, a "Portrait of Madame, the Baroness." She has painted many portraits, and is extremely successful in her pictures of flowers and fruit.

Among her principal works are "Diana and Her Dog," "Going out of Church," "Ophelia," "Sleep," "The Fall of the Leaves," and "Manon."

She has also painted many pictures in water-colors. Since 1890 she has exhibited at the Champ-de-Mars. Her illustrations in water-colors for "L'Abbé Constantin" and for an edition of "Flirt" are very attractive.

Her "Roses" at the Salon of 1903 were especially fine, so fresh and brilliant that they seemed to be actual blossoms.

This artist, not many months ago, called to mind the celebrated Greek supper of Mme. Lebrun, which was so famous in the time of that artist. The following is an account of the entertainment given by Mme. Lemaire:

"A most fascinating banquet was given in Paris quite recently by Madeleine Lemaire, in her studio, and Parisians pronounce it the most artistic fete that has occurred for many a moon. Athens was reconstructed for a night. A Greek feast, gathering at the same board the most aristocratic moderns, garbed in the antique peplum, as the caprice of a great artist. The invitation cards, on which the hostess had drawn the graceful figure of an Athenian beauty, were worded: 'A Soirée in Athens in the Time of Pericles. Madeleine Lemaire begs you to honor with your presence the Greek fête which she will give in her humble abode on Tuesday. Banquet, dances, games, and cavalcade. Ancient Greek costume de rigueur.' Every one invited responded yes, and from the Duchess d'Uzès, in a superb robe of cloth of gold and long veil surmounted by a circlet of diamonds, to that classic beauty Mme. Barrachin, in white draperies with a crown of pink laurel, the costumes were beautiful. One graceful woman went as Tanagra. The men were some of them splendid in the garb of old Greek warriors, wearing cuirass and helmet of gold. At dessert a bevy of pretty girls in classic costume distributed flowers and fruits to the guests, while Greek choruses sung by female choristers alternated with verses admirably recited by Bartel and Reichenberg. After the banquet Emma Calvé and Mme. Litoinne sang passages from 'Philémon et Bacus,' and then there were Greek dances executed by the leading dancers of the Opera. After supper and much gayety, the evening came to a close by an animated farandole danced by all present. It takes an artist like Madeleine Lemaire to design and execute such a fete, and beside it how commonplace appear the costly functions given by society in Newport and New York."

[*No reply to circular.*]

Levick, Ruby Winifred. At the South Kensington Royal College of Art this artist gained the prize for figure design; the medal for a study of a head from life, besides medals and other awards in the National Competition; British Institution scholarship for modelling, 1896; gold medal and the Princess of Wales scholarship, 1897; gold medal in national competition, 1898. Member of the Ridley Art Club. Born in Llandaff, Glamorganshire.

This sculptor has exhibited regularly at the Royal Academy since 1898. Among her works are "Boys Wrestling," group in the round; "Study of a Boy," a statuette; "Fishermen Hauling in a Net," "Boys Fishing," "The Hammer Thrower," "Rugby Football," and the "Sea Urchin," a statuette.

Miss Levick has executed a panel for the reredos in St. Brelade's Church, Jersey; and another for St. Gabriel's Church, Poplar. She exhibited at the Academy, 1903, "Sledgehammers: Portion of a Frieze in Relief."

Lewis, Edmonia. Born in the State of New York. This artist descended from both Indian and African ancestors. She had comparatively no instruction, when, in 1865, she exhibited in Boston a portrait bust of Colonel Shaw, which at once attracted much attention. In 1867 she exhibited a statue called the "Freedwoman." Soon after this she took up her residence in Rome and very few of her works were seen in the United States. She sent to the Philadelphia exhibition, in 1876, the "Death of Cleopatra," in marble. The Marquis of Bute bought her "Madonna with the Infant Christ," an altar-piece. Her "Marriage of Hiawatha" was purchased by a New York lady.

Among her other works are "An Old Arrow-Maker and His Daughter," "Asleep," and terra-cotta busts of Charles Sumner, Longfellow, John Brown, and others.

"Among Miss Lewis's works are two small groups illustrating Longfellow's poem of Hiawatha. Her first, 'Hiawatha's Wooing,' represents Minnehaha seated, making a pair of moccasins, and Hiawatha by her side with a world of love and longing in his eyes. In the 'Marriage' they stand side by side with clasped hands. In both the Indian type of feature is carefully preserved, and every detail of dress, etc., is true to nature. The sentiment equals the execution. They are charming bits, poetic, simple, and natural, and no happier illustrations of Longfellow's most original poem were ever made than these by the Indian sculptor." – *Revolution*, April, 1871.

"This was not a beautiful work – 'Cleopatra' – but it was very original and very striking, and it merits particular comment, as its ideal was so radically different from those adopted by Story and Gould in their statues of the Egyptian Queen... The effects of death are represented with such skill as to be absolutely repellent. Apart from all questions of taste, however, the striking qualities of the work are undeniable, and it could only have been produced by a sculptor of very genuine endowments." – *Great American Sculptors*.

Ley, Sophie. Third-class medal at Melbourne; honor diplomas, Karlsruhe. Member of the Künstlerbund, Karlsruhe. Born at Bodman am Bodensee, 1859. Pupil of the Art School in Stuttgart, where she received several prizes; and of Gude and Bracht in Karlsruhe.

Some flower pieces by this artist are in the collection of the Grand Duke of Baden; others belong to the Hereditary Grand Duke and to the Queen of Saxony; still others are in various private galleries.

A recently published design for the wall decoration of a school, "Fingerhut im Walde," was awarded a prize. Fräulein Ley receives young women students in her atelier in Karlsruhe.

Licata-Faccioli, Orsola. A first-class and several other medals as a student of the Academy at Venice. Member of the Academies of Venice and Perugia, 1864. Born in Venice, 1826. In 1848 she married and made a journey with her husband through Italy. Three pictures which she exhibited at Perugia, in 1864, won her election to the Academy; the Marquis Ala-Ponzoni purchased these. The Gallery at Vicenza has several of her views of Venice and Rome, and there are others in the municipal palace at Naples. Her pictures have usually sold immediately upon their exhibition, and are scattered through many European cities. At Hamburg is a view of Capodimonte; at Venice a large picture showing a view of San Marcellino; and at Capodimonte the "Choir of the Capuchins at Rome." Private collectors have also bought many of her landscapes. Since 1867 she has taught drawing in the Royal Institute at Naples. Two of the Signora's later pictures are "Arum Italicum," exhibited at Milan in 1881, and a "Park at Capodimonte," shown at the International Exposition in Rome – the latter is a brilliant piece of work. Her style is vigorous and robust, and her touch sure. Family cares seem never to have interrupted her art activity, for her work has been constant and of an especially high order.

Lindegren, Amalia. Member of the Academy of Stockholm. Honorary member of the London Society of Women Artists. Born in Stockholm. 1814-1891. A student in the above-named Academy, she was later a pupil of Cogniet and Tissier, in Paris, and afterward visited Rome and Munich. Her pictures are portraits and genre subjects. In the Gallery at Christiania are her "Mother and Child" and "Grandfather and Granddaughter." "The Dance in a Peasant Cottage" is in the Museum of Stockholm, where are also her portraits of Queen Louise and the Crown Princess of Denmark, 1873.

"With her unpretentious representations of the joy of children, the smiling happiness of parents, sorrow resigned, and childish stubbornness, Amalia Lindegren attained great national popularity, for without being a connoisseur it is possible to take pleasure in the fresh children's faces in her pictures." – *History of Modern Painters.*

Lippincott, Margarette. Honorable mention and Mary Smith Prize at Pennsylvania Academy of Fine Arts. Member of Philadelphia Water-Color Club and Plastic Club. New York Water-Color Club. Born in Philadelphia. Pupil of Pennsylvania Academy of Fine Arts and Art Students' League, New York.

This artist has painted flowers especially, but of late has taken up genre subjects and landscapes. Among her pictures is one of "Roses," in the Academy of Fine Arts, and "White Roses," in the Art Club of Philadelphia. "Sunset in the Hills" is in a private collection, and "The West Window" is owned in Detroit.

Liszewska, Anna Dorothea. Married name was Therbusch. Member of the Academies of Paris and Vienna and of the Institute of Bologna. Born in Berlin. 1722-1782. Was court painter at Stuttgart, and later held the same office under Frederick the Great, whose portrait she painted, 1772. Her picture of "Diana's Return from the Chase" was also painted for Frederick. Her early studies were conducted by her father. After leaving the court of Stuttgart she studied four years in Paris. In the Louvre is her picture of "A Man Holding a Glass of Water"; in the Brunswick Gallery is her portrait of herself; and several of her works are in the Schwerin Gallery. Her pictures of "A Repentant Maiden," 1781, and of "Ariadne at Naxos" attracted much attention.

Liszewska, Anna Rosina. Member of the Dresden Academy. Born in Berlin. 1716-1783. Pupil of her father. She executed forty portraits of women for the "Hall of Beauty" at Zerbst. One of her portraits, painted in 1770, is in the Gallery at Brunswick. She travelled in Holland in 1766, but was too much occupied with commissions to find time for foreign journeys. She painted a picture called "Artemisia" and a second of "Monime Pulling Down Her Diadem," which were interesting and excellent examples of her style of painting.

Locatelli, or Lucatelli, Maria Caterina. Of Bologna. Died in 1723. She studied under Pasinelli, and in the Church of St. Columba in Bologna are two pictures by her – a "St. Anthony" and a "St. Theresa."

Loewenthal, Baroness Anka. Born at Ogulin, Croatia, 1853. Pupil of Karl von Blaas and Julius von Payer. Some portraits by this artist are in the Academy of Arts and Sciences at Agram. But religious subjects were most frequently treated by her, and a number of these are in the Croatian churches. The "Madonna Immaculata" is in the Gymnasial Kirche, Meran, and a "Mater Dolorosa" in the Klosterkirche, Bruck a. d. Meer.

Longhi, Barbara. Born in Ravenna. 1552-1619(?). Daughter of Luca Longhi. She was an excellent artist and her works were sought for good collections. A portrait by her is in the Castellani Collection, dated 1589; "St. Monica," "Judith," and the "Healing of St. Agatha" are in the Ravenna Academy; a "Virgin and Child" is in the Louvre, and "Mary with the Children" in the Dresden Gallery.

Longman, E. B. This sculptor has a commission to execute a statue of Victory for a dome at the St. Louis Exposition.
[*No reply to circular.*]

Loop, Mrs. Henry A. Elected an associate of the National Academy of Design in 1875. Born in New Haven, 1840. Pupil of Professor Louis Bail in New Haven, of Henry A. Loop in New York, later spending two years in study in Paris, Venice, and Rome.

Mrs. Loop is essentially a portrait painter, but occasionally has painted figure pictures, such as "Baby Belle," "A Little Runaway," "A Bouquet for Mama," etc. Her portraits of Professors Low and Hadley of New Haven were much admired; those of Mrs. Joseph Lee, Miss Alexander, and other ladies were exhibited at the Academy.

"Mrs. Loop's picture is an honest, unpretending work, well drawn, naturally posed, and clearly, solidly colored. There is not a trace of affectation about it. The artistic effects are produced in the most straightforward way." – *Clarence Cook, in New York Tribune.*

"Mrs. Loop is certainly the leading portrait painter among our lady artists. She is vigorous, conscientious, and perceptive." – *Chicago Times*, 1875.

Lotz, Matilda. Gold medal at School of Design, California. Born in Franklin, Tennessee. This artist is sometimes called "the Rosa Bonheur of America." She began to draw pictures of animals when seven years old. Later she studied under Virgil Williams in San Francisco and under M. Barrios and Van Marcke in Paris.

She has travelled extensively in the East, painting camels, dromedaries, etc. Her work has a vigor and breadth well suited to her subjects, while she gives such attention to details as make her pictures true to life. One critic writes: "Her oxen and camels, like Rosa Bonheur's horses, stand out from canvas as living things. They have been the admiration of art lovers at the Salon in Paris, the Royal Academy in London, and at picture exhibitions in Austria-Hungary and Germany."

Among her works are "Oxen at Rest," "The Artist's Friends," "Hounds in the Woods," painted in California. "Mourning for Their Master," "The Sick Donkey," and other less important pictures are in private collections in Hungary. "The Early Breakfast" is in a gallery in Washington, D. C. She has painted portraits of famous horses owned by the Duke of Portland, which are in England, as is her picture called "By the Fireside."

Loud, May Hallowell. Member of the Copley Society and Boston Water-Color Club. Born in West Medford, Massachusetts, 1860. Pupil of the School of Museum of Fine Arts, Boston; Julian Academy, Paris; Cowles Art School, Boston. In Paris, under Tony Robert-Fleury, Giacomotti, and Louis Deschamps. Later under Abbott Thayer and Denman W. Ross.

Mrs. Loud's works are principally portraits, and are in private hands. Her picture called "The Singer" was purchased by the Atlanta Exposition, and is in a collection in that city. She works mostly in oils, but has been successful in portraits in pastel; two admirable examples were exhibited in Boston recently, and were favorably noticed for their color and "temperance in the use of high relief."

Louise, Princess. See Argyll.

Lusk, Marie K.
[*No reply to circular.*]

Lutmer, Emmy. Medal at Munich, 1888. Born at Elberfeld, 1859. Pupil of the School of Art Industries at Munich and of the Museums of Berlin and Vienna. This skilled enamel painter has her studio in Berlin, where she executes fine and beautiful work.

MacChesney, Clara Taggart. Two medals at Chicago Exposition, 1893; Dodge prize, National Academy, New York, 1894; gold medal, Philadelphia Art Club, 1900; Hallgarten prize, National Academy, 1901; bronze medal, Buffalo Exposition, 1901. Three medals at Colarossi School, Paris. Member of National Art Club, Barnard Club, and Water-Color Club, all of New York. Born in Brownsville, California. Pupil of Virgil Williams in San Francisco Art School; of H. C. Mowbray, J. C. Beckwith, and William Chase in Gotham Art School; and of G. Courtois, A. Girardot, and R. X. Prinet in Colarossi School, Paris. Exhibited at

Paris Salon, Beaux Arts, in 1896, 1898, and at the Exposition in 1900.

This artist paints figure subjects. Among these are "Retrospection," Boston Art Club; "Tired," Erie Art Club; "A Good Story," National Arts Club, New York; "The Old Cobbler," etc.

Her prize picture at the National Academy, New York, 1894, was called "The Old Spinner." This picture had been refused by the committee of the Society of American Artists, only to be thought worthy a prize at the older institution.

Macgregor, Jessie. The gold medal in the Royal Academy Schools for historical painting, a medal given biennially, and but one other woman has received it. Born in Liverpool. Pupil of the Schools of the Royal Academy; her principal teachers were the late Lord Leighton, the late P. H. Calderon, R.A., and John Pettie, R.A.

Her principal works are "In the Reign of Terror" and "Jephthah's Vow," both in the Liverpool Permanent Collection; "The Mistletoe Bough"; "Arrested, or the Nihilist"; "Flight," exhibited at Royal Academy in 1901; "King Edward VII.," 1902.

Miss Macgregor is a lecturer on art in the Victoria University Extension Lecture Scheme, and has lectured on Italian painting and on the National Gallery in many places.

At the London Academy in 1903 she exhibited "The Nun," "If a Woman Has Long Hair, it is a Glory to Her," I Cor. xi. 15; "Behind the Curtain," "Christmas in a Children's Hospital," and "Little Bo-peep."

Mackubin, Florence. Bronze medal and diploma, Tennessee Exposition, 1897. Vice-president of Baltimore Water-Color Club. Born in Florence, Italy. Studied in Fontainebleau under M. Lainé, in Munich under Professor Herterich, and in Paris under Louis Deschamps and Julius Rolshoven; also with Mlle. J. Devina in miniature painting.

Miss Mackubin has exhibited at the Paris Salon, the London Academy, and the National Academy, New York. Her works are portraits in miniature, pastel, and oil colors.

She was appointed by the Board of Public Works of Maryland to copy the portrait of Queen Henrietta Maria, for whom Maryland was named. The portrait is by Vandyck and in Warwick Castle. Miss Mackubin's copy is in the State House at Annapolis.

Her portraits are numerous. Among them are those of Mrs. Charles J. Bonaparte, Justice Horace Gray, Hon. George F. Hoar, Mrs. Thomas F. Bayard, and many others. In England she painted portraits of the Countess of Warwick, the Marchioness of Bath, and several other ladies.

Miss Mackubin's portrait of Cardinal Gibbons, exhibited in Baltimore in 1903, is much praised. He is sitting in an armchair near a table on which are books. The pose of the figure is natural, the drawing excellent, the flesh tints well handled, and the likeness satisfactory to an unusual degree. The accessories are justly rendered and the values well preserved – the texture of the stuffs, the ring on the hand, the hand delicate and characteristic; in short, this is an excellent example of dignified portraiture.

MacMonnies, Mary Fairchild. Awarded a scholarship in Paris by the St. Louis School of Fine Arts; medal at Chicago, 1893; bronze medal at Paris Exposition, 1900; bronze medal at Buffalo, 1901; gold medal at Dresden, 1902; Julia M. Shaw prize, Society of American Artists, New York, 1902. Associate member of Société Nationale des Beaux-Arts, Paris; member of the Society of American Artists, New York. Born at New Haven, Connecticut, about 1860.

Pupil of School of Fine Arts, St. Louis, Academy Julian, Paris, and of Carolus Duran.

Exhibited at Salon des Beaux-Arts, 1902, "The October Sun," "The Last Rays," and "The Rain"; in 1903, "A Snow Scene."

[*No reply to circular.*]

Macomber, Mary L. Bronze medal, Massachusetts Charitable Mechanics' Association, 1895; bronze medal, Cotton State and International Exposition, 1895; Dodge prize, National Academy, New York, 1897; honorable mention, Carnegie Institute, 1901. Member of the Copley Society, Boston. Born in Fall River, Massachusetts, 1861. Pupil of Robert Dunning, School of Boston Art Museum under Otto Grundmann and F. Crowninshield, and of Frank Duveneck.

This artist paints figure subjects. Her "Saint Catherine" is in the Boston Museum of Fine Arts; "Spring Opening the Gate to Love" was in the collection of the late Mrs. S. D. Warren; "The Annunciation" is in the collection of Mrs. D. P. Kimball, Boston. Other works of hers are a triptych, the "Magdalene," "Death and the Captive," "The Virgin of the Book," etc.

"One feels, on looking at the Madonnas, Annunciation, or any of Miss Macomber's pictures,... that she must have lived with and in her subject. Delicate coloring harmonizes with refined, spiritual conceptions... Her most generally liked picture is her 'Madonna.' All the figures wear a sweet, solemn sadness, illumined by immortal faith and love." – *Art Interchange,* April, 1899.

Magliani, Francesca. Born at Palermo in 1845, and studied painting there under a private teacher. Going later to Florence she was a pupil of Bedussi and of Gordigiani. Her early work consisted of copies from the Italian and other masters, and these were so well done that she soon began to receive orders, especially for portraits, from well-known people. Among them were G. Baccelli – the Minister of Public Instruction – King Humbert, and Queen Margherita, the latter arousing much interest when exhibited in Florence. Portraits of her mother, and of her husband, who was the Minister of Finance, were also recognized as admirable examples of portraiture. "Modesty and Vanity" is one of her genre pictures.

Mangilla, Ada. Gold medal at Ferrara for a "Bacchante," which is now in the Gallery there; gold medal at Beatrice, in Florence, 1890, for the "Three Marys." Born in Florence in 1863. Pupil of Cassioli. One of her early works was a design for two mosaic figures in the left door of the Cathedral in Florence, representing Bonifazio Lupi and Piero di Luca Borsi; this was exhibited in 1879, and was received with favor by the public.

This artist has had much success with Pompeian subjects, such as "A Pompeian Lady at Her Toilet," and "A Pompeian Flower-Seller." She catches with great accuracy the characteristics of the Pompeian type; and this facility, added to the brilliancy of her color and the spirit and sympathy of her treatment, has given these pictures a vogue. Two of them were sold in Holland. "Floralia" was sold in Venice. To an exhibition of Italian artists in London, in 1889, she contributed "The Young Agrippa," which was sold to Thomas Walker. Her grace and fancy appear in the drawings which she finds time to make for "Florentia," and in such pictures as "The Rose Harvest."

This highly accomplished woman, who has musical and literary talent, is the wife of Count Francessetti di Mersenile.

Mankiewicz, Henriette. Chevalier of the Legion of Honor. A series of her mural decorations was exhibited in various German cities, and finally shown at the Paris Exposition of 1890(?), where they excited such applause that the above honor was accorded her. These decorations are in the form of panels, in which water, in its varying natural aspects, supplies the subordinate features, while the fundamental motive is vegetation of every description. The artist has evidently felt the influence of Markart in Vienna, and some of her conceptions remind one of H. von Preusschen. Her technique is a combination of embroidery, painting, and applications on silk. Whether this combination of methods is desirable is another question, but as a means of decoration it is highly effective.

At an exhibition of paintings by women of Saxony, held in

Dresden under the patronage of Queen Carola in the fall of 1892, this artist exhibited another decorative panel, done in the same manner, which seems to have been a great disappointment to those who had heard wonderful accounts of the earlier cycle of panels. It was too full of large-leaved flowers, and the latter were too brilliant to serve as a foreground to the Alhambra scenes, which were used as the chief motive.

Manly, Alice Elfrida. A national gold medal and the Queen's gold medal, at the Royal Female School of Art, London. Member of the Dudley Gallery Art Society and the Hampstead Art Society. Born in London. Pupil of the above-mentioned School and of the Royal Academy Schools.

This artist has exhibited at the Academy, at the Royal Institute of Painters in Water Colors, and other exhibitions. Her pictures have frequently been sold from the exhibitions and reproduced. Among these are "Sympathy," sold as first prize in Derby Art Union; "Diverse Attractions"; "Interesting Discoveries"; "Coming," sold from the Royal Academy; "Gossips"; "The Wedding Gown," etc.

Miss Manly has done much work for publishers, which has been reproduced in colors and in black and white. She usually combines figures and landscape.

Mantovani, Signora S. Rome.
[*No reply to circular.*]

Maraini, Adelaide. Gold medal in Florence, at Beatrice Exposition, 1903. Born in 1843. This sculptor resides in Rome, where her works have been made. An early example of her art, "Camilla," while it gave proof of her artistic temperament, was unimportant; but her later works, as they have followed each other, have constantly gained in excellence, and have won her an enviable reputation. Among her statues are "Amleto," "The Sulamite Woman," and "Sappho." The last was enthusiastically received in Paris in 1878, and is the work which gained the prize at Florence, where it was said to be the gem of the exhibition. She has also executed a monument to Attilio Lemmi, which represents "Youth Weeping over the Tomb of the Dead," and is in the Protestant Cemetery at Florence; a bas-relief, the "Angels of Prayer and of the Resurrection"; a group, "Romeo and Juliet"; and portraits of Carlo Cattanei, Giuseppe Civinini, Signora Allievi, Senator Musio, the traveller De Albertis, and Victor Emmanuel.

Marcelle, Adèle, Duchess of Castiglione-Colonna, family name d'Affry. Born at Fribourg, Switzerland, 1837, and died at Castellamare, 1879. Her early manner was that of the later Cinquecento, but she afterward adopted a rather bombastic and theatrical style. Her only statue, a Pythia, in bronze was placed in the Grand Opera at Paris (1870). In the Luxembourg Museum are marble busts of Bianca Capello (1863) and an "Abyssinian Sheikh" (1870). A "Gorgon" (1865), a "Saviour" (1875), "La Bella Romana" (1875) are among her other works. She left her art treasures, valued at about fifty thousand francs, to the Cantonal Museum at Fribourg, where they occupy a separate room, called the Marcello Museum.

Marcovigi, Clementina. Born in Bologna, where she resides. Flower pieces exhibited by her at Turin in 1884 and at Venice in 1887 were commended for perfection of design and charm of color.

Maria Feodorovna, wife of the Czar Peter I. As Princess Dorothea Auguste Sophie of Würtemberg she was born at Trepton in 1759, and died at Petersburg in 1858. She studied under Leberecht, and engraved medals and cameos, many of which are portraits of members of the royal family and are in the royal collection at Petersburg. She was elected to the Berlin Academy in 1820.

Mariani, Virginia. Honorary member of the Umbrian Academy and of the Academy of the Virtuosi of the Pantheon. Born in Rome, 1824, where she has met with much success in decorating pottery, as well as in oil and water-color paintings. The Provincial Exposition at Perugia in 1875 displayed her "Mezze Figure," which was highly commended. She has decorated cornices, with flowers in relief, as well as some vases that are very beautiful. Besides teaching in several institutions and receiving private pupils, she has been an inspector, in her own department of art, of the municipal schools of Rome.

Marie, Duchess of Würtemberg. Daughter of Louis Philippe, and wife of Duke Frederick William Alexander of Würtemberg. Born at Palermo, 1813, and died at Pisa, 1839. She studied drawing with Ary Scheffer. Her statue of "Jeanne d'Arc" is at Versailles; in the Ferdinand Chapel, in the Bois de Boulogne, is the "Peri as a Praying Angel"; in the Saturnin Chapel at Fontainebleau is a stained-glass window with her design of "St. Amalia." Among her other works are "The Dying Bayard," a relief representing the legend of the Wandering Jew, and a bust of the Belgian Queen. Many of her drawings are in possession of her family. She also executed some lithographs, such as "Souvenirs of 1812," 1831, etc.

Marie Louise, Empress of France. 1791-1846. She studied under Prud'hon. Her "Girl with a Dove" is in the Museum of Besançon.

Marlef, Claude. Bronze medal at Paris Exposition, 1900. Associate of the French National Society of Fine Arts (Beaux-Arts). Born at Nantes. Pupil of A. Roll, Benjamin Constant, Puvis de Chavannes, and Dagnaux.

Mme. Marlef is a portrait painter. Her picture, "Manette Salomon," is in the Hotel de Ville, Paris; the "Nymphe Accroupie" is in the Municipal Museum of Nantes. Among her portraits of well-known women are those of Jane Hading, Elsie de Wolfe, Bessie Abbott of the Opera, Rachel Boyer of the Theatre Français, Marguerite Durand, Editeur de la Fronde, Mlle. Richepin, and many others.

Mme. Marlef has the power of keen observation, so necessary to a painter of portraits. Although there is a certain element of soft tenderness in her pictures, the bold virility of her drawing misled the critics, who for a time believed that her name was used to conceal the personality of a man. A critic in the Paris *World* writes of this artist: "She has exquisite color sense and delights in presenting that *exaltation de la vie*, that love, radiance, and joy of life, which are at once the secret of the success and the keynote of the masterful canvases of Roll, in whose studio were first developed Claude Marlef's delicate qualities of truthful perception in the portraiture of woman... Her perceptions being rapid, she has a remarkable instantaneous insight, enabling her to fix the dominant feature and soul of expression in each of the various types among her numerous sitters."

Mme. Marlef's family name is Lefebure. Her husband died in 1891, the year after their marriage, and she then devoted herself to the serious study of painting, which she had practised from childhood. She first exhibited at the Salon, 1895, and has exhibited annually since then. In 1902 she sent her own portrait, and in 1903 that of Bessie Abbott, to the Exhibition of the Société Nationale des Beaux-Arts.

Martin de Campo, Victoria. Member of the Academy of Fine Arts of Cadiz, her native city. In the different expositions of this and other Andalusian capitals she has exhibited since 1840 many works, including portraits, genre, historical pictures, and copies. Among them may be mentioned "Susanna in the Bath," "David Playing the Harp before Saul," a "Magdalen," a "Cupid," a "Boy with a Linnet," and a "Nativity." Some of these were awarded prizes. In the Chapel of Relics in the new Cathedral at Cadiz are her "Martyrdom of St. Lawrence" and a "Mater Dolorosa."

Martineau, Edith. Associate of Royal Society of Painters in Water-Colors; member of the Hampstead Art Society. Born in Liverpool, where she made her first studies in the School of Art, and later became a pupil of the Royal Academy Schools, London.

Her pictures are not large and are principally figures or figures in landscape, and all in water-colors. She writes very modestly that so many are sold and in private hands that she will give no list of subjects.

Massari, Luigia. Medal at Piacenza, 1869, and several other medals from art societies. Born at Piacenza, 1810. Pupil of A. Gemmi. Her works are in a number of churches: "St. Martin" in the church at Altoé; "St. Philomena" in the church at Busseto; the "Madonna del Carmine" and "St. Anna" in the church at Monticelli d'Ongina. This artist was also famous for her beautiful embroidery, as seen in her altar-cloths, one of which is in the Guastafredda Chapel at Piacenza. The fruits and flowers produced by her needle are marvellously like those in her pictures.

Massey, Mrs. Gertrude. Member of the Society of Miniaturists. Born in London, 1868. Has studied with private teachers in London and Paris.

This painter has made a specialty of miniatures and of pictures of dogs. She has been extensively employed by various members of the royal family, of whom she painted eleven miniatures, among which was one of the late Queen.

She sends me a list of several pictures of dogs and "Pets," all belonging to titled English ladies; also a long list of miniatures of gentlemen, ladies, and children of high degree, several being of the royal family, in addition, I suppose, to the eleven mentioned above.

She writes me: "Constantly met King and Queen and other members. Sittings took place at Windsor Castle, Sandringham, Marlborough House, Osborne, and Balmoral. One dog died after first sitting; had to finish from dead dog. Live in charming little cottage with *genuine* old-fashioned garden in St. John's Wood."

Mrs. Massey has exhibited at the Royal Academy and New Gallery, and has held a special exhibition of her pictures of dogs at the Fine Art Society, New Bond Street, London.

Massip, Marguerite. Member of the Society of Swiss Painters and Sculptors and of the Society of Arts and Letters, Geneva. Born at Geneva. Made her studies in Florence and Paris under the professors in the public schools. Her picture of "Le Buveur" is in the Museum of Geneva; "Five o'Clock Tea," also in a Geneva Museum; "La Bohemienne" is at Nice; "The Engagement" – a dancer – at St. Gall, and a large number of portraits in various cities, belonging to their subjects and their families.

Her portrait of Mme. M. L. was very much praised when exhibited in proximity with the works of some of the famous French artists. One critic writes: "The painting is firm and brilliant. The hands are especially beautiful; we scarcely know to whom we can compare Mme. Massip, unless to M. Paul Dubois. They have the same love of art, the same soberness of tone, the same scorn of artifice… The woman who has signed such a portrait is a great artist." It is well known that the famous sculptor is a remarkable portraitist.

In a review of the Salon at Nice we read: "A portrait by Mme. Massip is a magnificent canvas, without a single stroke of the charlatan. The pose is simple and dignified; there is the serenity and repose of a woman no longer young, who makes no pretension to preserve her vanishing beauty; the costume, in black, is so managed that it would not appear superannuated nor ridiculous at any period. The execution is that of a great talent and an artistic conscience. It is not a portrait for a bedchamber, still less for a studio; it is a noble souvenir for a family, and should have a place in the salon, in which, around the hearth, three generations may gather, and in this serene picture may see the wife, the mother, and the grandmother, when they mourn the loss of her absolute presence."

Massolien, Anna. Born at Görlitz, 1848. A pupil of G. Gräf and of the School of Women Artists in Berlin. Her portraits of Field Marshal von Steinmetz, Brückner, and G. Schmidt by their excellence assured the reputation of this artist, whose later portraits are greatly admired.

Mathilde, Princess. Medal at Paris Salon, 1865. Daughter of King Jerome Bonaparte. Born at Trieste, 1820; died at Paris, 1904. Pupil of Eugene Giraud. She painted genre subjects in water-colors. Her medal picture, "Head of a Young Girl," is in the Luxembourg; "A Jewess of Algiers," 1866, is in the Museum of Lille; "The Intrigue under the Portico of the Doge's Palace" was painted in 1865.

Mathilde Caroline, Grand Duchess of Hesse. Was born Princess of Bavaria. 1813-1863. Pupil of Dominik Onaglio. In the New Gallery at Munich are two of her pictures – "View of the Magdalen Chapel in the Garden at Nymphenburg," 1832, and "Outlook on the Islands, Procida and Ischia," 1836.

Matton, Ida. Two grand prizes and a purse, also a travelling purse from the Government of Sweden; honorable mention at the Paris Salon, 1896; honorable mention, Paris Exposition, 1900; prize for sculpture at the Union des femmes peintres et sculpteurs, 1903. Decorated with the "palmes académique" of President Loubet, 1903. Member of the Union des femmes peintres et sculpteurs, Paris. Born at Gefle, Sweden. Pupil of the Technical School, Stockholm, and of H. Chapu, A. Mercie, and D. Puech at Paris.

Among the works of this artist are "Mama!" a statue in marble; "Loké," a statue; "Dans les Vagues," a marble bust; "Funeral Monument," in bronze, in Gefle, Sweden; and a great number of portrait busts and various subjects in bas-relief.

At the Salon des Artistes Français, 1902, she exhibited four portraits, and in 1903, "Confidence."

Maury, Cornelia F. Member of St. Louis Artists' Guild and Society of Western Artists. Born in New Orleans, Louisiana. Pupil of St. Louis School of Fine Arts and of Julian Academy, under Collin and Merson. At the Salon of 1900 her picture, "Mother and Child," was hung on the line.

Miss Maury has made an especial study of child life. Among her pictures are "Little Sister," "Choir Boy," "Late Breakfast," and "First Steps." The latter picture and the "Baby in a Go-Cart" have been published in the Copley Prints.

"Cornelia F. Maury is most successful in portrayals of childhood. Her small figures are simple, unaffected, with no suggestion of pose. They convey that delightful feeling of unconsciousness in the subject that is always so charming either in nature or in artistic expression. The pastel depicting the flaxen-haired child in blue dress drawing a tiny cart is exceedingly artistic, and the same may be said of a pastel showing a small child in a Dutch high-chair near a window. A third picture – also a pastel – represents a choir-boy in a red robe, red cap, and white surplice, sitting in a high-backed, carved chair, holding a book in his hand. Miss Maury really has produced nothing finer than this last. It is a most excellent work." – *The Mirror, St. Louis,* April 10, 1902.

Mayreder-Obermayer, Rose. Born in Vienna, 1858. Pupil of Darnaut and Charmont. The works of this successful painter of flowers and still-life have been exhibited in Berlin, Vienna, Dresden, and Chicago. She has a broad, sure touch quite unusual in water-colors. She has also executed some notable decorative works, one of which, "November," has attracted much attention.

McCrossan, Mary. Silver and bronze medals, Liverpool; silver medal and honorable mention, Paris. Has exhibited at Royal Academy, London, at Royal Institute of Oil Colors, and many other English and Scotch exhibitions. Member of Liverpool Academy of Arts and of the Liverpool Sketching Club. Born in Liverpool. Studied at Liverpool School of Art under John Finnie; Paris, under M. Delécluse; St. Ives, Cornwall, under Julius Ollson.

The principal works of this artist are marine subjects and landscapes, and are mostly in private collections.

In the *Studio,* November, 1900, we read: "Miss McCrossan's exhibition of pictures and sketches displayed a pleasant variety of really clever work, mostly in oils, with a few water-colors and pastels. In each medium her color is strong, rich, and luminous, and her drawing vigorous and certain.

"While this artist's landscape subjects are intelligently selected and attractively rendered, there is unusual merit in her marine pictures, composed mainly from the fisher-craft of the Isle of Man and the neighborhood of St. Ives, and recording effects of brilliant sunshine lighting up white herring boats lying idly on intensely reflective blue sea, or aground on the harbor mud at low tide. There is a fascination in the choice color treatment of these characteristic pictures."

Mclaughlin, Mary Louise M. Honorable mention, Paris Salon, 1878; silver medal, Paris Exposition, 1889; gold medal, Atlanta, 1895; bronze medal, Buffalo, 1900. Member of the Society of Arts, London; honorary member of National Mineral Painters' League, Cincinnati. Born in Cincinnati, Ohio. Pupil of Cincinnati Art Academy and of H. F. Farny and Frank Duveneck in private classes.

Miss McLaughlin has painted in oil and water-colors and exhibited in various places, as indicated by the honors she has received. Having practised under- and over-glaze work on pottery, as well as porcelain etching and decorative etching on metals, she is now devoting herself to making the porcelain known as Losanti Ware.

Of a recent exhibition, 1903, a critic wrote: "Perhaps the most beautiful and distinguished group in the exhibition is that of Miss

McLaughlin, one of the earliest artistic workers in clay of the United States. She sends a collection of lovely porcelain vases, of a soft white tone and charming in contour. Some of these have open-work borders, others are decorated in relief, and the designs are tinted with delicate jade greens, dark blues, or salmon pinks. This ware goes by the name of Losanti, from the early name of Cincinnati, L'Osantiville."

This artist has written several books on china painting and pottery decoration.

McManus Mansfield, Blanche. Diplomas from the New Orleans Centennial and the Woman's Department, Chicago, 1903. Member of the New Vagabonds, London, and the Touring Club of France. Born in East Feliciana Parish, Louisiana, this artist has made her studies in London and Paris. Her principal work has been done in book illustrations. The following list gives some of her most important publications:

"Alice in Wonderland" and "Through the Looking-Glass." De Luxe edition in color. New York, 1899.

"The Calendar of Omar Khayyam." In color. New York, 1900.

"The Altar Service." Thirty-six wood-cut blocks printed on Japan vellum. London, 1902.

"The Coronation Prayer-Book." (Wood-cut borders.) Oxford University Press, 1902.

"Cathedrals of Northern France." In collaboration with Francis Miltoun. Boston and London, 1903.

"Cathedrals of Southern France." In collaboration with Francis Miltoun. Sold for publication in London and Boston, 1904.

"A Dante Calendar." London, 1903.

"A Rubaiyat Calendar." Boston, 1903.

"The King's Classics." (Designs and Decorations.) London, 1902-1903.

"The Book of Days." A Calendar. Sold in London for 1904.

After speaking of several works by Miss McManus, a notice from London says: "A more difficult or at least a more intricate series were the designs cut on wood for 'The Altar Service Book,' just issued in London by that newly founded venture, the De La More Press; which has drawn unto itself such scholars as Dr. Furnival, Professor Skeat, and Israel Gollancz. These designs by Miss McManus were printed direct from the wood blocks in very limited editions, on genuine vellum, on Japanese vellum, and a small issue on a real sixteenth-century hand-made paper. The various editions were immediately taken up in London on publication; hence it is unlikely that copies will be generally seen in America.

"We learn, however, that the original wood blocks will be shown at the St. Louis Exposition, in the section to be devoted to the work of American artists resident abroad. We suggest that all lovers of latter-day bookmaking 'make a note of it,' recalling meanwhile that it was this successful American designer who produced also the decorative wood-cut borders and initials which were used in 'The Coronation Prayer-Book of King Edward VII.,' issued from the celebrated Oxford University Press. There were forty initials or headings, embodying the coronation regalia, including the crown, sceptre, rose, thistle, shamrock, etc. The magnificent cover for the book was also designed by this artist.

"Among the American artists who have made a distinctive place in art circles, not only in America but on 'the other side,' is Mrs. M. F. Mansfield, formerly Blanche McManus of Woodville, Mississippi.

"In London she is widely known as a skilful, able, and versatile artist, and her remarkable success there is an illustration of 'the American invasion.' Little has been written in America, especially in the South, of what this talented Southern woman has accomplished. She has never sought personal advertisement; on the contrary, she has shrunk from any kind of publicity – even that which would have accrued from a proper valuation of her work.

"She is one of those artists whose talent is equalled only by her modesty, who, enamoured of her art and aiming at a patient, painstaking realization of her ideal, has been content to work on in silence. In the estimation of art connoisseurs, Blanche McManus is an artist of unquestionable talent and varied composition, who has already done much striking work. Her execution in the various branches has attracted international attention.

"She paints well in water-colors and in oil, and her etching is considered excellent. Her drawing is stamped good, and every year she has showed rapid improvement in design. She is a highly cultivated woman, with a close and accurate observation. A sincere appreciation of nature was revealed in her earliest efforts, and for some years she devoted much time to its study."

Moring's *Quarterly* says in regard to the special work which Mrs. Mansfield has done: "It is so seldom that an artist is able to take in hand what may be termed the entire decoration of a book – including in that phrase cover, illustration, colophon, head- and tail-pieces, initial letters, and borders – that it is a pleasure to find in the subject of our paper a lady who may be said to be capable of taking all these points into consideration in the embellishment of a volume."

Medici, Marie de'. Wife of Henry IV. Born at Florence, 1573; died at Cologne, 1642. A portrait of herself, engraved on wood, bears the legend, "Maria Medici F. MDLXXXII." Another portrait of a girl, attributed to her, is signed, "L. O. 1617." It may be considered a matter of grave doubt whether the nine-year-old girl drew and engraved with her own hand the first-named charming picture, which has been credited to her with such frank insouciance.

Mengs, Anna Maria. Member of the Academy of San Fernando. She was a daughter of Anton Rafael Mengs, and was born in Dresden in 1751, where she received instruction from her father. In 1777 she married the engraver Salvador Carmona in Rome, and went with him to Spain, where she died in 1790. Portraits and miniatures of excellent quality were executed by her, and on them her reputation rests.

Merian, Maria Sibylla. Born at Frankfort-on-the-Main in 1647. This artist merits our attention, although her art was devoted to an unusual purpose. Her father was a learned geographer and engraver whose published works are voluminous. Her maternal grandfather was the eminent engraver, Theodore de Bry or Brie.

From her childhood Anna Sibylla Merian displayed an aptitude for drawing and a special interest in insect life. The latter greatly disturbed her mother, but she could not turn the child's attention from entomology, and was forced to allow that study to become her chief pursuit.

The flower painter, Abraham Mignon, was her master in drawing and painting; but at an early age, before her studies were well advanced, she married an architect, John Andrew Graf, of Nuremberg, with whom she lived unhappily. She passed nearly twenty years in great seclusion, and, as she tells us in the preface to one of her books, she devoted these years to the examination and study of various insects, watching their transformations and making drawings from them. Many of these were in colors on parchment and were readily sold to connoisseurs.

Her first published work was called "The Wonderful Transformations of Caterpillars." It appeared in 1679, was fully illustrated by copper plate engravings, executed by herself from her own designs. About 1684 she separated from her husband, and with her daughters returned to Frankfort. Many interesting stories are told of her life there.

She made a journey to Friesland and was a convert to the doctrines of Labadie, but she was still devoted to her study and research. She was associated with the notable men of her time, and became the friend of the father of Rachel Ruysch. Although Madame Merian, who had taken her maiden name, was seventeen years older than the gifted flower painter, she became to her an example of industry and devotion to study.

Madame Merian had long desired to examine the insects of Surinam, and in 1699, by the aid of the Dutch Government, she made the journey – of which a French poet wrote:

"Sibylla à Surinam va chercher la nature,
Avec l'esprit d'un Sage, et le coeur d'un Heros"

– which indicates the view then held of a journey which would now attract no attention.

While in Guiana some natives brought her a box filled with "lantern flies," as they were then called. The noise they made at night was so disturbing that she liberated them, and the flies, regaining liberty, flashed out their most brilliant light, for which Madame Merian was unprepared, and in her surprise dropped the box. From this circumstance a most exaggerated idea obtained concerning the illuminating power of the flies.

The climate of Surinam was so unhealthy for Madame Merian that she could remain there but two years, and in that time she gathered the materials for her great work called "Metamorphoses Insectorum Surinamensium," etc. The illustrations were her own, and she pictured many most interesting objects – animals and vegetables as well as insects – which were quite unknown in Europe. Several editions of this book were published both in German and French. Her plates are still approved and testify to the scope and thoroughness of her research, as well as to her powers as an artist.

Her chief work, however, was a "History of the Insects of Europe, Drawn from Nature, and Explained by Maria Sibylla Merian." The illustrations of this work were beautiful and of great interest, as the insects, from their first state to their last, were represented with the plants and flowers which they loved, each object being correctly and tastefully pictured. Most of the original paintings for these works are in the British Museum. In the Vienna Gallery is a "Basket of Flowers" by this artist, and in the Basle Museum a picture of "Locust and Chafers."

The daughters of this learned artist naturalist, Joanna Maria Helena and Dorothea, shared the pursuits and labors of their mother, and it was her intention to publish their drawings as an appendix to her works. She did not live to do this, and later the daughters published a separate volume of their own.

This extraordinary woman, whose studies and writings added so much to the knowledge of her time, was neither beautiful nor graceful. Her portraits present a woman with hard and heavy features, her hair in short curls surmounted by a stiff and curious headdress, made of folds of some black stuff.

Merritt, Mrs. Anna Lea. Honorable mention, Paris Exposition, 1889; two medals and a diploma, Chicago Exposition, 1893. In 1890 her picture of "Love Locked Out" was purchased by the Chantry fund, London, for two hundred and fifty pounds. This honor has been accorded to few women, and of these I think Mrs. Merritt was first. Member of the Royal Society of Painter-Etchers. Born in Philadelphia. Pupil of Heinrich Hoffman in Dresden, and of Henry Merritt – whom she married – in London.

Mrs. Merritt has a home in Hampshire, England, but is frequently in Philadelphia, where she exhibits her pictures, which have also been seen at the Royal Academy since 1871.

This artist is represented by her pictures in the National Gallery of British Art, in the Pennsylvania Academy of Fine Arts, and by her portrait of Mr. James Russell Lowell in Memorial Hall, Harvard University.

[*No reply to circular.*]

Michis, Maria. See Cattaneo.

Milbacher, Louise von. Prize at Berlin in 1886. Born at Böhmischbrod, 1845. Pupil of Pönninger and Eisenmenger. A painter of portraits and of sacred and genre subjects. Three of her portraits are well known – those of Baron Thienen, General von Neuwirth, and Baron Eber-Eschenbach. The altar-piece in the chapel of the Vienna Institute, a "Holy Family," is by this artist. She has also painted still-life and animal subjects.

Modigliani, Signorina Corinna. Silver medal at Turin Exposition, 1898; silver medal at the Exposition of Feminine Art, 1899, 1900; diploma at Leghorn, 1901; gold medal. Member of the International Artistic Association. Born in Rome. Pupil of Professore Commendatore Pietro Vanni.

This artist has exhibited her works in the Expositions of Rome, Turin, Milan, Leghorn, Munich, Petersburg, and Paris since 1897, and will contribute to the St. Louis Exposition. Her pictures have been sold in Paris, London, and Ireland, as well as in Rome and other Italian cities, where many of them are in the collections of distinguished families.

Moldura, Lilla. A Neapolitan painter. Her father was an Italian and her mother a Spaniard. She was instructed in the elements of art by various excellent teachers, and then studied oil painting under Maldarelli and water-color under Mancini. She has often exhibited pictures in Naples, to the satisfaction of both artists and critics, and has also won success in London. She has been almost equally happy in views of the picturesque Campagna, and in interiors, both in oil and water-colors. The interior of the Chapel of the Immaculate Conception, in the Church of the Gerolamini, is strong in execution and good in drawing and color.

Möller, Agnes Slott. Born in 1862. Resides in Copenhagen. The especial work of this artist, by which her reputation is world-wide, is the illustration of old legends for children's books.

Montalba, Clara. Associate of the Society of Painters in Water-Colors, London, and of the Belgian Society of Water-Colorists. Born in Cheltenham, 1842. Pupil of Isabey in Paris. Her professional life has been spent in London and Venice. She has sent her pictures to the Academy and the Grosvenor Gallery exhibitions since 1879. "Blessing a Tomb, Westminster," was at the Philadelphia Exposition, 1876; "Corner of St. Mark's" and "Fishing Boats, Venice," were at Paris, 1878.

In 1874 she exhibited at the Society of British Artists, "Il Giardino Publico" – the Public Garden – of which a writer in the *Art Journal* said: "'Il Giardino Publico' stands foremost among the few redeeming features of the exhibition. In delicate perception of natural beauty the picture suggests the example of Corot. Like the great Frenchman, Miss Montalba strives to interpret the sadder moods of nature, when the wind moves the water a little mournfully and the outlines of the objects become uncertain in the filmy air."

[*No reply to circular.*]

Moretto, Emma. Venetian painter, exhibited at Naples, in 1877, "Abbey of St. Gregory at Venice"; at Turin, in 1880, a fine view of the "Canal of the Giudecca," and "Canal of S. Giorgio"; at the National Exposition in Milan, 1881, "Sunset" and a marine view; at Rome, in 1883, "Excursion on the Lagoon." Still others of the same general character are: "A Gondola," "At St. Mark's," "Grand Canal," "Morning at Sea," etc.

Moron, Therese Concordia. Born in Dresden, 1725; died in Rome, 1806. Pupil, of her father, Ismael Mengs. Her attention was divided between enamel painting and pastel, much of the latter being miniature work. In the Dresden Gallery are two of her pastel portraits and two copies in miniature of Correggio, viz., a half-length portrait of herself and a portrait of her sister, Julie Mengs; a copy of St. Jerome, or "The Day" – original in Parma – and "The Night."

A curious story has recently been published to the effect that in 1767 this artist sent word to Duke Xavier of Saxony that during the Seven Years' War she painted a copy in miniature of Correggio's "Holy Mother with the Christ Child, Mary Magdalen, Hieronymus, and Two Angels," which she sent by Cardinal

Albani to the Duke's father – Frederick Augustus II. of Saxony and Augustus III. of Poland – at Warsaw. It was claimed that two hundred and fifty ducats were due her. Apparently the demand was not met; but, on the other hand, the lady seems to have received for some years a pension of three hundred thalers from the Electorate of Saxony without making any return. Probably her claim was satisfied by this pension.

Moser, Mary. One of the original members of the London Academy. The daughter of a German artist, who resided in London. She was as well known for her wit as for her art. A friend of Fuseli, she was said to be as much in love with him as he was in love with Angelica Kauffman. Dr. Johnson sometimes met Miss Moser at the house of Nollekens, where they made merry over a cup of tea.

Queen Charlotte commissioned this painter to decorate a chamber, for which work she paid more than nine hundred pounds, and was so well pleased that she complimented the artist by commanding the apartment to be called "Miss Moser's Room."

Mott, Mrs. Alice. Born at Walton on Thames. Pupil of the Slade School and Royal Academy in London, and of M. Charles Chaplin in Paris in his studio. A miniaturist whose works are much esteemed. Her work is life-like, artistic, and strong in drawing, color, and composition. After finishing her study under masters she took up miniature painting by herself, studying the works of old miniaturists.

Recently she writes me: "I have departed from the ordinary portrait miniature, and am now painting what I call picture miniatures. For instance, I am now at work on the portrait of Miss D. C., who is in old-fashioned dress, low bodice, and long leg-of-mutton sleeves. She is represented as running in the open, with sky and tree background. She has a butterfly net over her shoulder, which floats out on the wind; she is looking up and smiling; her hair and her sash are blown out. It is to be called, 'I'd be a Butterfly.' The dress is the yellow of the common butterfly. It is a large miniature. I hope to send it, with others, to the St. Louis Exposition."

Her miniatures are numerous and in private hands. A very interesting one belongs to the Bishop of Ripon and is a portrait of Mrs. Carpenter, his mother.

Muntz, Laura A.
[*No reply to circular.*]

Murray, Elizabeth. Member of the Institute of Painters in Water-Colors, London, and of the American Society of Water-Color Painters, New York. Her pictures are of genre subjects, many of them being of Oriental figures. Among these are "Music in Morocco," "A Moorish Saint," "The Greek Betrothed," etc. Other subjects are "The Gipsy Queen," "Dalmatian Peasant," "The Old Story in Spain," etc.

Nathan, Signora Liliah Ascoli. Rome.
[*No reply to circular.*]

Negro, Teresa. Born in Turin, where she resides. She has made a study of antique pottery and has been successful in its imitation. Her vases and amphorae have been frequently exhibited and are praised by connoisseurs and critics. At the Italian National Exposition, 1880, she exhibited a terra-cotta reproduction of a classic design, painted in oils; also a wooden dish which resembled an antique ceramic.

Nelli, Plautilla. There is a curious fact connected with two women artists of Florence in the middle of the sixteenth century. In that city of pageants – where Ghirlandajo saw, in the streets, in churches, and on various ceremonial occasions, the beautiful women with whom he still makes us acquainted – these ladies, daughters of noble Florentine families, were nuns.

No Shakespearean dissector has, to my knowledge, affirmed that Hamlet's advice to Ophelia, "Get thee to a nunnery," and his assertion, "I have heard of your paintings, too," prove that Ophelia was an artist and a nunnery a favorable place in which to set up a studio. Yet I think I could make this assumption as convincing as many that have been "proved" by the *post obitum* atomizers of the great poet's every word.

But we have not far to seek for the reasons which led Plautilla Nelli and Maria Maddalena de' Pazzi to choose the conventual life. The subjects of their pictures prove that their thoughts were fixed on a life quite out of tune with that which surrounded them in their homes. If they pictured rich draperies and rare gems, it was but to adorn with them the Blessed Virgin Mother and the holy saints, in token of their belief that all of pomp and value in this life can but faintly symbolize the glory of the life to come.

Plautilla Nelli, born in Florence in 1523, entered the convent of St. Catherine of Siena, in her native city, and in time became its abbess. Patiently, with earnest prayer, she studied and copied the works of Fra Bartolommeo and Andrea del Sarto, until she was able to paint an original "Adoration of the Magi" of such excellence as to secure her a place among the painters of Florence.

Many of her pictures remained in her convent, but she also painted a "Madonna Surrounded by Saints" for the choir of Santa Lucia at Pistoja. There are pictures attributed to Plautilla Nelli in Berlin – notably the "Visit of Martha to Christ," – which are characterized by the earnestness, purity, and grace of her beloved Fra Bartolommeo. Her "Adoration of the Wise Men" is at Parma; the "Descent from the Cross" in Florence; the "Last Supper" in the church of Santa Maria Novella, Florence.

There are traditions of her success as a teacher of painting in her convent, but of this we have no exact knowledge such as we have of the work of the "Suor Plautilla," the name by which she came to be known in all Italy.

Nemes-Ransonnett, Countess Elisa. Born at Vienna, 1843. She

studied successively with Vastagh, Lulos, Aigner, Schilcher, Lenbach, Angeli, and J. Benczur, and opened her studio at Kun Szent Miklos near Budapest. The "Invitation to the Wedding" was well received, and her portraits of Schiller and Perczel are in public galleries – the former in the Vienna Künstlerhaus, and the latter in the Deputy House at Budapest.

Newcomb, Maria Guise. Born in New Jersey. Pupil of Schenck, Chialiva, and Edouard Detaille in Paris. Travelled in Algeria and the Sahara, studying the Arab and his horses. Very few artists can be compared with Miss Newcomb in representing horses. She has a genius for portraying this animal, and understands its anatomy as few painters have done.

She was but a child when sketching horses and cattle was her pastime, and so great was her fondness for it that the usual dolls and other toys were crowded out of her life. Her studies in Paris were comprehensive, and her work shows the results and places her among the distinguished painters of animals.

[*No reply to circular.*]

Ney, Elisabeth. Born in 1830. After studying at the Academy in Berlin, this sculptor went to Munich, where she was devoted to her art. She then came to Texas and remained some years in America. She returned to Berlin in 1897. Among her best known works are busts of Garibaldi, of J. Grimm, 1863, "Prometheus Bound," 1868, and a statue of Louis II. of Bavaria.

Nicholls, Mrs. Rhoda Holmes. Queen's Scholarship, Bloomsbury Art School, London; gold medal, Competitive Prize Fund Exhibition, New York; medal, Chicago Exposition, 1893; medal, Tennessee Exposition, 1897; bronze medal at Buffalo Exposition, 1901. Member of American Water-Color Society, New York Water-Color Society, Woman's Art Club, American Society of Miniature Painters, Pen and Brush Club; honorable member of Woman's Art Club, Canada. Born in Coventry, England. Pupil of

Bloomsbury School of Art, London; of Cannerano and Vertunni in Rome, where she was elected to the Circolo Artistico and the Società degli Aquarelliste.

Her pictures are chiefly figure subjects, among which are "Those Evening Bells," "The Scarlet Letter," "A Daughter of Eve," "Indian after the Chase," "Searching the Scriptures," etc.

In the *Studio*, March, 1901, in writing of the exhibition of the American Water-Color Society, the critic says: "In her two works, 'Cherries' and 'A Rose,' Mrs. Rhoda Holmes Nicholls shows us a true water-color executed by a master hand. The subject of each is slight; each stroke of her brush is made once and for all, with a precision and dash that are inspiriting; and you have in each painting the sparkle, the deft lightness of touch, the instantaneous impression of form and coloring that a water-color should have."

Mrs. Nicholls is also known as an illustrator. Harold Payne says of her: "Rhoda Holmes Nicholls, although an illustrator of the highest order, cannot be strictly classed as one, for the reason that she is equally great in every other branch of art. However, as many of her best examples of water-colors are ultimately reproduced for illustrative purposes, and as even her oil paintings frequently find their way into the pages of art publications, it is not wrong to denominate her as an illustrator, and that of the most varied and prolific type. She may, like most artists, have a specialty, but a walk through her studio and a critical examination of her work – ranging all along the line of oil paintings, water-colors of the most exquisite type, wash drawings, crayons, and pastels – would scarcely result in discovering her specialty... As a colorist she has few rivals, and her acute knowledge of drawing and genius for composition are apparent in everything she does."

Nichols, Catherine Maude, R. E. The pictures of this artist have been hung on the line at the Royal Academy exhibitions a dozen times at least. From Munich she has received an official letter thanking her for sending her works to exhibitions in that city. Fellow of the Royal Painter-Etchers' Society; president of the

Woodpecker Art Club, Norwich; Member of Norwich Art Circle and of a Miniature Painters' Society and the Green Park Club, London. Born in Norwich. Self-taught. Has worked in the open at Barbizon, in Normandy, in Cornwall, Devon, London, and all around the east coast of Norfolk.

Miss Nichols has held three exhibitions of her pictures both in oil and water-colors in London. She has executed more than a hundred copper plates, chiefly dry-points. The pictures in oils and water-colors, the miniatures and the proofs of her works have found purchasers, almost without exception, and are in private hands. Most of the plates she has retained.

Miss Nichols has illustrated some books, her own poems being of the number, as well as her "Old Norwich." She has also made illustrations for journals and magazines.

One is impressed most agreeably with the absence of mannerism in Miss Nichols' work, as well as with the pronounced artistic treatment of her subjects. Her sketches of sea and river scenery are attractive; the views from her home county, Norfolk, have a delightful feeling about them. "Norwich River at Evening" is not only a charming picture, but shows, in its perspective and its values, the hand of a skilful artist. "Mousehold Heath," showing a rough and broken country, is one of her strongest pictures in oils; "Stretching to the Sea" is also excellent. Among the water-colors "Strangers' Hall," Norwich, and "Fleeting Clouds," merit attention, as do a number of others. One could rarely see so many works, with such varied subjects, treated in oils, water-colors, dry point, etc., by the same artist.

I quote the following paragraph from the *Studio* of April, 1903: "Miss C. M. Nichols is an artist of unquestionable talent, and her work in the various mediums she employs deserves careful attention. She paints well both in water-colors and in oil, and her etchings are among the best that the lady artists of our time have produced. Her drawing is good, her observation is close and accurate, and she shows year by year an improvement in design. Miss Nichols was for several years the only lady fellow of the

Royal Society of Painter-Etchers."

Her "Brancaster Staithe" and "Fir Trees, Crown Point," dry points, are in the Norwich Art Gallery, presented by Sir Seymour Haden, president of the Royal Society of Painter-Etchers. Two of her works, a large oil painting of "Earlham" and a water-color of "Strangers' Hall," have been purchased by subscription and presented to the Norwich Castle Art Gallery.

Nicolau y Parody, Teresa. Member of the Academy of San Fernando and of the Academy of San Carlos of Valencia. This artist, who was born in Madrid, early showed an enthusiasm for painting, which she at first practised in various styles, but gradually devoted herself entirely to miniature. She has contributed to many public exhibitions, and has received many prizes and honorable mentions, as well as praise from the critics. Among her portraits are those of Isabel de Braganza, Washington, Mme. de Montespan, Mme. Dubarry, Queen Margaret of Austria, and Don Carlos, son of Philip II. Her other works include a "Magdalen in the Desert," "Laura and Petrarch," "Joseph with the Christ-Child," "Francis I. at the Battle of Pavia," and many good copies after celebrated painters.

Niederhäusen, Mlle. Sophie. Medal at the Swiss National Exposition, 1896. Member of the Exposition permanente de l'Athénée, Geneva. Born at Geneva. Pupil of Professor Wymann and M. Albert Gos, and of M. and Mme. Demont-Breton in France.

Mlle. Niederhäusen paints landscapes principally, and has taken her subjects from the environs of Geneva, in the Valais, and in Pas-de-Calais, France.

Her picture, called the "Bord du Lac de Genève," was purchased by the city and is in the Rath Museum. She also paints flowers, and uses water-colors as well as oils.

Nobili, Elena. Silver medal at the Beatrice Exposition,

Florence, 1890. Born in Florence, where she resides. She is most successful in figure subjects. She is sympathetic in her treatment of them and is able to impart to her works a sentiment which appeals to the observer. Among her pictures are "Reietti," "The Good-Natured One," "September," "In the Country," "Music," and "Contrasts."

Normand, Mrs. Ernest – Henrietta Rae. Medals in Paris and at Chicago Exposition, 1893. Born in London, 1859. Daughter of T. B. Rae, Esquire. Married the artist, Ernest Normand, 1884. Pupil of Queen's Square School of Art, Heatherley's, British Museum, and Royal Academy Schools. Began the study of art at the age of thirteen. First exhibited at the Royal Academy in 1880, and has sent important pictures there annually since that time.

Mrs. Normand executed decorative frescoes in the Royal Exchange, London, the subject being "Sir Richard Whittington and His Charities."

In the past ten years she has exhibited "Mariana," 1893; "Psyche at the Throne of Venus," 1894; "Apollo and Daphne," 1895; "Summer," 1896; "Isabella," 1897; "Diana and Calisto," 1899; "Portrait of Marquis of Dufferin and Ava," 1901; "Lady Winifred Renshaw and Son," and the "Sirens," 1903, which is a picture of three nude enchantresses, on a sandy shore, watching a distant galley among rocky islets.

[*No reply to circular.*]

Nourse, Elizabeth. Medal at Chicago Exposition, 1903; Nashville Exposition, 1897; Carthage Institute, Tunis, 1897; elected associate of the Beaux-Arts, Paris, 1895; silver medal, Paris Exposition, 1900; elected Sociétaire des Beaux-Arts, 1901. Born in Cincinnati, Ohio, where she began her studies, later going to the Julian Academy, under Boulanger and Lefebvre, and afterward studying with Carolus Duran and Henner. This artist idealizes the subjects of every-day, practical life, and gives them a poetic quality which is an uncommon and delightful attainment.

At the Salon des Beaux-Arts, 1902, Miss Nourse exhibited "The Children," "Evening Toilet of the Baby," "In the Shade at Pen'march," "Brother and Sister at Pen'march," "The Madeleine Chapel at Pen'march." In 1903, "Our Lady of Joy, Pen'march," "Around the Cradle," "The Little Sister," and "A Breton Interior."

[*No reply to circular.*]

Oakley, Violet. Member of Pennsylvania Academy of Fine Arts, Philadelphia Water-Color Club, Plastic Club, Philadelphia. Born in New Jersey, but has lived in New York, where she studied at the Art Students' League under Carroll Beckwith. Pupil of Collin and Aman-Jean in Paris and Charles Lasar in England; also in Philadelphia of Joseph de Camp, Henry Thouron, Cecilia Beaux, and Howard Pyle.

Miss Oakley has executed mural decorations, a mosaic reredos, and five stained-glass windows in the Church of All Saints, New York City, and a window in the Convent of the Holy Child, at Sharon Hill, Pennsylvania.

In the summer of 1903 she was commissioned to decorate the walls of the Governor's reception room in the new Capitol at Harrisburg. Before engaging in this work – the first of its kind to be confided to an American woman – Miss Oakley went to Italy to study mural painting. She then went to England to thoroughly inform herself concerning the historical foundation of her subject, the history of the earliest days of Pennsylvania. At Oxford and in London she found what she required, and on her return to America established herself in a studio in Villa Nova, Pennsylvania, to make her designs for "The Romance of the Founding of the State," which is to be painted on a frieze five feet deep. The room is seventy by thirty feet, and sixteen feet in height.

The decoration of this Capitol is to be more elaborate and costly than that of any other public edifice in the United States. In mural decoration Miss Oakley will be associated with Edwin A. Abbey, but the Governor's room is to be her work entirely, and will doubtless occupy her during several years.

Mr Charles A. Caffin, in his article upon the exhibition of the New York Water-Color Club, January, 1904, says: "Miss Oakley has had considerable experience in designing stained-glass windows, and has reproduced in some of her designs for book covers a corresponding treatment of the composition, with an attempt, not very logical or desirable, considering the differences between paint and glass, to reproduce also something of her window color schemes... But for myself, her cover, in which some girls are picking flowers, is far more charming in its easy grace of composition, choice gravity of color, and spontaneity of feeling. Here is revealed a very *naïve* imagination, free of any obsessions."

Occioni, Signora Lucilla Marzolo. Diploma of gold medal at the Women's Exhibition, Earl's Court, London, 1900. Born in Trieste. Pupil, in Rome, of Professor Giuseppe Ferrari.

This artist paints figure subjects, portraits, landscapes, and flowers, in both oils and water-colors, and also makes pen-drawings. Her works are in many private galleries. She gives me no list of subjects. Her pictures have been praised by critics.

O'Connell, Frederique Emilie Auguste Miethe. Born in Potsdam. 1823-1885. She passed her early life in her native city, having all the advantages of a solid and brilliant education. She early exhibited a love of drawing and devoted herself to the study of anatomical plates. She soon designed original subjects and introduced persons of her own imagination, which early marked her as powerful in her fancy and original in her manner of rendering her ideas.

A picture of "Raphael and the Fornarina," which she executed at the age of fifteen, was so satisfactory as to determine her fate, and she was allowed to study art.

When about eighteen years old she became the pupil of Charles Joseph Begas, a very celebrated artist of Berlin. Under his supervision she painted her first picture, called the "Day of the Dupes," which, though full of faults, had also virtues enough to secure much attention in the exhibition. It was first hung in a disadvantageous position, but the crowd discovered its merits and would have it noticed. She received a complimentary letter from the Academy of Berlin, and the venerable artist Cornelius made her a visit of congratulation.

About 1844 she married and removed to Brussels. Here she came into an entirely new atmosphere and her manner of painting was changed. She sought to free herself from all outer influence and to express her own feeling. She studied color especially, and became an imitator of Rubens. She gained in Brussels all the medals of the Belgian expositions, and there began two historical pictures, "Peter the Great and Catherine" and "Maria Theresa and Frederick the Great." These were not finished until after her removal to Paris in 1853. They were bought by Prince Demidoff for the Russian Government.

She obtained her first triumph in Paris, at the Salon of 1853, by a portrait of Rachel. She represented the famous actress dressed entirely in white, with the worn expression which her professional exertions and the fatal malady from which she was already suffering had given to her remarkable face. The critics had no words for this portrait which were not words of praise, and two years later, in 1855, Madame O'Connell reached the height of her talent. "A Faunesse," as it was called, in the exposition of that year, was a remarkable work, and thus described by Barty:

"A strong and beautiful young woman was seated near a spring, where beneath the shade of the chestnut trees the water lilies spread themselves out upon the stream which flowed forth. She was nude and her flesh palpitated beneath the caresses of the sun. With feminine caprice she wore a bracelet of pearls of the style of the gold workers of the Renaissance. Her black hair had lights of golden brown upon it, and she opened her great brown eyes with an expression of indifference. A half smile played upon her rosy lips and lessened the oval of the face like that of the

'Dancing Faun.' The whole effect of the lines of the figure was bold and gave an appearance of youth, the extremities were studiously finished, the skin was fine, and the whole tournure elegant. It was a Faunesse of Fontainebleau of the time of the Valois."

Mme. O'Connell then executed several fine portraits – two of Rachel, one of M. O'Connell, others of Charles Edward and Théophile Gautier, which were likened to works of Vandyck, and a portrait in crayon of herself which was a *chef-d'oeuvre*. She excelled in rendering passionate natures; she found in her palette the secret of that pallor which spreads itself over the faces of those devoted to study – the fatigues of days and nights without sleep; she knew how to kindle the feverish light in the eyes of poets and of the women of society. She worked with great freedom, used a thick pâte in which she brushed freely and left the ridges thus made in the colors; then, later, she put over a glaze, and all was done. Her etchings were also executed with great freedom, and many parts, especially the hair, were remarkably fine. She finished numerous etchings, among which a "St. Magdalen in the Desert" and a "Charity Surrounded by Children" are worthy of particular notice.

After Madame O'Connell removed to Paris she opened a large atelier and received many pupils. It was a most attractive place, with gorgeous pieces of antique furniture, loaded with models of sculpture, books, albums, engravings, and so on, while draperies, tapestries, armor, and ornaments in copper and brass all lent their colors and effects to enhance the attractions of the place. Many persons of rank and genius were among the friends of the artist and she was much in society.

In spite of all her talent and all her success the end of Madame O'Connell's life was sad beyond expression. Her health suffered, her reason tottered and faded out, yet life remained and she was for years in an asylum for the insane. Everything that had surrounded her in her Paris home was sold at auction. No time was given and no attempt was made to bring her friends together. No one who had known or loved her was there to shed a tear or to bear away a memento of her happy past. All the beautiful things of which we have spoken were sacrificed and scattered as unconscionably as if she had never loved or her friends enjoyed them.

In the busy world of Paris no one remembered the brilliant woman who had flashed upon them, gained her place among them, and then disappeared. They recalled neither her genius nor her womanly qualities which they had admired, appreciated, and so soon forgotten!

Oosterwyck, Maria van. The seventeenth century is remarkable for the perfection attained in still-life and flower painting. The most famous masters in this art were William van Aelst of Delft, the brothers De Heem of Utrecht, William Kalf and the Van Huysums of Amsterdam. The last of this name, however, Jan van Huysum, belongs to the next century.

Maria van Oosterwyck and Rachel Ruysch disputed honors with the above named and are still famous for their talents.

The former was a daughter of a preacher of the reformed religion. She was born at Nootdorp, near Delft, in 1630. She was the pupil of Jan David de Heem, and her pictures were remarkable for accuracy in drawing, fine coloring, and an admirable finish.

Louis XIV. of France, William III. of England, the Emperor Leopold of Germany, and Augustus I. of Poland gave her commissions for pictures. Large prices were paid her in a most deferential manner, as if the tributes of friendship rather than the reward of labor, and to these generous sums were added gifts of jewels and other precious objects.

Of Maria van Oosterwyck Kugler writes: "In my opinion she does not occupy that place in the history of the art of this period that she deserves, which may be partly owing to the rarity of her pictures, especially in public galleries. For although her flower pieces are weak in arrangement and often gaudy in the combination of color, she yet represents her flowers with the utmost truth of drawing, and with a depth, brilliancy, and juiciness of local coloring *unattained by any other flower painter"*

A picture in the Vienna Gallery of a sunflower with tulips and poppies, in glowing color, is probably her best work in a public collection. Her pictures are also in the galleries of Dresden, Florence, Carlsruhe, Copenhagen, the Schwerin Gallery, and the Metropolitan Museum of New York.

There is a romantic story told of Maria van Oosterwyck, as follows. William van Aelst, the painter of exquisite pictures of still-life, fruits, glass, and objects in gold and silver, was a suitor for her hand. She did not love him, but wishing not to be too abrupt in her refusal, she required, as a condition of his acceptance, that he should work ten hours a day during a year. This he readily promised to do. His studio being opposite that of Maria, she watched narrowly for the days when he did not work and marked them down on her window-sash. At the close of the year Van Aelst claimed her as his bride, assuming that he had fulfilled her condition; but she pointed to the record of his delinquencies, and he could but accept her crafty dismissal of his suit.

Osenga, Giuseppina. This artist resides in Parma, and has there exhibited landscapes that are praised for their color and for the manner in which they are painted, as well as for the attractive subjects she habitually chooses. "A View near Parma," the "Faces of Montmorency," and the "Bridge of Attaro" are three of her works which are especially admired.

Ostertag, Blanche. Member of Society of Western Artists; Arts Club, Chicago; Municipal Art League. Born in St. Louis. From 1892-1896 pupil of Laurens and Raphael Collin in Paris, where her works were hung on the line at the New Gallery, Champ de Mars.

A decorative artist who has executed mural decoration in a

private house in Chicago, and has illustrated "Max Müller's Memories" and other publications. For use in schools she made a color print, "Reading of the Declaration of Independence before the Army."

Her calendars and posters are in demand by collectors at home and in foreign countries. Miss Ostertag has designed elaborate chimney pieces to be executed in mosaic and glass. Her droll conceits in "Mary and Her Lamb," the "Ten Little Injuns," and other juvenile tales were complimented by Boutet de Monvel, who was so much interested in her work that he gave her valuable criticism and advice without solicitation.

O'Tama-Chiovara. Gold medal at an exhibition of laces in Rome and prizes at all the exhibitions held in Palermo by the Art Club. Born in Tokio, where she came to the notice of Vicenzo Ragusa, a Sicilian sculptor in the employ of the Japanese Government at Tokio. He taught her design, color, and modelling, and finally induced her to go with his sister to Palermo. Here her merit was soon recognized in a varied collection of water-colors representing flowers and fruits, which were reproduced with surpassing truth. When the School of Applied Art was instituted at Palermo in 1887, she was put in charge of the drawing, water-color, and modelling in the Women's Section.

She knows the flowers of various countries – those of Japan and Sicily wonderfully well, and her fancy is inexhaustible; her exquisite embroideries reflect this quality. She has many private pupils, and is as much beloved for her character as she is admired for her talents. When she renounced Buddhism for Christianity, the Princess of Scalca was her godmother.

Paczka-Wagner, Cornelia. Honorable mention, Berlin, 1890. Born in Göttingen, 1864. She has been, in the main, her own instructor, living for some years in Rome for the purpose of study. In 1895 she settled in Berlin, where she has made a specialty of women's and children's portraits in olgraphy (?) and lithography. Beautiful drawings by her were exhibited at the International Water-Color Exhibition in Dresden, 1892.

An interesting account of a visit to the studio of the Hungarian painter Paczka and his German wife tells of a strong series of paintings in progress there, under the general title, "A Woman's Soul." In freedom and boldness of conception they were said to remind one of Klinger, but in warmth and depth of feeling to surpass him. Frau Paczka had just finished a very large picture, representing the first couple after the expulsion from Paradise. The scene is on the waste, stony slope of a mountain; the sun shines with full force in the background, while upon the unshadowed rocks of the foreground are the prostrate Adam and his wife – more accusing than complaining.

In 1899 Frau Paczka exhibited in Berlin, "Vanitas," which excels in richness of fancy and boldness of representation, while wanting somewhat in detail; the ensemble presents a remarkably fine, symbolic composition, which sets forth in rich color the dance of mankind before the golden calf, and the bitter disillusions in the struggle for fame, wealth, and happiness.

Parlaghy, Vilma, or the Princess Lwoff. Great gold medal from the Emperor of Austria, 1890; great gold medal, 1894; small gold medal at Berlin, 1890, adjudged to her portrait of Windhorst. Born at Hadju-Dorogh in 1863, and studied in Budapest, Munich, Venice, Florence, and Turin. Her portraits having found great favor at the Court of Berlin, she removed her studio from Munich to that capital.

One of her instructors was Lenbach, and she is said by some critics to have appropriated his peculiarities as a colorist and his shortcomings in drawing, without attaining his geniality and power of divination. In 1891 her portrait of Count von Moltke, begun shortly before his death and finished afterward, was sent to the International Exposition at Berlin, but was rejected. The Emperor, however, bought it for his private collection, and at his request it was given a place of honor at the Exposition, the incident causing much comment. She exhibited a portrait of the Emperor William at Berlin in 1893, which Rosenberg called careless in drawing and modelling and inconceivable in its unrefreshing, dirty-gray color.

In January, 1895, she gave an exhibition of one hundred and four of her works, mostly portraits, including those of the Emperor, Caprivi, von Moltke, and Kossuth, which had previously been exhibited in Berlin, Munich, and Paris. The proceeds of this exhibition went to the building fund of the Emperor William Memorial Church.

Of a portrait exhibited in 1896, at Munich, a critic said that while it was not wholly bad, it was no better than what hundreds of others could do as well, and hundreds of others could do much better.

Pasch, Ulricke Friederika. Member of the Academy of Fine Arts of Sweden. Born in Stockholm. 1735-1796. A portrait of Gustavus-Adolphus II. by this artist is in the Castle at Stockholm. She was a sister of Lorenz Pasch.

Pascoli, Luigia. This Venetian painter has exhibited in various Italian cities since 1870, when she sent a "Magdalen" to Parma. "First Love" appeared at Naples in 1877, and "The Maskers" – pastel – at Venice in 1881. A "Girl with a Cat," a "Roman Girl," and a "Seller of Eggs" – the latter in Venetian costume – are works of true value. Her copies of Titian's "St. Mark" and of Gian Bellini's "Supper at Emmaus" have attracted attention and are much esteemed.

Passe, Magdalena van de. Born at Utrecht about 1600; she died at the age of forty. This engraver was a daughter of Crispus van de Passe, the elder. She practised her art in Germany, England, Denmark, and the Netherlands, and was important as an artist. Her engraving was exceedingly careful and skilful.

Among her plates are "Three Sibyls," 1617; an "Annunciation," "Cephalus and Procris," "Latona," and landscapes after the works of Bril, Savery, Willars, etc.

Pattison, Helen Searle. Born in Burlington, Vermont. Daughter of Henry Searle, a talented architect who moved to Rochester, New York, where his daughter spent much of her girlhood. She held the position of art teacher in a school in Batavia, New York, while still a girl herself.

About 1860 she became the pupil of Herr Johan Wilhelm Preyer, the well-known painter of still-life, fruit, and flowers. Preyer was a dwarf and an excellent man, but as a rule took no pupils. He was much interested in Miss Searle, and made an exception in her case. She soon acquired the technique of her master and painted much as he did, but with less minute detail, finer color, and far more sentiment.

In 1876 Miss Searle married the artist, James William Pattison, now on the staff of the Art Institute, Chicago. After their marriage Mr. and Mrs. Pattison resided at Écouen, near Paris. Returning to America in 1882, they spent some time in Chicago and New York City, removing to Jacksonville, Illinois, in 1884. Here Mr. Pattison was at the head of the School of Fine Arts.

Mrs. Pattison lived but a few months in Jacksonville, dying in November, 1884.

Mrs. Pattison's artistic reputation was well established and her works were exhibited at the Paris Salon and in all the German cities of importance. They were frequently seen in England and at the National Academy of Design in New York. Her subjects were still-life, fruit, and flowers, and her works are widely distributed.

Pazzi, Caterina de, whose conventual name was Maria Maddalena. Was born in Florence in 1566. It would be interesting to know the relation that this gentle lady bore to those Pazzi who had earned a fame so unlike hers fourscore years before she saw the light.

Caterina de Pazzi, when a mere girl, entered a convent which stood on the site of the church known by her name in the Via Pinti. The cell of Santa Maddalena – now a chapel – may still be visited. She was canonized by Pope Alexander VIII. in 1670, sixty-two years after her death.

The Florentines have many lovely legends associated with her memory. One of these relates that she painted pictures of sacred subjects when asleep. Be this as it may, we know that her pictures were esteemed in the days when the best artists lived and worked beside her. Examples of her art may still be seen in churches in Rome and Parma, as well as in the church of her native city which bears her name.

Peale, Anna C. Made her mark as a miniature painter and for some years was the only professional woman artist in Philadelphia. Her portrait of General Jackson made in 1819 was well considered. She also made portraits of President Monroe, Henry Clay, R. M. Johnson, John Randolph of Roanoke, and other prominent men. Miss Peale married in 1829 the Rev. William Staughton, a Baptist clergyman, the president of the theological college at Georgetown, Kentucky. He lived but three months after their marriage, and she returned to Philadelphia and again pursued her artistic labors. She married a second husband, General William Duncan, and from this time gave up professional painting.

Peale, Sara M. 1860-1885. Daughter of James Peale, under whose teaching she made her first studies. She was also a pupil of her uncle, the founder of Peale's Museum, Philadelphia. Miss Peale painted portraits and spent some years in Baltimore and Washington. Among her portraits are those of Lafayette, Thomas Benton, Henry A. Wise, Caleb Cushing, and other distinguished men. From 1847 she resided in St. Louis thirty years and then went to Philadelphia. Her later works were still-life subjects, especially fruits.

Pelichy, Geertruida. Honorary member of the Academy of Vienna. Born in Utrecht, 1744; died in Brügge, 1825. Pupil of P. de Cock and Suvée. In 1753, she went to Brügge with her father, and later to Paris and Vienna. She painted portraits of the Emperor Joseph II. and Maria Theresa, some good landscapes, and animal studies. Two of her pictures are in the Museum at Brügge.

Pellegrino, Itala. Born at Milan, 1865. Pupil of Battaglia. Her pictures are of genre and marine subjects. At the great exhibition at Turin, 1884, she exhibited a marine view which was bought by Prince Amadeo. Another marine view exhibited at Milan was acquired by the Società Promotrice. In 1888 she sent to the exhibition at Naples, where she resides, a view of Portici, which was added to the Royal Gallery. The excellence of her work is in the strength and certainty of touch and the sincerity and originality of composition. She has painted a "Marine View of Naples," "In the Gulf," "Fair Weather," and "Evening at Sea"; also a genre picture, "Frusta là," which was sold while in an exhibition in Rome.

Penicke, Clara. Born at Berlin in 1818, where she died in 1899. She studied first with Remy and later with Carl Begas and Edward Magnus. Her work was largely confined to portrait and historical painting. In the Gallery at Schwerin is her "Elector Frederick of Saxony Refusing to Accept the Interim." Another good example of her historical work is the "Reconciliation of Charlemagne with Thassilo of Bavaria." A well-known and strongly modelled portrait of Minister Von Stoach and several Luther portraits, "Luther's Family Devotion" and "Luther Finds the First Latin Bible," show her facility in this branch of art. She also painted a "Christ on the Cross."

Perelli, Lida. A landscape painter living in Milan, who has become well known by pictures that have been seen at the exhibitions in several Italian cities, especially through some

Roman studies that appeared at Florence and Turin in 1884. "A View of Lecco, Lake Como," "Casolare," and "A Lombard Plain" are among her best works.

Perman, Louise E. Born at Birkenshaw, Renfrewshire. Studied in Glasgow. This artist paints roses, and roses only, in oils. In this art she has been very successful. She has exhibited at the Royal Academy and the New Gallery, London; at the Royal Scottish Academy, Glasgow; at art exhibits in Munich, Dresden, Berlin, Prague, Hanover, etc., and wherever her works have been seen they have been sold. In May, 1903, a collection of twenty-five rose pictures were exhibited by a prominent dealer, and but few were left in his hands.

A critic in the *Studio* of April, 1903, writing of the exhibition at the Ladies' Artists' Club, Glasgow, says: "Miss Louise Perman's rose pictures were as refined and charming as ever. This last-named lady certainly has a remarkable power of rendering the beauties of the queen of flowers, whether she chooses to paint the sumptuous yellow of the 'Maréchal Niel,' the blush of the 'Katherine Mermet,' or the crimson glory of the 'Queen of Autumn.' She seems not only to give the richness of color and fulness of contour of the flowers, but to capture for the delight of the beholder the very spiritual essence of them." To the London Academy, 1903, she sent a picture called "York and Lancaster."

Perrier, Marie. Mention honorable at Salon des Artistes Français, 1899; Prix Marie Bashkirtseff, 1899; honorable mention, Paris Exposition, 1900; numerous medals from foreign and provincial exhibitions; medals in gold and silver at Rouen, Nîmes, Rennes, etc.; bronze medals at Amiens and Angers. Member of the Société des Artistes Français; perpetual member of the Baron Taylor Association, section of the Arts of Painting, etc. Born at Paris. Pupil of Benjamin Constant, Jules Lefebvre, and J. P. Laurens.

Mlle. Perrier's picture of "Jeanne d'Arc" is in a provincial museum; several pictures by her belonging to the city of Paris are scenes connected with the schools of the city – "Breakfast at the Communal School"; "After School at Montmartre" were at the Salon des Artistes Français, 1903; others are "Manual Labor at the Maternal School," "Flowers," and "Recreation of the Children at the Maternal School." Of the last Gabriel Moury says, "It is one of the really good pictures in the Salon."

This artist decorated a villa near Nîmes with four large panels representing the "Seasons," twelve small panels, the "Hours," and pictures of the labors of the fields, such as the gathering of grapes and picking of olives.

She has painted numerous portraits of children and a series of pictures illustrating the "Life of the Children of Paris." They are "Children at School and after School," "Children on the Promenade and Their Games," and "Children at Home."

Perry, Clara Greenleaf. Member of the Copley Society. Born at Long Branch, New Jersey. Pupil of Boston Art Museum School, under Mr. Benson and Mr. Tarbell; in Paris pupil of M. Raphael Collin and Robert Henri.

Miss Perry has exhibited her portrait of Mrs. U. in the Salon of the Société Nationale des Beaux-Arts and in Philadelphia. She paints landscapes and portraits.

Perry, Lilla Cabot. Pupil in Boston of Dennis Bunker and Alfred Collins; in Paris of Alfred Stevens, Robert Fleury, Bouguereau, and Courtois; in Munich of Fritz von Uhde.

Mrs. Perry is essentially a portrait painter, but has painted landscapes, especially in Japan, where she spent some years. The scenery of Japan and its wonderfully beautiful Fuziyama would almost compel an artist to paint landscapes.

Mrs. Perry says that her pictures of French and Japanese types are, in fact, portraits as truly as are those she is asked to paint.

Her picture of a "Japanese Lacemaker" belongs to Mr. Quincy

A. Shaw. It has been much admired in the exhibitions in which it has been seen.

In the Water-Color Exhibition of the Boston Art Club, 1903, Mrs. Perry's portrait of Miss S. attracted much attention. The delicate flesh tones, the excellent modelling of the features, and what may be called the whole atmosphere of the picture combine in producing an effective and pleasing example of portraiture.

Perugini, Caterina E. An Italian painter living in London, where she frequently exhibits her excellent pictures. Among them are "A Siesta," "Dolce far Niente," "Multiplication," and portraits of Guy Cohn, son of Sir Guy Campbell, Bart., and of Peggy and Kitty Hammond, two charming children.

At the Academy, 1903, she exhibited "Faith" and "Silken Tresses."

Perugini, Mrs. Kate Dickens. Younger daughter of Charles Dickens and wife of Charles Edward Perugini. This artist has exhibited at the Royal Academy and at other exhibitions since 1877. Her pictures are of genre subjects, such as the "Dolls' Dressmaker," "Little-Red-Cap," "Old Curiosity Shop," etc. At the Academy, 1903, she exhibited "Some Spring Flowers."
[*No reply to circular.*]

Peters, Anna. Medals at Vienna, 1873; London, 1874; Munich, 1876; Amsterdam and Antwerp, 1877. Born at Mannheim, 1843. Pupil of her father, Pieter Francis Peters, in Stuttgart. Miss Peters travelled over Europe and was commissioned to decorate apartments in the royal castles at Stuttgart and Friedrichshafen.

Her picture of "Roses and Grapes" is in the National Gallery, London; and one of "Autumn Flowers" in the Museum at Stuttgart.

Pillini, Margherita. An Italian painter living in Paris. Her most successful exhibitions have been those at Rome, in 1883, when her "Silk-cocoon Carder of Quimper" and "Charity" appeared; and at Turin, in 1884, when "The Three Ages," "The Poor Blind Man," and a portrait of the Prince of Naples were shown, all exquisite in sentiment and excellent in execution. The "Silk-cocoon Carder of Quimper" has been thus noticed by De Rengis: "If I am not mistaken, Signora Margherita Pillini has also taken this road, full of modernity, but not free from great danger. Her 'Silk-cocoon Carder' is touched with great disdain for every suggestion of the old school. Rare worth – if worth it is – that a young woman should be carried by natural inclination into such care for detail."

Pinto-Sezzi, Ida. Silver medal at the Beatrice Exposition, Florence, 1890. Since 1882 pictures by this artist have been seen in various Italian exhibitions. In the Beatrice of that year she exhibited "Cocciara," and in 1887 "A Friar Cook." Her "Fortune-Teller" attracted general attention at Venice in 1887.

This artist has also given some time to the decoration of terra-cotta in oil colors. An amphora decorated with landscape and figures was exhibited at the Promotrice in Florence in 1889 (?) and much admired.

Poetting, Countess Adrienne. Born in Chrudim, Bohemia, 1856. The effect of her thorough training under Blass, Straschiripka, and Frittjof Smith is seen in her portraits of the Deputy-Burgomaster Franz Khume, which is in the Rathhaus, Vienna, as well as in those of the Princess Freda von Oldenburg and the writer, Bertha von Suttner. Her excellence is also apparent in her genre subjects, "In the Land of Dreams" being an excellent example of these.

Popert, Charlotte. Silver medal at the Beatrice, Florence, 1890. Born in Hamburg, 1848. Pupil in Weimar of the elder Preller and Carl Gherts; of P. Joris in Rome, and Bonnat in Paris. After extensive travels in the Orient, England, the Netherlands, and

Spain, she established herself in Rome and painted chiefly in water-colors. Her "Praying Women of Bethlehem" is an excellent example of her art.

In 1883 she exhibited at Rome, "In the Temple at Bethlehem"; at Turin in 1884, "In the Seventeenth Century" and "The Nun"; at Venice in 1887, an exquisite portrait in water-colors.

Poppe-Lüderitz, Elizabeth. Honorable mention, Berlin, 1891. For the second time only the Senate of the Berlin Academy conferred this distinction upon a woman. The artist exhibited two portraits, "painted with Holbein-like delicacy and truthfulness" – if we may agree with the critics.

This artist was born in Berlin in 1858, and was a pupil of Gussow. Her best pictures are portraits, but her "Sappho" and "Euphrosine" are excellent works.

Popp, Babette. Born in Regensburg, 1800; died about 1840. Made her studies in Munich. In the Cathedral of Regensburg is her "Adoration of the Kings."

Powell, Caroline A. Bronze medal at Chicago, 1893; silver medal at Buffalo, 1901. Member of the Society of American Wood-Engravers and of the Boston Society of Arts and Crafts. Born in Dublin, Ireland. Pupil of W. J. Linton and Timothy Cole.

Miss Powell was an illustrator of the *Century Magazine* from 1880 to 1895. The engraving after "The Resurrection" by John La Farge, in the Church of St. Thomas, New York, is the work of this artist. She also illustrated "Engravings on Wood," by William M. Laffan, in which book her work is commended.

Miss Powell is now employed by Messrs. Houghton, Mifflin & Co., and writes me: "So far as I know, I am, at present, the only woman in America engaged in the practise of engraving as a fine art."

Prestel, Maria Catharina; family name Holl. Born in

Nuremburg, 1747. Her husband, Johan Prestel, was her teacher, and she was of great assistance in the work which he produced at Frankfort-on-the-Main, in 1783. In 1786, however, she separated from him and went to London, where she devoted herself to aquatints. She executed more than seventy plates, some of them of great size.

Prestel, Ursula Magdalena. Born in Nuremburg. 1777-1845. Daughter of the preceding artist. She worked in Frankfort and London, travelled in France and Switzerland, and died in Brussels. Her moonlight scenes, some of her portraits, and her picture of the "Falls of the Rhine near Laufen," are admirable.

Preuschen, Hermine von Schmidt; married name, Telman. Born at Darmstadt, 1857. Pupil of Ferdinand Keller in Karlsruhe. Travelled in Spain, France, Italy, the Netherlands, and Denmark. She remained some time in Munich, Berlin, and Rome, establishing her studio in these cities and painting a variety of subjects. Her flower pictures are her best works. Her "Mors Imperator" created a sensation by reason of its striking qualities rather than by intrinsic artistic merit. In the gallery at Metz is her picture of "Irene von Spilimberg on the Funeral Gondola."

In 1883 she exhibited in Rome, "Answered," a study of thistles; "In Autumn," a variety of fruits; and "Questions," a charming study of carnations. At Berlin, in 1890, "Meadow Saffron and Cineraria" was praised for its glowing color and artistic arrangement. A Viennese critic, the same year, lamented that an artist of so much talent should paint lifeless objects only. In Berlin, in 1894, she held an exhibition, in which her landscapes and flower pieces were better than her still-life pictures. Frau Preuschen is also a musician and poet.

The painting of flower pieces is a delightful art for man or woman, but so many such pictures which are by amateurs are seen in exhibitions – too good to be refused but not of a satisfactory quality – that one can scarcely sympathize with the critic who would have Mme. Preuschen paint other subjects than these charming blossoms, so exquisite in form and color, into which she paints so much delightful sentiment.

Puehn, Sophie. Born at Nuremberg, 1864. This artist studied in Paris and Munich and resides in the latter city. At the International Exhibition, Vienna, 1894, her portrait of a "Lady Drinking Tea" was praised by the critics without exception, and, in fact, her portraits are always well considered. That she is also skilful in etching was shown in her "Forsaken," exhibited in 1896.

Putnam, Sarah Goold. Member of the Copley Society. Born in Boston. Pupil in Boston and New York of J. B. Johnston, F. Duveneck, Abbott Thayer, and William Chase; in Scheveningen, of Bart. J. Blommers; and in Munich, of Wilhelm Dürr.

Miss Putnam's portrait of Hon. John Lowell is in the District Court Room in Post-Office Building, Boston; that of William G. Russell, in the Law Library in the Court House, Pemberton Square, same city; that of General Charles G. Loring, for many years Director of Boston Museum of Fine Arts, belongs to his family; among her other portraits are those of Dr. Henry P. Bowditch, Francis Boott, George Partridge Bradford, Edward Silsbee, Mrs. Asa Gray, and Lorin Deland. In addition to the above she has painted more than one hundred portraits of men, women, and children, which belong to the families of the subjects.

Puyroche, Mme. Elise. Born in Dresden, 1828. Resided in Lyons, France, where she was a pupil of the fine colorist, Simon St. Jean. Mme. Puyroche excelled her master in the arrangement of flowers in her pictures and in the correctness of her drawing, while she acquired his harmonious color. Her picture called the "Tom Wreath," painted in 1850, is in the Dresden Gallery.

Questier, Catherine. Born in Amsterdam. In 1655 she published two comedies which were illustrated by engravings of her own design and execution. She achieved a good reputation for painting, copper engraving, and modelling in wax, as well as for her writings.

Raab, Doris. Third-class medal, Nuremberg; also second-class medal, 1892. Born in Nuremberg, 1851. Pupil of her father, Johann Leonhard Raab, in etching and engraving. She has engraved many works by Rubens, Van Dyck, and Cuyp; among her plates after works of more recent artists are Piloty's "Death Warrant of Mary Stuart," Lindenschmidt's "In Thought," and Laufberger's "Hunting Fanfare." This artist resides in Munich.

Radovska, Baroness Annetta, of Milan. Her interesting genre pictures are seen in most of the Italian exhibitions. "Old Wine, Young Wife," was at Milan, 1881; in same city, 1883, "An Aggression," "The Visit," "The Betrothed." She also sent to Rome, in 1883, two pictures, one of which, "The Harem," was especially noteworthy. In 1884, at Turin, she exhibited "Tea" and the "Four Ages"; these, were excellent in tone and technique and attractive in subject. At Milan, 1886, her "Will He Arrive?" was heartily commended in the art journals.

Rae, Henrietta. See Normand, Mrs. Ernest

Ragusa, Eleanora. See O'Tama.

Rapin, Aimée. At the Swiss National Exposition, 1896, a large picture of a "Genevese Watchmaker" by this artist was purchased; By the Government and is in the Museum at Neuchâtel. In 1903 the city of Geneva commissioned her to paint a portrait of Philippe Plantamour, which is in the Museum Mon-Repos, at Geneva. Member of the Société des Beaux-Arts of Lausanne, Société des Femmes peintres et sculpteurs de la Suisse romande, Société de l'exposition permanente des Beaux-Arts, Geneva. Born at Payerne, Canton de Vaud. Studied at Geneva under M. Hebert and Barthelmy Menn, in painting; Hugues Bovy, modelling.

Mlle. Rapin writes me: "I am, above all, a portrait painter, and my portraits are in private hands." She names among others of her sitters, Ernest Naville, the philosopher; Raoul Pictet, chemist; Jules Salmson, sculptor, etc. She mentions that she painted a portrait of the present Princess of Wales at the time of her marriage, but as it was painted from photographs the artist has no opinion about its truth to life. Mlle. Rapin has executed many portraits of men, women, and children in Paris, London, and Germany, as well as in Switzerland. She refers me to the following account of herself and her art. In the *Studio* of April, 1903, R. M. writes: "The subject of these notes is a striking example of the compensations of Nature for her apparent cruelty; also of what the genuine artist is capable of achieving notwithstanding the most singular disadvantages. Some years ago in the little town of Payerne, Canton Vaud, a child was born without arms. One day the mother, while standing near a rose-bush with her infant in her arms, was astonished to observe one of its tiny toes clasp the stem of the rose. Little did she guess at the time that these prehensile toes were destined one day to serve an artist, in the execution of her work, with the same marvellous facility as hands. As the child grew up the greatest care was bestowed upon her education. She early manifested unmistakable artistic promise, and at the age of sixteen was sent to the École des Beaux Arts, Geneva... For reasons already mentioned Mlle. Rapin holds a unique position amongst that valiant and distinguished group of Swiss lady artists to whose work we hope to have the opportunity of referring... She is a fine example of that singleness of devotion which characterizes the born artist. Her art is the all-absorbing interest of her life. It is not without its limitations, but within these limitations the artist has known how to be true to herself. Drawing her inspiration direct from nature, she has held on her independent way, steadily faithful to the gift she possesses of evoking a character in a portrait or of making us feel how the common task, when representative of genuine human effort and touched with the poetry of national tradition, of religion, and of nature, becomes a subject of noble artistic treatment. She has kept unimpaired that *merveilleux frisson de sensibilité* which is one of the most precious gifts of the artistic temperament, and which is quick to respond to the ideal in the real. There are some artists who, though possessed of extraordinary mastery over the materials of their art, bring to their work a spirit which beggars and belittles both art and life; there are others who seem to work with an ever-present sense of the noble purpose of their vocation and the pathos and dignity of existence. Mlle. Rapin belongs to the second category. Her 'L'Horloger' is an example of this. A Genevese watchmaker is bending to his work at a bench covered with tools. Through the window of the workshop one perceives in the blue distance Mont Saléve, and nearer the time-honored towers of the Cathedral of St. Pierre. Here is a composition dealing with simple life – a composition which, from the point of execution, color, and harmony of purpose, leaves little or nothing to be desired. But this is not all. It is, so to speak, an artistic *résumé* of the life and history of the old city, and that strongly portrayed national type gathers dignity from his alliance with the generations who helped to make one of the main interests of the city, and from his relationship to that eventful past suggested by the Cathedral and the Mountain.

"Mlle. Rapin is unmistakably one of the best Swiss portraitists, working for the most part in pastels, her medium by predilection; she has at the same time modelled portraits in bas-relief. We are not only impressed by the intensely living quality of her work as a portraitist, but by the extraordinary power with which she has seized and expressed the individual character and history of each of her subjects."

Mlle. Rapin has exhibited her works with success in Paris, Munich, and Berlin. The few specimens of her bas-reliefs which I have seen prove that did she prefer the art of sculpture before that of painting, she would be as successful with her modelling tools as she has been with her brush.

Rappard, Clara von. Second-class medal, London. Born at Wabern, near Berne, 1857. After studying with Skutelzky and Dreber, she worked under Gussow in Berlin. She spent some time in travel, especially in Germany and Italy, and then, choosing Interlaken as her home, turned her attention to the illustration of books, as well as to portrait and genre painting. In the Museum at Freiburg is her "Point-lace-maker." A series of sixteen "Phantasies" by this artist has been published in Munich.

Rath, Henriette. Honorary member of the Société des Arts, 1801. Born in 1772, she died in 1856 at Genf, where, with her sister, she founded the Musée Rath. She studied under Isabey, and was well and favorably known as a portrait and enamel painter.

Ream, Vinnie. See Hoxie.

Redmond, Frieda Voelter. Medal at the Columbian Exhibition, Chicago. Member of the Woman's Art Club. Born in Thun, Switzerland. Studies made in Switzerland and in Paris. A painter of flowers and still-life.

"Mrs. Redmond is a Swiss woman, now residing in New York. She has exhibited her works in the Paris Salon, in the National Academy of Design, at the Society of American Artists' exhibitions, etc., and was awarded a medal at the World's Fair in Chicago. Her work is not only skilful and accurate in description and characterization; it is done with breadth and freedom, and given a quality of fine decorative distinction. Her subjects are roses, cyclamen, chrysanthemums, nasturtiums, double larkspurs, cinneraria, etc., and she makes each panel a distinct study in design, with a background and accessories of appropriate character. For example, the three or four large panels of roses painted at Mentone have a glimpse of the Mediterranean for background, and a suggestion of trellis-work for the support of the vine or bush; and in another rose panel we have a tipped-over Gibraltar basket with its luscious contents strewed about in artful confusion. The double larkspurs make very charming panels for decorative purposes. They are painted with delightful fulness of color and engaging looseness and crispness of touch." – *Boston Transcript.*

Regis, Emma. This Roman painter has given special attention to figures, and has executed a number of portraits, one of the best of which is that of the Marchioness Durazzo Pallavicini. She has exhibited some delightful work at Turin and at Rome, such as "The Lute-Player," "All is not Gold that Glitters," "Humanity," and "In illo Tempore?"
[*No reply to circular.*]

Reinhardt, Sophie. Born at Kirchberg, 1775; died at Karlsruhe, 1843. Pupil of Becker. She travelled in Austro-Hungary and Italy. In the Kunsthalle at Karlsruhe is her picture of "St. Elizabeth and the Child John." Among her best works are "The Death of St. Catherine of Alexandria," "The Death of Tasso," and twelve illustrations for a volume of Hebel's poems.

Remy, Marie. Born in Berlin, 1829. Daughter of Professor August Remy of the Berlin Academy. Pupil of her father, Hermine Stilke, and Theude Grönland. She travelled extensively in several European countries, making special studies in flowers and still-life, from which many of her water-colors were painted; twenty of these are in the Berlin National Gallery.

Reuter, Elizabeth. Born in Lubeck, 1853. Pupil of Zimmermann in Munich, A. Schliecker in Hamburg, and of H. Eschke in Berlin. She also went to Düsseldorf to work in the Gallery there. Later she travelled in Scandinavia. Her best pictures are landscapes. Among them is a charming series of six water-colors of views in the park of Friedrichsruhe.

Revest, Cornelia Louisa. Second-class medals in 1819 and 1831 in Paris. Born in Amsterdam, 1795; died in Paris, 1856. Pupil of Sérangély and Vafflard in Paris. In 1814 she painted a "Magdalen at the Feet of Christ" for a church in Marseilles. She also painted many good portraits and a picture called "The Young Mother Playing the Mandolin."

Richard, Mme. Hortense. Honorable mention, Exposition of 1889; third-class medal, 1892; silver medals at Antwerp and Barcelona, and gold medal in London. Born at Paris, 1860. Pupil of James Bertrand, Jules Lefebvre, and Bouguereau. Has exhibited regularly since 1875. Her picture of "Cinderella" is in the Museum of Poitiers; "At Church in Poitou" is in the Luxembourg. She has painted many portraits.

Richards, Anna Mary. Norman Dodge prize, National Academy, New York, 1890. Member of the '91 Art Club, London. Born at Germantown, Pennsylvania, 1870. Pupil of Dennis Bunker in Boston, H. Siddons Mowbray and La Farge in New York, Benjamin Constant and J. P. Laurens in Paris, and always of her father, W. T. Richards.

Miss Richards' work is varied. She is fond of color when suited to her subject; she also works much in black and white. When representing nature she is straightforward in her rendering of its aspects and moods, but she also loves the "symbolic expression of emotion" and the so-called "allegorical subjects." The artist writes: "I simply work in the way that at the moment it seems to me fitting to work to express the thing I have in mind. Where the object of the picture is one sort of quality, I use the method that seems to me to emphasize that quality."

When but fourteen years old this artist exhibited at the National Academy, New York, a picture of waves, "The Wild Horses of the Sea," which was immediately sold and a duplicate ordered. In England Miss Richards has exhibited at the Academy, and her pictures have been selected for exhibitions in provincial galleries. Miss Richards is earnestly devoted to her art, and has in mind an end toward which she diligently strives – not to become a painter distinguished for clever mannerism, but "to attain a definite end; one which is difficult to reach and requires widely applied effort."

Judging from what she has already done at her age, one may predict her success in her chosen method. In February, 1903, Miss Richards and her father exhibited their works in the Noe Galleries. I quote a few press opinions.

"Miss Richards paints the sea well; she infuses interest into her figures; she has a love of allegory; her studies in Holland and Norway are interesting. Her 'Whitby,' lighted by sunset, with figures massed in the streets in dark relief against it, is beautiful. Her 'Friends,' showing two women watching the twilight fading from the summits of a mountain range, the cedared slopes and river valley below meantime gathering blueness and shadow, is of such strength and sweetness of fancy that it affects one like a strain of music."

"Miss Richards becomes symbolic or realistic by turn. Some of her figures are creatures of the imagination, winged and iridescent, like the 'Spirit of Hope.' Again, she paints good, honest Dutchmen, loafing about the docks. Sometimes she has recourse to poetry and quotes Emerson for a title... If technically she is not always convincing, it is apparent that the artist is doing some thinking for herself, and her endeavors are in good taste."

Miss Richards has written "Letter and Spirit," containing fifty-seven "Dramatic Sonnets of Inward Life."

These she has illustrated by sixty full-page pictures. Of these drawings the eminent artist, G. F. Watts, says: "In imaginative comprehension they are more than illustrations; they are interpretations. I find in them an assemblage of great qualities – beauty of line, unity and abundance in composition, variety and appreciation of natural effects, with absence of manner; also unusual qualities in drawing, neither academical nor eccentric –

all carried out with great purity and completeness."

Richards, Signora Emma Gagiotti. Rome.
[*No reply to circular.*]

Ries, Therese Feodorowna. Bronze medal at Ekaterinburg; Karl Ludwig gold medal, Vienna; gold medal, Paris Exposition, 1900. Officer of the Academy. Born in Moscow. Pupil of the Moscow Academy and of Professor Hellmer, Vienna, women not being admitted to the Vienna Academy.

A critic in the *Studio* of July, 1901, who signs his article A. S. L., writes as follows of this remarkable artist: "Not often does it fall to the lot of a young artist to please both critic and public at the same time, and, having gained their interest, to continue to fill their expectations. But it was so with Feodorowna Ries, a young Russian artist who some eight months ago had never even had a piece of clay in her hand, but who, by dint of 'self,' now stands amongst the foremost of her profession. It was chance that led Miss Ries to the brush, and another chance which led her to abandon the brush for the chisel. Five years ago she was awarded the Carl Ludwig gold medal for her 'Lucifer,' and at the last Paris Exhibition she gained the gold medal for her 'Unbesiegbaren' (The Unconquerable).

"Miss Ries was born and educated in Moscow, but Vienna is the city of her adoption. She first studied painting at the Moscow Academy, her work there showing great breadth of character and power of delineation. At the yearly Exhibition in Moscow, held some five months after she had entered as a student, she took the gold medal for her 'Portrait of a Russian Peasant.' She then abandoned painting for sculpture, and one month later gained the highest commendations for a bust of 'Ariadne.' She then began to study the plastic art from life. Dissatisfied with herself, although her 'Somnambulist' gained a prize, Miss Ries left Moscow for Paris, but on her way stayed in Vienna, studying under Professor Hellmer. One year later, at the Vienna Spring Exhibition, she exhibited her 'Die Hexe.' Here is no traditional witch, though the broomstick on which she will ride through the air is *en evidence*. She is a demoniac being, knowing her own power, and full of devilish instinct. The marble is full of life, and one seems to feel the warmth of her delicate, powerfully chiselled, though soft and pliable limbs."

"'Die Unbesiegbaren' is a most powerful work, and stood out in the midst of the sculpture at Paris in 1900 with the prominence imparted by unusual power in the perception of the *whole* of a subject and the skill to render the perception so that others realize its full meaning. There are four figures in this group – men drawing a heavy freight boat along the shore by means of a towline passed round their bodies, on which they throw their weight in such a way that their legs, pressed together, lose their outline – except in the case of the leader – and are as a mass of power. They also pull on the line with their hands. The leader bends over the rope until he looks down; the man behind him raises his head and looks up with an appealing expression; the two others behind are exerting all their force in pulling on the rope, but have twisted the upper part of the body in order to look behind and watch the progress of their great burden. There is not the least resemblance of one to the other, either in feature or expression, and to me it would seem that the woman who had conceived and executed this group might well be content to rest on her laurels.

"But an artistic creator who is really inspired with his art and not with himself is never satisfied; he presses on and on – sometimes after he has expressed the best of his talent. This is not yet reached, I believe, by Miss Ries, and we shall see still greater results of her inspiration."

The Austrian Government commissioned this artist to execute the figure of a saint. One may well prophesy that there will be nothing conventional in this work. She has already produced a striking "Saint Barbara." Her portrait busts include those of Professor Wegr, Professor Hellmer, Mark Twain, Countess

Kinsky, Countess Palffs, Baron Berger, and many others.

Rijutine, Elisa. A bronze and a gold medal at the Beatrice Exposition, Florence, 1890. Born in Florence, where she resides and devotes herself to painting in imitation of old tapestries. An excellent example of her work is in water-colors and is called "The Gardener's Children." In 1888 and 1889 she exhibited "The Coronation of Esther" and a picture of "Oleanders."

Roberts, Elizabeth Wentworth.
[*No reply to circular.*]

Robinson, Mrs. Imogene Morrell. Medals at the Mechanics' Fair, Boston, and at the Centennial Exhibition, Philadelphia, 1876. Born in Attleborough, Massachusetts. Pupil of Camphausen in Düsseldorf, and of Couture in Paris, where she resided several years. Among her important works are "The First Battle between the Puritans and Indians" and "Washington and His Staff Welcoming a Provision Train," both at Philadelphia. Mrs. Morrell continued to sign her pictures with her maiden name, Imogene Robinson.

A critic of the New York *Evening Post* said of her pictures at Philadelphia: "In the painting of the horses Mrs. Morrell has shown great knowledge of their action, and their finish is superb. The work is painted with great strength throughout, and its solidity and forcible treatment will be admired by all who take an interest in Revolutionary history... In the drawing of the figures of Standish and the chief at his side, and the dead and dying savages, there is a fine display of artistic power, and the grouping of the figures is masterly... In color the works are exceedingly brilliant."

Robusti, Marietta. Born in Venice. 1560-1590. The parentage of this artist would seem to promise her talent and insure its culture. She was the daughter of Jacopo Robusti, better known as "Il

Tintoretto," who has been called "the thunder of art," and who avowed his ambition to equal "the drawing of Michael Angelo and the coloring of Titian."

The portrait of Marietta Robusti proves her to have been justly celebrated for her beauty. Her face is sweet and gentle in expression. She was sprightly in manner and full of enthusiasm for anything that interested and attracted her; she had a good talent for music and a charming voice in singing.

Her father's fondness for her made him desire her constant companionship, and at times he permitted her to dress as a boy and share with him certain studies that she could only have made in this disguise. Tintoretto carefully cultivated the talents of his daughter, and some of the portraits she painted did her honor. That of Marco dei Vescovi first turned public attention to her artistic merits. The beard was especially praised and it was even said by good judges that she equalled her father. Indeed, her works were so enthusiastically esteemed by some critics that it is difficult to make a just estimate of her as an artist, but we are assured of her exquisite taste in the arrangement of her pictures and of the rare excellence of her coloring.

It soon became the fashion in the aristocratic circles of Venice to sit for portraits to this fascinating artist. Her likeness of Jacopo Strada, the antiquarian, was considered a worthy gift for the Emperor Maximilian, and a portrait of Marietta was hung in the chamber of his Majesty. Maximilian, Philip II. of Spain, and the Archduke Ferdinand, each in turn invited Marietta to be the painter of his Court.

Tintoretto could not be induced to be separated from his daughter, and the honors she received so alarmed him that he hastened to marry her to Mario Augusti, a wealthy German jeweller, upon the condition that she should remain at home.

But the Monarch who asks no consent and heeds no refusal claimed this daughter so beloved. She died at thirty, and it is recorded that both her father and her husband mourned for her so long as they lived. Marietta was buried in the Church of Santa

Maria dell' Orto, where, within sight of her tomb, are several of her father's pictures.

Tintoretto painting his daughter's portrait after her death has been the subject of pictures by artists of various countries, and has lost nothing of its poetic and pathetic interest in the three centuries and more that have elapsed since that day when the brave old artist painted the likeness of all that remained to him of his idolized child.

Rocchi, Linda. Born in Florence; she resides in Geneva. Two of her flower pieces, in water-color, were seen at the Fine Arts Exposition, Milan, 1881. In 1883, also in Milan, she exhibited "A Wedding Garland," "Hawthorne," etc. The constantly increasing brilliancy of her work was shown in three pictures, flowers in water-colors, seen at the Milan Exposition, 1886. To Vienna, 1887, she sent four pictures of wild flowers, which were much admired.

Rocco, Lili Rosalia. Honorable mention, a bronze medal, and four silver medals were accorded this artist at the Institute of Fine Arts in Naples, where she studied from 1880 to 1886, and was also a pupil of Solari. Born in Mazzara del Vallo, Sicily, 1863. In 1886 she exhibited, at Naples, "Cari Fiori!" at Palermo, "Flora"; and in Rome, "A Sicilian Contadina." In 1888 her picture, "Spring," was exhibited in London. Two of her works were in the Simonetti Exposition, 1889, one being a marine view from her birthplace. She has painted many portraits, both in oils and water-colors, and has been appointed a teacher in at least two Government schools in Naples.

Rodiana, Onorata. Was a contemporary of the saintly Caterina de Vigri, but was of quite another order of women. She had one quality which, if not always attractive, at least commands attention. She was unique, since we know of no other woman who was at the same time a successful artist and a valiant soldier!

Born in Castelleone, near Cremona, early in the fifteenth

century, she was known as a reputable artist while still young, and was commissioned to decorate the palace of the tyrant, Gabrino Fondolo, at Cremona. The girlish painter was beautiful in person, frank and engaging in manner, and most attractive to the gentlemen of the tyrant's court.

One day when alone and absorbed in the execution of a wall-painting, a dissolute young noble addressed her with insulting freedom. She could not escape, and in the struggle which ensued she drew a dagger and stabbed her assailant to the heart.

Rushing from the palace, she disguised herself in male attire and fled to the mountains, where she joined a company of Condottieri. She soon became so good a soldier that she was made an officer of the band.

Fondolo raged as tyrants are wont to do, both on account of the murder and of the escape. He vowed the direst vengeance on Onorata if ever she were again in his power. Later, when his anger had cooled and he had no other artist at command who could worthily complete her decorations, he published her pardon and summoned her to return to his service.

Onorata completed her work, but her new vocation held her with a potent spell, and henceforth she led a divided life – never entirely relinquishing her brush, and remaining always a soldier.

When Castelleone was besieged by the Venetians, Onorata led her band thither and was victorious in the defence of her birthplace. She was fatally wounded in this action and died soon after, in the midst of the men and women whose homes she had saved. They loved her for her bravery and deeply mourned the sacrifice of her life.

Few stories from real life are so interesting and romantic as this, yet little notice has been taken of Onorata's talent or of her prowess, while many less spirited and unusual lives have been commemorated in prose and poetry.

Rodriguez de Toro, Luisa. Honorable mention, Madrid, 1856,

for a picture of "Queen Isabel the Catholic Reading with Doña Beatriz de Galindo"; honorable mention, 1860, for her "Boabdil Returning from Prison."

Born in Madrid; a descendant of the Counts of Los Villares, and wife of the Count of Mirasol. Pupil of Cárlos Ribera.

Ronner, Mme. Henriette. Medals and honorable mentions and elections to academies have been showered on Mme. Ronner all over Europe. The King of Belgium decorated her with the Cross of the Order of Leopold. Born in Amsterdam in 1821. The grandfather of this artist was Nicolas Frederick Knip, a flower painter; her father, Josephus Augustus Knip, a landscape painter, went blind, and after this misfortune was the teacher of his daughter; her aunt, for whom she was named, received medals in Paris and Amsterdam for her flower pictures. What could Henriette Knip do except paint pictures? Hers was a clear case of predestination!

At all events, almost from babyhood she occupied herself with her pencil, and when she was twelve years old her blind father began to teach her. Even at six years of age it was plainly seen that she would be a painter of animals. When sixteen she exhibited a "Cat in a Window," and from that time was considered a reputable artist.

In 1850 she was married and settled in Brussels. From this time for fifteen years she painted dogs almost without exception. Her picture called "Friend of Man" was exhibited in 1850. It is her most famous work and represents an old sand-seller, whose dog, still harnessed to the little sand-wagon, is dying, while two other dogs are looking on with well-defined sympathy. It is a most pathetic scene, wonderfully rendered.

About 1870 she devoted herself to pictures of cats, in which specialty of art she has been most important. In 1876, however, she sent to the Philadelphia Exposition a picture of "Setter Dogs." "A Cart Drawn by Dogs" is in the Museum at Hanover; "Dog and Pigeon," in the Stettin Museum; "Coming from Market" is in a private collection in San Francisco.

Mme. Ronner has invented a method of posing cats that is ingenious and of great advantage. To the uninitiated it would seem that one could only take the portrait of a sleeping cat, so untiring are the little beasts in their gymnastic performances. But Mme. Ronner, having studied them with infinite patience, proceeded to arrange a glass box, in which, on a comfortable cushion, she persuades her cats to assume the positions she desires. This box is enclosed in a wire cage, and from the top of this she hangs some cat attraction, upon which the creature bounds and shows those wonderful antics that the artist has so marvellously reproduced in her painting. Mme. Ronner has two favorite models, "Jem" and "Monmouth." The last name is classical, since the cat of Mother Michel has been made immortal.

Miss Winslow, in "Concerning Cats," says that "Mme. Ronner excels all other cat painters, living or dead. She not only infuses a wonderful degree of life into her little figures, but reproduces the shades of expression, shifting and variable as the sands of the sea, as no other artist of the brush has done. Asleep or awake, her cats look to the" felinarian "like cats with whom he or she is familiar. Curiosity, drowsiness, indifference, alertness, love, hate, anxiety, temper, innocence, cunning, fear, confidence, mischief, earnestness, dignity, helplessness – they are all in Mme. Ronner's cats' faces, just as we see them in our own cats."

It is but a short time ago that Mme. Ronner was still painting in Brussels, and had not only cats, but a splendid black dog and a cockatoo to bear her company, while her son is devoted to her. Her house is large and her grounds pleasant, and her fourscore years did not prevent her painting several hours a day, and, like some other ladies of whom we know, she was "eighty years young."

The editor of the *Magazine of Art*, M. H. Spielman, in an article on the Royal Academy Exhibition, 1903, writes: "What the dog is to Mr. Riviere, to Madame Ronner is the cat. With what unerring truth she records delightful kittenly nature, the feline nobility of haughty indifference to human approval or discontent, the subtlety of expression, and drawing of heads and bodies, the exact quality and tone of the fur, the expressive eloquence of the tail! With all her eighty years, Madame Ronner's hand, vision, and sensibility have not diminished; only her sobriety of color seems to have increased." Her pictures of this year were called "The Ladybird" and "Coaxing." To the Exhibition of the Beaux-Arts in Brussels, 1903, Mme. Ronner sent pictures of cats, full of life and mischief.

Roosenboom, Margarite Vogel. Second-class medal, Munich, 1892. Born in 1843 and died in 1896, near The Hague. She spent a large part of her life near Utrecht, devoting herself mainly to the painting of flowers. One of her works is in the Royal Museum at Amsterdam, and another in the Museum at Breslau.

Rope, Ellen M. This English sculptor executed four large panels for the Women's Building at the Chicago Exhibition. They represented Faith, Hope, Charity, and Heavenly Wisdom. They are now in the Ladies' Dwelling, Cherries Street, London. A "Memorial" by her is in Salisbury Cathedral. Her reliefs of children are, however, her best works; that of a "Boy on a Dolphin" is most attractive. "Christ Blessing Little Children" is charmingly rendered.

At the Academy, 1903, she exhibited a panel for an organ chamber, in low relief.

Rosa, Aniella di. 1613-1649. A pupil in Naples of Stanzioni, who, by reason of her violent death, has been called the Neapolitan Sirani. She acquired a good reputation as a historical painter and doubtless had unusual talent, but as she worked in conjunction with Stanzioni and with her husband, Agostino Beltrano, it is difficult to speak of works entirely her own.

Two pictures that were acknowledged to be hers represented

the birth and death of the Virgin; these were praised and were at one time in a church in Naples, but in a recent search for them I was unable to satisfy myself that the pictures I saw were genuine.

Another pupil in the studio of Stanzioni was the Beltrano whom Aniella married. He painted in fresco, Aniella in oils, and they were frequently employed together. The fine picture of San Biagio, in the church of Santa Maria della Sanità, was one of their joint works.

Their early married life was very happy, but Aniella was beautiful and Beltrano grew jealous; it is said without cause, through the influence of a woman who loved him and hated Aniella; and in spite of the efforts she made to merit her husband's confidence, his distrust of her increased. Her base rival, by her art and falsehood, finally succeeded in convincing Beltrano that Aniella was unworthy, and in his rage he fatally stabbed her, when, at thirty-six, she was in the prime of her beauty and talent. She survived long enough to convince her husband of her innocence and to pardon him for his crime, but he fled from Italy and lived the life of an outcast during ten years. He then returned to Naples, where after seven years, tormented by remorse, death came to his release.

Domenici generously praised the works of Aniella, and quoted her master, Stanzioni, as saying that she was the equal of the best painters of her time.

Rosalba. See Carriera.

Rossi, Properzia de. Born in Bologna. 1490-1530. This artist was the first woman to succeed as a sculptor whose works can still be seen. Pupil of Raimondi, she was more or less influenced by Tribolo. In the Church of San Petronio, in her native city, in the eleventh chapel, is a beautiful bas-relief of two angels, executed by Properzia. They are near Tribolo's "Ascension." A relief and a portrait bust in the same church are also ascribed to her.

Her first work in sculpture was a minute representation of the

Crucifixion on a peach stone! The executioners, women, soldiers, and disciples were all represented in this infinitesimal space. She also inserted in a coat of arms a double-headed eagle in silver filigree; eleven peach stones on each side, one set representing eleven apostles with an article of the creed underneath, the other set eleven virgins with the name of a saint and her special attribute on each. Some of these intaglios are still in a private collection in Bologna.

At length Properzia saw the folly of thus belittling her talent, and when the facade of San Petronio was to be enriched with sculpture she asked for a share in the work and presented a bust she had made as a pledge of her ability; she was appointed to execute a portion of the decorations. She made a bas-relief, the subject being "Joseph and Potiphar's Wife," which Vasari called "a lovely picture, sculptured with womanly grace, and more than admirable."

By this time the jealousy of other artists was aroused, and a story was diligently repeated to the effect that Properzia loved a young nobleman who did not care for her, and that the above work, so much admired, represented her own passion. Albertini and other artists waged an absolute crusade against her, and so influenced the superintendents of the church that Properzia was obliged to leave the work and her relief was never put in place. Through mortification and grief her health failed, and she died when but forty years old.

In spite of her persecution she was known in all Italy, not only for her sculpture, but for her copper-plate engraving and etching. When Pope Clement VII. went to Bologna for the coronation of Charles V. he asked for Properzia, only to hear that she had been buried that very week.

Her story has been told by Vasari and other writers. She was handsome, accomplished in music, distinguished for her knowledge of science, and withal a good and orderly housewife. "Well calculated to awaken the envy, not of women only, but also of men." Canova ardently admired the work of Properzia that remained in his day, and esteemed her early death as one of the chief misfortunes to the advance of the fine arts in Italy.

Rotky, Baroness Hanna. Born at Czernowitz in 1857. She studied portrait painting under Blaas, Swerdts, and Trentino, and has worked principally in Vienna. Her portrait of Freiherr von Sterneck is in the Military Academy at Wiener-Neustadt.

Rudder, Mme. de. This lady has made an art of her embroidery, and may be said to have revived this decorative specialty and to have equalled the ancient productions which are so beautiful and valuable. After her marriage to the well-known sculptor this gifted couple began their collaboration. M. P. Verneuil, in *Brush and Pencil*, November, 1903, writes: "The first result of this joint work was shown in 1894 at the Exposition Cercle pour l'Art, in the form of a panel, called 'The Eagle and the Swan.' It was exhibited afterward at the Secession in Vienna, where it was purchased by a well-known amateur and connoisseur. Other works were produced in succession, each more interesting than its predecessor. Not daunted by difficulties that would have discouraged the most ambitious and audacious craftswoman, Mme. de Rudder took for a subject 'The Fates,' to decorate a screen. Aside from the artistic interest attaching to this work, it is remarkable for another quality. The artist yielded to the instinctive liking that she had for useful art – she ornamented a useful article – and in mastering the technical difficulties of her work she created the new method called 're-embroidery.' For the dresses of her 'Fates' ancient silks were utilized for a background. Some of the pieces had moth-holes, which necessitated the addition of 'supplementary ornamental motives,' 'embroidered on cloth to conceal the defects.' The discovery of 're-embroidery' was the result of this enforced expedient.

"This screen, finished in 1896, was exhibited at the Cercle Artistique, Brussels, where the mayor, M. Buls, saw it. Realizing the possibilities of the method and the skill of the artist, he gave an order to Mme. de Rudder to decorate the Marriage Hall of the Hotel de Ville. This order was delivered in 1896. During this period Mme. de Rudder worked feverishly. About the same time that the order for the Hotel de Ville was given, she received from M. Van Yssendyck, architect of the Hotel Provincial in Ghent, a commission to design and embroider six large allegorical panels. One of them represented 'Wisdom' in the habiliments of Minerva, modernized, holding an olive branch. The five others were 'Justice,' holding a thistle, symbolizing law; 'Eloquence,' crowned with roses and holding a lyre; 'Strength,' bending an oak branch; 'Truth,' crushing a serpent and bearing a mirror and some lilies; and 'Prudence,' with the horn of plenty and some holly. These six panels are remarkable for the beautiful decorative feeling that suffuses their composition. The tricks of workmanship are varied, and all combine to give a wonderful effect. Contrary to the form of presenting the 'Fates,' all the figures are draped."

Her next important commission was for eight large panels, intended to decorate the Congo Free State department in the Brussels Exposition. These panels represent the "Triumph of Civilization over Barbarism," and are now in the Museum at Tervueren. They are curious in their symbols of fetichism, and have an attraction that one can scarcely explain. The above are but a part of her important works, and naturally, when not absorbed by these, Mme. de Rudder executes some smaller pieces which are marvels of patience in their exquisite detail.

Perhaps her panels of the "Four Seasons" may be called her *chef-d'oeuvre*. The writer quoted above also says:

"To Mme. de Rudder must be given the credit for the interpretation of work demanding large and varied decorative effect, while in the creation of true artistic composition she easily stands at the head of the limited coterie of men and women who have mastered this delicate and difficult art. She is a leader in her peculiar craft."

Rude, Mme. Sophie Frémiet. 1797-1867. Medal at Paris Salon,

1833. Born in Dijon. This artist painted historical and genre subjects as well as portraits. Her picture of the "Sleeping Virgin," 1831, and that of the "Arrest of the Duchess of Burgundy in Bruges," 1841, are in the Dijon Museum.

Ruysch, Rachel. The perfection of flower-painting is seen in the works of Rachel Ruysch. The daughter of a distinguished professor of anatomy, she was born at Amsterdam in 1664. She was for a time a pupil of William van Aelst, but soon studied from nature alone. Some art critics esteem her works superior to those of De Heem and Van Huysum. Let that be as it may, the pictures with which she was no doubt dissatisfied when they passed from her hand more than two centuries ago are greatly valued to-day and her genius is undisputed.

When thirty years old Rachel Ruysch married the portrait painter, Julian van Pool. She bore him ten children, but in the midst of all her cares she never laid her brush aside. Her reputation extended to every court of Europe. She received many honors, and was elected to the Academical Society at The Hague. She was received with distinguished courtesies on the two occasions when she visited Düsseldorf.

The Elector John of Pfalz appointed her painter at his court, and beyond paying her generously for her pictures, bestowed valuable gifts on her. The Elector sent several of her works to the Grand Duke of Tuscany and to other distinguished rulers of that day.

The advance of years in no wise dulled her powers. Her pictures painted when eighty years old are as delicately finished as those of many years earlier. She died when eighty-six, "respected by the great, beloved even by her rivals, praised by all who knew her."

The pictures by Rachel Ruysch are honorably placed in many public galleries; in those of Florence and Turin, as well as at Amsterdam, The Hague, Berlin, Dresden, Vienna, and Munich, they are much valued. Although these pictures are characterized by extreme delicacy of touch, softness, and lightness, this artist knew how so to combine these qualities as to impart an effect of strength to her painting. Her rendering of separate flowers was exquisite, and her roses, either by themselves or combined with other flowers, are especially beautiful. She painted fruits in perfection, and the insects and butterflies which she sometimes added are admirably executed.

The chief criticism that can be made of her pictures is that she was less skilful in the grouping of her flowers than in their painting. Many of her works are in private galleries, especially in Holland. They are rarely sold; in London, about thirty years ago, a small "Bouquet of Flowers with Insects" was sold for more than two thousand dollars, and is now of double that value.

Her pictures have the same clearness and individuality that are seen in her portrait, in which she has short hair, a simple low-cut dress, with a necklace of beads about the throat.

Salles, Adelheid. Born in Dresden, 1825; died in Paris, 1890. Pupil of Bernhard and Jacquand, she established her studio in Paris. Many of her works are in museums: "Elijah in the Desert," at Lyons; "The Legend of the Alyscamps," at Nîmes; "The Village Maiden," at Grenoble; "Field Flowers," at Havre, etc. She also painted portraits and historical subjects, among which are "Psyche in Olympus," "The Daughters of Jerusalem in the Babylonian Captivity," and the "Daughter of Jairus."

She was a sister of E. Puyroche-Wagner.

Sartain, Emily. Medal at Philadelphia Exhibition, 1876; Mary Smith prize at the Pennsylvania Academy for best painting by a woman, in 1881 and 1883. Born in Philadelphia, 1841. Miss Sartain has been the principal of the Philadelphia School of Design for Women since 1886.

She studied engraving under her father, John Sartain, and with Luminais in Paris. She engraved and etched book illustrations and numerous larger prints. She is also a painter of portraits and genre pictures, and has exhibited at the Salon des Beaux-Arts, Paris. Miss Sartain has been appointed as delegate from the United States to the International Congress on Instruction in Drawing to be held at Berne next August. Her appointment was recommended by the Secretary of the Interior, the United States Commissioner of Education, and Prof. J. H. Gore. Miss Sartain has also received letters from Switzerland from M. Leon Genoud, president of the Swiss Commission, begging her to accept the appointment.

Schaefer, Maria. First-class medal, Bene-merenti, Roumania. Born in Dresden, 1854. Her first studies were made in Darmstadt under A. Noack; later she was a pupil of Budde and Bauer in Düsseldorf, and finally of Eisenmenger in Vienna. After travelling in Italy in 1879, she settled in Darmstadt. She made several beautiful copies of Holbein's "Madonna," one for the King of Roumania, and one as a gift from the city of Darmstadt to the Czarina Alexandra. Among her most excellent portraits are those of Friedrich von Schmidt and his son Henry. Several of her religious paintings ornament German churches: "St. Elizabeth" is at Biedenkopf, "Mary's Departure from the Tomb of Christ" is at Nierstein, and "Christ with St. Louis and St. Elizabeth" and a Rosary picture are in the Catholic church at Darmstadt.

Scheffer, Caroline. The daughter of Ary Lamme and wife of J. B. Scheffer was an artist in the last decades of the eighteenth century, but the special interest connected with her is the fact that she was the mother of Ary and Henry Scheffer. From her artistic standpoint she had an appreciation of what was needed for the benefit of her sons. She took them to Paris to study, devoted herself entirely to their welfare, and died in Paris in 1839.

Schleh, Anna. Born in Berlin, 1833. Her principal studies were made in her native city under Schrader, although she went to Rome in 1868, and finally took up her residence there. She had, previous to her work in Rome, painted "The Marys at the Grave." Her later pictures include "The Citron-Vender" and a number of portraits for the Henkel family of Donnersmark.

Schmitt-Schenkh, Maria. Born in Baden, 1837. She studied her art in Munich, Carlsruhe, and Italy. She established herself in Munich and painted pictures for churches, which are in Kirrlach, Mauer, Ziegelhausen, and other German towns. She also designed church windows, especially for the Liebfrauenkirche at Carlsruhe.

Schumann, Anna Maria. Was called by the Dutch poets their Sappho and their Corneille. She was born in 1607, but as her family were Protestants and frequently changed their residence in order to avoid persecution, the place of her birth is unknown. When Anna Maria was eight years old, they went permanently to Utrecht.

This distinguished woman was one of the exceptions said to prove rules, for though a prodigy in childhood she did not become a commonplace or stupid woman. Learning was her passion and art her recreation. It is difficult to repeat what is recorded of her unusual attainments and not feel as if one were being misled by a Munchausen! But it would be ungracious to lessen a fame almost three centuries old.

We are told that Anna Maria could speak in Latin when seven years old, and translated from Seneca at ten. She acquired the Hebrew, Greek, Samaritan, Arabic, Chaldaic, Syriac, Ethiopian, Turkish, and Persian languages with such thoroughness that her admirers claim that she wrote and spoke them all. She also read with ease and spoke with finished elegance Italian, Spanish, English, and French, besides German and her native tongue.

Anna Maria Schurmann wrote verses in various languages, but the chief end which her exhaustive studies served was to aid her in theological research; in this she found her greatest satisfaction and deepest interest. She was respectfully consulted upon important questions by the scholars of different countries.

At the University of Utrecht an honorable place was reserved for her in the lecture-rooms, and she frequently took part in the learned discussions there. The professors of the University of Leyden paid her the compliment of erecting a tribune where she could hear all that passed in the lecture-room without being seen by the audience.

As an artist the Schurmann reached such excellence that the painter Honthorst valued a portrait by her at a thousand Dutch florins – about four hundred and thirty dollars – an enormous sum when we remember that the works of her contemporary, Albert Cuyp, were sold for thirty florins! and no higher price was paid for his works before the middle of the eighteenth century. A few years ago his picture, called "Morning Light," was sold at a public sale in London for twenty-five thousand dollars. How astonishing that a celebrated artist like Honthorst, who painted in Utrecht when Cuyp painted in Dort, should have valued a portrait by Anna Maria Schurmann at the price of thirty-three works by Cuyp! Such facts as these suggest a question regarding the relative value of the works of more modern artists. Will the judgments of the present be thus reversed in the future?

This extraordinary woman filled the measure of possibilities by carving in wood and ivory, engraving on crystal and copper, and having a fine musical talent, playing on several instruments. When it is added that she was of a lovable nature and attractive in manner, one is not surprised that her contemporaries called her "the wonder of creation."

Volsius was her friend and taught her Hebrew. She was intimately associated with such scholars as Salmatius and Heinsius, and was in correspondence with scholars, philosophers, and theologians regarding important questions of her time.

Anna Maria Schurmann was singularly free from egotism. She rarely consented to publish her writings, though often urged to do so. She avoided publicity and refused complimentary attentions which were urged upon her, conducting herself with a modesty as rare as her endowments.

In 1664, when travelling with her brother, she became acquainted with Labadie, the celebrated French enthusiast who preached new doctrines. He had many disciples called Labadists. He taught that God used deceit with man when He judged it well for man to be deceived; that contemplation led to perfection; that self-mortification, self-denial, and prayer were necessary to a godly life; and that the Holy Spirit constantly made new revelations to the human beings prepared to receive them.

Anna Maria Schurmann heard these doctrines when prostrated by a double sorrow, the deaths of her father and brother. She put aside all other interests and devoted herself to those of the Labadists. It is said that after the death of Labadie she gathered his disciples together and conducted them to Vivert, in Friesland. William Penn saw her there, and in his account of the meeting he tells how much he was impressed by her grave solemnity and vigorous intellect.

From this time she devoted her fortune to charity and died in poverty at the age of seventy-one. Besides her fame as an artist and a scholar, her name was renowned for purity of heart and fervent religious feeling. Her virtues were many and her few faults were such as could not belong to an ignoble nature.

Scudder, Janet. Medal at Columbian Exposition, 1893. Two of her medallion portraits are in the Luxembourg, Paris. Member of the National Sculpture Society, New York. Born in Terre Haute, Indiana. Pupil of Rebisso in Cincinnati, of Lorado Taft in Chicago, and of Frederic MacMonnies in Paris.

At the Chicago Exposition Miss Scudder exhibited two heroic-sized statues representing Illinois and Indiana. The portraits purchased by the French Government are of American women and are the first work of an American woman sculptor to be admitted to the Luxembourg. These medallions are in bas-relief in marble, framed in bronze. Casts from them have been made in gold and silver. The first is said to be the largest medallion ever made in gold; it is about four inches long.

To the Pan-American Exposition Miss Scudder contributed four boys standing on a snail, which made a part of the "Fountain of Abundance." She has exhibited in New York and Philadelphia a fountain, representing a boy dancing hilariously and snapping his fingers at four huge frogs round his pedestal. The water spurts from the mouths of the frogs and covers the naked child.

Miss Scudder is commissioned to make a portrait statue of heroic size for the St. Louis Exposition. She will no doubt exhibit smaller works there. Portraits are her specialty, and in these she has made a success, as is proved by the appreciation of her work in Paris.

A memorial figure in marble is in Woodlawn Cemetery, also a cinerary urn in stone and bronze; a bronze memorial tablet is in Union College. Miss Scudder also made the seal for the Bar Association of New York.

Sears, Sarah C. Medal at Chicago, 1893; William Evans prize, American Water-Color Society, New York; honorable mention, Paris Exposition, 1900; bronze medal at Buffalo, 1901; silver medal at Charleston, South Carolina. Member of the New York Water-Color Club, Boston Art Students' Association, National Arts Club, Boston Water-Color Club. Born in Cambridge, Massachusetts. Pupil of Ross Turner, Joseph de Camp, Edmund C. Tarbell, and George de Forest Brush. Mrs. Sears has also studied by herself with the criticism of masters.

She paints portraits, figures, and flowers, and is much interested in the applied arts. Of her exhibition at the Boston Art Club, 1903, a critic writes: "Nothing could be more brilliant in point of color than the group of seven water-color pictures of a sunny flower-garden by Mrs. Sears. In these works pure and limpid color has been pushed to its extreme capacity, under full daylight conditions, with a splendor of brightness which never crosses the line of crudity, but holds the same relative values as we see in nature, the utmost force of local color courageously set forth and contrasted without apparent artifice, blending into an harmonious unity of tone. Two of these pictures are especially fine, with their cool backgrounds of sombre pines to set off the magnificent masses of flowers in the foreground."

At the exhibition of the Philadelphia Water-Color Club, 1903, the *Press* said: "These brilliant and overpowering combinations of color carry to a limit not before reached the decorative possibilities of flowers."

Mrs. Sears' honors have been awarded to her portraits.

Seidler, Caroline Luise. Born in Jena, 1786; died in Weimar, 1866. Her early studies were made in Gotha with Doell; in 1811 she went to Dresden, where she became a pupil of G. von Kügelgen; in 1817 Langer received her into his Munich studio; and between 1818 and 1823 she was in Italy, making special studies of Vanucci and Raphael. In 1823 she was appointed instructor of the royal princesses at Weimar, and in 1824 inspector of the gallery there, and later became court painter. Among her works are a portrait of Goethe, a picture of "Ulysses and the Sirens," and one of "Christ, the Compassionate," which is in the church at Schestadt, Holstein.

Serrano y Bartolomé, Joaquina. Born in Fermoselle. Pupil in Madrid of Juan Espalter, of the School of Arts and Crafts, and of the School of Painting. She sent four pictures to the Exposition of 1876 in Madrid: the portrait of a young woman, a still-life subject, a bunch of grapes, and a "Peasant Girl" – the last two are in the Museum of Murcia. In 1878 she sent "A Kitchen Maid on Saturday," a study, a flower piece, and two still-life pictures; and in 1881 two portraits and some landscapes. Her portrait of the painter Fortuny, which belongs to the Society of Authors and Artists, gained her a membership in that Society. Two other excellent portraits are those of her teacher, Espalter, and General Trillo.

Sewell, Amanda Brewster. Bronze medal, Chicago, 1893; bronze medal, Buffalo, 1901; silver medal, Charleston; Clarke prize, Academy of Design, 1903. Member of the Woman's Art Club and an associate of National Academy of Design. Born in Northern New York. Pupil at Cooper Union under Douglas Volk and R. Swain Gifford, and of Art Students' League under William Chase and William Sartain; also of Julian's Academy under Tony Robert Fleury and Bouguereau, and of Carolus Duran.

Mrs. Sewell's "A Village Incident" is owned by the Philadelphia Social Art Club; "Where Roses Bloom" is in the Boston Art Club; portrait of Professor William R. Ware is in the Library of Columbia University. Her portrait of Amalia Küssner will be exhibited and published.

Mrs. Sewell is the first woman to take the Clarke prize. She has been a careful student in the arrangement of portraits in order to make attractive pictures as well as satisfactory likenesses. Of the pictures she exhibited at the Academy of Design, winter of 1903, Charles H. Caffin writes:

"The portrait of Mrs. Charles S. Dodge, by Mrs. A. Brewster Sewell, is the finest example in the exhibition of pictorial treatment, the lady being wrapped in a brown velvet cloak with broad edges of brown fur, and seated before a background of dark foliage. It is a most distinguished canvas, though one may object to the too obvious affectation of the arrangement of the hands and of the gesture of the head – features which will jar upon many eyes and detract from the general handsomeness. The same lady sends a large classical subject, the 'Sacred Hecatomb,' to which the Clarke prize was awarded. It represents a forest scene lit by slanting sunlight, through which winds a string of bulls, the foremost accompanied by a band of youths and maidens with dance and song. The light effects are managed very skilfully and with convincing truth, and the figures are free and animated in movement, though the flesh tints are scarcely agreeable. It is a decorative composition that might be fitly placed in a large hall in some country house."

Seydelmann, Apollonie. Member of the Dresden Academy. Born at Trieste about 1768; died in Dresden, 1840. Pupil of J. C. Seydelmann, whom she married. Later she went to Italy and there studied miniature painting under Madame Maron.

She is best known for her excellent copies of old pictures, and especially by her copy of the Sistine Madonna, from which Müller's engraving was made.

Shaw, Annie C. The first woman elected Academician in the Academy of Design, Chicago, 1876. Born at Troy, New York. Pupil of H. C. Ford. Landscape painter. Among her works are "On the Calumet," "Willow Island," "Keene Valley, New York," "Returning from the Fair," 1878, which was exhibited in Chicago, New York, and Boston. To the Centennial, Philadelphia, 1876, she sent her "Illinois Prairie."

"Returning from the Fair" shows a group of Alderney cattle in a road curving through a forest. At the time of its exhibition an art critic wrote: "The eye of the spectator is struck with the rich mass of foliage, passing from the light green of the birches in the foreground, where the light breaks through, to the dark green of the dense forest, shading into the brownish tints of the early September-tinged leaves. Farther on, the eye is carried back through a beautiful vista formed by the road leading through the centre of the picture, giving a fine perspective and distance through a leafy archway of elms and other forest trees that gracefully mingle their branches overhead, through which one catches a glimpse of deep blue sky. As the eye follows this roadway to its distant part the sun lights up the sky, tingeing with a mellow light the group of small trees and willows, contrasting beautifully with the almost sombre tones of the dense forest in the middle distance."

Shrimpton, Ada M. Has exhibited at the Royal Academy, Royal Institute of Water-Colors, British Artists, and principal provincial galleries in England and in Australia; also at the Paris Salon. Member of Society of Women Artists, London. Born in Old Alresford, Hampshire. Pupil of John Sparkes at South Kensington, and of Jean Paul Laurens and Benjamin Constant in Paris.

This artist has painted principally figure subjects, among which are "Cedric's Daughter," "Thoughts of Youth are Long Thoughts," "Dream of the Past," "Pippa Passes," "Dorothy's Bridesmaid's Dress," etc., etc. Recently she has devoted herself to portraits of ladies and children, in both oil and water-colors.

Sirani, Elisabetta. Has been praised as a woman and as an artist by Lanzi, Malvasia, Picinardi, and other writers until one must believe that in spite of the exaggeration of her personal qualities and her artistic genius, she was a singularly admirable woman and a gifted artist.

She was born in Bologna about 1640, and, like Artemisia Gentileschi, was the daughter of a painter of the school of Guido Reni, whose follower Elisabetta also became. From the study of her master she seems to have acquired the power to perceive and reproduce the greatest possible beauty with which her subjects could be invested.

She worked with such rapidity that she was accused of profiting by her father's assistance, and in order to refute this accusation it was arranged that the Duchess of Brunswick, the Duchess of Mirandola, Duke Cosimo, and others should meet in her studio, on which occasion Elisabetta charmed and astonished her guests by the ease and perfection with which she sketched in and shaded drawings of the subjects which one person after another suggested to her.

Her large picture of the "Baptism of Christ" was completed when the artist was but twenty years old. Malvasia gives a list of one hundred and twenty pictures executed by Elisabetta, and yet she was but twenty-five when her mysterious death occurred.

In the Pinacoteca of Bologna is the "St. Anthony Adoring the Virgin and Infant Jesus," by the Sirani, which is much admired;

several other works of hers are in her native city. "The Death of Abel" is in the Gallery of Turin; the "Charity," in the Sciarra Palace in Rome; "Cupids" and a picture of "Martha and Mary," in the Vienna Gallery; an "Infant Jesus" and a picture called "A Subject after Guido" are in the Hermitage at Petersburg.

Her composition was graceful and refined, her drawing good, her color fresh and sweet, with a resemblance to Guido Reni in the half tones. She was especially happy in the heads of the Madonna and the Magdalene, imparting to them an expression of exalted tenderness.

Her paintings on copper and her etchings were most attractive; indeed, all her works revealed the innate grace and refinement of her nature.

Aside from her art the Sirani was a most interesting woman. She was very beautiful in person, and the sweetness of her temper made her a favorite with her friends, while her charming voice and fine musical talent added to her many attractions. Her admirers have also commended her taste in dress, which was very simple, and have even praised her moderation in eating! She was skilled in domestic matters and accustomed to rise at dawn to attend to her household affairs, not permitting her art to interfere with the more homely duties of her life. One writer says that "her devoted filial affection, her feminine grace, and the artless benignity of her manners rounded out a character regarded as an ideal of perfection by her friends."

It may be that her tragic fate caused an exaggerated estimate to be made of her both as a woman and an artist. The actual cause of her death is unknown. There have been many theories concerning it. It was very generally believed that she was poisoned, although neither the reason for the crime nor the name of its perpetrator was known.

By some she was believed to have been sacrificed to the same professional jealousy that destroyed Domenichino; others accepted the theory that a princely lover who had made unworthy proposals to her, which she had scorned, had revenged himself by her murder. At length a servant, Lucia Tolomelli, who had been a long time in the Sirani family, was suspected of having poisoned her young mistress, was arrested, tried, and banished. But after a time the father of Elisabetta, finding no convincing reason to believe her guilty, obtained her pardon.

Whatever may have been the cause of the artist's death, the effect upon her native city was overwhelming and the day of her burial was one of general mourning, the ceremony being attended with great pomp. She was buried beside Guido Reni, in the Chapel of Our Lady of the Rosary, in the magnificent Church of the Dominicans.

Poets and orators vied with each other in sounding her praises, and a book called "Il Penello Lagrimato," published at Bologna soon after her death, is a collection of orations, sonnets, odes, epitaphs, and anagrams, in Latin and Italian, setting forth the love which her native city bore to this beautiful woman, and rehearsing again and again her charms and her virtues.

In the Ercolani Gallery there is a picture of Elisabetta painting a portrait of her father. It is said that she also painted a portrait of herself looking up with a spiritual expression, which is in a private collection and seen by few people.

Smith, Jessie Willcox. Mary Smith prize, Pennsylvania Academy of Fine Arts, 1903. Member of the Plastic Club and a fellow of the Academy, Philadelphia. Born in Philadelphia, where she was a pupil of the Academy; also studied under Thomas Eakins, Thomas P. Anschutz, and Howard Pyle.

Miss Smith is essentially an illustrator and her work is seen in all the leading American magazines. "The Child's Calendar" is the work of this artist.

Sonrel, Mlle. E. Honorable mention, Paris, 1893; third-class medal, 1895; bronze medal, Paris Exposition, 1900. At the Salon des Artistes Français, 1902, she exhibited "Sybille" and "Monica"; in 1903, "The Dance of Terpsichore" and "Princesse Lointaine."

[*No reply to circular.*]

Spanò, Maria. Silver medal, Naples, 1859, for a picture of a "Contadina of Sorrento." Born in Naples, 1843. Pupil of her father, Raffaele Spanò, under whose direction she made a thorough study of figure painting, the results of which are evident in her excellent portraits and historical subjects. She has also been greatly interested in landscape painting, in which she has been successful. "A Confidence" was bought by the Gallery at Capodimonte, and two of her pictures were acquired by the Provincial Council of Naples – a "Contadina," life size, and a "Country Farmyard." One of her best pictures is "Bice at the Castle of Rosate."

Spilimberg, Irene di. Born in Udina, 1540. Her family was of German origin and exalted position. She was educated in Venice with great care and all the advantages that wealth could command. She was much in the society of learned men, which she preferred before that of the world of fashion.

Titian was her roaster in painting. Lanzi and Rudolfi praised her as an artist, and her fame now rests on the testimony of those who saw her works rather than on the pictures themselves, some of which are said to be in private collections in Italy. Titian painted her portrait as a tribute to her beauty; Tasso celebrated her intellectual charm in a sonnet, and yet she was but nineteen years old when she died.

Twenty years later a collection of orations and poems was published, all of which set forth her attractions and acquirements, and emphasized the sadness of her early death and the loss that the world had suffered thereby. When one remembers how soon after death those who have done a life work are forgotten, such a memorial to one so young is worthy of note.

Spurr, Gertrude E. Associate member of Royal Canadian Academy and member of the Ontario Society of Arts. Born in

Scarborough, England. Pupil of the Lambeth Art School in drawing, of E. H. Holder in painting, in England; also of George B. Bridgman in New York. This artist usually paints small pictures of rural scenery in England and Wales – little stone cottages, bridges, river and mountain scenes. "Castle Rock, North Devon," was exhibited at Buffalo, and is owned by Herbert Mason, Esq., of Toronto. "A Peep at Snowdon" and "Dutch Farm Door, Ontario," are in Montreal collections. Her works have been exhibited in London at the Royal Society of British Artists and the Society of Lady Artists, and have been sold from these exhibitions.

I quote from the *Queen*, in reference to one of Miss Spurr's London exhibitions: "We know of no more favorite sketching-ground in N. Wales for the artist than Bettws-y-coed. Every yard of that most picturesque district has been painted and sketched over and over again. The artist in this instance reproduces some of the very primitive cottages in which the natives of the principality sojourn. The play of light on the modest dwelling-places is an effective element in the cleverly rendered drawing now in the Society of Artists' Exhibition. Miss Spurr, the daughter of a Scarboro lawyer, commenced her art studies with Mr. E. H. Holder, in the winter painting dead birds, fruit, and other natural objects, and in summer spending her time on the coast or in the woods or about Rievaulx Abbey. Any remaining time to be filled up was occupied by attending the Scarboro School of Art under the instruction of Mr. Strange. In a local sketching club Miss Spurr distinguished herself and gained several prizes, and she has at length taken up her abode in the metropolis, where she has attended the Lambeth Schools, studying diligently both from casts and life."

Stacey, Anna L. Honorable mention at Exhibition of Chicago Artists, 1900; Young Fortnightly Club prize, 1902; Martin B. Cahn prize, Exhibition at Art Institute, Chicago, 1902. Member of Chicago Society of Artists. Born in Glasgow, Missouri.

Pupil of Art Institute in Chicago. Paints portraits, figure subjects, and landscapes. The Cahn prize was awarded to the "Village at Twilight." "Florence" is owned by the Klio Club; "Trophies of the Fields," by the Union League Club, Chicago.

Recently Miss Stacey has painted a number of successful portraits.

Stading, Evelina. Born in Stockholm. 1803-1829. She was a pupil of Fahlcrantz for a time in her native city, and then went to Dresden, where she made a thorough study and some excellent copies of the works of Ruisdael. In 1827 she went to Rome, making studies in Volzburg and the Tyrol *en route*. She painted views in Switzerland and Italy, and two of her landscapes are in the gallery in Christiania.

Stanley, Lady Dorothy. Member of the Ladies' Athenæum Club. Born in London. Pupil of Sir Edward Poynter – then Mr. Poynter – and of M. Legros, at Slade School, University College, London; also of Carolus Duran and Henner in Paris.

Lady Stanley has exhibited at the Royal Academy, the new Gallery, at the English provincial exhibitions, and at the Salon, Paris.

Her picture, "His First Offence," is in the Tate National Gallery; "Leap Frog," in the National Gallery of Natal, Pietermaritzburg. Other pictures of hers are "A Water Nymph," "The Bathers," etc., which are in private galleries. "Leap Frog" was in the Academy exhibition, 1903.

Stebbins, Emma. 1815-1882. Born in New York. As an amateur artist Miss Stebbins made a mark by her work in black and white and her pictures in oils. After a time she decided to devote herself to sculpture. In Rome she studied this art and made her first success with a statuette of "Joseph." This was followed by "Columbus" and "Satan Descending to tempt Mankind." For Central Park, New York, she executed a large fountain, the subject being "The Angel of the Waters."

Stephens, Mrs. Alice Barber. Mary Smith prize, 1890. Pupil of the Pennsylvania Academy of Fine Arts and of the Julian Academy, Paris. An illustrator whose favorite subjects are those of every-day home life – the baby, the little child, the grandmother in cap and spectacles, etc.

[No reply to circular.]

Stevens, Edith Barretto. Two scholarships and a prize of one hundred dollars from the Art Students' League, of which she is a member. Born in Houston, Virginia, in 1878. Studied at Art Students' League and under Daniel C. French and George Gray Barnard.

Miss Stevens mentions as her principal works "A Candlestick Representing a Girl Asleep under a Poppy," "Figure of Spring," and the "Spirit of Flame."

Miss Stevens is one of the women sculptors who have been selected to share in the decoration of the buildings for the St. Louis Exposition. She is to make two reclining figures on the pediment over the main entrance to the Liberal Arts Building. She has in her studio two reclining figures which will probably serve to fulfil this commission.

Miss Stevens is modest about her work and does not care to talk much about this important commission, even suggesting that her design may not be accepted; if she is successful it will certainly be an unusual honor for a woman at her age, whose artistic career covers less than five years.

Stevens, Mary. Bronze medal at the Crystal Palace. Member of the Dudley Gallery, London. Born at Liverpool. Pupil of William Kerry and of her husband, Albert Stevens, in England, and of the Julian Academy, Paris.

Mrs. Stevens' pictures were well considered when she exhibited a variety of subjects; of late, however, she has made a specialty of pictures of gardens, and has painted in many famous English and French gardens, among others, those of Holland House, Warwick Castle, and St. Anne's, Dublin. In France, the gardens of the Duchesse de Dino and the Countess Foucher de Careil.

Mrs. Stevens – several of whose works are owned in America – has commissions to paint in some American gardens and intends to execute them in 1904.

Stillman, Marie Spartali. Pupil of Ford Madox Brown. This artist first exhibited in public at the Dudley Gallery, London, in 1867, a picture called "Lady Pray's Desire." In 1870 she exhibited at the Royal Academy, "Saint Barbara" and "The Mystic Tryst." In 1873 she exhibited "The Finding of Sir Lancelot Disguised as a Fool" and "Sir Tristram and La Belle Isolde," both in water-colors. Of these, a writer in the *Art Journal* said: "Mrs. Stillman has brought imagination to her work. These vistas of garden landscape are conceived in the true spirit of romantic luxuriance, when the beauty of each separate flower was a delight. The figures, too, have a grace that belongs properly to art, and which has been well fitted to pictorial expression. The least satisfactory part of these clever drawings is their color. There is an evident feeling of harmony, but the effect is confused and the prevailing tones are uncomfortably warm."

W. M. Rossetti wrote: "Miss Spartali has a fine power of fusing the emotion of her subject into its color and of giving aspiration to both; beyond what is actually achieved one sees a reaching toward something ulterior. As one pauses before her work, a film in that or in the mind lifts or seems meant to lift, and a subtler essence from within the picture quickens the sense. In short, Miss Spartali, having a keen perception of the poetry which resides in beauty and in the means of art for embodying beauty, succeeds in infusing that perception into the spectator of her handiwork."

[*No reply to circular.*]

Stocks, Minna. Born in Scheverin, 1846. Pupil of Schloepke in Scheverin, Stiffeck in Berlin, E. Bosch in Düsseldorf, and J. Bauck in Munich. Her "Lake of Scheverin" is in the Museum of her native city.

Her artistic reputation rests largely on her pictures of animals. She exhibits at the Expositions of the Society of Women Artists, Berlin, and among her pictures seen there is "A Journey through Africa," which represents kittens playing with a map of that country. It was attractive and was praised for its artistic merit. In fact, her puppies and kittens are most excellent results – have been called masterpieces – of the most intimate and intelligent study of nature.

Among her works are "A Quartet of Cats," "The Hostile Brothers," and "The Outcast."

Stokes, Marianna. Honorable mention at Paris Salon, 1884; gold medal in Munich, 1890; medal at Chicago in 1893. Member of the Society of Painters in Tempera. Born in Graz-Styria. Pupil of Professor W. von Lindenschmit in Munich, of M. Dagnan Bouveret and M. Courtois in Paris.

Her picture, "A Parting," is in the Liverpool Gallery; "Childhood's Wonder," in the Nottingham Gallery; "Aucassin and Nicolette," in the Pittsburg Gallery, etc.

Mrs. Stokes writes me that she has taken great interest in the revival of tempera painting in recent years. In reviewing the exhibition in the New Gallery, London, the *Spectator* of May 2, 1903, speaks of the portraits by Mrs. Stokes as charming, and adds: "They are influenced by the primitive painters, but in the right way. That is, the painter has used a formal and unrealistic style, but without any sacrifice of artistic freedom." Of a portrait of a child the same writer says: "It would be difficult to imagine a happier portrait of a little child,... and in it may be seen how the artist has used her freedom; for although she has preserved a primitive simplicity, the sky, sea, and windmill have modern qualities of atmosphere. The picture is very subtle in drawing and color, and the sympathy for child-life is perfect, seen as it is both in the hands and in the eyes.

"Another portrait by the same artist is hung on a marble pillar at the top of the stairs leading up to the balcony. The admirable qualities of decoration are well shown by the way it is hung... Is a fine piece of strong and satisfactory color, but the decorative aspect in no way takes precedence of the portraiture. We think of the man first and the picture afterward."

At the Academy, in 1903, Mrs. Stokes exhibited a portrait of J. Westlake, Esq., K.C.

Storer, Mrs. Maria Longworth. Gold medal at Paris Exposition, 1900. Born in Cincinnati, Ohio. Pupil of the Cincinnati Art School, which her father, Joseph Longworth, endowed with three hundred thousand dollars.

After working four years, making experiments in clay decoration at the Dallas White Ware Pottery, Mrs. Storer, "who had the enthusiasm of the artistic temperament coupled with fixity of purpose and financial resources,... had the courage to open a Pottery which she called Rookwood, the name of her father's place on the hills beyond. This was in 1880."

Nine years later this pottery had become self-supporting, and Mrs. Storer then dissolved her personal association with it, leaving it in charge of Mr. William Watts Taylor, who had collaborated with her during six years.

At the Paris Exposition Mrs. Storer exhibited about twenty pieces of pottery mounted in bronze – all her own work. It was an exquisite exhibition, and I was proud that it was the work of one of my countrywomen.

In 1897 Mr. Storer was appointed United States minister to Belgium, and Mrs. Storer took a Japanese artist, Asano, to Brussels, to instruct her in bronze work. Two years later Mr. Storer's mission was changed to Spain, and there Mrs. Storer continued, under Asano's guidance, her work in bronze, some of the results being seen in the mounting of her pottery.

At present Mr. Storer is our Ambassador to Austria, and Mrs. Storer writes me that she hopes to continue her work in bronze in Vienna.

In the summer of 1903 Mrs. Storer was in Colorado Springs, where she was much interested in the pottery made by Mr. Van Briggle. She became one of the directors of the Van Briggle Pottery Company, and encouraged the undertaking most heartily.

Stumm, Maud. Born in Cleveland, Ohio. Pupil of Art Students' League under Kenyon Cox and Siddons Mowbray, and of Oliver Merson in Paris, where her painting was also criticised and approved by Whistler. Her earliest work was flower painting, in which she gained an enviable reputation.

In Paris she began the study of figure painting, and her exhibition at the Salon was favorably received, the purity and brilliancy of her coloring being especially commended.

Several of Miss Stumm's pictures are well known by reproductions. Among these is the "Mother and Child," the original of which is owned by Mr. Patterson, of the Chicago *Tribune*. Her calendars, too, are artistic and popular; some of these have reached a sale of nearly half a million.

A series of studies of Sarah Bernhardt, in pastel, and a portrait of Julia Marlowe are among her works in this medium. Many of her figure subjects, such as "A Venetian Matron" and "A Violinist," are portraits, not studies from professional models.

This artist has painted an unusual variety of subjects, but is ambitious in still another department of painting – decorative art – in which she believes she could succeed.

Her works are seen in the exhibitions of the Society of American Artists and of the American Water-Color Society.

Swoboda, Josephine. Born in Vienna, 1861. Pupil of Laufberger and I. V. Berger. This portrait artist has been successful and numbers among her subjects the Princess Henry of

Prussia, the late Queen of England, whose portrait she painted at Balmoral in 1893, the Minister Bauhaus, and several members of the royal house of Austria. The portrait of Queen Victoria was exhibited at the Water-Color Club, Vienna.

She also paints charming miniatures. Her pictures are in both oil and water-colors, and are praised by the critics of the exhibitions in which they are seen.

Swope, Mrs. Kate. Honorable mention at National Academy of Design, 1888; honorable mention and gold medal, Southern Art League, 1895; highest award, Louisville Art League, 1897. Member of Louisville Art League. Born in Louisville, Kentucky. Pupil of Edgar Ward and M. Flagg in New York, and later of B. R. Fitz.

Mrs. Swope devotes herself almost entirely to sacred subjects. The pictures that have been awarded medals are Madonnas. She prefers to paint her pictures out of doors and in the sunlight, which results in her working in a high key and, as she writes, "in tender, opalescent color."

One of her medal pictures is the "Head of a Madonna," out of doors, in a hazy, blue shadow, against a background of grapevine foliage. The head is draped in white; the eyes are cast down upon the beholder. A sun spot kisses the white draperies on the shoulder. It is a young, girlish face, but the head is suggestive of great exaltation.

A second picture which received an award was a "Madonna and Child," out of doors. The figure is half life size. Dressed in white, the Madonna is stretched at full length upon the grass. Raised on one arm, she gazes into the face of the infant Christ Child.

Mrs. Swope has had success in pastel, in which, not long since, she exhibited a "Mother and Child," which was much admired. The mother – in an arbor – held the child up and reverently kissed the cheek. It was called "Love," and was exhibited in New York, Philadelphia, and Chicago.

Mrs. Swope's most ambitious work – five by three feet in size – represents an allegorical subject and is called "Revelation."

Sues, Mlle. Lea. Three silver medals from the School of Arts, Geneva; diploma of honor at the National Swiss Exposition, 1896. Member of l'Athénée, Geneva. Born at Genoa and studied there under Professors Gillet, Poggy, and Castan.

This artist paints landscapes, Swiss subjects principally. Her pictures of Mont Blanc and Chamounix are popular and have been readily sold. They are in private collections in several countries, and when exhibited have been praised in German and French as well as in Swiss publications.

Syamour, Mme. Marguerite. Honorable mention, 1887; bronze medal at Exposition at Lyons. Born at Bréry, 1861. Pupil of Mercié. Her principal works are a plaster statue, "New France," 1886, in the Museum of Issoudun; a statue of Voltaire; a plaster statue, "Life"; a plaster group, the "Last Farewells"; a statue of "Diana," in the Museum of Amiens; a great number of portrait busts, among them those of Jules Grévy, Flammarion, J. Claretie, etc.

At the Salon, Artistes Français, 1902, this artist exhibited a "Portrait of M. G. L.," and in 1904 "A Vision" and "La Dame aux Camelias."

Taylor, Elizabeth V. Sears prize, Boston Art Museum; bronze medal, Nashville Exposition, 1897. Member of the Copley Society, Boston. Pupil of E. C. Tarbell and Joseph de Camp in the School of the Museum of Fine Arts, Boston.

This artist paints portraits in miniature and in life size. Her works are numerous and have been seen in many exhibitions.

Thaulow, Mme. Alexandra. Wife of the great Scandinavian painter. This lady is an artist in bookbinding and her work is much admired. A writer, H. F., says, in the *Studio*, December,

1903: "When the exhibition of bookbinding was held some time ago at the Musée Galliera, Madame Thaulow's showcase attracted attention by its variety and its grace. The charm of these bindings lies in the fact that they have none of the massive heaviness of so many productions of this kind. One should be able to handle a book with ease, and not be forced to rest content with beholding it displaying its beauties behind glass or on the library shelf; and Madame Thaulow understood this perfectly when she executed the bindings now reproduced here. But these bindings are interesting not only from the standpoint of their utility and intelligent application; their ornamentation delights one by its graceful interpretation of Nature, rendered with a very special sense of decoration; moreover, the coloring of these mosaics of leather is restrained and fresh, and the hollyhocks and the hortensias, the bunches of mistletoe and the poppies, which form some of her favorite *motifs*, go to make up a delicious symphony."

Thevenin, Marie Anne Rosalie. Medals at the Salons of 1849, 1859, 1861. Born at Lyons. Pupil of Leon Cogniet. Portrait and figure painter. Among her pictures the following are noticeable: "Flora McIvor and Rose Bradwardine," 1848; "Portrait of Abbé Jacquet," 1859; "Portrait of a Lady," 1861.

Thomas-Soyer, Mme. Mathilde. Honorable mention, 1880; third-class medal, 1881; bronze medal, Exposition, 1889. Born at Troyes, 1859. Pupil of Chapu and Cain. The principal works of this sculptor are: "A Russian Horse"; "Lost Dogs"; "Russian Greyhounds"; "Huntsmen and a Poacher," in the Museum of Semur; "Combat of Dogs," purchased by the Government; "Cow and Calf," in the Museum of Nevers; "Stag and Bloodhound," in the Museum of Troyes, etc.

At the Salon, Artistes Français, 1902, Mme. Thomas-Soyer exhibited "An Irish Setter and a Laverock," and in 1903 "Under the White Squall."

Thornycroft, Mary. Born 1814; died 1895. Daughter of John Francis, the sculptor, whose pupil she was. This artist exhibited at the Royal Academy when very young. Her first important work was a life-size figure called "The Flower-Girl." In 1840 she married Thomas Thornycroft, and went to Rome two years later, spending a year in study there. Queen Victoria, after her return, commissioned her to execute statues of the royal children as the Four Seasons. These were much admired when exhibited at the Academy. Later she made portrait statues and busts of many members of the royal family, which were also seen at the Academy Exhibition.

In his "Essays on Art," Palgrave wrote: "Sculpture has at no time numbered many successful followers among women. We have, however, in Mrs. Thornycroft, one such artist who, by some recent advance and by the degrees of success which she has already reached, promises fairly for the art. Some of this lady's busts have refinement and feeling."

Thurber, Caroline Nettleton. Born in Oberlin, Ohio. Pupil of Howard Helmick in Washington, and of Benjamin Constant and Jean Paul Laurens in Paris.

In 1898 Mrs. Thurber took a studio in Paris, where her first work was the portrait of a young violinist, which was exhibited in the Salon of the following spring. This picture met with immediate favor with the public, the art critics, and the press. The Duchess of Sutherland, upon seeing it, sent for the artist and arranged for a portrait of her daughter, which was painted the following autumn while Mrs. Thurber was a guest at Dunrobin Castle. This portrait was subsequently exhibited in London and Liverpool.

Mrs. Thurber has painted portraits of many persons of distinction in Paris, among them one of Mlle. Ollivier, only daughter of Émile Ollivier, president of the Académie Française. Monsieur Ollivier, in a personal note to the artist, made the following comment upon the portrait of his daughter: "How much

I thank you for the portrait of my daughter; it lives, so powerfully is it colored, and one is tempted to speak to it." Mrs. Thurber is an exhibitor in the Salon, Royal Academy, and New Gallery, London, and other foreign exhibitions, as well as in those of this country.

She now has a studio in the family home at Bristol, Rhode Island, on Narragansett Bay, where she works during half the year. In winter she divides her time among the larger cities as her orders demand. While Mrs. Thurber's name is well known through her special success in the portraiture of children, she has painted many prominent men and women in Chicago, New York, Philadelphia, Washington, and New England.

Among her later portraits are those of Mrs. James Sullivan, one of the lady commissioners of the St. Louis Exposition; Lieut.-Gen. Nelson A. Miles; Albert, son of Dr. Shaw, editor of the *Review of Reviews*; Mrs. A. A. F. Johnston, former Dean of Oberlin College; Augustus S. Miller, mayor of Providence; Hon. L. F. C. Garvin, governor of Rhode Island; and Judge Austin Adams, late of the Supreme Court of Iowa.

Thurwanger, Felicité Chastanier. This remarkable artist, not long since, when eighty-four years old, sent to the exhibition at Nice – which is, in a sense, a branch of the Paris Salon – three portraits which she had just finished. "They were hung in the place of honor and unanimously voted to belong to the first class."

Mme. Thurwanger was the pupil of Delacroix during five years. The master unconsciously did his pupil an injury by saying to her father: "That daughter of yours is wonderfully gifted, and if she were a man I would make a great artist of her." Hearing this, the young artist burst into tears, and her whole career was clouded by the thought that her sex prevented her being a really great artist, and induced in her an abnormal modesty. This occurred about forty-five years ago; since then we have signally changed all that!

Delacroix, who was an enthusiast in color, was the leader of one school of his time, and was opposed by Ingres, who was so wanting in this regard that he was accused of being color-blind.

Mme. Thurwanger had a curious experience with these artists. When but seventeen she was commissioned by the Government to copy a picture in the Louvre. One morning, when she was working in the Gallery, Ingres passed by and stopped to look at her picture. He examined it carefully, and with an expression of satisfaction said: "I am so very glad to see that you have the true idea of art! Remember always that there is no color in Nature; the outline is all; if the outline is good, no matter about the coloring, the picture will be good."

This story would favor the color-blind theory, as Ingres apparently saw color neither in the original nor the copy.

An hour later Delacroix came to watch the work of his pupil, and after a few minutes exclaimed: "I am so happy, my dear girl, to see that you have the true and only spirit of art. Never forget that in Nature there is no line, no outline; everything is color!"

In 1852 Mme. Thurwanger was in Philadelphia and remained more than two years. She exhibited her pictures, which were favorably noticed by the Philadelphia *Enquirer*. In July of the above year her portraits were enthusiastically praised. "Not a lineament, not a feature, however trivial, escapes the all-searching eye of the artist, who has the happy faculty of causing the expression of the mind and soul to beam forth in the life-like and speaking face."

In October, 1854, her picture of a "Madonna and Child" was thus noticed by the same paper: "For brilliancy, animation, maternal solicitude, form, grace, and feature, it would be difficult to imagine anything more impressive. It is in every sense a gem of the pictorial art, while the execution and finish are such as genius alone could inspire."

Tirlinks, Liewena. Born in Bruges, a daughter of Master Simon. This lady was not only esteemed as an artist in London, but she won the heart of an English nobleman, to whom she was given in marriage by Henry VIII. Her miniatures were much admired and greatly in fashion at the court. Some critics have thought the Tirlinks to be the same person with Liewena Bennings or Benic, whose story, as we know it, is much the same as the above.

Tormoczy, Bertha von. Diploma of honor, Budapest and Agram. Born at Innspruck, 1846. Pupil of Hausch, Her, and Schindler. Among her pictures are "Girl in the Garden," "Blossoming Meadows," "Autumn Morning," and a variety of landscapes.

Toro, Petronella. A painter of miniatures on ivory which have attained distinction. Among those best known are the portraits of the Prince of Carignano, Duke Amadeo, and the Duchess d'Aosta with the sons of the Prince of Carignano. She has painted a young woman in an antique dress and another in a modern costume. Her works are distinguished by firmness of touch and great intelligence. She has executed some most attractive landscapes.

Treu, or Trey, Katharina. Born at Bamberg. 1742-1811. A successful painter of flowers and still-life. Her talent was remarkable when but a child, and her father, who was her only master, began her lessons when she was ten years old. When still young she was appointed court painter at Mannheim, and in 1776 was made a professor in the Academy at Düsseldorf. Her pictures are in the Galleries of Bamberg and Carlsruhe, and in the Darmstadt and Stuttgart Museums.

Urrutia de Urmeneta, Ana Gertrudis de. Member of the Academy of Fine Arts, Cadiz, 1846. Born in Cadiz. 1812-1850. She began the study of drawing with Javier, and after her marriage to Juan José de Urmeneta, professor of painting and sculpture and director of the Cadiz Academy, continued her work under his direction. A "St. Filomena" and "Resurrection of the Body," exhibited in 1846, are among her best pictures. Her "St. Jeronimo" is in the new cathedral at Cadiz, and the Academy has shown respect to her memory by placing her portrait in the room in which its sessions are held.

Viani, Maria. Born at Bologna. 1670-1711. I find no reliable biographical account of this artist, whose name appears in the catalogue of the Dresden Gallery as the painter of the "Reclining Venus, lying on a blue cushion, with a Cupid at her side."

Verelst, Marian. Born in 1680. This artist belonged in Antwerp and was of the celebrated artistic family of her name. She was a pupil of her father, Hermann, and her uncle, Simon Verelst. She became famous for the excellent likenesses she made and for the artistic qualities of her small portraits.

Like so many other artists, she was distinguished for accomplishments outside her art. She was a fine musician and a marvel in her aptitude in acquiring both ancient and modern languages. A very interesting anecdote is related of her, as follows: When in London, one evening at the theatre she sat near six German gentlemen, who expressed their admiration of her in the most flattering terms of their language, and at the same time observed her so closely as to be extremely rude. The artist, in their own tongue, remarked that such extravagant praise was the opposite of a compliment. One of them repeated his words in Latin, when she again replied in the same language. The strangers then asked her if she would give them her name. This she did and further told them that she lived with her uncle, Simon Verelst. In the end she painted the portrait of each of these men, and the story of their experience proved the reason for the acquaintance of the artist being sought by people of culture and position. Walpole speaks in praise of her portraits and also mentions her unusual attainments in languages.

Vigée, Marie Louise Elizabeth. Member of the French

Academy. Born in Paris in 1755. That happy writer and learned critic, M. Charles Blanc, begins his account of her thus: "All the fairies gathered about the cradle of Elizabeth Vigée, as for the birth of a little princess in the kingdom of art. One gave her beauty, another genius; the fairy Gracious offered her a pencil and a palette. The fairy of marriage, who had not been summoned, told her, it is true, that she should wed M. Le Brun, the expert in pictures – but for her consolation the fairy of travellers promised her that she should bear from court to court, from academy to academy, from Paris to Petersburg, and from Rome to London, her gayety, her talent, and her easel – before which all the sovereigns of Europe and all those whom genius had crowned should place themselves as subjects for her brush."

It is difficult to write of Madame Le Brun in outline because her life was so interesting in detail. Though she had many sorrows, there is a halo of romance and a brilliancy of atmosphere about her which marks her as a prominent woman of her day, and her autobiography is charming – it is so alive that one forgets that she is not present, telling her story!

The father of this gifted daughter was an artist of moderate ability and made portraits in pastel, which Elizabeth, in her "Souvenirs," speaks of as good and thinks some of them worthy of comparison with those of the famous Latour. M. Vigée was an agreeable man with much vivacity of manner. His friends were numerous and he was able to present his daughter to people whose acquaintance was of value to her. She was but twelve years old at the time of his death, and he had already so encouraged her talents as to make her future comparatively easy for her.

Elizabeth passed five years of her childhood in a convent, where she constantly busied herself in sketching everything that she saw. She tells of her intense pleasure in the use of her pencil, and says that her passion for painting was innate and never grew less, but increased in charm as she grew older. She claimed that it was a source of perpetual youth, and that she owed to it her acquaintance and friendship with the most delightful men and women of Europe.

While still a young girl, Mlle. Vigée studied under Briard, Doyen, and Greuze, but Joseph Vernet advised her to study the works of Italian and Flemish masters, and, above all, to study Nature for herself – to follow no school or system. To this advice Mme. Le Brun attributed her success.

When sixteen years old she presented two portraits to the French Academy, and was thus early brought to public notice.

When twenty-one she married M. Le Brun, of whom she speaks discreetly in her story of her life, but it was well known that he was of dissipated habits and did not hesitate to spend all that his wife could earn. When she left France, thirteen years after her marriage, she had not so much as twenty francs, although she had earned a million!

She painted portraits of many eminent people, and was esteemed as a friend by men and women of culture and high position. The friendship between the artist and Marie Antoinette was a sincere and deep affection between two women, neither of whom remembered that one of them was a queen. It was a great advantage to the artist to be thus intimately associated with her sovereign lady. Even in the great state picture of the Queen surrounded by her children, at Versailles, one realizes the tenderness of the painter as she lovingly reproduced her friend.

Marie Antoinette desired that Mme. Le Brun should be elected to the Academy; Vernet approved it, and an unusual honor was shown her in being made an Academician before the completion of her reception picture. At that time it was a great advantage to be a member of the Academy, as no other artists were permitted to exhibit their works in the Salon of the Beaux-Arts.

Mme. Le Brun had one habit with which she allowed nothing to interfere, which was taking a rest after her work for the day was done. She called it her "calm," and to it she attributed a large share of her power of endurance, although it lost her many pleasures. She could not go out to dinner or entertain at that hour.

The evening was her only time for social pleasures. But when one reads her "Souvenirs," and realizes how many notable people she met in her studio and in evening society, it scarcely seems necessary to regret that she could not dine out!

Mme. Le Brun was at one period thought to be very extravagant, and one of her entertainments caused endless comments. Her own account of it shows how greatly the cost was exaggerated. She writes that on one occasion she invited twelve or fifteen friends to listen to her brother's reading during her "calm." The poem read was the "Voyage du jeune Anacharsis en Grèce," in which a dinner was described, and even the receipts for making various sauces were given. The artist was seized with the idea of improvising a Greek supper.

She summoned her cook and instructed her in what had been read. Among her guests were several unusually pretty ladies, who attired themselves in Greek costumes as nearly as the time permitted. Mme. Le Brun retained the white blouse she wore at her work, adding a veil and a crown of flowers. Her studio was rich in antique objects, and a dealer whom she knew loaned her cups, vases, and lamps. All was arranged with the effect an artist knows how to produce.

As the guests arrived Mme. Le Brun added here and there an element of Grecian costume until their number was sufficient for an effective *tableau vivant*. Her daughter and a little friend were dressed as pages and bore antique vases. A canopy hung over the table, the guests were posed in picturesque attitudes, and those who arrived later were arrested at the door of the supper-room with surprise and delight.

It was as if they had been transported to another clime. A Greek song was chanted to the accompaniment of a lyre, and when the honey, grapes, and other dishes were served *à la Grecque*, the enchantment was complete. The poet recited odes from Anacreon and all passed off delightfully.

The fame of this novel supper was spread over Paris, and marvellous tales were told of its magnificence and its cost. Mme.

Le Brun writes: "Some ladies asked me to repeat this pleasantry. I refused for various reasons, and several of them were disturbed by my refusal. Soon a report that the supper had cost me twenty thousand francs was spread abroad. The King spoke of it as a joke to the Marquis of Cubières, who fortunately had been one of the guests and was able to convince His Majesty of the folly of such a story. Nevertheless, the modest sum of twenty thousand at Versailles became forty thousand at Rome; at Vienna the Baroness de Strogonoff told me that I had spent sixty thousand francs for my Greek supper; you know that at Petersburg the price at length was fixed at eighty thousand francs, and the truth is that it cost me about fifteen francs!"

Early in 1789, when the warnings of the horrors about to take place began to be heard, Mme. Le Brun went to Italy. In each city that she visited she was received with great kindness and many honors were shown her. In Florence she was invited to paint her own portrait, to be hung in that part of the Uffizi set apart for the portraits of famous painters. Later she sent the well-known portrait, near that of Angelica Kauffman. It is interesting to read Goethe's comparison of the two portraits.

Speaking of Angelica's first, he writes: "It has a truer tone in the coloring, the position is more pleasing, and the whole exhibits more correct taste and a higher spirit in art. But the work of Le Brun shows more careful execution, has more vigor in the drawing, and more delicate touches. It, has, moreover, a clear though somewhat exaggerated coloring. The Frenchwoman understands the art of adornment – the headdress, the hair, the folds of lace on the bosom, all are arranged with care and, as one might say, *con amore*. The piquant, handsome face, with its lively expression, its parted lips disclosing a row of pearly teeth, presents itself to the beholder's gaze as if coquettishly challenging his admiration, while the hand holds the pencil as in the act of drawing.

"The picture of Angelica, with head gently inclined and a soft, intellectual melancholy pervading the countenance, evinces higher genius, even if, in point of artistic skill, the preference should be given to the other."

Mme. Le Brun found Rome delightful and declared that if she could forget France she should be the happiest of women. She writes of her fellow artist: "I have been to see Angelica Kauffman, whom I greatly desired to know. I found her very interesting, apart from her fine talent, on account of her mind and her general culture... She has talked much with me during the two evenings I have passed at her house. Her manner is gentle; she is prodigiously learned, but has no enthusiasm, which, considering my ignorance, has not electrified me... I have seen several of her works; her sketches please me more than her pictures, because they are of a Titianesque color."

Mme. Le Brun received more commissions for portraits than she could find time to paint in the three years she lived in Italy. She tells us: "Not only did I find great pleasure in painting surrounded by so many masterpieces, but it was also necessary for me to make another fortune. I had not a hundred francs of income. Happily I had only to choose among the grandest people the portraits which it pleased me to paint." Her account of her experiences in Italy is very entertaining, but at last the restlessness of the exile overcame her and impelled her to seek other scenes. She went to Vienna and there remained three other years, making many friends and painting industriously until the spirit of unrest drove her to seek new diversions, and she went to Russia.

She was there received with great cordiality and remained six years – years crowded with kindness, labor, honor, attainment, joy, and sorrow. Her daughter was the one all-absorbing passion – at once the joy and the grief of her life. She was so charming and so gifted as to satisfy the critical requirements of her mother's desires. In Petersburg, where the daughter was greatly admired and caressed, the artist found herself a thousand times more happy than she had ever been in her own triumphs.

Mme. Le Brun was so constantly occupied and the need of

earning was so great with her, that she was forced to confide her daughter to the care of others when she made her début in society. Thus it happened that the young girl met M. Nigris, whom she afterward married. Personally he was not agreeable to Mme. Le Brun and his position was not satisfactory to her. We can imagine her chagrin in accepting a son-in-law who even asked her for money with which to go to church on his wedding-day! The whole affair was most distasteful, and the marriage occurred at the time of the death of Mme. Le Brun's mother. She speaks of it as a "time devoted to tears."

Her health suffered so much from this sadness that she tried the benefit of change of scene, and went to Moscow. Returning to Petersburg, she determined – in spite of the remonstrances of her friends, and the inducements offered her to remain – to go to France. She several times interrupted her journey in order to paint portraits of persons who had heard of her fame, and desired to have her pictures.

She reached Paris in 1801 and writes thus of her return: "I shall not attempt to express my emotions when I was again upon the soil of France, from which I had been absent twelve years. Fright, grief, joy possessed me, each in turn, for all these entered into the thousand varying sentiments which swept over my soul. I wept for the friends whom I had lost upon the scaffold, but I was about to see again those who remained. This France to which I returned had been the scene of atrocious crimes; but this France was my Native Land!"

But the new régime was odious to the artist, and she found herself unable to be at home, even in Paris. After a year she went to London, and remained in England three years. She detested the climate and was not in love with the people, but she found a compensation in the society of many French families who had fled from France as she had done.

In 1804 Mme. Nigris was in Paris and her mother returned to see her. The young woman was very beautiful and attractive, very fond of society, entirely indifferent to her husband, and not always wise in the choice of her companions. Mme. Le Brun, always hard at work and always having great anxieties, at length found herself so broken in health, and so nervously fatigued that she longed to be alone with Nature, and in 1808 she went to Switzerland. Her letters written to the Countess Potocka at this time are added to her "Souvenirs," and reveal the very best of her nature. Feeling the need of continued repose, she bought a house at Louveciennes, where she spent much time. In 1818 M. Le Brun died, and six years later the deaths of her daughter and her brother left her with no near relative in the world.

For a time she sought distractions in new scenes and visited the Touraine and other parts of France, but though she still lived a score of years, she spent them in Paris and Louveciennes. She had with her two nieces, who cared for her more tenderly than any one had done before. One of these ladies was a portrait painter and profited much by the advice of Mme. Le Brun, who wrote of this period and these friends: "They made me feel again the sentiments of a mother, and their tender devotion diffused a great charm over my life. It is near these two dear ones and some friends who remain to me that I hope to terminate peacefully a life which has been wandering but calm, laborious but honorable."

During the last years of her life the most distinguished society of Paris was wont to assemble about her – artists, litterateurs, savants, and men of the fashionable world. Here all essential differences of opinion were laid aside and all met on common ground. Her "calm" seemed to have influenced all her life; only good feeling and equality found a place near her, and few women have the blessed fortune to be so sincerely mourned by a host of friends as was Elizabeth Vigée Le Brun, dying at the age of eighty-seven.

Mme. Le Brun's works numbered six hundred and sixty portraits – fifteen genre or figure pictures and about two hundred landscapes painted from sketches made on her journeys. Her portraits included those of the sovereigns and royal families of all Europe, as well as the most famous authors, artists, singers, and the learned men in Church and State.

As an artist M. Charles Blanc thus esteems her: "In short, Mme. Le Brun belonged entirely to the eighteenth century – I wish to say to that period of our time which rested itself suddenly at David. While she followed the counsels of Vernet, her pencil had a certain suppleness, and her brush a force; but she too often attempted to imitate Greuze in her later works and she weakened the resemblance to her subjects by abusing the *regard noyé* (cloudy or indistinct effect). She was too early in vogue to make all the necessary studies, and she too often contented herself with an ingenuity a little too manifest. Without judging her as complacently as the Academy formerly judged her, we owe her an honorable place, because in spite of revolutions and reforms she continued to her last day the light, spiritual, and French Art of Watteau, Nattier, and Fragonard."

Vigri, Caterina de. Lippo Dalmasii was much admired by Malvasia, who not only extols his pictures, but his spirit as well, and represents him as following his art as a religion, beginning and ending his daily work with prayer. Lippo is believed to have been the master of Caterina de Vigri, and the story of her life is in harmony with the influence of such a teacher.

She is the only woman artist who has been canonized; and in the Convent of the Corpus Domini, in Bologna, which she founded, she is known as "La Santa," and as a special patron of the Fine Arts.

Caterina was of a noble family of Ferrara, where she was born in 1413. She died when fifty years old; and so great was the reverence for her memory that her remains were preserved, and may still be seen in a chapel of her convent. There are few places in that ever wonderful Italy of such peculiar interest as this chapel, where sits, clothed in a silken robe, with a crown of gold on the head, the incorrupt body of a woman who died four hundred and forty years ago. The body is quite black, while the nails are still pink. She holds a book and a sceptre. Around her, in the well-lighted chapel, are several memorials of her life: the viola on which she played, and a manuscript in her exquisite chirography, also a service book illuminated by Caterina, and, still more important, one of her pictures, a "Madonna and Child," inserted in the wall on the left of the chapel, which is admirable for the beauty of expression in the face of the Holy Mother.

We cannot trace Caterina's artist life step by step, but she doubtless worked with the same spirit of consecration and prayer as did that Beato whom we call Angelico, in his Florentine convent, a century earlier.

Caterina executed many miniatures, and her easel pictures were not large. These were owned by private families. She is known to us by two pictures of "St. Ursula folding her Robe about her Companions." One is in the Bologna Gallery, the other in the Academy in Venice. The first is on a wooden panel, and was painted when the artist was thirty-nine years old. The Saint is represented as unnaturally tall, the figures of her virgins being very small. The mantle and robe of St. Ursula are of rich brocade ornamented with floral designs, while on each side of her is a white flag, on which is a red cross. The face of the saint is so attractive that one forgets the elongation of her figure. There is a delicacy in the execution, combined with a freedom and firmness of handling fully equal to the standard of her school and time. Many honors were paid to the memory of Caterina de Vigri. She was chosen as the protectress of Academies and Art Institutions, and in the eighteenth century a medal was coined, on which she is represented as painting on a panel held by an angel. How few human beings are thus honored three centuries after death!

Vincent, Mme. See Labille.

Visscher, Anna and Maria. These daughters of the celebrated Dutch engraver were known as "the Dutch Muses." They made their best reputation by their etchings on glass, but they were also well known for their writing of both poetry and prose. They were associated with the scholars of their time and were much admired.

Volkmar, Antonie Elizabeth Cæcilia. Born in Berlin, 1827. She studied with Schroder in her native city, with L. Cogniet in Paris, and later in Italy. She returned to Berlin, where she painted portraits and genre subjects. Her picture of the "Grandmother telling Stories" is in the Museum of Stettin. Among her works are "An Artist's Travels" a "German Emigrant," and "School Friends."

Vonnoh, Bessie Potter. Bronze medal, Paris Exposition, 1900; Second Prize at Tennessee Centennial. Honorable mention at Buffalo Exposition, 1901. Member of the National Sculpture Society and National Arts Club. Born in St. Louis, Missouri, 1872.

This sculptor is a pupil of the Art Institute, Chicago. Among her best works are "A Young Mother"; "Twin Sisters"; "His First Journey"; "Girl Reading," etc.

In the *Century Magazine*, September, 1897, Arthur Hoeber wrote: "There were shown at the Society of American Artists in New York, in the Spring of 1896, some statuettes of graceful young womanhood, essentially modern in conception, singularly naïve in treatment, refined, and withal intensely personal... While the disclosure is by no means novel, Miss Potter makes us aware that in the daily prosaic life about us there are possibilities conventional yet attractive, simple, but containing much of suggestion, waiting only the sympathetic touch to be responsive if the proper chord is struck."

This author also notices the affiliation of this young woman with the efforts of the Tanagra workers, and says: "But if the inspiration of the young woman is evident, her work can in no way be called imitative."

Vos, Maria. Born in Amsterdam, 1824. Pupil of P. Kiers. Her pictures were principally of still-life, two of which are seen in the Amsterdam Museum.

Wagner, Maria Dorothea; family name Dietrich. 1728-1792. The gallery of Wiesbaden has two of her landscapes, as has also the Museum at Gotha. "Der Mühlengrund," representing a valley with a brook and a mill, is in the Dresden Gallery.

Ward, Miss E. This sculptor has a commission to make a statue of G. R. Clark for the St. Louis Exposition.
[*No reply to circular.*]

Ward, Henrietta Mary Ada. Gold and silver medals at the Crystal Palace; bronze medal at the Vienna Exposition, 1873. Born in Newman Street, London, when that street and the neighborhood was the quarter in which the then celebrated artists resided. Mrs. Ward was a pupil of the Bloomsbury Art School and of Sak's Academy. Her grandfather, James Ward, was a royal Academician, and one of the best animal painters of England. While Sir Thomas Lawrence lived, Mrs. Ward's father, who was a miniaturist, was much occupied in copying the works of Sir Thomas on ivory, as the celebrated portrait painter would permit no other artist to repeat them. After the death of Sir Thomas, Mr. Ward became an engraver. Her mother was also a miniature painter. Her great-uncles were William Ward, R.A., and George Morland; John Jackson, R.A., was her uncle; and her husband, Edward M. Ward, to whom she was married at sixteen, was also a Royal Academican.

From 1849, Mrs. Ward exhibited at the Royal Academy during thirty years, without a break, but her husband's death caused her to omit some exhibitions, and since that time her exhibits have been less regular. For some years Mrs. Ward has had successful classes for women at Chester Studios, which have somewhat interfered with her painting.

Mrs. Ward's subjects have been historical and genre, some of which are extensively known by prints after them. Among these are "Joan of Arc," "Palissy the Potter," and "Mrs. Fry and Mary

Saunderson visiting Prisoners at Newgate," the last dedicated by permission to Queen Victoria. This picture was purchased by an American.

Of her picture of "Mary of Scotland, giving her infant to the Care of Lord Mar," Palgrave wrote: "This work is finely painted, and tells its tale with clearness." Among her numerous works are: "The Poet Hogg's First Love"; "Chatterton," the poet, in the Muniment Room, Bristol; "Lady Jane Grey refusing the Crown of England"; "Antwerp Market"; "Queen Mary of Scots' farewell to James I."; "Washing Day at the Liverpool Docks"; "The Princes in the Tower"; "George III. and Mrs. Delayney, with his family at Windsor"; "The Young Pretender," and many others.

When sixteen Mrs. Ward exhibited two heads in crayon. In 1903, at the Academy, she exhibited "The Dining-room, Kent House, Knightsbridge." Mrs. Ward painted for Queen Victoria two portraits of the Princess Beatrice, and a life-size copy of a portrait of the Duke of Albany. She also painted a portrait of Princess Alice of Albany, who is about to marry Prince Alexander of Teck.

Edward VII. has commissioned this artist to make two copies of the state portrait, painted by S. Luke Fildes, R.A.

Mrs. Ward had two more votes for her admission to the Royal Academy than any other woman of her time has had.

Wasser, Anna. Born at Zürich, 1676, is notable among the painters of her country. She was the daughter of an artist, and early developed a love of drawing and an unusual aptitude in the study of languages. In painting she was a pupil of Joseph Werner. After a time she devoted herself to miniature painting; her reputation extended to all the German courts, as well as to Holland and England, and her commissions were so numerous that her father began to regard her as a mine of riches. He allowed her neither rest nor recreation, and was even unwilling that she should devote sufficient time to her pictures to finish them properly. Under this pressure of haste and constant labor her health gave way and she became melancholy.

She was separated from her father, and in more agreeable surroundings her health was restored and she resumed her painting. Her father then insisted that she should return to him. On her journey home she had a fall, from the effects of which she died at the age of thirty-four.

Fuseli valued a picture by Anna Wasser, which he owned, and praised her correctness of design and her feeling for color.

Waters, Sadie P. 1869-1900. Honorable mention Paris Exposition, 1900. Born in St. Louis, Missouri. This unusually gifted artist made her studies entirely in Paris, under the direction of M. Luc-Olivier Merson.

Her earlier works were portraits in miniature, in which she was very successful. That of Jane Hading was much admired. She also excelled in illustrations, but in her later work she found her true province, that of religious subjects. A large picture on ivory, called "La Vierge au Lys," was exhibited in Paris, London, Brussels, and Ghent, and attracted much attention.

Her picture of the "Vierge aux Rosiers," reproduced here, was in the Salon, 1899, and in the exhibition of Religious Art in Brussels in 1900, after which it was exhibited in New York; and wherever seen it was especially admired.

Miss Waters' pictures were exhibited in the Salon Français, Champs Elysées, from 1891 until her death. From the earliest days of childhood she was remarkable for her skill in drawing and in working out, from her own impressions, pictures of events passing about her. If at the theatre she saw a play that appealed to her, she made a picture symbolic of the play, and constantly startled her friends by her original ideas and the pronounced artistic temperament, which was very early the one controlling power in her life. Mr. Carl Gutherz thus speaks of her good fortune in studying with M. Merson.

"As the Master and Student became more and more acquainted, and the great artist found in the student those kindred qualities which subsequently made her work so refined and beautiful,... he took the utmost care in developing her drawing – the fidelity of line and of expression, and the ever-pervading purity in her work. The sympathy with all good was reflected in the student, as it was ever present with the master, and only those who are acquainted with M. Merson can appreciate how fortunate it was for Art that the young artist was under a master of his character and temperament."

One of her pictures, called "La Chrysanthème," represents a nude figure of a young girl, seated on the ground, leaning against a large basket of chrysanthemums, from which she is plucking blossoms. The figure is beautiful, and shows the deep study the artist had made, although still so young.

The following estimate of her work is made by one competent to speak of such matters: "In this epoch of feverish uncertainty, of heated discussions and rivalries in art matters, the quiet, calm figure of Sadie Waters has a peculiar interest and charm generated by her tranquil and persistent pursuit of an ideal – an ideal she attained in her later works, an ideal of the highest mental order, mystical and human, and so far removed from the tendencies of our time that one might truthfully say, it stands alone. Her talents were manifold. She was endowed with the best of artistic qualities. She cultivated them diligently, and slowly acquired the handicraft and skill which enabled her to express herself without restriction. In her miniatures she learned to be careful, precise, and delicate; in her work from nature she was human; and in her studies of illuminating she gained a perfect understanding of ornamental painting and forms; and the subtle ambiance of the beautiful old churches and convents where she worked and pored over the ancient missals, and softly talked with the princely robed Monsignori, no doubt did much to develop her love for the Beautiful Story, the delicate myth of Christianity – and all this, all these rare qualities and honest efforts we find in her last picture, The Virgin.

"The beauty and preciseness of this composition, the divine

feeling not without a touch of motherly sentiment, its delicacy so rare and so pure, the distinction of its coloring, are all past expression, and give it a place unique in the nineteenth century." – *Paul W. Bartlett*, Paris, 1903.

Wegmann, Bertha. Honorable mention, Paris Salon, 1880; third-class medal, 1882; Thorwaldsen medal at Copenhagen; small gold medal, Berlin, 1894. Born at Soglio, Switzerland, 1847. Studied in Copenhagen, Munich, Paris, and Florence.

She paints portraits and genre subjects. Her pictures, seen at Berlin in 1893, were much admired. They included portraits, figure studies, and Danish interiors. At Munich, in 1894, her portraits attracted attention, and were commended by those who wrote of the exhibition. Among her works are many portraits: "Mother and Child in the Garden," and "A Widow and Child," are two of her genre subjects.

Weis, Rosario. Silver medal from the Academy of San Fernando, 1842, for a picture called "Silence." Member of the Academy. Pupil of Goya, who early recognized her talent. In 1823, when Goya removed to Burdeos, she studied under the architect Tiburcio Perez. After a time she joined Goya, and remained his pupil until his death in 1828. She then entered the studio Lacour, where she did admirable work. In 1833, for the support of her mother and herself, she made copies of pictures in the Prado on private commissions.

In 1842 she was appointed teacher of drawing to the royal family, in which position she did not long continue, her death occurring in 1843.

Among her pictures are "Attention!" an allegorical figure; "An Angel"; "A Venus"; and "A Diana." Among her portraits are those of Goya, Velasquez, and Figaro.

Wiegmann, Marie Elisabeth; family name Hancke. Small gold medal, Berlin. Born 1826 at Solberberg, Silesia; died, 1893, at

Düsseldorf. In 1841 she began to study with Stilke in Düsseldorf; later with K. Sohn. She travelled extensively in Germany, England, Holland, and Italy, and settled with her husband, Rudolph Wiegmann, in Düsseldorf. In the Museum at Hanover is "The Colonist's Children Crowning a Negro Woman," and in the National Gallery at Berlin a portrait of Schnaase. Some children's portraits, and one of the Countess Hatzfeld, should also be mentioned among her works.

In portraiture her work was distinguished by talent, spirit, and true artistic composition; in genre – especially the so-called ideal genre – she produced some exquisite examples.

Wentworth, Marquise Cecilia de. Gold medal, Tours National Exposition, Lyons and Turin; Honorable mention, Paris Salon, 1891; Bronze medal, Paris Exposition, 1900; Chevalier of the Legion of Honor, 1901. Born in New York. Pupil of the Convent of the Sacred Heart and of Cabanel, in Paris. This artist has painted portraits of Leo XIII., who presented her with a gold medal; of Cardinal Ferrata; of Challemel-Lacour, President of the Senate at the time when the portrait was made, and of many others. Her picture of "Faith" is in the Luxembourg Gallery. At the Salon des Artistes Français, 1903, Madame de Wentworth exhibited the "Portrait of Mlle. X.," and "Solitude."

[*No reply to circular.*]

Wheeler, Janet. First Toppan Prize and Mary Smith Prize at Academy of Fine Arts, Philadelphia; Gold medal, Philadelphia Art Club. Fellow of Academy of Fine Arts, and member of Plastic Club, Philadelphia. Born in Detroit, Michigan. Pupil of Academy of Fine Arts, Philadelphia, and of the Julian Academy in Paris.

This artist paints portraits almost entirely, which are in private hands. I know of but one figure picture by her, which is called "Beg for It." She was a miniaturist several years before taking up larger portraits.

White, Florence. Silver medal at Woman's Exhibition, Earl's Court; silver medal for a pastel exhibited in Calcutta. Born at Brighton, England. Pupil of Royal Academy Schools in London, and of Bouguereau and Perrier in Paris.

In 1899 this artist exhibited a portrait in the New Gallery; in 1901 a portrait of Bertram Blunt, Esq., at the Royal Academy; and in 1902 a portrait of "Peggy," a little girl with a poodle.

She has sent miniatures to the Academy exhibitions several years; that of Miss Lyall Wilson was exhibited in 1903.

Whitman, Sarah de St. Prix. Bronze medal at Columbian Exposition, Chicago, 1893; gold and bronze medals at Atlanta Exposition; diploma at Pan-American, Buffalo, 1901. Member of the Society of American Artists, New York; Copley Society, Boston; Water-Color Club, Boston. Born in Baltimore, Maryland. Pupil of William M. Hunt and Thomas Couture.

Mrs. Whitman has painted landscapes and portraits, and of recent years has been much occupied with work in glass. Windows by her are in Memorial Hall, Cambridge; in the Episcopal Church in Andover, Massachusetts, etc. An altar-piece by her is in All Saints' Church, Worcester.

Her portrait of Senator Bayard is in the State Department, Washington.

Whitney, Anne. Born in Watertown, Massachusetts. Made her studies in Belmont and Boston, and later in Paris and Rome.

Miss Whitney's sculptures are in many public places. A heroic size statue of Samuel Adams is in Boston and Washington, in bronze and marble; Harriet Martineau is at Wellesley College, in marble; the "Lotos-Eaters" is in Newton and Cambridge, in marble; "Lady Godiva," a life-size statue in marble, is in a private collection in Milton; a statue of Leif Eriksen, in bronze, is in Boston and Milwaukee; a bust of Professor Pickering, in marble, is in the Observatory, Cambridge; a statue, "Roma," is in Albany, Wellesley, St. Louis, and Newton, in both marble and bronze; Charles Sumner, in bronze of heroic size, is in Cambridge; a bust of President Walker, bronze, is also in Cambridge; President Stearns, a bust in marble, is in Amherst; a bust of Mrs. Alice Freeman Palmer is in Cambridge; a bust of Professor Palmer is on a bronze medal; the Calla Fountain, in bronze, is in Franklin Park; and many other busts, medals, etc., in marble, bronze, and plaster, are in private collections.

Wilson, Melva Beatrice. Prize of one hundred dollars a year for three successive years at Cincinnati Art Museum. Honorable mention, Paris Salon, 1897. Born in Cincinnati, 1875. Pupil of Cincinnati Art Museum, under Louis T. Rebisso and Thomas Noble; in Paris, of Rodin and Vincent Norrottny.

By special invitation this sculptor has been an exhibitor at the National Sculpture Society, New York. Her principal works are: "The Minute Man," in Corcoran Art Gallery, Washington, D. C.; "The Volunteer," which was given by the State of New York as a military prize to a Vermont Regiment; an equestrian statue of John F. Doyle, Jr.; "Bull and Bear" and the "Polo Player" in bronze, owned by Tiffany & Co.; "Retribution" in a private collection in New York.

Miss Wilson has been accorded the largest commission given any woman sculptor for the decoration of the buildings of the St. Louis Exposition. She is to design eight spandrils for Machinery Hall, each one being twenty-eight by fifteen feet in size, with figures larger than life. The design represents the wheelwright and boiler-making trades. Reclining nude figures, of colossal size, bend toward the keystone of the arch, each holding a tool of a machinist. Interlaced cog-wheels form the background.

Wirth, Anna Marie. Member of the Munich Art Association. Born in St. Petersburg, 1846. Studied in Vienna under Straschiripka – commonly known as Johann Canon – and in Paris, although her year's work in the latter city seems to have left no trace upon her manner of painting. The genre pictures, in which she excels, clearly show the influence of the old Dutch school. A writer in "Moderne Kunst" says, in general, that she shows us real human beings under the "précieuses ridicules," the languishing gallants and the pedant, and often succeeds in individualizing all these with the sharpness of a Chodowiecki, though at times she is merely good-natured, and therefore weak.

Sometimes, like Terborch, by her anecdotical treatment, she can set a whole romantic story before you; again, in the manner of Gerard Dow, she gives you a penetrating glimpse into old burgher life – work that is quite out of touch with the dilettantism that largely pervades modern art.

The admirers of this unusual artist seek out her genre pictures in the exhibitions of to-day, much as one turns to an idyl of Heinrich Voss, after a dose of the "storm and stress" poets. Most of her works are in private galleries.

One of her best pictures will be seen at the St. Louis Exposition.

Wisinger-Florian, Olga. Bavarian Ludwig medal, 1891; medal at Chicago, 1893. Born in Vienna, 1844. Pupil of Schäffer and Schwindler. She has an excellent reputation as a painter of flowers. In the New Gallery, Munich, is one of her pictures of this sort; and at Munich, 1893, her flower pieces were especially praised in the reports of the exhibition.

She also paints landscapes, in which she gains power each year; her color grows finer and her design or modelling stronger. At Vienna, 1890, it was said that her picture of the "Bauernhofe" was, by its excellent color, a disadvantage to the pictures near it, and the shore motive in "Abbazia" was full of artistic charm. At Vienna, 1893, she exhibited a cycle, "The Months," which bore witness to her admirable mastery of her art.

Among her works are some excellent Venetian subjects: "On the Rialto"; "Morning on the Shore"; and "In Venice."

Wolff, Betty. Honorable mention, Berlin, 1890. Member of the

Association of Women Artists and Friends of Art; also of the German Art Association. Born in Berlin, where she was a pupil of Karl Stauffer-Bern; she also studied in Munich under Karl Marr.

Besides numerous portraits of children, in pastel, this artist has painted portraits in oils of many well-known persons, among whom are Prof. H. Steinthal, Prof. Albrecht Weber, and General von Zycklinski.

Wolters, Henrietta, family name Van Pee. Born in Amsterdam. 1692-1741. Pupil of her father, and later made a special study of miniature under Christoffel le Blond. Her early work consisted largely in copies from Van de Velde and Van Dyck. Her miniatures were so highly esteemed that Peter the Great offered her a salary of six thousand florins as his court painter; and Frederick William of Prussia invited her to his court, but nothing could tempt her away from her home in Amsterdam. She received four hundred florins for a single miniature, a most unusual price in her time.

Wood, Caroline S. Daughter of Honorable Horatio D. Wood, of St. Louis. This sculptor has made unusual advances in her art, to which she has seriously devoted herself less than four years. She has studied in the Art School of Washington University, the Art Institute, Chicago, and is now a student in the Art League, New York.

She has been commissioned by the State of Missouri to make a statue to represent "The Spirit of the State of Missouri," for the Louisiana Purchase Exposition.

[*No reply to circular.*]

Woodbury, Marcia Oakes. Prize at Boston Art Club; medals at Mechanics' Association Exhibition, Atlanta and Nashville Expositions. Member of the New York and Boston Water-Color Clubs. Born at South Berwick, Maine. Pupil of Tommasso Juglaris, in Boston, and of Lasar, in Paris.

Mrs. Woodbury paints in oils and water-colors; the latter are genre scenes, and among them are several Dutch subjects. She has painted children's portraits in oils. Her pictures are in private hands in Boston, New York, Chicago, and Cincinnati. "The Smoker," and "Mother and Daughter," a triptych, are two of her principal pictures.

Woodward, Dewing. Grand prize of the Academy Julian, 1894. Member of Water-Color Club, Baltimore; Charcoal Club, Baltimore; L'Union des Femmes Peintres et Sculpteurs de France. Born at Williamsport, Pennsylvania. Pupil of Pennsylvania Academy a few months; in Paris, of Bouguereau, Robert-Fleury, and Jules Lefebvre.

Her "Holland Family at Prayer," exhibited at the Paris Salon, 1893, and "Jessica," belong to the Public Library in Williamsport; "Clam-Diggers Coming Home – Cape Cod" was in the Venice Exhibition, 1903; one of her pictures shows the "Julian Academy, Criticism Day."

She has painted many portraits, and her work has often been thought to be that of a man, which idea is no doubt partly due to her choosing subjects from the lives of working men. She is of the modern school of colorists.

Wright, Ethel. This artist contributed annually to the exhibitions of the London Academy from 1893 to 1900, as follows: In 1893 she exhibited "Milly" and "Echo"; in 1894, "The Prodigal"; in 1895, a water-color, "Lilies"; in 1896, "Rejected"; in 1897, a portrait of Mrs. Laurence Phillips; in 1898, "The Song of Ages," reproduced in this book; in 1899, a portrait of Mrs. Arthur Strauss; and in 1900, one of Miss Vaughan.

[*No reply to circular.*]

Wright, Mrs. Patience. Born at Bordentown, New Jersey, 1725, of a Quaker family. When left a widow, with three children to care for, she went to London, where she found a larger field for her art than she had in the United States, where she had already made a good reputation as a modeller in wax. By reason of this change of residence she has often been called an English sculptress.

Although the imaginative and pictorial is not cultivated or even approved by Quakers, Patience Lovell, while still a child, and before she had seen works of art, was content only when supplied with dough, wax, or clay, from which she made figures of men and women. Very early these figures became portraits of the people she knew best, and in the circle of her family and friends she was considered a genius.

Very soon after Mrs. Wright reached London she was fully employed. She worked in wax, and her full-length portrait of Lord Chatham was placed in Westminster Abbey, protected by a glass case. This attracted much attention, and the London journals praised the artist. She made portraits of the King and Queen, who, attracted by her brilliant conversation, admitted her to an intimacy at Buckingham House, which could not then have been accorded to an untitled English woman.

Mrs. Wright made many portraits of distinguished people; but few, if any, of these can now be seen, although it is said that some of them have been carefully preserved by the families who possess them.

To Americans Mrs. Wright is interesting by reason of her patriotism, which amounted to a passion. She is credited with having been an important source of information to the American leaders in the time of the Revolution. In this she was frank and courageous, making no secret of her views. She even ventured to reprove George III. for his attitude toward the Colonists, and by this boldness lost the royal favor.

She corresponded with Franklin, in Paris, and new appointments, or other important movements in the British army, were speedily known to him.

Washington, when he knew that Mrs. Wright wished to make a bust of him, replied in most flattering terms that he should think himself happy to have his portrait made by her. Mrs. Wright very much desired to make likenesses of those who signed the Treaty of Peace, and of those who had taken a prominent part in making it. She wrote: "To shame the English king, I would go to any trouble and expense, and add my mite to the honor due to Adams, Jefferson, and others."

Though so essentially American as a woman, the best of her professional life was passed in England, where she was liberally patronized and fully appreciated. Dunlap calls her an extraordinary woman, and several writers have mentioned her power of judging the character of her visitors, in which she rarely made a mistake, and chose her friends with unusual intelligence.

Her eldest daughter married in America, and was well known as a modeller in wax in New York. Her younger daughter married the artist Hoppner, a rival in portraiture of Stuart and Lawrence, while her son Joseph was a portrait painter. His likeness of Washington was much admired.

Wulfraat, Margaretta. Born at Arnheim. 1678-1741. Was a pupil of Caspar Netscher of Heidelberg, whose little pictures are of fabulous value. Although he was so excellent a painter he was proud of Margaretta, whose pictures were much admired in her day. Her "Musical Conversation" is in the Museum of Schwerin. Her "Cleopatra" and "Semiramis" are in the Gallery at Amsterdam.

Yandell, Enid. Special Designer's Medal, Chicago, 1893; silver medal, Tennessee Exposition; Honorable Mention, Buffalo, 1901. Member of National Sculpture Society; Municipal Art Society; National Arts Club, all of New York. Born in Louisville, Kentucky. Graduate of Cincinnati Art Academy. Pupil of Philip Martiny in New York, and in Paris of Frederick McMonnies and Auguste Rodin.

The principal works of this artist are the Mayor Lewis monument at New Haven, Connecticut; the Chancellor Garland

Memorial, Vanderbilt University, Nashville; Carrie Brown Memorial Fountain, Providence; Daniel Boone and the Ruff Fountain, Louisville.

Richard Ladegast, in January, 1902, wrote a sketch of Miss Yandell's life and works for the *Outlook*, in which he says that Miss Yandell was the first woman to become a member of the National Sculpture Society. I quote from his article as follows: "The most imposing product of Miss Yandell's genius was the heroic figure of Athena, twenty-five feet in height, which stood in front of the reproduction of the Parthenon at the Nashville Exposition. This is the largest figure ever designed by a woman.

"The most artistic was probably the little silver tankard which she did for the Tiffany Company, a bit of modelling which involves the figures of a fisher-boy and a mermaid. The figure of Athena is large and correct; those of the fisher-boy and mermaid poetic and impassioned... The boy kisses the maid when the lid is lifted. He is always looking over the edge, as if yearning for the fate that each new drinker who lifts the lid forces upon him."

Of the Carrie Brown Memorial Fountain he says: "The design of the fountain represents the struggle of life symbolized by a group of figures which is intended to portray, according to Miss Yandell, not the struggle for bare existence, but 'the attempt of the immortal soul within us to free itself from the handicaps and entanglements of its earthly environments. It is the development of character, the triumph of intellectuality and spirituality I have striven to express.' Life is symbolized by the figure of a woman, the soul by an angel, and the earthly tendencies – duty, passion, and avarice – by male figures. Life is represented as struggling to free herself from the gross earthly forms that cling to her. The figure of Life shows a calm, placid strength, well calculated to conquer in a struggle; and the modelling of her clinging robes and the active muscle of the male figures is firm and life-like. The mantle of truth flows from the shoulders of the angel, forming a drapery for the whole group, and serving as a support for the basin, the edges of which are ornamented with dolphins spouting water.

"The silhouette formed by the mass of the fountain is most interesting and successful from all points of view. The lines of the composition are large and dignified, especially noticeable in the modelling of the individual figures, which is well studied and technically excellent."

At Buffalo, where this fountain was exhibited, it received honorable mention.

Miss Yandell has been commissioned to execute a symbolical figure of victory and a statue of Daniel Boone for the St. Louis Exposition.

Ykens, Laurence Catherine. Elected to the Guild of Antwerp in 1659. Born in Antwerp. Pupil of her father, Jan Ykens. Flowers, fruits, and insects were her favorite subjects, and were painted with rare delicacy. Two of these pictures are in the Museo del Prado, at Madrid. They are a "Festoon of Flowers and Fruits with a Medallion in the Centre, on which is a Landscape"; and a "Garland of Flowers with a Similar Medallion."

Ziesensis, Margaretta. There were few women artists in the Scandinavian countries in the early years of the eighteenth century. Among them was Margaretta Ziesensis, a Danish lady, who painted a large number of portraits and some historical subjects.

She was best known, however, for her miniature copies of the works of famous artists. These pictures were much the same in effect as the "picture-miniatures" now in vogue. Her copy of Correggio's Zingarella was much admired, and was several times repeated.

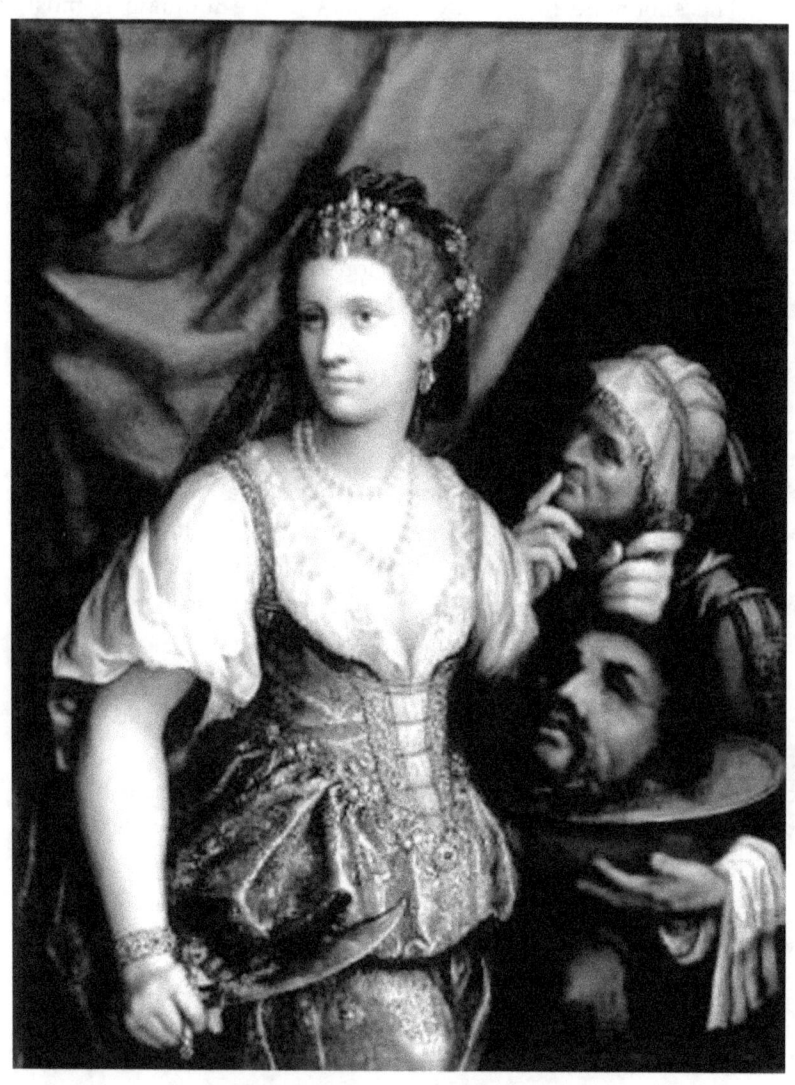

Fede Galizia, Judith with the Head of Holofernes,
Museum of Art, Sarasota, Florida

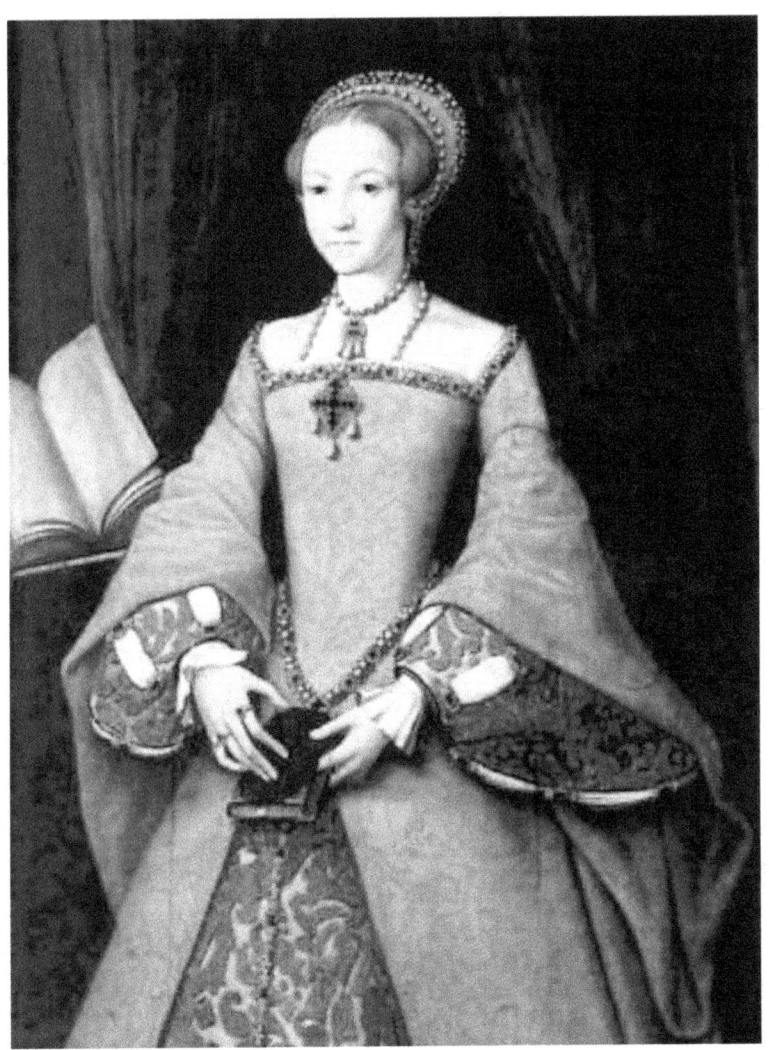

Levina Teerline (a Flemish painter)

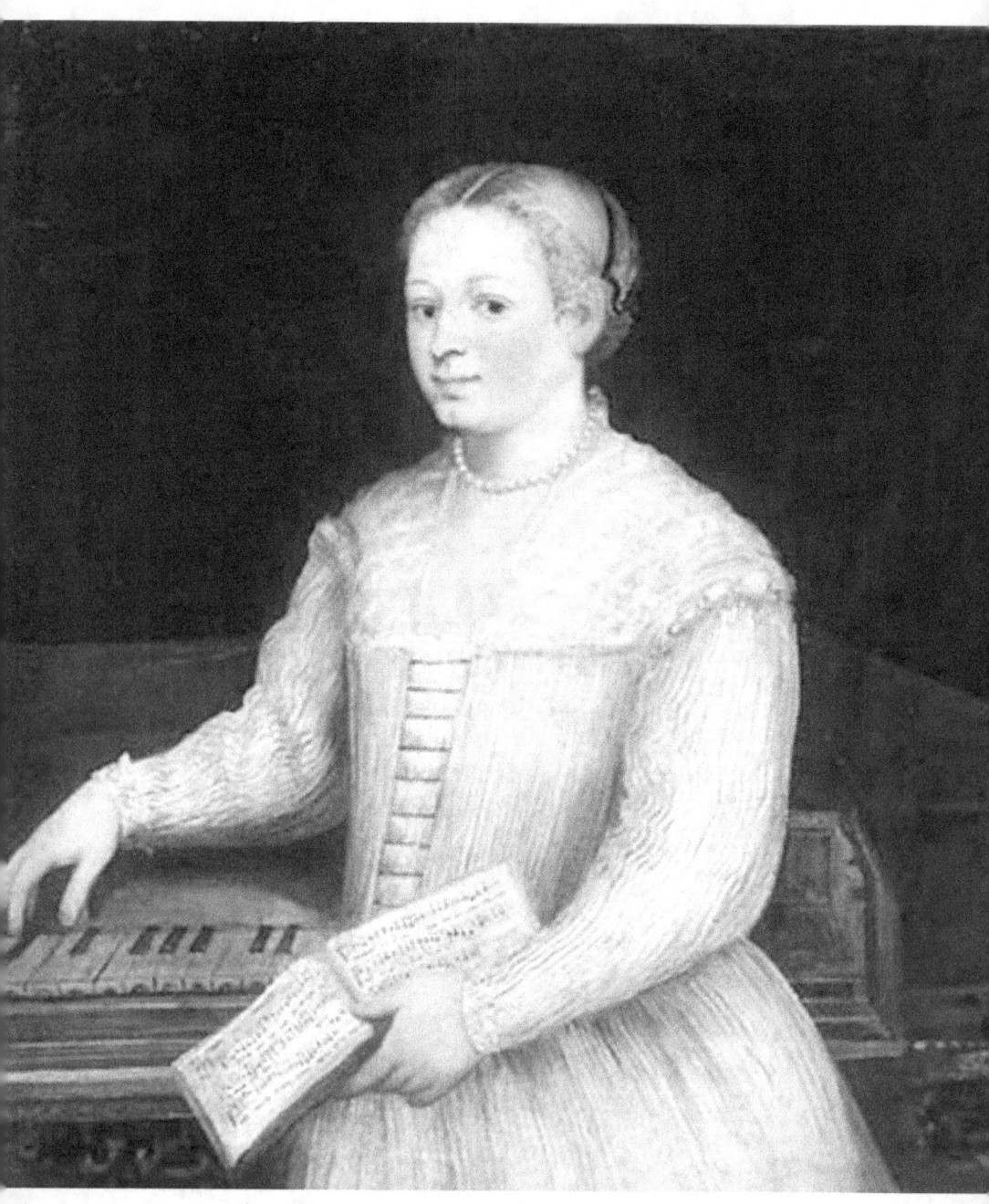

Marietta Robusti, Self-Portrait, 1589, Uffizi

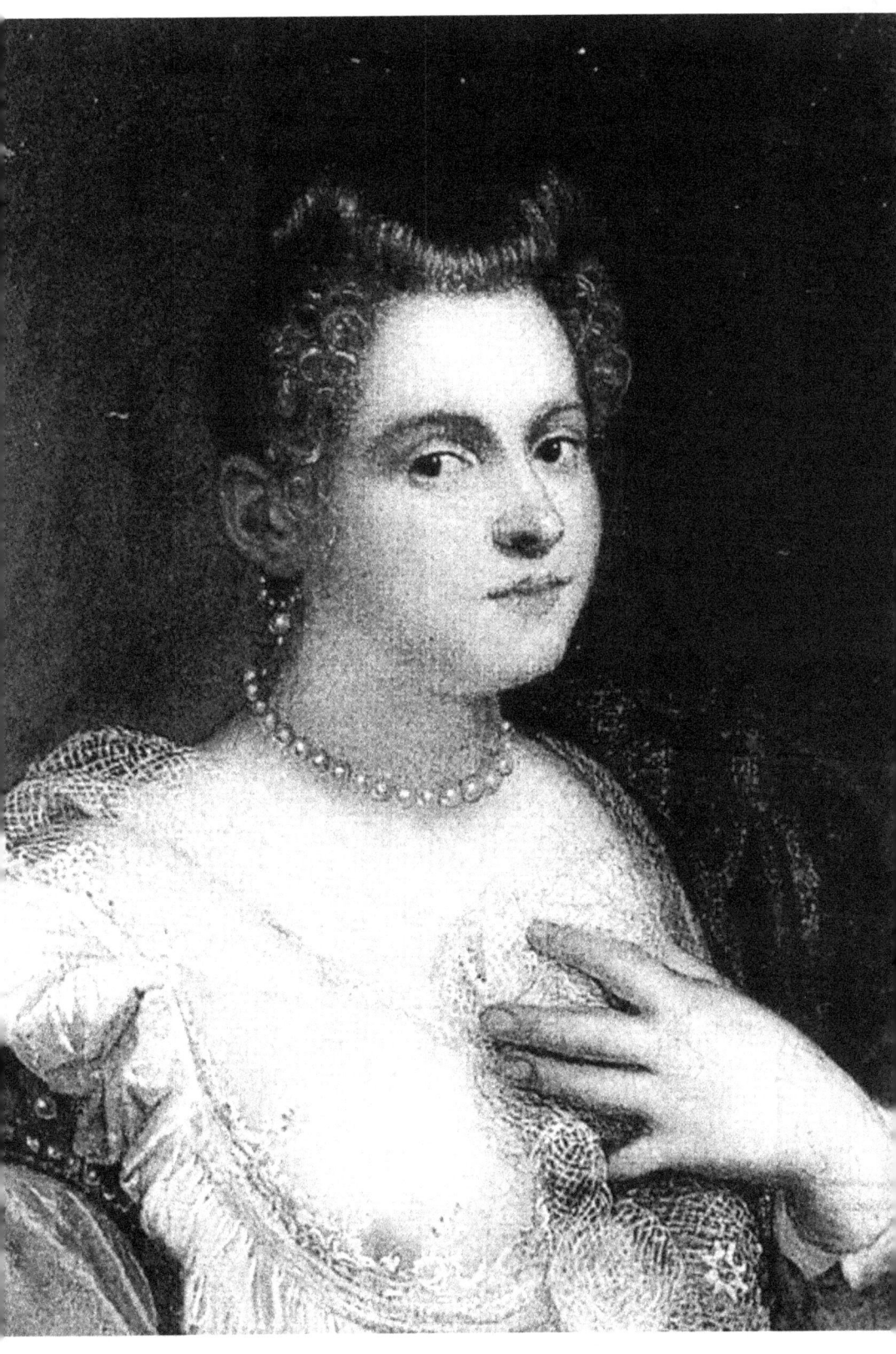

Marietta Robusti, Self-Portrait, Prado, Madrid

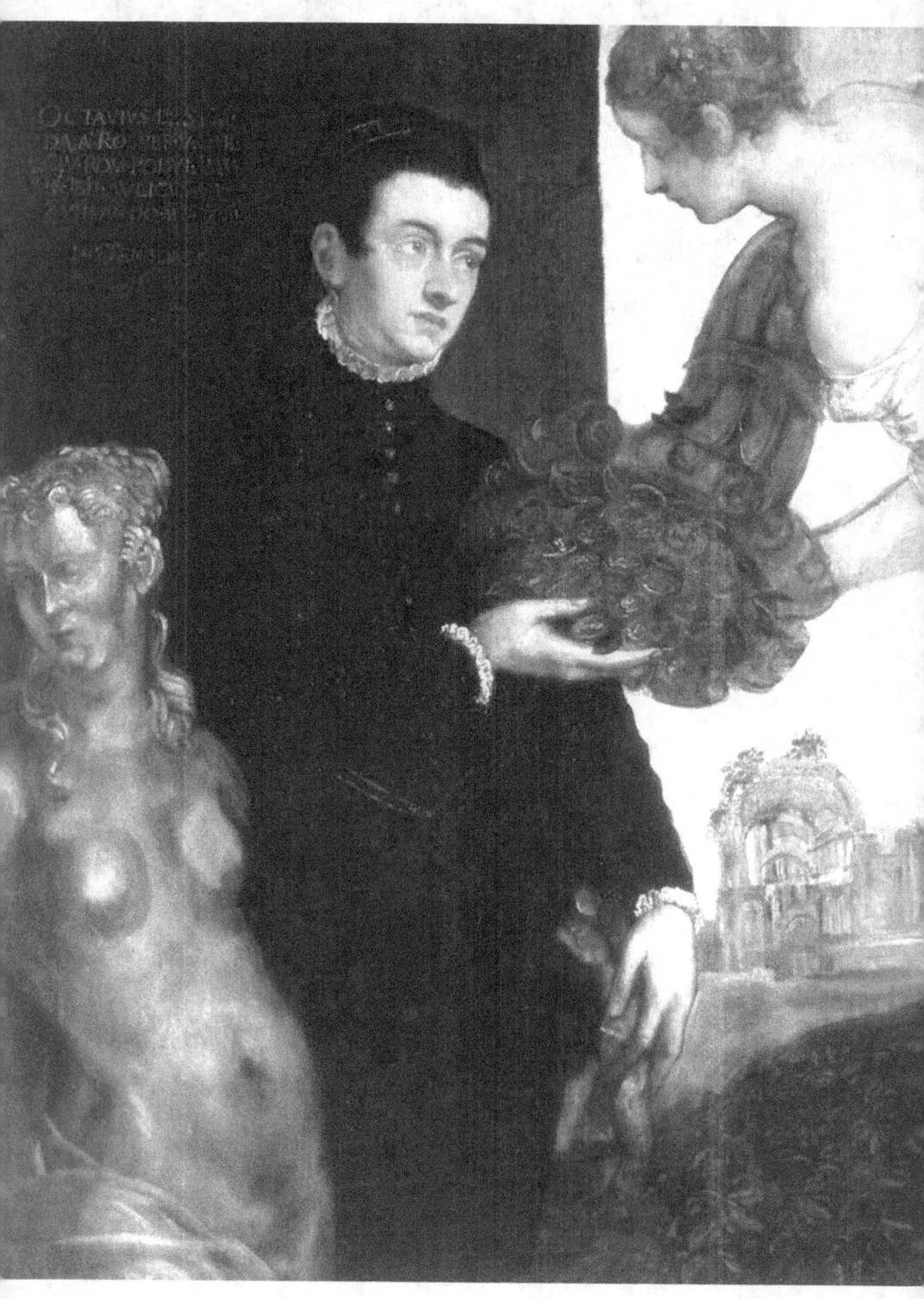

Marietta Robusti, Portrait of Ottavio Strada, 1567-68, Amsterdam

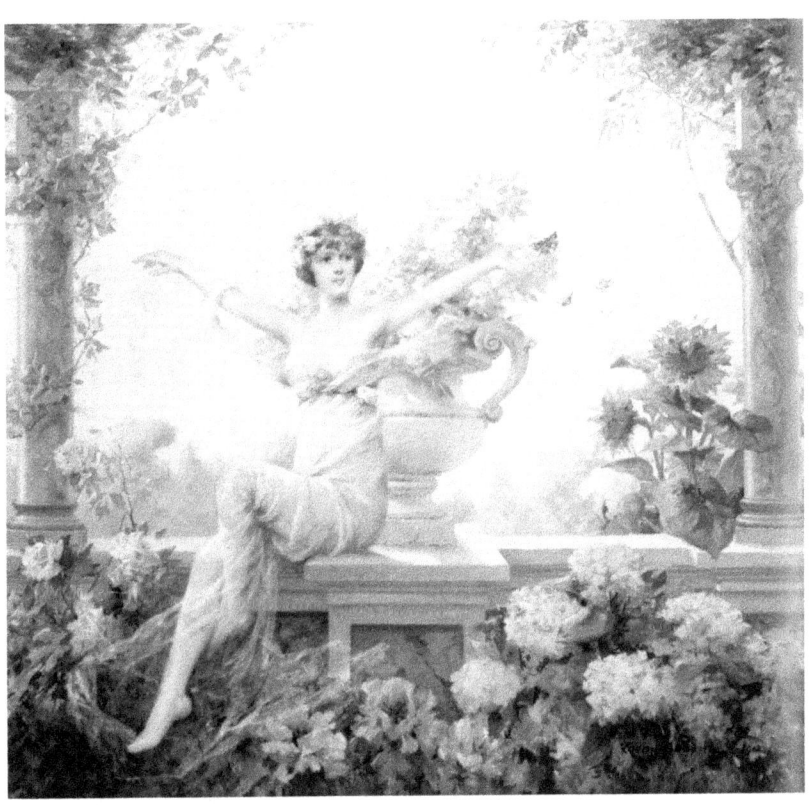

Louise Abbema, Flora, 1913

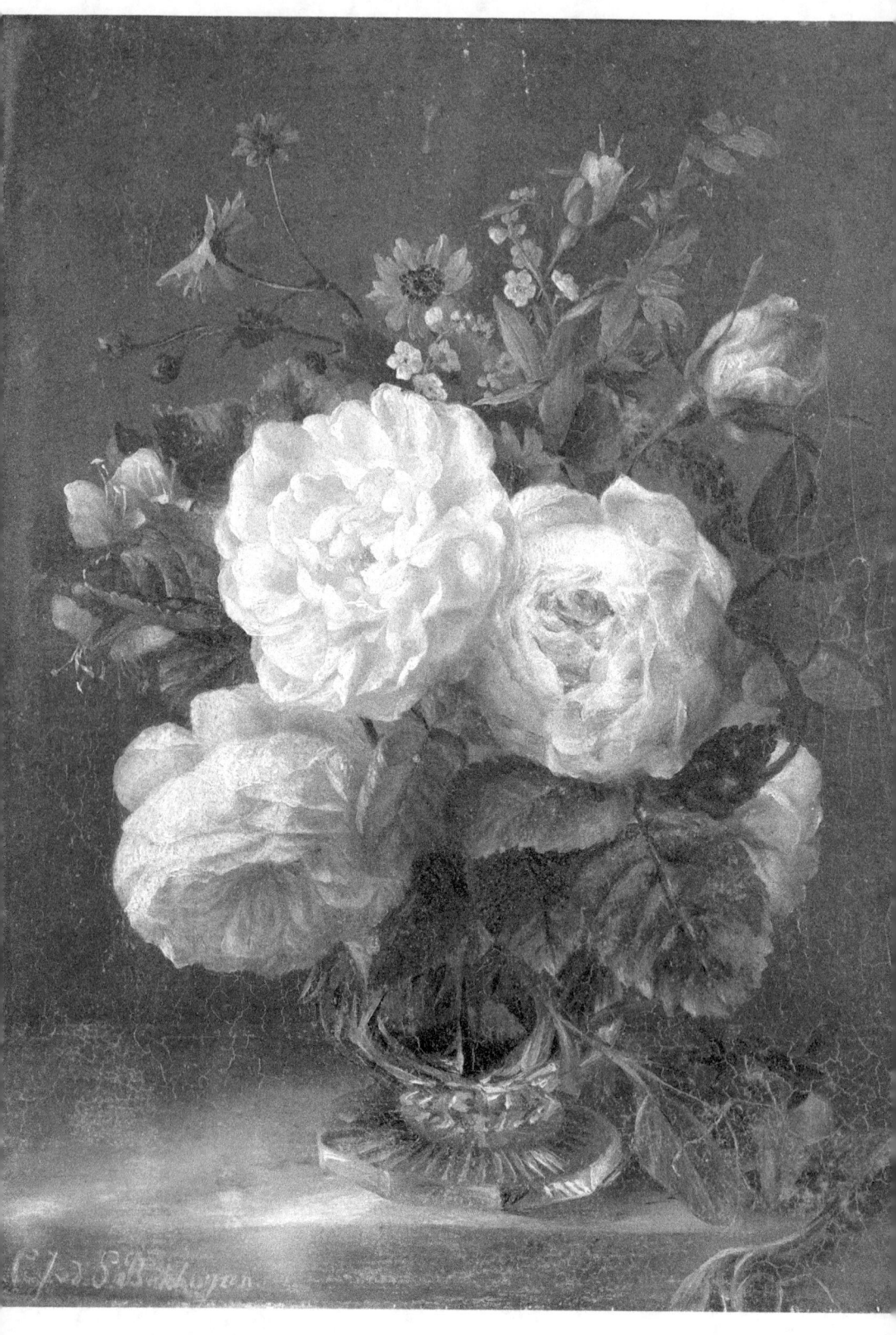

J.G.J. Bakhuyzen, Stilleven met bloemen in een kristallen vaas, 1850-60,
Rijksmuseum, Amsterdam

Angelica Kauffmann, Self-Portrait, 1770-75.

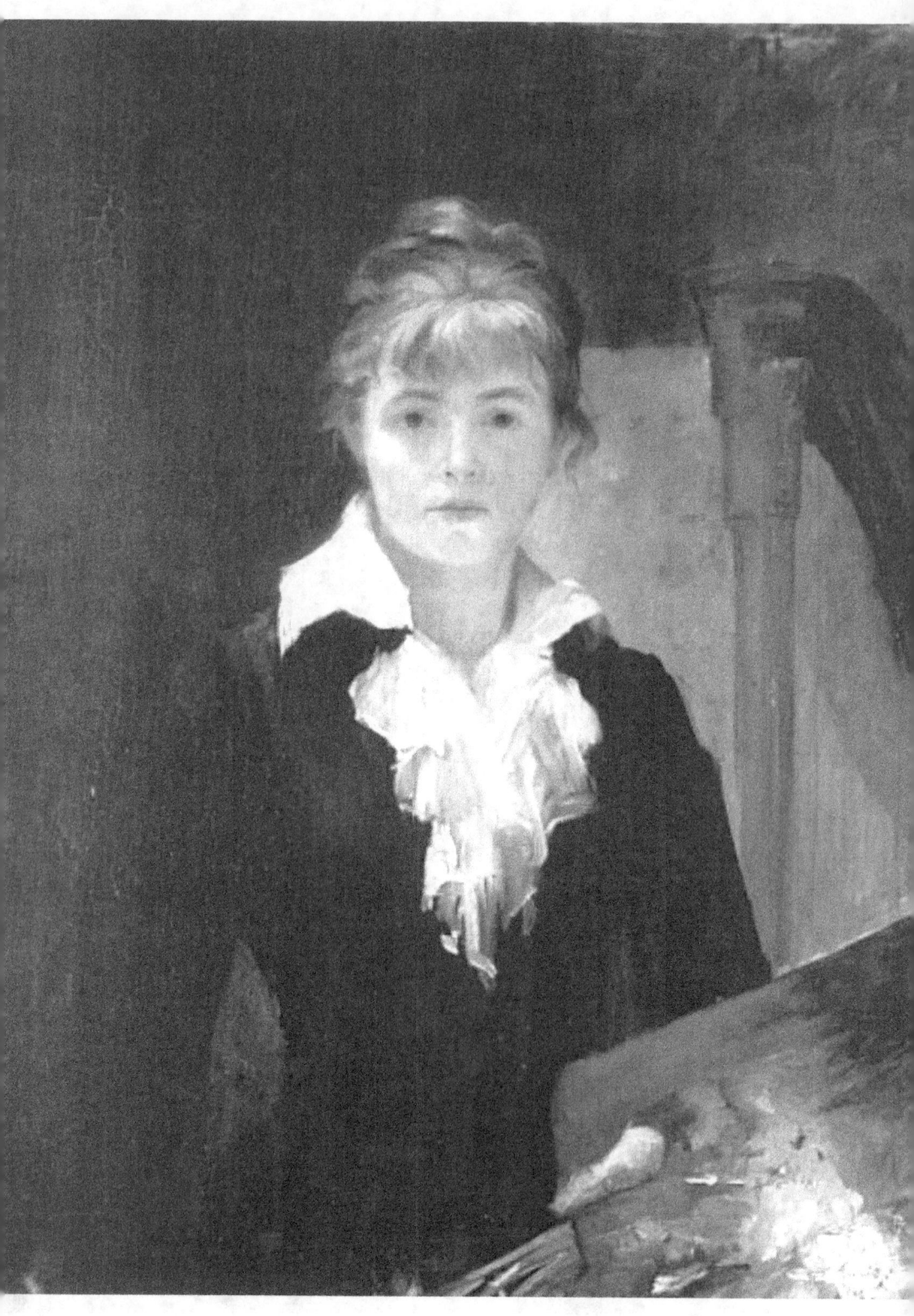

Marie Bashkirtseff, Self-Portrait, 1880

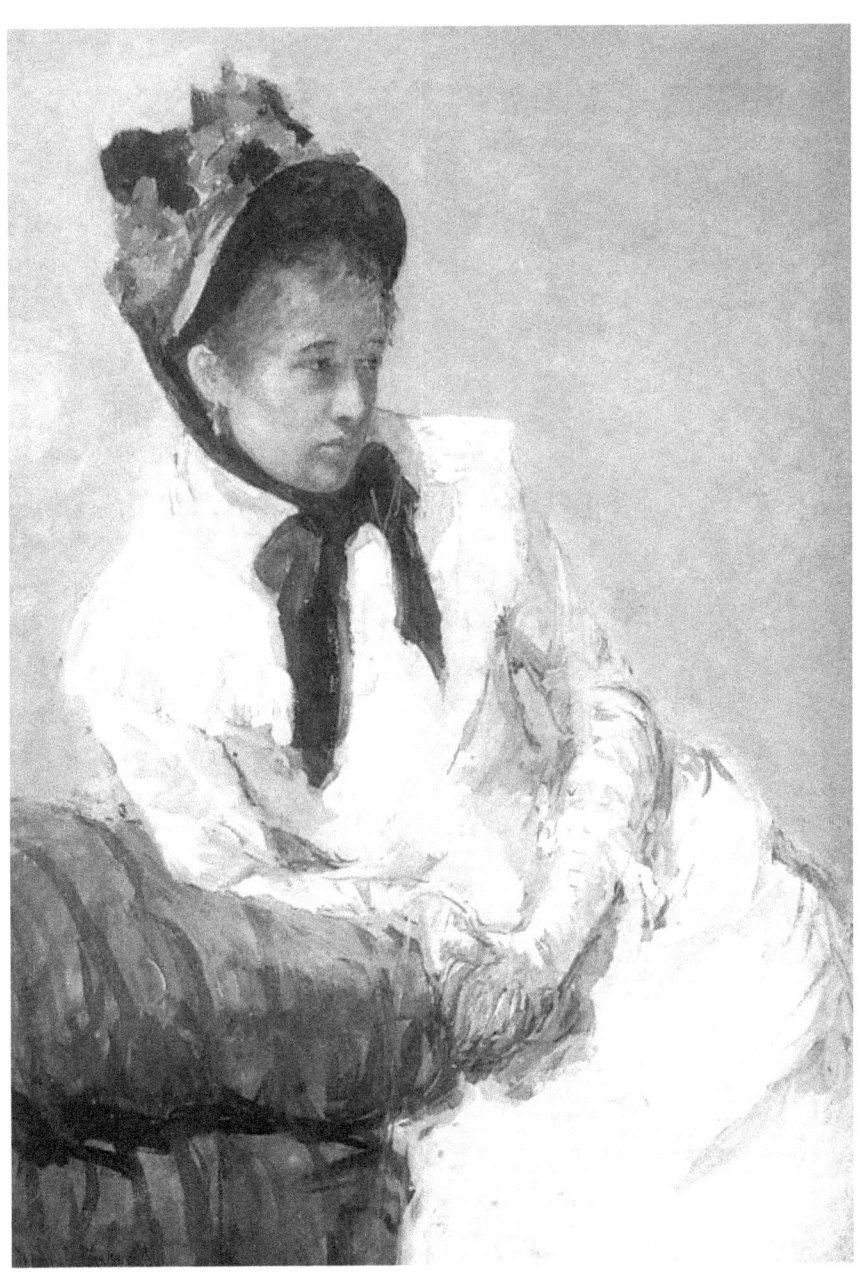

Mary Cassatt, Self-Portrait, 1878,
Metropolitan Museum of Art, New York City

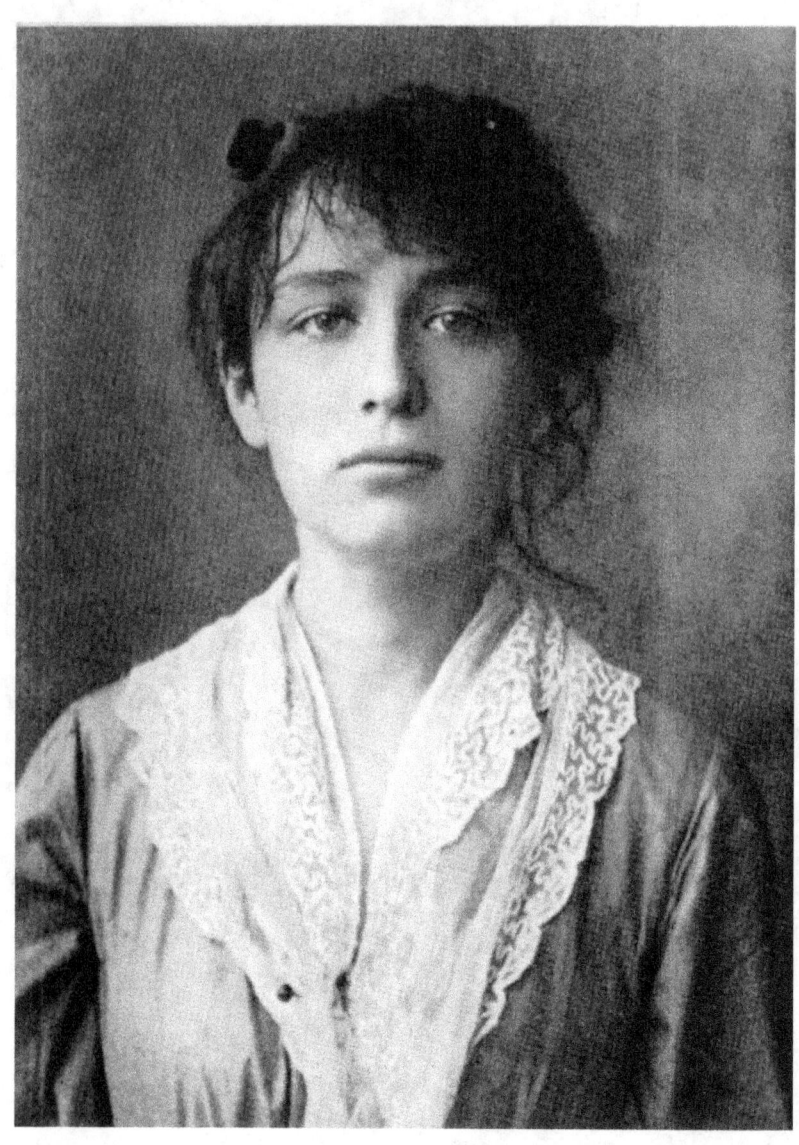

Camille Claudel

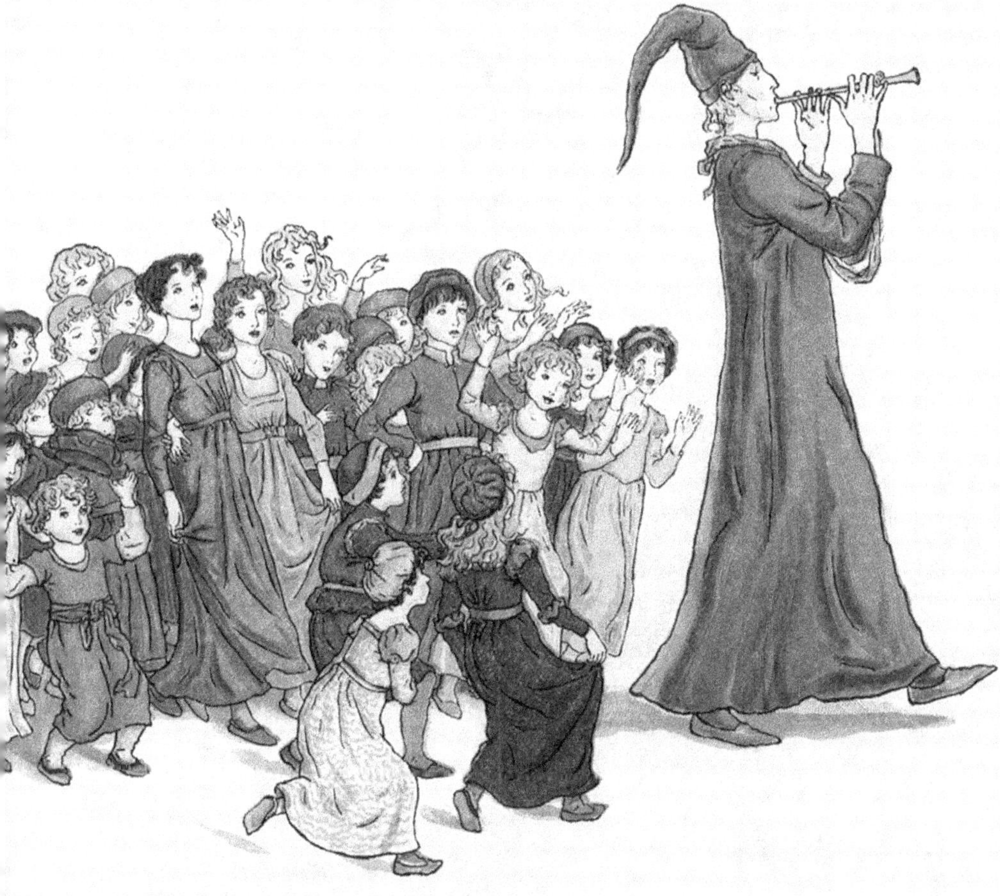

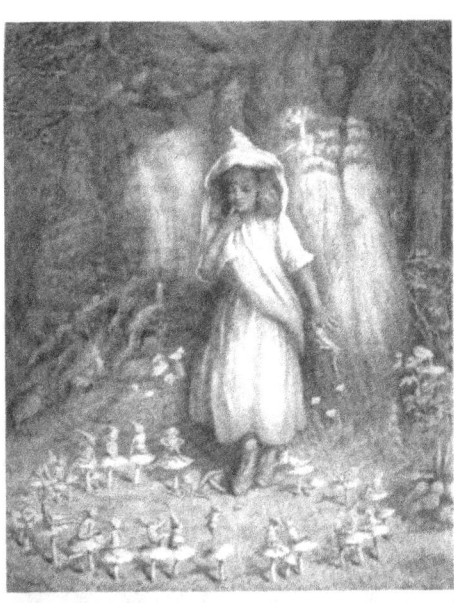

Kate Greenaway, The Pied Piper, 1888
(above). The Elf-Ring (left).

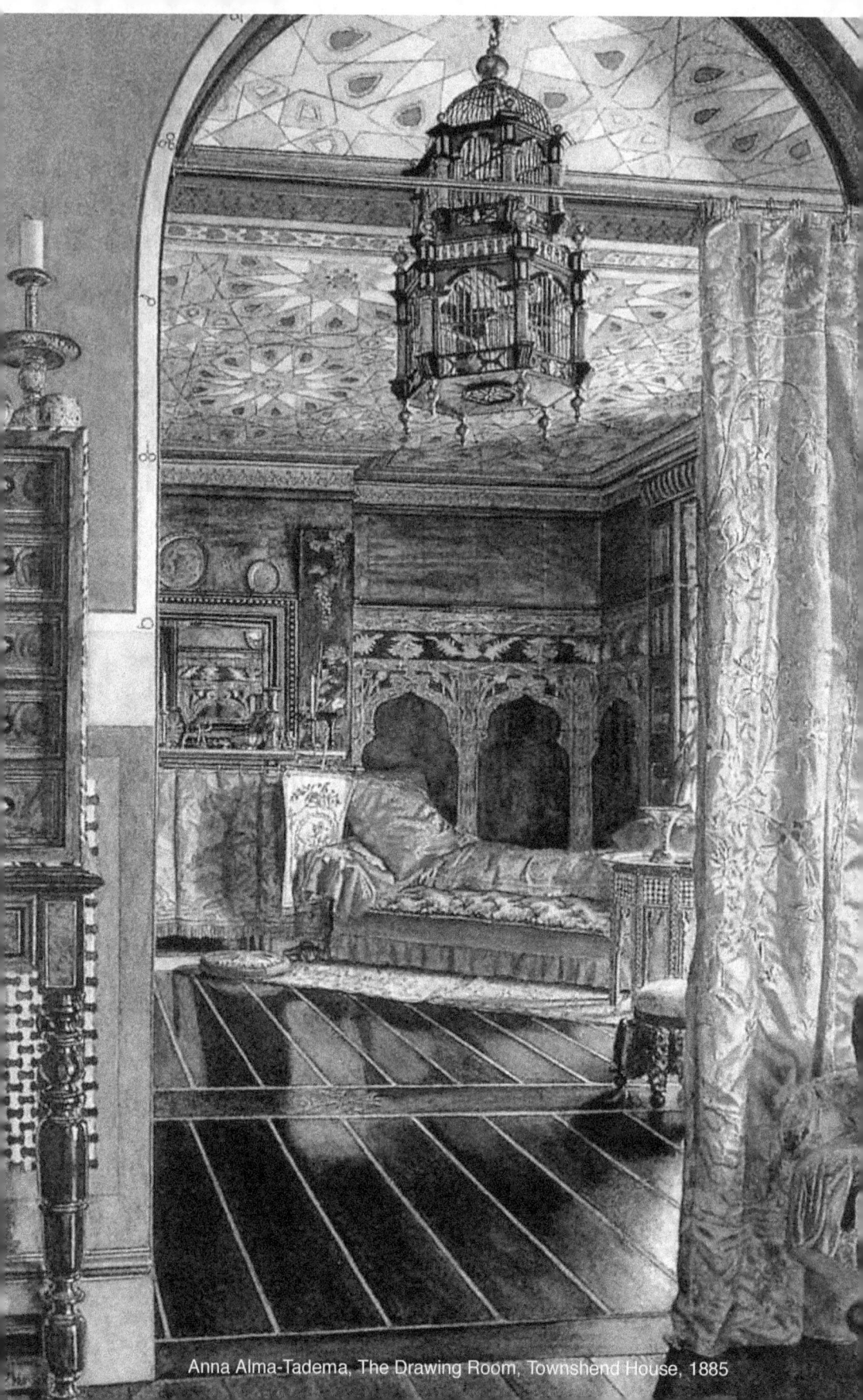

Anna Alma-Tadema, The Drawing Room, Townshend House, 1885

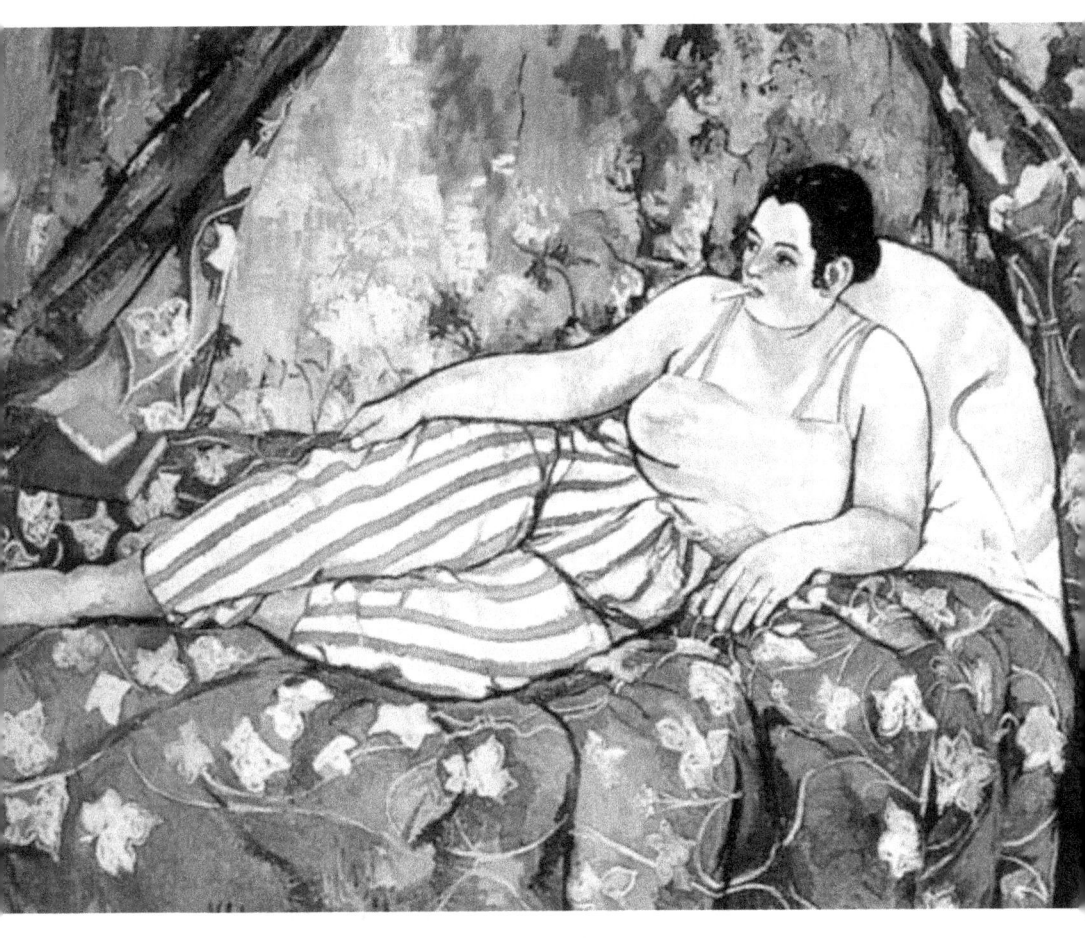

Suzanne Valadon, The Blue Room, 1923

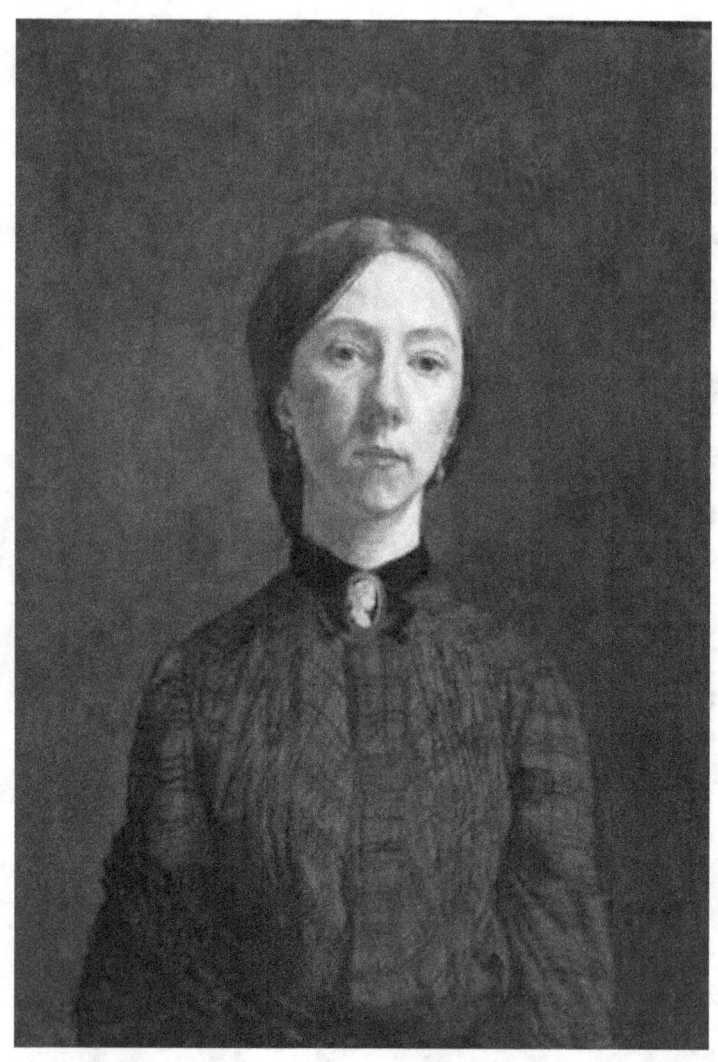

Gwen John, Self-Portrait, National Portrait Gallery, London

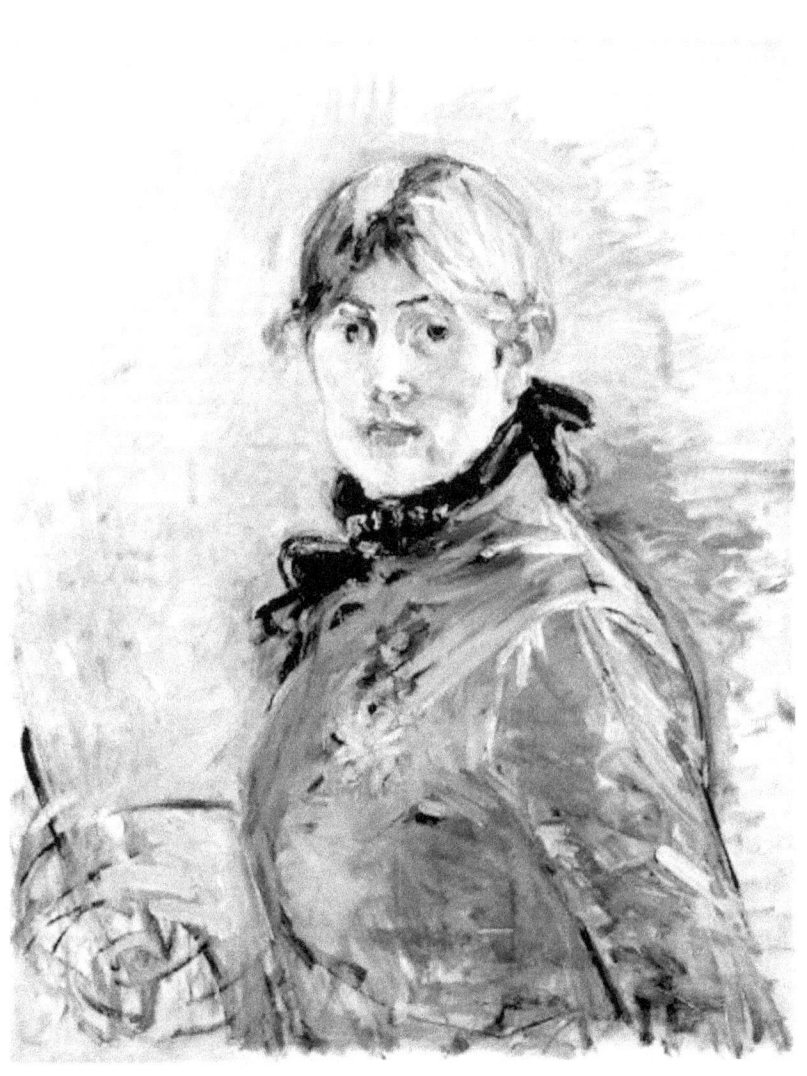

Berthe Morisot, Self-Portrait, 1885

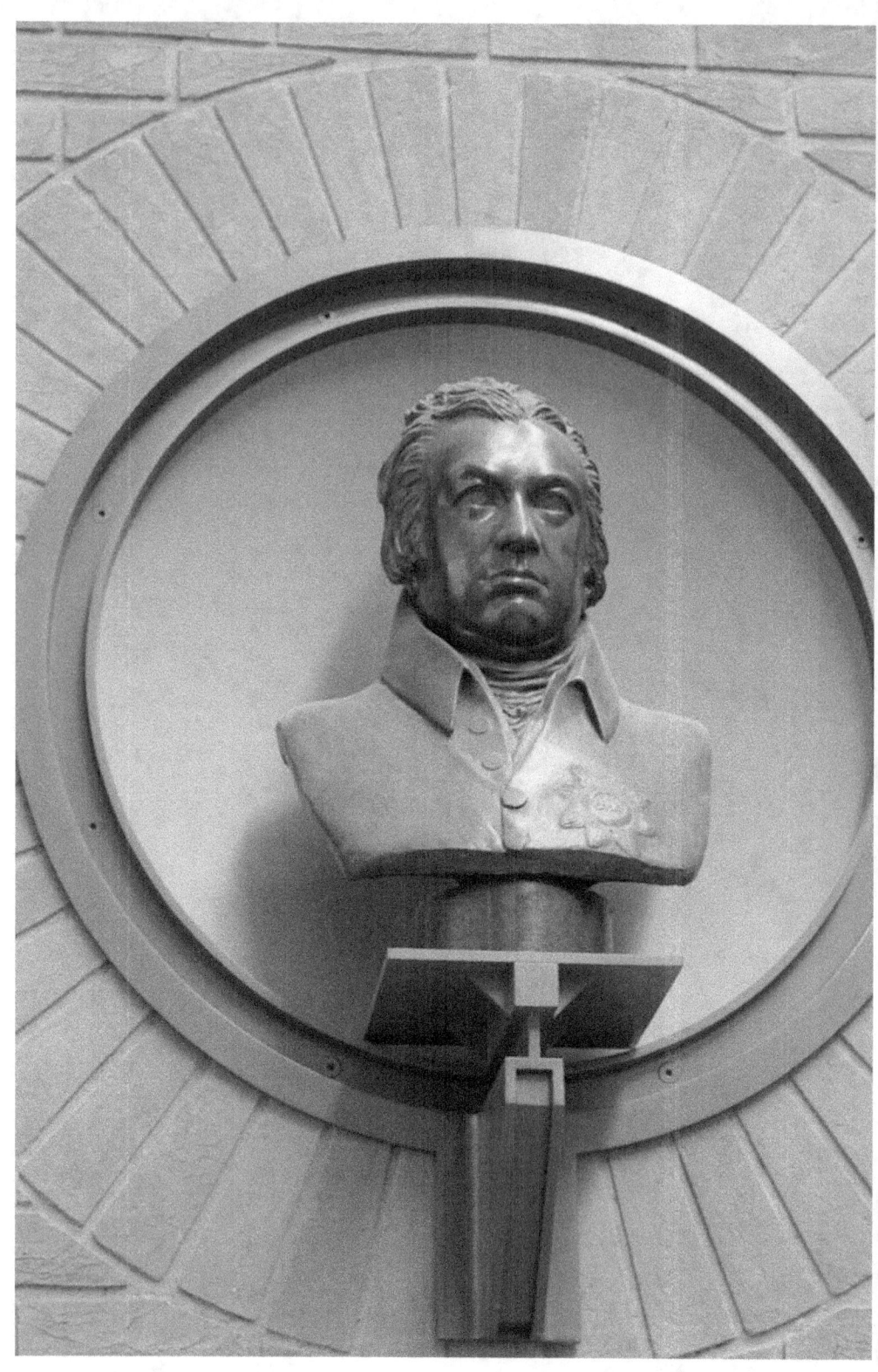

Sir Joseph Banks by Anne Seymour Damer

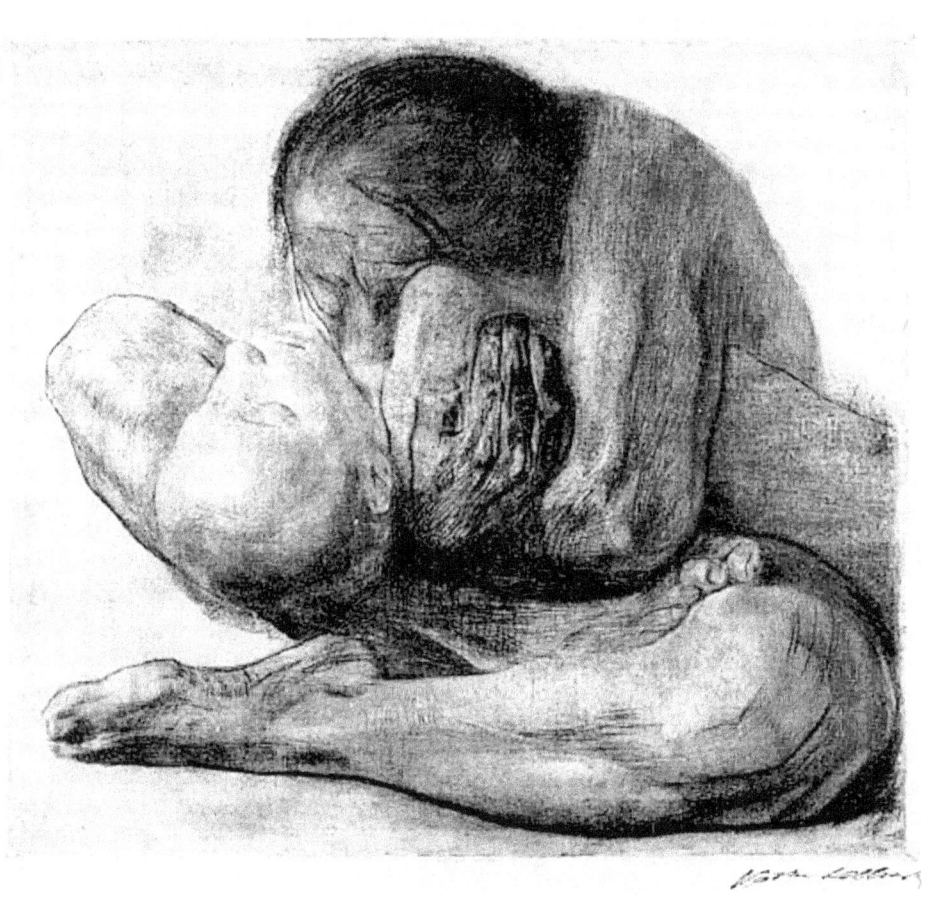

Käthe Kollwitz, Woman With Dead Child, 1903

SUPPLEMENT

Containing names previously omitted and additions. The asterisk (*) denotes preceding mention of the artist.

*Bilders, Marie van Bosse. This celebrated landscape painter became an artist through her determination to be an artist rather than because of any impelling natural force driving her to this career.

After patient and continuous toil, she felt that she was developing an artistic impulse. The advice of Van de Sande-Bakhuyzen greatly encouraged her, and the candid and friendly criticism of Bosboom inspired her with the courage to exhibit her work in public.

In the summer of 1875, in Vorden, she met Johannes Bilders, under whose direction she studied landscape painting. This master took great pains to develop the originality of his pupil rather than to encourage her adapting the manner of other artists. During her stay in Vorden she made a distinct gain in the attainment of an individual style of painting.

After her return to her home at The Hague, Bilders established a studio there and showed a still keener interest in his pupil. This artistic friendship resulted in the marriage of the two artists, and in 1880 they established themselves in Oosterbeck.

Here began the intimate study of the heath which so largely influenced the best pictures by Frau Bilders. In the garden of the picturesque house in which the two artists lived was an old barn, which became her studio, where, early and late, in all sorts of weather, she devotedly observed the effects later pictured on her canvases. At this time she executed one of her best works, now in the collection of the Prince Regent of Brunswick. It is thus described by a Dutch writer in Rooses' "Dutch Painters of the Nineteenth Century":

"It represents a deep pool, overshadowed by old gnarled willows in their autumnal foliage, their silvery trunks bending over, as if to see themselves in the clear, still water. On the edge of the pool are flowers and variegated grasses, the latter looking as if they wished to crowd out the former – as if *they* were in the right and the flowers in the wrong; as if such bright-hued creatures had no business to eclipse their more sombre tones; as if *they* and *they* alone were suited to this silent, forsaken spot."

Johannes Bilders was fully twenty-five years older than his wife, and the failure of both his physical and mental powers in his last days required her absolute devotion to him. In spite of this, the garden studio was not wholly forsaken, and nearly every day she accomplished something there. After her husband's death she had a long illness. On her recovery she returned to The Hague and took the studio which had been that of the artist Mauve.

The life of the town was wearisome to her, but she found a compensation in her re-union with her old friends, and with occasional visits to the heath she passed most of her remaining years in the city.

Her favorite subjects were landscapes with birch and beech trees, and the varying phases of the heath and of solitary and unfrequented scenes. Her works are all in private collections. Among them are "The Forester's Cottage," "Autumn in Doorwerth," "The Old Birch," and the "Old Oaks of Wodan at Sunset."

Boznanska, Olga. Born in Cracow, where she was a pupil of Matejko. Later, in Munich, she studied with Kricheldorf and Dürr. Her mother was a French woman, and critics trace both Polish and French characteristics in her work.

She paints portraits and genre subjects. She is skilful in seizing salient characteristics, and her chief aim is to preserve the individuality of her sitters and models. She skilfully manages the side-lights, and by this means produces strong effects. After the first exhibition of her pictures in Berlin, her "God-given talent" was several times mentioned by the art critics.

At Munich she made a good impression by her pictures exhibited in 1893 and 1895; at the Exposition in Paris, 1889, her portrait and a study in pastel were much admired and were generously praised in the art journals.

*Cox, Louise. The picture by Mrs. Cox, reproduced in this book, illustrates two lines in a poem by Austin Dobson, called "A Song of Angiola in Heaven."

> "Then set I lips to hers, and felt, –
> Ah, God, – the hard pain fade and melt."

De Morgan, Emily. Family name Pickering. When sixteen years old, this artist entered the Slade School, and eighteen months later received the Slade Scholarship, by which she was entitled to benefit for three years. At the end of the first year, however, she resigned this privilege because she did not wish to accept the conditions of the gift.

As a child she had loved the pictures of the precursors of Raphael, in the National Gallery, and her first exhibited picture, "Ariadne in Naxos," hung in the Grosvenor Gallery in 1877, proved how closely she had studied these old masters. At this time she knew nothing of the English Pre-Raphaelites; later, however, she became one of the most worthy followers of Burne-Jones.

About the time that she left the Slade School one of her uncles took up his residence in Florence, where she has spent several winters in work and study.

One of her most important pictures is inscribed with these lines:

"Dark is the valley of shadows,
Empty the power of kings;
Blind is the favor of fortune,
Hungry the caverns of death.
Dim is the light from beyond,
Unanswered the riddle of life."

This pessimistic view of the world is illustrated by the figure of a king, who, in the midst of ruins, places his foot upon the prostrate form of a chained victim; Happiness, with bandaged eyes, scatters treasures into the bottomless pit, a desperate youth being about to plunge into its depths; a kneeling woman, praying for light, sees brilliant figures soaring upward, their beauty charming roses from the thorn bushes.

Other pictures by this artist remind one of the works of Botticelli. Of her "Ithuriel" W. S. Sparrow wrote: "It may be thought that this Ithuriel is too mild – too much like Shakespeare's Oberon – to be in keeping with the terrific tragedy depicted in the first four books of the 'Paradise Lost.' Eve, too, lovely as she is, seems to bear no likelihood of resemblance to Milton's superb mother of mankind. But the picture has a sweet, serene grace which should make us glad to accept from Mrs. De Morgan another Eve and another Ithuriel, true children of her own fancy."

The myth of "Boreas and Orithyia," though faulty perhaps in technique, is good in conception and arrangement.

Mrs. De Morgan has produced some impressive works in sculpture. Among these are "Medusa," a bronze bust; and a "Mater Dolorosa," in terra-cotta.

Deschly, Irene. Born in Bucharest, the daughter of a Roumanian advocate. She gave such promise as an artist that a government stipend was bestowed on her, which enabled her to study in Paris, where she was a pupil of Laurens and E. Carrière.

Her work is tinged with the melancholy and intensity of her nature – perhaps of her race; yet there is something in her grim conceptions, or rather in her treatment of them, that demands attention and compels admiration. Even in her "Sweet Dream," which represents the half-nude figure of a young girl holding a rose in her hand, there is more sadness than joy, as though she said, "It is only a dream, after all." "Chanson," exhibited at the Paris Exposition, 1900, displays something of the same quality.

Eristow-Kasak, Princess Marie. Among the many Russian portraits in the Paris Exposition, 1900, two, the work of this pupil of Michel de Zichys, stood out in splendid contrast with the crass realism or the weak idealism of the greater number. One was a half-length portrait of the laughing Mme. Paquin; full of life and movement were the pose of the figure, the fall of the draperies, and the tilt of the expressive fan. The other was the spirited portrait of Baron von Friedericks, a happy combination of cavalier and soldier in its manly strength.

When but sixteen years old, the Princess Marie roused the admiration of the Russian court by her portrait of the Grand Duke Sergius. This led to her painting portraits of various members of the royal family while she was still a pupil of De Zichys.

After her marriage she established herself in Paris, where she endeavors to preserve an incognito as an artist in order to work in the most quiet and devoted manner.

Goebeler, Elise. This artist studied drawing under Steffeck and color under Dürr, in Munich. Connoisseurs in art welcome the name of Elise Goebeler in exhibitions, and recall the remarkable violet-blue lights and the hazy atmosphere in her works, out of which emerges some charming, graceful figure; perhaps a young girl on whose white shoulders the light falls, while a shadow half conceals the rest of the form. These dreamy, Madonna-like beauties are the result of the most severe and protracted study. Without the remarkable excellence of their technique and the unusual quality of their color they would be the veriest sentimentalities; but wherever they are seen they command admiration.

Her "Cinderella," exhibited in Berlin in 1880, was bought by the Emperor; another picture of the same subject, but quite different in effect, was exhibited in Munich in 1883. In the same year, in Berlin, "A Young Girl with Pussy-Willows" and "A Neapolitan Water Carrier" were seen. In 1887, in Berlin, her "Vanitas, Vanitatum Vanitas" and the "Net-Mender" were exhibited, and ten years later "Cheerfulness" was highly commended. At Munich, in 1899, her picture, called "Elegie," attracted much attention and received unusual praise.

*Herbelin, Jeane Mathilde. This miniaturist has recently died at the age of eighty-four. In addition to the medals and honors she had received previous to 1855, it was that year decided that her works should be admitted to the Salon without examination. She was a daughter of General Habert, and a niece of Belloc, under whom she studied her art while still very young. Her early ambition was to paint large pictures, but Delacroix persuaded her to devote herself to miniature painting, in which art she has been called "the best in the world."

She adopted the full tones and broad style to which she was accustomed in her larger works, and revolutionized the method of miniature painting in which stippling had prevailed. When eighteen years old, she went to Italy, where she made copies from the masters and did much original work as well.

Among her best portraits are those of the Baroness Habert, Guizot, Rossini, Isabey, Robert-Fleury, M. and Mme. de Torigny, Count de Zeppel, and her own portrait. Besides portraits, she painted a picture called "A Child Holding a Rose," "Souvenir," and "A Young Girl Playing with a Fan."

Johnson, Adelaide. Born at Plymouth, Illinois. This sculptor first studied in the St. Louis School of Design, and in 1877, at the St. Louis Exposition, received two prizes for the excellence of her wood carving. During several years she devoted herself to interior decoration, designing not only the form and color to be used in decorating edifices, but also the furniture and all necessary details to complete them and make them ready for use.

Being desirous of becoming a sculptor, Miss Johnson went, in 1883, to England, Germany, and Italy. In Rome she was a pupil of Monteverde and of Altini, who was then president of the Academy of St. Luke.

After two years she returned to America and began her professional career in Chicago, where she remained but a year before establishing herself in Washington. Her best-known works are portrait busts, which are numerous. Many of these have been seen in the Corcoran Art Gallery and in other public exhibitions.

Of her bust of Susan B. Anthony, the sculptor, Lorado Taft, said: "Your bust of Miss Anthony is better than mine. I tried to make her real, but you have made her not only real, but ideal." Among her portraits are those of General Logan, Dr. H. W. Thomas, Isabella Beecher Hooker, William Tebb, Esq., of London, etc.

Koegel, Linda. Born at The Hague. A pupil of Stauffer-Bern in Berlin and of Herterich in Munich. Her attachment to impressionism leads this artist to many experiments in color – or, as one critic wrote, "to play with color."

She apparently prefers to paint single figures of women and young girls, but her works include a variety of subjects. She also practises etching, pen-and-ink drawing, as well as crayon and water-color sketching. The light touch in some of her genre pictures is admirable, and in contrast, the portrait of her father – – the court preacher – displays a masculine firmness in its handling, and is a very striking picture.

In 1895 she exhibited at the Munich Secession the portrait of a woman, delicate but spirited, and a group which was said to set aside every convention in the happiest manner.

Kroener, Magda. The pictures of flowers which this artist paints prove her to be a devoted lover of nature. She exhibited at Düsseldorf, in 1893, a captivating study of red poppies and another of flowering vetch, which were bought by the German Emperor. The following year she exhibited two landscapes, one of which was so much better than the other that it was suggested that she might have been assisted by her husband, the animal painter, Christian Kroener.

One of her most delightful pictures, "A Quiet Corner," represents a retired nook in a garden, overgrown with foliage and flowers, so well painted that one feels that they must be fragrant.

Lepsius, Sabina. Daughter of Gustav Graf and wife of the portrait painter, Lepsius. She was a pupil of Gussow, then of the Julian Academy in Paris, and later studied in Rome. Her pictures have an unusual refinement; like some other German women artists, she aims at giving a subtle impression of character and personality in her treatment of externals, and her work has been said to affect one like music.

The portrait of her little daughter, painted in a manner which suggests Van Dyck, is one of the works which entitle her to consideration.

Leyster, Judith. A native of Haarlem on Zandam, the date of her birth being unknown. She died in 1660. In 1636 she married the well-known artist, Jan Molemaer. She did her work at a most interesting period in Dutch painting. Her earliest picture is dated 1629; she was chosen to the Guild of St. Luke at Haarlem in 1633.

Recent investigations make it probable that certain pictures which have for generations been attributed to Frans Hals were the work of Judith Leyster. In 1893 a most interesting lawsuit, which occurred in London and was reported in the *Times*, concerned a picture known as "The Fiddlers," which had been sold as a work of Frans Hals for £4,500. The purchasers found that this claim was not well founded, and sought to recover their money.

A searching investigation traced the ownership of the work back to a connoisseur of the time of William III. In 1678 it was sold for a small sum, and was then called "A Dutch Courtesan Drinking with a Young Man." The monogram on the picture was called that of Frans Hals, but as reproduced and explained by C. Hofstede de Groot in the *"Jahrbuch für Königlich-preussischen Kunst-Sammlungen"* for 1893, it seems evident that the signature is J. L. and not F. H.

Similar initials are on the "Flute Player," in the gallery at Stockholm; the "Seamstress," in The Hague Gallery, and on a picture in the Six collection at Amsterdam.

It is undeniable that these pictures all show the influence of Hals, whose pupil Judith Leyster may have been, and whose manner she caught as Mlle. Mayer caught that of Greuze and Prud'hon. At all events, the present evidence seems to support the claim that the world is indebted to Judith Leyster for these admirable pictures.

Mach, Hildegarde von. This painter studied in Dresden and Munich, and under the influence of Anton Pepinos she developed her best characteristics, her fine sense of form and of color. She admirably illustrates the modern tendency in art toward individual expression – a tendency which permits the following of original methods, and affords an outlet for energy and strength of temperament.

Fräulein Mach has made a name in both portrait and genre painting. Her "Waldesgrauen" represents two naked children in an attitude of alarm as the forest grows dark around them; it gives a vivid impression of the mysterious charm and the possible dangers which the deep woods present to the childish mind.

Mayer, Marie Françoise Constance. As early as 1806 this artist received a gold medal from the Paris Salon, awarded to her picture of "Venus and Love Asleep." Born 1775, died 1821. She studied under Suvée, Greuze, and Prud'hon. There are various accounts of the life of Mlle. Mayer. That of M. Charles Guenllette is the authority followed here. It is probable that Mlle. Mayer came under the influence of Prud'hon as early as 1802, possibly before that time.

Prud'hon, a sensitive man, absorbed in his art, had married at twenty a woman who had no sympathy with his ideals, and when she realized that he had no ambition, and was likely to be always poor, her temper got the better of any affection she had ever felt for him. Prud'hon, in humiliation and despair, lived in a solitude almost complete.

It was with difficulty that Mlle. Mayer persuaded this master to receive her as a pupil; but this being gained, both these painters had studios in the Sorbonne from 1809 to 1821. At the latter date all artists were obliged to vacate the Sorbonne ateliers to make room for some new department of instruction. Mlle. Mayer had been for some time in a depressed condition, and her friends had been anxious about her. Whether leaving the Sorbonne had a tendency to increase her melancholy is not known, but her suicide came as a great surprise and shock to all who knew her, especially to Prud'hon, who survived her less than two years.

Prud'hon painted several portraits of Mlle. Mayer, the best-known being now in the Louvre. It represents an engaging personality, in which vivacity and sensibility are distinctly indicated.

Mlle. Mayer had made her début at the Salon of 1896 with a portrait of "Citizeness Mayer," painted by herself, and showing a sketch for the portrait of her mother; also a picture of a "Young Scholar with a Portfolio Under His Arm," and a miniature. From this time her work was seen at each year's salon.

Her pictures in 1810 were the "Happy Mother" and the "Unhappy Mother," which are now in the Louvre; the contrast between the joyousness of the mother with her child and the anguish of the mother who has lost her child is portrayed with great tenderness. The "Dream of Happiness," also in the Louvre, represents a young couple in a boat with their child; the boat is guided down the stream of life by Love and Fortune. This is one of her best pictures. It is full of poetic feeling, and the flesh tints are unusually natural. The work of this artist is characterized by delicacy of touch and freshness of color while pervaded by a peculiar grace and charm. Her drawing is good, but the composition is less satisfactory.

It is well known that Prud'hon and his pupil painted many pictures in collaboration. This has led to an under-valuation of her ability, and both the inferior works of Prud'hon and bad imitations of him have been attributed to her. M. Guenllette writes that when Mlle. Mayer studied under Greuze she painted in his manner, and he inclines to the opinion that some pictures attributed to Greuze were the work of his pupil. In the same way she imitated Prud'hon, and this critic thinks it by no means certain that the master finished her work, as has been alleged.

In the Museum at Nancy are Mlle. Mayer's portraits of Mme. and Mlle. Voiant; in the Museum of Dijon is an ideal head by her, and in the Bordeaux Gallery is her picture, called "Confidence." "Innocence Prefers Love to Riches" and the "Torch of Venus" are well-known works by Mlle. Mayer.

Mesdag-van Houten, S. Gold medal at Amsterdam, 1884; bronze medal, Paris Exposition, 1889. Born at Groningen, 1834. In 1856 she married Mesdag, who, rather late in life decided to follow the career of a painter. His wife, not wishing to be separated from him in any sense, resolved on the same profession, and about 1870 they began their study. Mme. Mesdag acquired her technique with difficulty, and her success was achieved only as the result of great perseverance and continual labor. The artists of Oosterbeck and Brussels, who were her associates, materially aided her by their encouragement. She began the study of drawing at the age of thirty, and her first attempt in oils was made seven years later. Beginning with single twigs and working over them patiently she at length painted whole trees, and later animals. She came to know the peculiarities of nearly all native trees.

She built a studio in the woods of Scheveningen, and there developed her characteristics – close observation and careful reproduction of details.

In the summer of 1872 M. and Mme. Mesdag went to Friesland and Drenthe, where they made numerous sketches of the heath, sheep, farmhouses, and the people in their quaint costumes. One of Mme. Mesdag's pictures, afterward exhibited at Berlin, is thus described: "On this canvas we see the moon, just as she has broken through a gray cloud, spreading her silvery sheen over the sleepy land; in the centre we are given a sheep-fold, at the door of which a flock of sheep are jostling and pushing each other, all eager to enter their place of rest. The wave-like movement of these animals is particularly graceful and cleverly done. A little shepherdess is guiding them, as anxious to get them in as they are to enter, for this means the end of her day's work. Her worn-out blue petticoat is lighted up by a moonbeam; in her hand she appears to have a hoe. It is a most harmonious picture; every line is in accord with its neighbor."

While residing in Brussels these two artists began to collect works of art for what is now known as the Mesdag Museum. In 1887 a wing was added to their house to accommodate their increasing treasures, which include especially good examples of modern French painting, pottery, tapestry, etc.

In 1889 an exhibition of the works of these painters was held. Here convincing proof was given of Mme. Mesdag's accuracy, originality of interpretation, and her skill in the use of color.

Möller, Agnes Slott, or Slott-Möller, Agnes. This artist follows the young romantic movement in Denmark. She has embodied in her work a modern comprehension of old legends. The landscape and people of her native land seem to her as eminently suitable motives, and these realities she renders in the spirit of a by-gone age – that of the national heroes of the sagas and epics of the country, or the lyric atmosphere of the folk-songs.

She may depict these conceptions, full of feeling, in the dull colors of the North, or in rich and glowing hues, but the impression she gives is much the same in both cases, a generally restful effect, though the faces in her pictures are full of life and emotion. Her choice of subjects and her manner of treatment almost inevitably introduce some archaic quality in her work. This habit and the fact that she cares more for color than for drawing are the usual criticisms of her pictures.

Her "St. Agnes" is an interesting rendering of a well-worn subject. "Adelil the Proud," exhibited at the Paris Exposition of 1889, tells the story of the Duke of Frydensburg, who was in love with Adelil, the king's daughter. The king put him to death, and the attendants of Adelil made of his heart a viand which they presented to her. When she learned what this singular substance was – that caused her to tremble violently – she asked for wine, and carrying the cup to her lips with a tragic gesture, in memory of her lover, she died of a broken heart. It is such legends as these that Mme. Slott-Möller revives, and by which she is widely known.

Morisot or Morizot, Berthe. Married name Manet. Born at Bourges, 1840, died in Paris, 1895. A pupil of Guichard and Oudinot. After her marriage to Eugène Manet she came under the influence of his famous brother, Édouard. This artist signed her pictures with her maiden name, being too modest to use that which she felt belonged only to Édouard Manet, in the world of art.

A great interest was, however, aroused in the private galleries, where the works of the early impressionists were seen, by the pictures of Berthe Morisot. Camille Mauclair, an enthusiastic admirer of this school of art, says: "Berthe Morizot will remain the most fascinating figure of Impressionism – the one who has stated most precisely the femininity of this luminous and iridescent art."

A great-granddaughter of Fragonard, she seems to have inherited his talent; Corot and Renoir forcibly appealed to her. These elements, modified by her personal attitude, imparted a strong individuality to her works, which divided honors with her personal charms.

According to the general verdict, she was equally successful in oils and water-colors. Her favorite subjects – although she painted others – were sea-coast views, flowers, orchards, and gardens and young girls in every variety of costume.

After the death of Édouard Manet, she devoted herself to building up an appreciation of his work in the public mind. So intelligent were her methods that she doubtless had great influence in making the memory of his art enduring.

Among her most characteristic works are: "The Memories of the Oise," 1864; "Ros-Bras," "Finistère," 1868; "A Young Girl at a Window," 1870; a pastel, "Blanche," 1873; "The Toilet," and "A Young Woman at the Ball."

ᴬNey, Elizabeth. The Fine Arts jury of the St. Louis Exposition have accepted three works by this sculptor to be placed in the Fine Arts Building. They are the Albert Sidney Johnston memorial; the portrait bust of Jacob Grimm, in marble; and a bronze statuette of Garibaldi. It is unusual to allow so many entries to one artist.

Pauli, Hanna, family name, Hirsch. Bronze medal at Paris Exposition, 1889. Born in Stockholm and pupil of the Academy of Fine Arts there; later, of Dagnan-Bouveret, in Paris. Her husband, also an artist, is Georg Pauli. They live in Stockholm, where she paints portraits and genre subjects.

At the Paris Exposition, 1900, she exhibited two excellent portraits, one of her father and another of Ellen Key; also a charming genre subject, "The Old Couple."

Romani, Juana, H. C. Born at Velletri, 1869. Pupil of Henner and Roybet, in Paris, where she lives. This artist is, *sui generis*, a daughter of the people, of unconventional tastes and habits. She has boldly reproduced upon canvas a fulness of life and joy, such as is rarely seen in pictures.

While she has caught something of the dash of Henner, and something of the color of Roybet, and gained a firm mastery of the best French technique, these are infused with the ardor of a Southern temperament. Her favorite subjects are women – either in the strength and beauty of maternity, or in the freshness of youth, or even of childhood.

Some critics feel that, despite much that is desirable in her work, the soul is lacking in the women she paints. This is no doubt due in some measure to certain types she has chosen – for example, Salome and Herodias, in whom one scarcely looks for such an element.

Her portrait of Roybet and a picture of "Bianca Capello" were exhibited at Munich in 1893 and at Antwerp in 1894. The "Pensierosa" and a little girl were at the Paris Salon in 1894, and were much admired. "Herodias" appeared at Vienna in 1894 and at Berlin the following year, while "Primavera" was first seen at the Salon of 1895. This picture laughs, as children laugh, with perfect abandon.

A portrait of Miss Gibson was also at the Salon of 1895, and "Vittoria Colonna" and a "Venetian Girl" were sent to Munich. These were followed by the "Flower of the Alps" and "Desdemona" in 1896; "Doña Mona," palpitating with life, and "Faustalla of Pistoia," with short golden hair and a majestic poise of the head, in 1897; "Salome" and "Angelica," two widely differing pictures in character and color, in 1898; "Mina of Fiesole," and the portrait of a golden-haired beauty in a costume of black and gold, in 1899; the portrait of Mlle. H. D., in 1900; "L'Infante," one of her most noble creations, of a remarkably fine execution, and a ravishing child called "Roger" – with wonderful blond hair – in 1901.

Mlle. Romani often paints directly on the canvas without preliminary sketch or study, and sells many of her pictures before they are finished. Some of her works have been purchased by the French Government, and there are examples of these in the Luxembourg, and in the Gallery of Mülhausen.

Rupprecht, Tini. After having lessons from private instructors, this artist studied under Lenbach. She has been much influenced by Gainsborough, Lawrence, and Reynolds, traces of their manner being evident in her work. She renders the best type of feminine seductiveness with delicacy and grace; she avoids the trivial and gross, but pictures all the allurements of an innocent coquetry.

Her portrait of the Princess Marie, of Roumania, was exhibited in Munich in 1901; its reality and personality were notable, and one critic called it "an oasis in a desert of portraits." "Anno 1793" and "A Mother and Child" have attracted much favorable comment in Munich, where her star is in the ascendant, and greater excellence in her work is confidently prophesied.

Schwartze, Therese. Honorable mention, Paris Salon, 1885; gold medal, 1889. Diploma at Ghent, 1892; gold medal, 1892. At International Exhibition, Barcelona, 1898, a gold medal. Made a Knight of the Order of Orange-Nassau, 1896. Born in Amsterdam about 1851. A pupil of her father until his death, when she became a student under Gabriel Max, in Munich, for a year. Returning to Amsterdam, she was much encouraged by Israels, Bilders, and Bosboom, friends of her father.

She went to Paris in 1878 and was so attracted by the artistic life which she saw that she determined to study there. But she did not succeed in finding a suitable studio, neither an instructor who pleased her, and she returned to Amsterdam. It was at this time that she painted the portrait of Frederick Müller.

In the spring of 1880 she went again to Paris, only to "feast on things artistic." A little later she was summoned to the palace at Soestdijk to instruct the Princess Henry of the Netherlands. In 1883 she served with many distinguished artists on the art jury of the International Exhibition at Amsterdam.

In 1884 she once more yielded to the attraction that Paris had for her, and there made a great advance in her painting. In 1885 she began to work in pastel, and one of her best portraits in this medium was that of the Princess (Queen) Wilhelmina, which was loaned by the Queen Regent for the exhibition of this artist's work in Amsterdam in 1890.

The Italian Government requested Miss Schwartze to paint her own portrait for the Uffizi Gallery. This was shown at the Paris Salon, 1889, and missed the gold medal by two votes. This portrait is thought by some good judges to equal that of Mme. Le Brun. The head with the interesting eyes, shaded by the hand which wards off the light, and the penetrating, observant look, are most impressive.

She has painted a portrait of Queen Emma, and sent to Berlin in 1902 a portrait of Wolmaran, a member of the Transvaal Government, which was esteemed a work of the first rank. She has painted several portraits of her mother, which would have made for her a reputation had she done no others. She has had many notable men and women among her sitters, and though not a robust woman, she works incessantly without filling all the commissions offered her.

Her pictures are in the Museums of Amsterdam and Rotterdam.

Her work is full of life and strength, and her touch shows her confidence in herself and her technical knowledge. She is, however, a severe critic of her own work and is greatly disturbed by indiscriminating praise. She is serious and preoccupied in her studio, but with her friends she is full of gayety, and is greatly admired, both as a woman and as an artist.

Van der Veer, Miss. "This artist," says a recent critic, "has studied to some purpose in excellent continental schools, and is endowed withal with a creative faculty and breadth in conception rarely found in American painters of either sex. Her genre work is full of life, light, color, and character, with picturesque grouping, faultless atmosphere, and a breadth of technical treatment that verges on audacity, yet never fails of its designed purpose."

The fifty pictures exhibited by Miss Van der Veer in Philadelphia, in February, 1904, included interiors, portraits – mostly in pastel – flower studies and sketches, treating Dutch peasant life. Among the most notable of these may be mentioned "The Chimney Corner," "Saturday Morning," "Mother and Child," and a portrait of the artist herself.

Waldau, Margarethe. Born in Breslau, 1860. After studying by herself in Munich, this artist became a pupil of Streckfuss in Berlin, and later, in Nuremberg, studied under the younger Graeb and Ritter. The first subject chosen by her for a picture was the "Portal of the Church of the Magdalene." Her taste for architectural motives was strengthened by travel in Russia, the Netherlands, Belgium, and Germany.

The fine old churches of Nuremberg and the venerable edifices of Breslau afforded her most attractive subjects, which she treated with such distinction that her pictures were sought by kings and princes as well as by appreciative connoisseurs.

Her success increased her confidence in herself and enhanced the boldness and freedom with which she handled her brush. An exhibition of her work in Berlin led to her receiving a commission from the Government to paint two pictures for the Paris Exposition, 1900. "Mayence at Sunset" and the "Leipzig Market-Place in Winter" were the result of this order, and are two of her best works.

Occasionally this artist has painted genre subjects, but her real success has not been in this direction.

CRESCENT MOON PUBLISHING

web: www.crmoon.com e-mail: cresmopub@yahoo.co.uk

ARTS, PAINTING, SCULPTURE

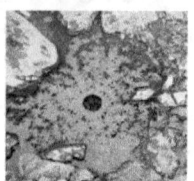

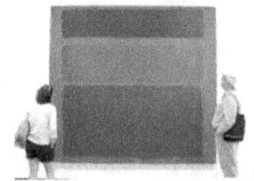

The Art of Andy Goldsworthy
Andy Goldsworthy: Touching Nature
Andy Goldsworthy in Close-Up
Andy Goldsworthy: Pocket Guide
Andy Goldsworthy In America
Land Art: A Complete Guide
The Art of Richard Long
Richard Long: Pocket Guide
Land Art In the UK
Land Art in Close-Up
Land Art In the U.S.A.
Land Art: Pocket Guide
Installation Art in Close-Up
Minimal Art and Artists In the 1960s and After
Colourfield Painting
Land Art DVD, TV documentary
Andy Goldsworthy DVD, TV documentary
The Erotic Object: Sexuality in Sculpture From Prehistory to the Present Day
Sex in Art: Pornography and Pleasure in Painting and Sculpture
Postwar Art
Sacred Gardens: The Garden in Myth, Religion and Art
Glorification: Religious Abstraction in Renaissance and 20th Century Art
Early Netherlandish Painting
Leonardo da Vinci
Piero della Francesca
Giovanni Bellini
Fra Angelico: Art and Religion in the Renaissance
Mark Rothko: The Art of Transcendence
Frank Stella: American Abstract Artist
Jasper Johns
Brice Marden
Alison Wilding: The Embrace of Sculpture
Vincent van Gogh: Visionary Landscapes
Eric Gill: Nuptials of God
Constantin Brancusi: Sculpting the Essence of Things
Max Beckmann
Caravaggio
Gustave Moreau
Egon Schiele: Sex and Death In Purple Stockings
Delizioso Fotografico Fervore: Works In Process 1
Sacro Cuore: Works In Process 2
The Light Eternal: J.M.W. Turner
The Madonna Glorified: Karen Arthurs

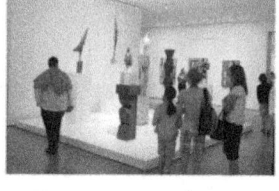

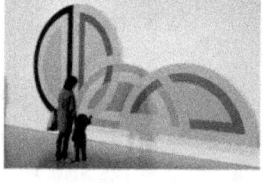

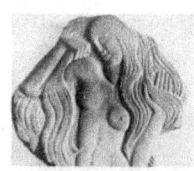

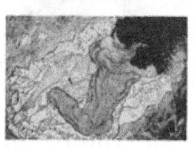

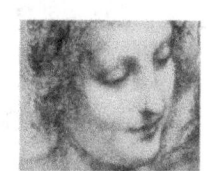

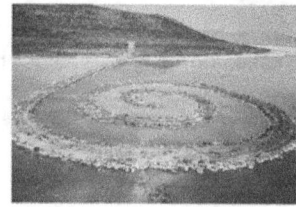

LITERATURE

J.R.R. Tolkien: The Books, The Films, The Whole Cultural Phenomenon
J.R.R. Tolkien: Pocket Guide
Tolkien's Heroic Quest
The *Earthsea* Books of Ursula Le Guin
Beauties, Beasts and Enchantment: Classic French Fairy Tales
German Popular Stories by the Brothers Grimm
Philip Pullman and *His Dark Materials*
Sexing Hardy: Thomas Hardy and Feminism
Thomas Hardy's *Tess of the d'Urbervilles*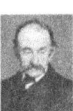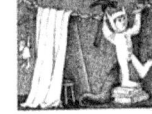
Thomas Hardy's *Jude the Obscure*
Thomas Hardy: The Tragic Novels
Love and Tragedy: Thomas Hardy
The Poetry of Landscape in Hardy
Wessex Revisited: Thomas Hardy and John Cowper Powys
Wolfgang Iser: Essays and Interviews
Petrarch, Dante and the Troubadours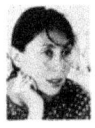
Maurice Sendak and the Art of Children's Book Illustration
Andrea Dworkin
Cixous, Irigaray, Kristeva: The *Jouissance* of French Feminism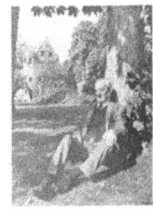
Julia Kristeva: Art, Love, Melancholy, Philosophy, Semiotics and Psychoanalysis
Hélène Cixous I Love You: The *Jouissance* of Writing
Luce Irigaray: Lips, Kissing, and the Politics of Sexual Difference
Peter Redgrove: Here Comes the Flood
Peter Redgrove: Sex-Magic-Poetry-Cornwall
Lawrence Durrell: Between Love and Death, East and West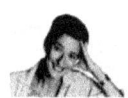
Love, Culture & Poetry: Lawrence Durrell
Cavafy: Anatomy of a Soul
German Romantic Poetry: Goethe, Novalis, Heine, Hölderlin
Feminism and Shakespeare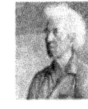
Shakespeare: Love, Poetry & Magic
The Passion of D.H. Lawrence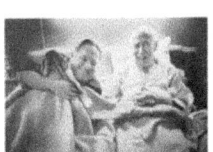
D.H. Lawrence: Symbolic Landscapes
D.H. Lawrence: Infinite Sensual Violence
Rimbaud: Arthur Rimbaud and the Magic of Poetry
The Ecstasies of John Cowper Powys
Sensualism and Mythology: The Wessex Novels of John Cowper Powys
Amorous Life: John Cowper Powys and the Manifestation of Affectivity (H.W. Fawkner)
Postmodern Powys: New Essays on John Cowper Powys (Joe Boulter)
Rethinking Powys: Critical Essays on John Cowper Powys
Paul Bowles & Bernardo Bertolucci
Rainer Maria Rilke
Joseph Conrad: *Heart of Darkness*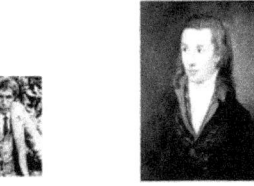
In the Dim Void: Samuel Beckett
Samuel Beckett Goes into the Silence
André Gide: Fiction and Fervour
Jackie Collins and the Blockbuster Novel
Blinded By Her Light: The Love-Poetry of Robert Graves
The Passion of Colours: Travels In Mediterranean Lands
Poetic Forms

POETRY

Ursula Le Guin: Walking In Cornwall
Peter Redgrove: Here Comes The Flood
Peter Redgrove: Sex-Magic-Poetry-Cornwall
Dante: Selections From the Vita Nuova
Petrarch, Dante and the Troubadours
William Shakespeare: Sonnets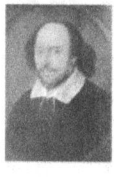
William Shakespeare: Complete Poems
Blinded By Her Light: The Love-Poetry of Robert Graves
Emily Dickinson: Selected Poems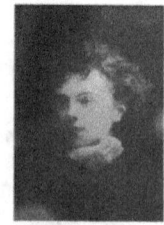
Emily Brontë: Poems
Thomas Hardy: Selected Poems
Percy Bysshe Shelley: Poems
John Keats: Selected Poems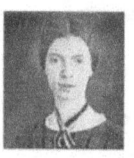
Joh n Keats: Poems of 1820
D.H. Lawrence: Selected Poems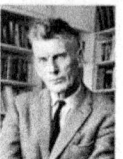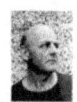
Edmund Spenser: Poems
Edmund Spenser: Amoretti
John Donne: Poems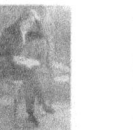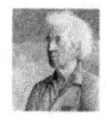
Henry Vaughan: Poems
Sir Thomas Wyatt: Poems
Robert Herrick: Selected Poems
Rilke: Space, Essence and Angels in the Poetry of Rainer Maria Rilke
Rainer Maria Rilke: Selected Poems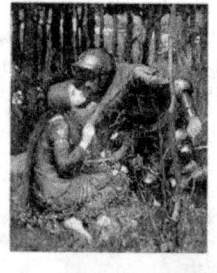
Friedrich Hölderlin: Selected Poems
Arseny Tarkovsky: Selected Poems
Arthur Rimbaud: Selected Poems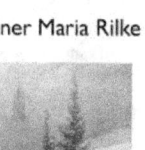
Arthur Rimbaud: A Season in Hell
Arthur Rimbaud and the Magic of Poetry
Novalis: Hymns To the Night
German Romantic Poetry
Paul Verlaine: Selected Poems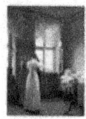
Elizaethan Sonnet Cycles
D.J. Enright: By-Blows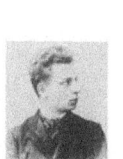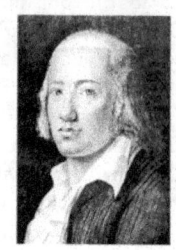
Jeremy Reed: Brigitte's Blue Heart
Jeremy Reed: Claudia Schiffer's Red Shoes
Gorgeous Little Orpheus
Radiance: New Poems
Crescent Moon Book of Nature Poetry
Crescent Moon Book of Love Poetry
Crescent Moon Book of Mystical Poetry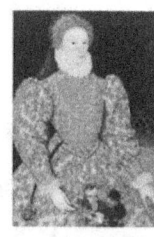
Crescent Moon Book of Elizabethan Love Poetry
Crescent Moon Book of Metaphysical Poetry
Crescent Moon Book of Romantic Poetry
Pagan America: New American Poetry

MEDIA, CINEMA, FEMINISM and CULTURAL STUDIES

J.R.R. Tolkien: The Books, The Films, The Whole Cultural Phenomenon
J.R.R. Tolkien: Pocket Guide
The *Lord of the Rings* Movies: Pocket Guide
The Cinema of Hayao Miyazaki
Hayao Miyazaki: *Princess Mononoke*: Pocket Movie Guide
Hayao Miyazaki: *Spirited Away*: Pocket Movie Guide
Tim Burton : Hallowe'en For Hollywood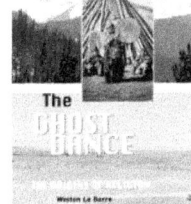
Ken Russell
Ken Russell: *Tommy*: Pocket Movie Guide
The Ghost Dance: The Origins of Religion
The Peyote Cult
Cixous, Irigaray, Kristeva: The *Jouissance* of French Feminism
Julia Kristeva: Art, Love, Melancholy, Philosophy, Semiotics and Psychoanalysis
Luce Irigaray: Lips, Kissing, and the Politics of Sexual Difference
Hélène Cixous I Love You: The *Jouissance* of Writing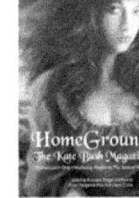
Andrea Dworkin
'Cosmo Woman': The World of Women's Magazines
Women in Pop Music
HomeGround: The Kate Bush Anthology
Discovering the Goddess (Geoffrey Ashe)
The Poetry of Cinema
The Sacred Cinema of Andrei Tarkovsky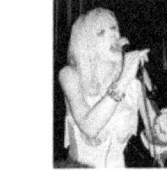
Andrei Tarkovsky: Pocket Guide
Andrei Tarkovsky: *Mirror*: Pocket Movie Guide
Andrei Tarkovsky: *The Sacrifice*: Pocket Movie Guide
Walerian Borowczyk: Cinema of Erotic Dreams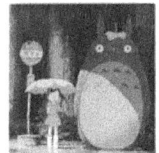
Jean-Luc Godard: The Passion of Cinema
Jean-Luc Godard: *Hail Mary*: Pocket Movie Guide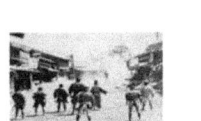
Jean-Luc Godard: *Contempt*: Pocket Movie Guide
Jean-Luc Godard: *Pierrot le Fou*: Pocket Movie Guide
John Hughes and Eighties Cinema
Ferris Bueller's Day Off: Pocket Movie Guide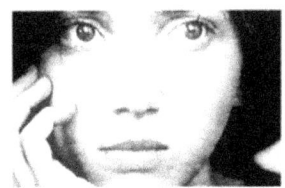
Jean-Luc Godard: Pocket Guide
The Cinema of Richard Linklater
Liv Tyler: Star In Ascendance
Blade Runner and the Films of Philip K. Dick
Paul Bowles and Bernardo Bertolucci
Media Hell: Radio, TV and the Press
An Open Letter to the BBC
Detonation Britain: Nuclear War in the UK
Feminism and Shakespeare
Wild Zones: Pornography, Art and Feminism
Sex in Art: Pornography and Pleasure in Painting and Sculpture
Sexing Hardy: Thomas Hardy and Feminism

The Light Eternal is a model monograph, an exemplary job. The subject matter of the book is beautifully
organised and dead on beam. (Lawrence Durrell)
It is amazing for me to see my work treated with such passion and respect. (Andrea Dworkin)

CRESCENT MOON PUBLISHING
P.O. Box 1312, Maidstone, Kent, ME14 5XU, Great Britain. www.crmoon.com

cresmopub@yahoo.co.uk   www.crescentmoon.org.uk

MEDIA, CINEMA, FEMINISM and CULTURAL STUDIES

J.R.R. Tolkien: The Books, The Films, The Whole Cultural Phenomenon
J.R.R. Tolkien: Pocket Guide
The *Lord of the Rings* Movies: Pocket Guide
The Cinema of Hayao Miyazaki
Hayao Miyazaki: *Princess Mononoke*: Pocket Movie Guide
Hayao Miyazaki: *Spirited Away*: Pocket Movie Guide
Tim Burton : Hallowe'en For Hollywood
Ken Russell
Ken Russell: *Tommy*: Pocket Movie Guide
The Ghost Dance: The Origins of Religion
The Peyote Cult
Cixous, Irigaray, Kristeva: The *Jouissance* of French Feminism
Julia Kristeva: Art, Love, Melancholy, Philosophy, Semiotics and Psychoanalysis
Luce Irigaray: Lips, Kissing, and the Politics of Sexual Difference
Hélene Cixous I Love You: The *Jouissance* of Writing
Andrea Dworkin
'Cosmo Woman': The World of Women's Magazines
Women in Pop Music
HomeGround: The Kate Bush Anthology
Discovering the Goddess (Geoffrey Ashe)
The Poetry of Cinema
The Sacred Cinema of Andrei Tarkovsky
Andrei Tarkovsky: Pocket Guide
Andrei Tarkovsky: *Mirror*: Pocket Movie Guide
Andrei Tarkovsky: *The Sacrifice*: Pocket Movie Guide
Walerian Borowczyk: Cinema of Erotic Dreams
Jean-Luc Godard: The Passion of Cinema
Jean-Luc Godard: *Hail Mary*: Pocket Movie Guide
Jean-Luc Godard: *Contempt*: Pocket Movie Guide
Jean-Luc Godard: *Pierrot le Fou*: Pocket Movie Guide
John Hughes and Eighties Cinema
Ferris Bueller's Day Off: Pocket Movie Guide
Jean-Luc Godard: Pocket Guide
The Cinema of Richard Linklater
Liv Tyler: Star In Ascendance
Blade Runner and the Films of Philip K. Dick
Paul Bowles and Bernardo Bertolucci
Media Hell: Radio, TV and the Press
An Open Letter to the BBC
Detonation Britain: Nuclear War in the UK
Feminism and Shakespeare
Wild Zones: Pornography, Art and Feminism
Sex in Art: Pornography and Pleasure in Painting and Sculpture
Sexing Hardy: Thomas Hardy and Feminism

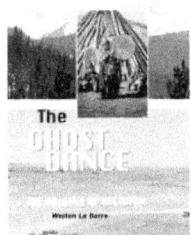
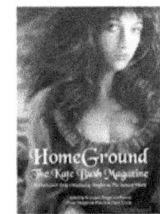
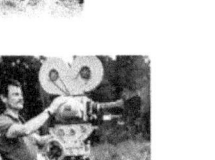
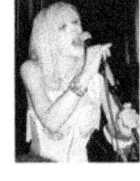
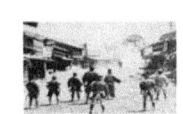
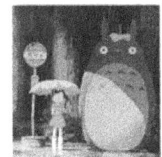
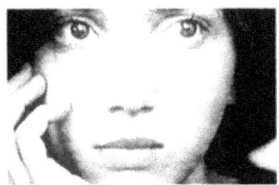

The Light Eternal is a model monograph, an exemplary job. The subject matter of the book is beautifully organised and dead on beam. (Lawrence Durrell)
It is amazing for me to see my work treated with such passion and respect. (Andrea Dworkin)

CRESCENT MOON PUBLISHING
P.O. Box 1312, Maidstone, Kent, ME14 5XU, Great Britain. www.crmoon.com

cresmopub@yahoo.co.uk   www.crescentmoon.org.uk

www.ingramcontent.com/pod-product-compliance
Lightning Source LLC
Chambersburg PA
CBHW072011230526
45468CB00021B/1186